Jaguar Books on Lat

Series Editors

⋔ W9-CFA-281

WILLIAM H. BEEZLEY, Professor of History, University of Arizona
COLIN M. MACLACHLAN, John Christy Barr Distinguished Professor of
History, Tulane University

Volumes Published

John E. Kicza, ed., *The Indian in Latin American History: Resistance,
Resilience, and Acculturation* (1993; rev. ed., 2000).
Cloth ISBN 0-8420-2822-6   Paper ISBN 0-8420-2823-4

Susan E. Place, ed., *Tropical Rainforests: Latin American Nature and
Society in Transition* (1993; rev. and updated ed., 2001).
Cloth ISBN 0-8420-2907-9   Paper ISBN 0-8420-2908-7

Paul W. Drake, ed., *Money Doctors, Foreign Debts, and Economic
Reforms in Latin America from the 1890s to the Present* (1994).
Cloth ISBN 0-8420-2434-4   Paper ISBN 0-8420-2435-2

John A. Britton, ed., *Molding the Hearts and Minds: Education,
Communications, and Social Change in Latin America* (1994).
Cloth ISBN 0-8420-2489-1   Paper ISBN 0-8420-2490-5

David J. Weber and Jane M. Rausch, eds., *Where Cultures Meet: Frontiers
in Latin American History* (1994). Cloth ISBN 0-8420-2477-8
Paper ISBN 0-8420-2478-6

Gertrude M. Yeager, ed., *Confronting Change, Challenging Tradition:
Women in Latin American History* (1994). Cloth ISBN 0-8420-2479-4
Paper ISBN 0-8420-2480-8

Linda Alexander Rodríguez, ed., *Rank and Privilege: The Military and
Society in Latin America* (1994). Cloth ISBN 0-8420-2432-8
Paper ISBN 0-8420-2433-6

Darién J. Davis, ed., *Slavery and Beyond: The African Impact on Latin
America and the Caribbean* (1995). Cloth ISBN 0-8420-2484-0
Paper ISBN 0-8420-2485-9

Gilbert M. Joseph and Mark D. Szuchman, eds., *I Saw a City Invincible:
Urban Portraits of Latin America* (1996). Cloth ISBN 0-8420-2495-6
Paper ISBN 0-8420-2496-4

Roderic Ai Camp, ed., *Democracy in Latin America: Patterns and Cycles* (1996). Cloth ISBN 0-8420-2512-X   Paper ISBN 0-8420-2513-8

Oscar J. Martínez, ed., *U.S.-Mexico Borderlands: Historical and Contemporary Perspectives* (1996). Cloth ISBN 0-8420-2446-8 Paper ISBN 0-8420-2447-6

William O. Walker III, ed., *Drugs in the Western Hemisphere: An Odyssey of Cultures in Conflict* (1996). Cloth ISBN 0-8420-2422-0 Paper ISBN 0-8420-2426-3

Richard R. Cole, ed., *Communication in Latin America: Journalism, Mass Media, and Society* (1996). Cloth ISBN 0-8420-2558-8 Paper ISBN 0-8420-2559-6

David G. Gutiérrez, ed., *Between Two Worlds: Mexican Immigrants in the United States* (1996). Cloth ISBN 0-8420-2473-5 Paper ISBN 0-8420-2474-3

Lynne Phillips, ed., *The Third Wave of Modernization in Latin America: Cultural Perspectives on Neoliberalism* (1998). Cloth ISBN 0-8420-2606-1   Paper ISBN 0-8420-2608-8

Daniel Castro, ed., *Revolution and Revolutionaries: Guerrilla Movements in Latin America* (1999). Cloth ISBN 0-8420-2625-8 Paper ISBN 0-8420-2626-6

Virginia Garrard-Burnett, ed., *On Earth as It Is in Heaven: Religion in Modern Latin America* (2000). Cloth ISBN 0-8420-2584-7 Paper ISBN 0-8420-2585-5

Carlos A. Aguirre and Robert Buffington, eds., *Reconstructing Criminality in Latin America* (2000). Cloth ISBN 0-8420-2620-7 Paper ISBN 0-8420-2621-5

Christon I. Archer, ed., *The Wars of Independence in Spanish America* (2000). Cloth ISBN 0-8420-2468-9   Paper ISBN 0-8420-2469-7

John F. Schwaller, ed., *The Church in Colonial Latin America* (2000). Cloth ISBN 0-8420-2703-3   Paper ISBN 0-8420-2704-1

Ingrid E. Fey and Karen Racine, eds., *Strange Pilgrimages: Exile, Travel, and National Identity in Latin America, 1800–1990s* (2000). Cloth ISBN 0-8420-2693-2   Paper ISBN 0-8420-2694-0

Tropical
Rainforests

Tropical Rainforests

Latin American Nature and Society in Transition

REVISED AND UPDATED EDITION

Susan E. Place
Editor

Jaguar Books on Latin America
Number 2

A Scholarly Resources Inc. Imprint
Wilmington, Delaware

Scholarly Resources Inc.
104 Greenhill Avenue
Wilmington, DE 19805-1897
www.scholarly.com

Library of Congress Cataloging-in-Publication Data

Tropical rainforests : Latin American nature and society in transition /
    Susan E. Place, editor. — Rev. and updated ed.
        p. cm. — (Jaguar books on Latin America ; no. 2)
    Includes bibliographical references.
        ISBN 0-8420-2907-9 (alk. paper) — ISBN 0-8420-2908-7 (pbk. :
alk. paper)
        1. Rain forests—Latin America. 2. Rain forests—Economic aspects
—Latin America. 3. Rain forest ecology—Latin America. 4. Rain forest
conservation—Latin America. 5. Deforestation—Latin America.
I. Place, Susan E., 1947–   II. Series.

SD153 .T76 2001
333.75'16'098—dc21   00-066107

∞ The paper used in this publication meets the minimum requirements of
the American National Standard for permanence of paper for printed library materials, Z39.48, 1984.

Acknowledgments

In producing this volume I have been assisted by those whose aid and encouragement I would like to recognize. A generous grant from the California State University, Chico, provided the time away from teaching that allowed me to edit the first edition of this book. Also at CSU, Chico, Christine Crown and Chuck Nelson of the Geographic Information Center of the Department of Geography and Planning worked cheerfully and expertly to create the map from a disorganized mass of unrelated information.

I would like to thank Bill Beezley, who provided the original inspiration for this volume and kindly allowed me the opportunity to develop his idea in my own way. The generosity of the authors in allowing me to use their work in this anthology is also greatly appreciated.

Finally, I dedicate this book to my son, Brendan O'Donnell. His challenging questions and wry sense of humor have enlivened my work on this volume and enriched my life.

About the Editor

Susan E. Place is professor of geography at California State University, Chico. For the past twenty years she has researched various aspects of the relationship between nature and society in Latin America, particularly in Costa Rica. Her research has explored the ecological and social impacts of deforestation, women's participation in agricultural restructuring, the relationship between newly created national parks and local communities, and ecotourism-based development.

Contents

Introduction

In the past decade, many people have begun to think in new ways about the relationship between nature and society. As 1992 marked five hundred years of interaction between Europe and the Americas, it inspired a reevaluation of the consequences of introducing European technologies, economic systems, and forms of social organization into the Americas. This reevaluation led more Westerners to appreciate the value of indigenous cultures and their resource management practices. Native Americans have also begun to assert their rights in a more public way, often utilizing modern technological innovations and the mass media to disseminate their points of view. For example, in April 2000 the news media provided widespread coverage of demonstrations by Indian tribes against Brazil's celebration of the 500th anniversary of the arrival of the Portuguese. Indigenous peoples frequently emphasize environmental relations in their self-representation to the Western world. In doing so, they highlight humanity's increasingly sophisticated and nuanced conceptualizations of the relationship between society and nature.

In the twentieth century, Latin America experienced a transformation in the relationship between society and nature due to the introduction of economic modernization. Originating in Europe and North America, modernization is based on the adoption of Western technology and emphasizes high rates of economic growth. Modernization set in motion processes that tended to exacerbate problems arising from historical patterns of social and environmental relations in Latin America. The push for economic growth and export diversification extended agribusiness operations into ever more remote, "backward" rural areas that included the last remaining stands of tropical rainforest as well as the homelands of indigenous peoples. High levels of foreign debt, incurred as part of the modernization approach to development, encouraged the expansion of modern commercial production into the forested frontier regions of Latin America.

Another major event of 1992 was the United Nations Conference on the Environment and Development (UNCED), or Earth Summit, held in Rio de Janeiro. The contentious nature of this conference revealed both the political aspects of environmental policy and the importance of a healthy environment to economic development. Nature clearly plays a vital but often unrecognized or seriously undervalued role in modern economies. As a result of decades of environmental degradation, however, the necessity of maintaining environmental health is becoming increasingly obvious to many people. What is not so obvious is how to accommodate the economic aspirations of the rural poor as well as the environmental goals of preserving remaining tropical forest. The term "sustainable development" refers to various approaches that combine concern for both environmental health and improvement of the quality of life for the poor. Such concerns challenge powerful economic and political interests that consider nature a free good that can (and even should) be used to increase economic output. Typically, proponents of development in Latin America have focused almost exclusively on economic growth, whether it be by exploitation of tropical rainforests for quick profit or conversion of the land to other forms of use, such as agriculture, ranching, or mining. Today, however, previously marginalized and silenced groups such as landless farmers and poor peasants, indigenous peoples, rubber tappers, and other forest dwellers are contesting powerful interests over the question of how to develop remaining forest zones. The environmental movement, often motivated to respond to the same destructive processes as social justice groups, may not always share the same goals. However, a number of environmental activists do recognize the commonality of their interests with social activists and are moving toward a more holistic approach to integrating environment and development.

Increasingly, what used to be local conflicts over land use and land tenure are becoming global. The political nature of economic development was highlighted in 1999 by demonstrations in Seattle, Washington, against WTO (World Trade Organization) policies. A few months later, in the spring of 2000, thousands of protesters demonstrated in front of the World Bank and International Monetary Fund (IMF) headquarters in Washington, DC. Their demands centered on debt reduction and environmental and social justice for the people of Third World countries. Various organizations dedicated to saving the rainforest were involved in these demonstrations, thus revealing a broadening of the horizon of the conservation movement. The selections in this book provide an overview of some of the issues involved in both the destruction and preservation of tropical rainforests in Latin America, including various causes of deforestation and alternative visions of development in rainforest regions.

The American tropics (known to biologists as Neotropics) include a wide variety of forest ecosystems, from cloud forests on wet tropical mountain slopes to seasonally dry tropical deciduous forests and woodlands on the Pacific side of Mexico and Central America, and pine forests on the Caribbean side of Honduras and Nicaragua. Because there is more information published about it than about any other type of neotropical forest, most of the selections offered here focus on the tropical rainforest. A number of other forest ecosystems in Latin America, however, are equally (or more) endangered by the same forces that threaten the tropical rainforest. While the natural distribution of rainforests in the Neotropics ranged from southern Mexico to southern Brazil (see map), the actual extent of rainforest today is much smaller—and shrinking rapidly.

Natural Distribution of Tropical Rainforest in Latin America

Humans have cleared vast areas of tropical forest in Latin America. Most of the forests of the seasonally dry zones of Central and South America have already disappeared, and tropical rainforests in the more accessible coastal areas have been decimated as well. Amazonia represents the last great contiguous expanse of tropical rainforest. Although perhaps only 20 percent has been removed so far, the rate of cutting has been accelerating so that now more than twenty thousand square kilometers are cleared each year. Projections based on current trends indicate that by the middle of the twenty-first century there will be no sustainable tropical rainforest left in Brazil. Only small, unsustainable remnants will stand. Because of the ecological characteristics of tropical rainforests, scientists now doubt that such patches of forest can survive in the long run, even if undisturbed by human activities.

Widespread tropical deforestation has a number of serious environmental, economic, and social implications. One of the most commonly discussed characteristics of the tropical rainforest is its high biodiversity. Occupying only about 6 percent of the Earth's surface, these forests are believed to contain at least 50 percent of the world's known plant and animal species. Amazonia, the largest and richest of the tropical rainforests, contains at least 20 percent of the world's higher plant varieties and an equal proportion of its bird species. Other areas in the Neotropics are also spectacularly rich in species, especially Central America, with the extra diversity of habitat in its mountainous terrain and because of its land-bridge position between North and South America. Costa Rica, smaller than the state of West Virginia, has more species of birds than all of North America.

Tropical rainforests are the most complex terrestrial ecosystems on the Earth. Structurally, they have many different life forms and are composed of several vertical layers of vegetation, each with associated faunas; this complexity allows a large number of different species to coexist in a given area. High biodiversity also implies that there is a large variety of genes and an abundance of different chemical compounds present in tropical rainforests. But a forest ecosystem is more than just an assemblage of species; it also represents the interactions between species, and the variety of interspecies interactions is particularly rich in tropical rainforests. Many tropical plants, for example, produce toxic compounds in order to evade the large number of creatures (especially insects) that try to eat them. Several selections in this book discuss the economic implications of biodiversity for medicine, agriculture, and industries of various kinds.

Latin America's tropical rainforests also have a high degree of horizontal diversity, meaning that the assemblage of species found in one area may differ from those found only a few miles away. Sometimes called "patchiness," this adds further complexity to species diversity. There are also centers of particularly high diversity in various parts of the Amazon and along the Brazilian coast. Scientists have postulated that these regions might represent Pleistocene refugia—forested areas where large numbers of forest-dependent species concentrated during past dry periods (corresponding to glacial advances during the Ice Ages), when grasslands expanded to cover much of Amazonia, leaving only islands of forest in favored zones. The forests that scientists would most like to see preserved in parks are these centers of diversity because they are especially vulnerable to species extinctions as a result of forest clearance.

Tropical rainforests interact with their physical environments in a number of ways that affect human well-being. They act as immense solar-powered engines that pump water, nutrients, and gases such as carbon dioxide and oxygen through the Earth's biosphere and atmosphere. Recent research indicates that by recycling water through the regional hydrological cycle, the Amazon rainforest generates about one-half of the rain that falls in the Amazon basin. Precipitation is captured by the forest and slowly returns by means of evaporation or transpiration as water va-por to the atmosphere, from which it can return to the forest as rain. Furthermore, the forest is like a giant sponge that holds a large amount of water not only in the vegetation but also in the leaf litter on the ground and in the soil. In this way it plays an important role in regional water cycles by helping to store a large percentage of the water from precipitation until it can be slowly released, either to the atmosphere (through the vegetation) or to feed streams and rivers from stored groundwater. When large-scale forest clearance occurs, the ecosystem's ability to store water decreases, and a high proportion of precipitation runs off the unprotected land. Local climates and water cycles, therefore, may experience greater extremes in cleared regions. Of particular concern to humans, drought conditions may begin to occur regularly, often alternating with floods produced by the rapid runoff during rainy periods.

The warm, wet climate of tropical rainforest regions creates the seeming paradox of incredibly luxuriant vegetation rooted in infertile soil. Over 75 percent of Amazonia's soils are classified as acid, infertile, or poorly drained, and only 8 percent are moderately fertile, well-drained soils suitable for agriculture. Most soils found under tropical rainforest conditions, except on floodplains or in certain volcanic areas, are deficient in nutrients because of the perpetually warm, rainy climate. The high temperatures of the tropics cause rapid decomposition of organic material—that is, downed trees, leaf litter, animal feces or carcasses—as well as of the inorganic parent material of the soil. Frequent heavy rains quickly leach the decomposing materials out of the root zone. Tropical rainforest plants have adapted by quickly taking up nutrients as they become available, which explains why most of the nutrients in a tropical rainforest are stored in the vegetation and not in the soil as they are in the middle latitudes, such as North America and Europe. Thus, a paradox faces humans who seek to make a living in the tropical rainforest: clearing the forest for farming removes the nutrients necessary to sustain crops over the long term.

Destruction of the forest clearly disrupts various ecological services upon which humans depend, such as regulation of the water cycle and the climate, and protection of the soil. Often people remain unaware of that dependence until environmental disruption causes them problems. The current debate over how to manage Latin America's remaining tropical rainforest derives from differences in how these indirect services are perceived. Many scientists, environmentalists, and forest dwellers emphasize the importance of the forest's ecological services and the need to maintain them by protecting the integrity of the natural forest. But divergent economic interests and different degrees of dependence upon and familiarity with the tropical rainforest lead to different assessments of the value of its conservation versus the value of conversion to other kinds of production. Those who wish to preserve the tropical rainforest often live in it (at least part of the time) and know it intimately. Many depend on the forest and its ecological services for their livelihoods and therefore have a personal stake in rainforest conservation.

On the other hand, proponents of economic growth tend to focus on the material goods produced by the forest or the land on which it grows and minimize the value of the indirect services provided by nature. Often living elsewhere, they seek to make money from logging forests and converting them to more profitable uses. The governments of countries with extensive tracts of forest are often faced with large foreign debts. The economic crises of the 1980s and ensuing structural adjustment programs encouraged them to increase production of export commodities, which led to expansion of commercial economic activity into remaining forested frontiers. The proponents of economic development also envision that these activities will improve the economic status of the rural poor by providing paid employment in commercial enterprises in the hinterlands.

A society's perception of the tropical rainforest underlies and motivates its particular way of interacting with it. Perspectives on the nature of the tropical rainforest have varied over Latin America's history and suggest considerable ambivalence toward it. Since the inception of contact between Eurasia and the Americas, Westerners have viewed tropical rainforests as lucrative sources of raw materials. Beginning with the gold fever of the colonial period, the myth of potential wealth lying under or in the tropical forest has fueled its periodic exploration and exploitation in a long sequence of economic booms and busts. In addition to the extraction of minerals and petroleum lying underground, the tropical rainforest itself has been exploited for dyewood, mahogany, rubber, and botanical specimens—a trend that continues today with the search for plants with medicinal and commercial properties.

Europeans have dreaded the tropical rainforest because of its plagues of insects and diseases as well as its sometimes fierce native inhabitants. Individuals, perhaps revealing more about themselves and their milieus than about the rainforest, reflect society's ambivalence in the variety of their perceptions of the forest. Contrast, for example, the views of Amazonia presented by José Eustasio Rivera and Katherine Milton in Part I. The former wrote early in the twentieth century about the wild, threatening, evil forest. The latter wrote somewhat wistfully late in the century that modern industrial society might benefit from lifestyles more like those of Amazonian Indians, who live in an environment portrayed as relatively benign. Milton's article demonstrates how subjective attitudes toward the forest spill over into scholarly analyses of the tropical rainforest and its economic potential. In the past, anthropologists, geographers, and other scholars have viewed the tropical rainforest as a limiting environment, one that prevented the development of large populations and complex cultures. Recent research, undertaken in an era with a more positive—

even romantic—perception of the rainforest and the people who live there, suggests that the tropical rainforest may have supported larger populations and more complex cultures in pre-Columbian times than previously realized. Furthermore, ethnographic fieldwork has revealed that contemporary Native American cultures utilize the tropical rainforest in complex and sophisticated ways, even though their material culture or technology tends to be simple.

Latin America's forested frontier regions have become contested arenas where different perspectives on development compete. Sparsely populated tropical rainforest zones have long been perceived as an "escape valve" for populations displaced by economic, social, political, and environmental problems in previously settled, more densely populated regions of Latin America. Recently, however, scholarly research and activism by environmentalists and human rights advocates have encouraged new conceptualizations of the tropical rainforest, its environmental characteristics, and economic potential. The rainforest is now perceived as providing many "free" goods and services that can be managed and exploited in a sustainable way. In some cases, research suggests that conversion of the tropical rainforest to other forms of land use, such as ranching or large-scale agriculture, may not produce as much income per hectare in the long run as natural forest managed sustainably. Extractive reserves—forests protected so that local inhabitants can exploit their renewable products such as rubber, nuts and fruits, and resins—may be one way of promoting forest conservation and local economic development simultaneously.

A current, heated debate over the role of extractive reserves in the economic development of the Amazon illustrates the range of opinions regarding appropriate land use in the tropical rainforest. Powerful economic and political interests continue to favor opening up the Amazon, in spite of ecological arguments on the side of forest preservation and of cost-benefit analyses that indicate that forest clearance may not be economically sensible in the long run. Large landholders and industrialists—both foreign and national—seek personal and corporate profits, while the landless and the unemployed seek a way to support themselves and their families by acquiring land of their own on the frontier. Unequal land tenure and high unemployment in the more densely populated zones of Latin America have traditionally pushed migrants into sparsely populated frontier zones. High rates of population growth over the past forty years, coupled with a development strategy that has further widened the gap between the rich and the poor, have increased the flow of migrants into the tropical rainforest.

Politicians try to maintain enough constituents to keep themselves in power by promoting the construction of roads into forested frontier regions, providing access to land without the necessity of implementing land reform elsewhere. With this policy they hope to simultaneously defuse popular unrest born of the misery and hopelessness of the underclass and curry favor with the powerful economic interests with a personal stake in the development of remaining forested land. In some countries, such as Brazil, the politically powerful military wants to secure existing borders and protect the resources of the hinterland by promoting effective occupation of forested frontier zones.

The appropriate metaphor for the Amazon and other rainforest frontiers appears to be not an escape valve, but rather a microcosm of the unresolved economic, political, social, and environmental problems that plague Latin America as a whole. As long as present conditions exist, the forces that fuel migration into the rainforest will continue. Concentration of land ownership and wealth, agricultural modernization, the need to make payments on large foreign debts, and the political goal of national integration (effective territorial occupation by members of a country's dominant culture) all increase the pressure to colonize remaining tropical rainforest zones—regardless of the environmental and social consequences for the people who have traditionally lived there and preserved the forest.

The selections that follow provide a sample of ideas about the nature of the tropical rainforest, the causes and consequences of tropical deforestation, and alternative approaches to developing Latin America's tropical rainforests on a more sustainable and equitable basis. Part I introduces the reader to a variety of perceptions of the rainforest. The selections in Part II describe the impacts of the dominant modern approach to economic development on tropical rainforests and the people who live in them. The implications of these impacts and the arguments for saving tropical rainforests are discussed in Part III. Finally, selections in Part IV present alternatives for future development in tropical rainforest zones of Latin America, many of which raise the possibility of development as a process in which natural environments and traditional cultures are preserved rather than destroyed in the name of "progress."

I

Perceptions of the Rainforest

Since their first encounters with Latin America, Europeans have expressed mixed feelings about the tropical rainforest. The lure of fabulous wealth and the hope of finding El Dorado have wrestled with the dread of mythical beings and horrible diseases in the "green hell." Accounts of the tropical rainforest, whether novels, travel journals, or scientific reports, reveal at least as much about their authors as they do about the forest. Every writer represents to a certain extent the prevailing worldview of his or her time and culture, but perceptions of the rainforest are also filtered through the lens of meanings created by the individual's experiences and beliefs.

The selections in Part I provide a sample of the variety of modern perceptions of the tropical rainforest. Henry Walter Bates, writing in the nineteenth century, represents the straightforward, "objective" approach of modern science (Selection 1). Excerpted from *The Naturalist on the River Amazons*, Bates's reading provides a factual description of the tropical rainforest environment where he collected specimens; it engages in relatively little editorializing. John Vandermeer and Ivette Perfecto (Selection 2) offer a summary of the current state of scientific knowledge about the workings of the tropical rainforest. This selection reveals how much science has evolved from its nineteenth-century emphasis on describing and cataloguing nature. Today's scientists endeavor to understand ecological relationships in nature. They are more likely to seek information that will support the preservation of the rainforest ecosystem than to seek commodities that will promote economic growth in industrialized countries, as was the case with nineteenth-century natural historians.

José Eustasio Rivera portrays the Amazon rainforest as the ultimate green hell in an excerpt from his novel, *The Vortex*, written in the early twentieth century (Selection 3). This novel, which chronicles the horrors of abusive labor relations during the rubber boom of the late nineteenth century, recognizes the role of nature in the social relations of production. Rivera shows how the oppressive rubber industry exploited both labor and nature. His horrific portrait of the tropical rainforest stands in marked contrast to the far more benevolent contemporary perception, which has sparked a global "Save the Rainforest" movement. The contemporary view of the traditional inhabitants of the rainforest has also changed. Once perceived as victims virtually enslaved by an oppressive system, rubber tappers are today often portrayed as effective social actors and protectors of the Amazon rainforest (despite their fluctuating economic circumstances due to volatile rubber prices).

Just as the tropical rainforest has been perceived in conflicting ways, so have its Native American inhabitants. Archaeologists and anthropologists frame their research in terms of the prevailing theories and conceptualizations of their times, and the past several decades have witnessed a marked shift in the way they see Native Americans. Betty J. Meggers and Clifford Evans (Selection 4) represent a previous generation of archaeologists and anthropologists who believed Amazonia to be a difficult and limiting environment that prevented the development of advanced cultures. In more recent years, however, archaeologists have begun to consider the region more complex and culturally varied than previously supposed, containing some areas that once supported fairly dense populations and advanced cultures. Support for the contemporary perspective also derives from recent ethnographic research, which views tribal cultures as sophisticated managers of the tropical rainforest environments in which they live. Katherine Milton (Selection 5) exemplifies the current scholarly perspective on indigenous people, which emphasizes their intimate knowledge of and adaptation to the natural environment. Selection 6, written by Gerardo Reichel-Dolmatoff, a Colombian anthropologist, provides a more personal and emotional account of the world of the indigenous peoples of Amazonia. It emphasizes their cosmology as a way of both understanding and managing the natural world without destroying it.

---

1 Henry Walter Bates ◆ Spring, Summer, and Autumn in One Tropical Day

Henry Walter Bates, a prominent nineteenth-century English naturalist, traveled to the Amazon in 1843 with Alfred Russel Wallace, cocreator with Charles Darwin of the theory of evolution by natural selection. This excerpt gives Bates's impressions from his first walk, with Wallace, in the tropical rainforest near Pará (now called Belém). He provides a good description of the sound and feel of the forest, as well as its appearance, and conveys a sense of the monotony of the tropical climate in his description of the daily routine of the two naturalists.

From Henry Walter Bates, *The Naturalist on the River Amazons* (1863; reprint New York: Dover, 1975), 26–32.

In this selection the modern reader can get some unintended insights into the midnineteenth-century world of the author—when vast herds of buffalo still roamed the great plains of North America and church domes towered over the other buildings of the great cities. Bates's passing references to these as unremarkable facts highlights the rapidity with which humans can reshape their environments—often in unforeseen ways. Can we imagine what Amazonia might look like a century from now? Will there still be extensive tracts of natural forest where future naturalists and scientists can explore and make discoveries, as Bates did?

The two hours before breakfast were devoted to ornithology. At that early period of the day the sky was invariably cloudless (the thermometer marking 72 degrees or 73 degrees Fahrenheit): the heavy dew or the previous night's rain, which lay on the moist foliage, becoming quickly dissipated by the glowing sun, which rising straight out of the east, mounted rapidly towards the zenith. All nature was fresh, new leaf and flower-buds expanding rapidly. Some mornings a single tree would appear in flower amidst what was the preceding evening a uniform green mass of forest—a dome of blossom suddenly created as if by magic. The birds were all active; from the wild-fruit trees, not far off, we often heard the shrill yelping of the Toucans. . . . Small flocks of parrots flew over on most mornings, at a great height, appearing in distinct relief against the blue sky, always two by two, chattering to each other, the pairs being separated by regular intervals; their bright colours, however, were not apparent at that height. After breakfast we devoted the hours from 10 A.M. to 2 or 3 P.M. to entomology; the best time for insects in the forest being a little before the greatest heat of the day.

The heat increased rapidly towards two o'clock (92 degrees and 93 degrees Fahrenheit), by which time every voice of bird or mammal was hushed; only in the trees was heard at intervals the harsh whirr of a cicada. The leaves, which were so moist and fresh in early morning, now become lax and drooping; the flowers shed their petals. Our neighbours, the Indian and Mulatto inhabitants of the open palm-thatched huts, as we returned home fatigued with our ramble, were either asleep in their hammocks or seated on mats in the shade, too languid even to talk. On most days in June and July a heavy shower would fall some time in the afternoon, producing a most welcome coolness. The approach of the rain-clouds was after a uniform fashion very interesting to observe. First, the cool sea-breeze, which commenced to blow about 10 o'clock, and which had increased in force with the increasing power of the sun, would flag and finally die away. The heat and electric tension of the atmosphere would then become almost insupportable. Languor and uneasiness would seize on every one; even the denizens of the forest betraying it by their motions. White clouds would appear in the east and gather into cumuli, with an increasing blackness along their lower portions. The whole eastern horizon would become almost suddenly black, and this would spread upwards, the sun at length become obscured. Then the rush of a mighty wind is heard through the forest, swaying the tree-tops; a vivid flash of lightning burst forth, then a crash of thunder, and down streams the deluging rain. Such storms soon cease, leaving bluish-black motionless clouds in the sky until night. Meantime all nature is refreshed; but heaps of flower-petals and fallen leaves are seen under the trees. Towards evening life revives again, and the ringing uproar is resumed from bush and tree. The following morning the sun again rises in a cloudless sky, and so the cycle is completed; spring, summer, and autumn, as it were, in one tropical day. The days are more or less like this throughout the year in this country. A little difference exists between the dry and wet seasons; but generally, the dry season, which lasts from July to December, is varied with showers, and the wet, from January to June, with sunny days. It results from this, that the periodical phenomena of plants and animals do not take place at about the same time in all species, or in the individuals of any given species, as they do in temperate countries. Of course, there is no hybernation; nor, as the dry season is not excessive, is there any summer torpidity as in some tropical countries. Plants do not flower or shed their leaves, nor do birds moult, pair, or breed simultaneously. In Europe, a woodland scene has its spring, its summer, its autumnal, and its winter aspects. In the equatorial forests the aspect is the same or nearly so every day in the year: budding, flowering, fruiting, and leaf-shedding are always going on in one species or other. The activity of birds and insects proceeds without interruption, each species having its own separate times. . . . It is never either spring, summer, or autumn, but each day is a combination of all three. With the day and night always of equal length, the atmospheric disturbances of each day neutralising themselves before each succeeding morn; with the sun in its course proceeding mid-way across the sky, and the daily temperature the same within two or three degrees throughout the year—how grand in its perfect equilibrium and simplicity is the march of Nature under the equator! . . .

The same unbroken forest extends all the way to Maranham and in other directions, as we were told, a distance of about three hundred miles southward and eastward of Pará. In almost every hollow part the road was crossed by a brook, whose cold, dark, leaf-stained waters were bridged over by tree trunks. The ground was carpeted, as usual, by Lycopodiums, but it was also encumbered with masses of vegetable debris and a thick coating of dead leaves. Fruits of many kinds were scattered about, amongst which were many sorts of beans, some of the pods a foot long, flat and leathery in texture, others hard as stone. . . .

What attracted us chiefly were the colossal trees. The general run of trees had not remarkably thick stems; the great and uniform height to which they grow without emitting a branch, was a much more noticeable feature than their thickness; but at intervals of a furlong or so a veritable giant towered up. Only one of these monstrous trees can grow within a given space; it monopolises the domain, and none but individuals of much inferior size can find a footing near it. The cylindrical trunks of these larger trees were generally about twenty to twenty-five feet in circumference. Von Martius mentions having measured trees in the Pará district, belonging to various species . . . which were fifty to sixty feet in girth at the point where they become cylindrical. The height of the vast column-like stems could not be less than one hundred feet from the ground to their lowest branch. Mr. Leavens, at the saw-mills, told me they frequently squared logs for sawing one hundred feet long. . . . The total height of these trees, stem and crown together, may be estimated at from 180 to 200 feet: where one of them stands, the vast dome of foliage rises above the other forest trees as a domed cathedral does above the other buildings in a city.

A very remarkable feature in these trees is the growth of buttress-shaped projections around the lower part of their stems. The spaces between these buttresses, which are generally thin walls of wood, form spacious chambers, and may be compared to stalls in a stable: some of them are large enough to hold half a dozen persons. The purpose of these structures is as obvious, at the first glance, as that of the similar props of brickwork which support a high wall. They are not peculiar to one species, but are common to most of the larger forest trees. Their nature and manner of growth are explained when a series of young trees of different ages is examined. It is then seen that they are the roots which have raised themselves ridge-like out of the earth; growing gradually upwards as the increasing height of the tree required augmented support. Thus they are plainly intended to sustain the massive crown and trunk in these crowded forests, where lateral growth of the roots in the earth is rendered difficult by the multitude of competitors. . . .

In some parts of the road ferns were conspicuous objects. But I afterwards found them much more numerous on the Maranham road, especially in one place where the whole forest glade formed a vast fernery; the ground was covered with terrestrial species, and the tree trunks clothed with climbing and epiphytous kinds. I saw no tree ferns in the Pará district; they belong to hilly regions; some occur, however, on the Upper Amazons.

Such were the principal features in the vegetation of the wilderness; but where were the flowers? To our great disappointment we saw none, or only such as were insignificant in appearance. Orchids are very rare in the dense forests of the lowlands. I believe it is now tolerably well ascertained that the majority of forest trees in equatorial Brazil have small and inconspicuous flowers. Flower-frequenting insects are also rare in the forest. Of course they would not be found where their favourite food was wanting, but I always noticed that even where flowers occurred in the forest, few or no insects were seen upon them. In the open country or campos of Santarem, on the Lower Amazons, flowering trees and bushes are more abundant, and there a large number of floral insects are attracted. The forest bees of South America . . . are more frequently seen feeding on the sweet sap which exudes from the trees, or on the excrement of birds on leaves, than on flowers.

We were disappointed also in not meeting with any of the larger animals in the forest. There was no tumultuous movement, or sound of life. We did not see or hear monkeys, and no tapir or jaguar crossed our path. Birds, also, appeared to be exceedingly scarce. . . .

I afterwards saw reason to modify my opinion, founded on these first impressions, with regard to the amount and variety of animal life in this and other parts of the Amazonian forests. There is, in fact, a great variety of mammals, birds, and reptiles, but they are widely scattered, and all excessively shy of man. The region is so extensive, and uniform in the forest clothing of its surface, that it is only at long intervals that animals are seen in abundance, where some particular spot is found which is more attractive than others. Brazil, moreover, is throughout poor in terrestrial mammals, and the species are of small size; they do not, therefore, form a conspicuous feature in its forests. The huntsman would be disappointed who expected to find here flocks of animals similar to the buffalo herds of North America, or the swarms of antelopes and herds of ponderous pachyderms of Southern Africa. The largest and most interesting portion of the Brazilian mammal fauna is arboreal in its habits. . . . The most intensely arboreal animals in the world are the South American monkeys of the family Cebidae, many of which have a fifth hand for climbing in their prehensile tails, adapted for this function by their strong muscular development, and the naked palms under their tips. This seems to teach us that the South American fauna has been slowly adapted to a forest life, and therefore, that extensive forests must have always existed since the region was first peopled by mammalia. . . .

We often read, in books of travels, of the silence and gloom of the Brazilian forests. They are realities, and the impression deepens on a longer acquaintance. The few sounds of birds are of that pensive or mysterious character which intensifies the feeling of solitude rather than imparts a sense of life and cheerfulness. Sometimes, in the midst of the stillness, a sudden yell or scream will startle one; this comes from some defenceless fruit-eating animal, which is pounced upon by a tiger-cat or stealthy boa-constrictor. Morning and evening the howling monkeys make a most fearful and harrowing noise, under which it is difficult to keep up one's buoyancy of spirit. The feeling of inhospitable wildness which the forest is calculated to inspire, is increased tenfold under this fearful uproar. Often, even in the still hours of midday, a sudden crash will be heard resounding afar through the wilderness, as some great bough or entire tree falls to the ground. There are, besides, many sounds which it is impossible to account for.

2 John Vandermeer and Ivette Perfecto ◆ A Spider Web or a House of Cards?

John Vandermeer and Ivette Perfecto provide a contemporary Western scientific viewpoint in this excerpt from their book Breakfast of Biodiversity. *They summarize the current ecological understanding of the tropical rainforest, revealing how much scientists have learned since Bates's travels in Amazonia during the nineteenth century. Vandermeer and Perfecto confront several popular notions about tropical rainforests, and in this selection they focus on the ecological characteristics. They contend that some of the conventional wisdom about these ecosystems is too simplistic; because of its extraordinary biodiversity, the rainforest is variously described as being stable (resilient) or fragile (easily disturbed). Vandermeer and Perfecto claim that the terms of this debate are misleading. Instead, they propose that six key functions of rainforests should be considered: high biodiversity, pollination systems, responses to herbivory, seed dispersal strategies, light gap dynamics, and adaptation to soil infertility. The authors offer this framework for understanding how rainforests function in order to build a solid foundation for the political work of preserving environmental health and promoting economic justice for the rural inhabitants of rainforest regions. Vandermeer and Perfecto show that a good understanding of rainforest functions helps to provide insight into the environmental implications of the political, economic, and social forces that promote deforestation.*

The tropics is the area between the Tropic of Cancer and the Tropic of Capricorn. The lowland humid tropics, site of the world's rain forests, account for less than one-third of tropical lands—deserts, savannahs, and mountains also occur there. Tropical rain forests are evergreen, or partially evergreen, forests in areas that receive no less than four inches of precipitation in any month for two out of three years, and have a mean annual temperature of more than 24 degrees with no frost.[1] Tropical rain forests are found in three general regions of the world [America, Asia,

From John Vandermeer and Ivette Perfecto, *Breakfast of Biodiversity: The Truth about Rainforest Destruction* (Oakland: Food First Books, 1995), 19–38. Figures omitted. Reprinted by permission of the Institute for Food and Development Policy.

and Africa]. . . . Worldwide, tropical rain forests occupy 7.8 million square kilometers of land area,[2] and are being destroyed at a rate of almost 0.5 million square kilometers per year.[3]

Rain forests are enormously complicated creatures. Neither the people who live in them, nor the scientists who study them, understand everything about how rain forests work, which undoubtedly contributes to our mystical feelings about them. Yet comprehension need not elude us completely. Few of us understand how our automobiles work, but we do know certain basics—the motor will start when we turn on the ignition, and the accelerator pedal is quite distinct from the brake pedal. In this sense we can also comprehend the way rain forests function. No one knows all the details, and all is not yet understood, but what is known with some certainty can be explained about as easily as explaining how to put the key in the ignition, or when to step on the brake rather than the accelerator.

Most popular accounts of rain forest loss and/or preservation emphasize either a romantic or a utilitarian notion of rain forests, concentrating mostly on the larger political forces driving their destruction. This has led to some confusion, and no little dogma about what can and cannot, or should and should not, be done to save or restore rain forests.

Extent of Today's Rain Forests and Rate of Deforestation

Region	Current extent	Rate of annual deforestation
America	4 million square kilometers	0.19 square kilometers
Asia	2 million square kilometers	0.22 square kilometers
Africa	1.8 million square kilometers	0.05 square kilometers

The Rain Forest: Stable Web or Fragile House of Cards?

Since ecology began to fire the popular imagination in the 1960s, two major perceptions about the nature of ecosystems have resurfaced with remarkable regularity. These two ideas are in fundamental opposition to one another, yet this conflict frequently escapes notice. On the one hand, ecosystems are thought to be fragile and easily damaged by the careless hand of man or woman. On the other hand, ecosystems are considered stable organisms, honed by evolution to be harmonious; the "balance of nature" is considered a stable equilibrium. If an ecosystem is stable, it is obviously not likely to be fragile. Yet these conflicting notions surface repeatedly in the popular ecology movement.

Perhaps nowhere are these two ideas applied with such misguided fervor as in the popular literature on tropical rain forests. Curiously, both the fragility and the stability of rain forests are attributed to their characteristic high biodiversity. Two common metaphors may help explain the rationale behind this idea. On the one hand, the immense biodiversity in a rain forest may be thought of as the filaments in a spider web; the more connections, the stronger the web. Thus, because the rain forest has so many strands and so many connections, it must be very stable. On the other hand, the immense biodiversity may be represented as a house of cards, each card balanced precariously on edge, all the cards supporting one another to keep the house standing. This house of cards may be balanced because of the large number of cards, but removing just one could very well cause the entire structure to come tumbling down.

So which metaphor makes the most sense in fact? Is the rain forest a highly connected web that gains its strength and stability from its multiplicity of connections? Or is the rain forest a house of cards, precariously balanced, and subject at any moment to total collapse if a single card is removed?

It may surprise anyone who has read a few books about rain forests to learn that both these popular visions are probably way off the mark. In the past ten years the science of ecology has learned a great deal about how rain forests work. Added to what has already been gleaned from fifty years of tropical forestry, and from the accumulation of hundreds of years of knowledge of the indigenous people who live in these ecosystems, we now have a relatively clear understanding of the basic functioning of tropical rain forests. To be sure, an enormous number of particulars remain enigmatic—something to be expected from the sheer quantity of elements involved. But the overall picture is probably better understood than might be surmised from a look at the rain forest picture book on Uncle Ed's coffee table. Many of us do not understand how a carburetor works, yet we can easily grasp the function of the accelerator pedal. Similarly, many details of rain forest function are still poorly understood, yet we can fully grasp the nuances of biodiversity and other general features of rain forest function—and perhaps we can use that knowledge to our benefit.

Six Key Factors in Rain Forest Function

The overall picture of rain forest function can be understood with six key ideas. First, as is commonly mentioned in popular accounts of rain forests, there exists an enormous amount of diversity—different kinds of plants and animals and other living things. This diversity in and of itself generates some problems for individual species. For example, if hundreds of distinct species are to exist in the same place, that means most of them must be rare. If there is just room for 200 trees in a plot of land, and you wish to fit in 100 species, each species, on average, can only be represented by two individuals.

This brings up the second factor: sex. How do such rare individuals find mates? The dominant elements of the forest are plants, and especially trees, and sex in plants happens through the process of pollination.

The third key factor is the problem (from the point of view of plants) of herbivores: the many insects and animals that enjoy eating leaves, shoots, and seeds. How plants deal with herbivores is a major piece of the story of how rain forests work. Herbivores tend to specialize on particular species of plants. For example, the mahogany moth eats nothing but mahogany trees. If mahogany trees are interspersed with numerous different species, as is the case when most species are rare, mahogany moths will have trouble finding their dinner. If mahogany trees are all clumped together, they make an excellent target for herbivores.

This leads to the fourth factor, the dispersal of offspring. If seeds just drop to the base of a plant, and the young plants grow there, any insect that happens to find the adult will find the offspring too. So plants have evolved various strategies to disperse their seeds.

The fifth item is death. In the context of the forest, a dead tree signifies much more than simply the passing away of one individual in a population. A dead tree means a gap in the canopy of the forest. Sunlight may now enter that gap and, for a time, the understory of the forest is quite different than it was before the death of the tree. Thus, a major element of rain forest function is the formation of light gaps by falling trees. What happens in these gaps is of utmost importance to the structure of the forest.

The sixth key factor in rain forest function is the soil. The matrix from which the trees must draw their sustenance is very special for tropical rain forest trees. The same physical forces that make the rain forest itself so incredibly lush also make the soils on which they live rather infertile—an apparent contradiction that we explain below.

So these six factors—high biodiversity, pollination, herbivory, seed dispersal, light gap dynamics, and soils—are the simple elements of how tropical rain forests function. We note in passing that each of these six key elements will play a part in any and all proposed management schemes of tropical rain forest areas. They will be useful in understanding the enigma of poor farming potential in the most lush ecosystem on Earth, the headaches of reforestation after commercial logging, and how to make good on the promise of food from the forest.

Biodiversity

We begin by examining the most obvious factor. In a forested area in Northern Michigan we found eight species of trees in a sample of one hectare (approximately 2.47 acres). In the same-size area in the rain forest of Nicaragua we have thus far encountered about 200 species of trees.[4] Entomologists netting insects in Kansas found 90 species of insects, whereas applying their nets in the same fashion in a rain forest in Costa

Rica they found 545 species.[5] In a Peruvian rain forest entomologist E. O. Wilson identified 43 species of ants in a single tree, almost as many as those reported for all the British Isles.[6] In the Americas, bird species increase approximately fivefold from mid latitudes to the tropics.[7] While there are exceptions to this rule (for example, the number of small rodents running around in the leaf litter of a tropical rain forest is about the same as, or even lower than, the number running around in a northern forest), this general pattern is repeated for most kinds of organisms one examines—trees, herbs, insects, birds, etc.[8]

Ecologists have been debating the significance of the high degree of rain forest biodiversity for a long time, and so far have not come up with a satisfying explanation. On the one hand, there is the persistent and enigmatic question of what causes this great amount of diversity. Initially it seemed that the high productivity afforded by large quantities of rainfall and hot temperatures would promote much diversity. However, when ecologists examined this idea closely it did not prove to be true. Indeed, there are convincing arguments that greater productivity could actually result in much lower diversity. From the point of view of how much material is actually produced per unit time, the most productive ecosystem in the world is a modern cornfield. Other ecologists have suggested that the longer duration the tropics have been free of the ice sheets that covered much of the temperate zone during the great Ice Ages has allowed for the evolution of more different kinds of organisms. But here, too, there are opposing arguments and this "time hypothesis" remains, at best, controversial. We could go on with a variety of other explanations, but the story is the same for each one of them. While [Isaac] Newton was able to explain the laws of gravity, and [Charles] Darwin explained how biological organisms evolved, no comparable explanation yet exists for why some places (like the tropics) have many species, while other places (like the Arctic) have so few.

Though the origin of this diversity remains an enigma, the answer to the related question of how all these species are maintained in the same system is slowly being worked out. As mentioned above, the assumption that the more things in a system, the more stable the system, has been accepted in the popular literature on rain forests for years. But a careful analysis of how ecosystems work has led us to the surprising conclusion that the fundamental theories of ecology actually predict the opposite. In fact, the more diverse the system, the more likely it is to be fragile. Our house-of-cards metaphor seems more likely to be true than the spider web.

Realizing that a high-biodiversity system, like a rain forest, is more likely to be fragile than stable, ecologists in the 1980s began trying to figure out how such diverse systems could be maintained. That is, rather than assuming that such complex systems were stable as a spider web and asking where they came from, we began admitting that maybe rain forests weren't so stable and asking how they could persist in the real world if they were house-of-cards fragile.

This is where ecology stands today regarding the issue of rain forest stability or fragility. The answers are certainly not yet well established, but the questions are clearer now than they have been before. Two research agendas appear to be dominating this issue today. First, many are asking questions about the particular way in which ecosystems are held together—the details of the balancing cards, so to speak—whether a tree with many rare herbivores can coexist in the neighborhood of a tree with a few common ones, or whether a beetle that eats a bug that eats an herb is more likely to persist in the long run than a beetle that eats a beetle that eats the bug that eats the herb.[9] Second, other ecologists are focusing on the role of disturbance events such as storms and landslides.[10] Since such disturbance events are as much a part of nature as the biological organisms that make up the ecosystem, it seems important to understand what their ultimate effect might be. How the diversity arose in the first place is something of an enigma.[11]

Pollination

Since the evolution of flowering plants over a hundred million years ago, terrestrial ecosystems have been dominated by a fundamental *mutualism*— animals help plants have sex and the plants reward the animals with food. The hummingbird drinks nectar from the flower of the wild banana plant and takes the pollen from one banana plant to another. The hummingbird gets fed and the banana plant has sex. Both species benefit from this interaction, the definition of mutualism. While the vast majority of plants in the world are pollinated by insects, the rain forest also contains special pollinating systems involving birds and bats.

In a rain forest, the problem of pollination is basically one of being rare and wanting to have sex (i.e., wanting to reproduce). The problem is solved in a variety of ways, but most commonly in one of four specific forms. First, particular species may be rare over a large range, but common in a local area. This leaves certain technical genetic problems unresolved and creates problems with elevated herbivory, but solves the simple problem of reproduction. Pollen can reach ova quite easily if a rare species always exists in a clump of its own.

Second, many rare species have evolved a process called *selfing*. Using a variety of mechanisms, many tree species are effectively hermaphrodites. This means that a single individual has the reproductive organs of both sexes. While this seems an obvious solution to the problem of reproduction, it creates enormous alternative complications associated with inbreeding. We all know what happens when cousins marry, and the genetic problems faced by the royal families who inbred are legion. Such problems are magnified enormously when an individual mates with itself. . . .

Third, many pollinating systems for rare plant species include synchronous mass flowering and a long-distance pollinator. For example, some tree species typically display all their flowers in unison, once per year, and all the individuals in the population of that species do so simultaneously. These trees use, as pollinators, bees capable of flying very long distances between meals. Thus, over an extended area, while the trees themselves occur only occasionally amongst a mass of other species, when it is time for sex, all the individuals in the extended population put out all their flowers at the same time. The bees are able to fly from one tree to the other, picking them out amidst the mass of greenery of all the other species because of the abundance of colorful flowers in their crowns.

The synchronous mass-flowering strategy has certain prerequisites. The pollinating bees must be supplied with a food source for the entire year. A particular species of tree will likely only flower for a week or two during that year. In order to have at least one species of tree flowering at all times during the year (an absolute necessity for the bee), there must be a minimum number of tree species in the forest. So, for example, if each of the tree species flowers for two weeks during the year, an absolute minimum of 26 tree species will be needed to maintain this particular form of pollination (assuming any overlap in flowering time is minimal). This requirement has dire consequences for any strategy that attempts to preserve small patches of forest. If, by accident, the patch is missing or loses just one of the necessary 26 species of trees, the whole system could collapse since the bees would die during that two-week period without food; and without their specialized pollinators, the trees would be unable to reproduce.

The fourth solution to the problem of reproduction for rare species is the habit of *trap-lining*. Some birds and insects are capable of creating a mental map in order to remember the locations of particular food sources. An individual plant that is currently producing flowers may be very far from others of its species, but a hummingbird, for example, may know exactly where the next individual of that species is located. The hummingbird thus has a number of individual plants in mind when she sets off in the morning to find food. She tanks up on nectar at the first site and then flies off to the next plant, remembering from day to day where these particular individual plants are located. She has, metaphorically, a trap line (trappers frequently refer to the series of traps they put out each night as a trap line) formed by the flowering plants she visits each day. The individual plants, in turn, produce only a few flowers each day, attracting the pollinator, but not monopolizing its attention, so that it may fly off to the next individual in the trap line.

These, then, are the four principal ways in which the problem of sex under conditions of rarity has been solved: local clumping, selfing, synchronous mass flowering, and trap-lining. Of course the details of pollination systems are far more complicated than we indicate here. But the basic patterns are really quite simple.

Herbivory

Herbivory as a way of life has existed for hundreds of millions of years. The spectacular elephants and lithe gazelles of the African savannas, or the cattle herds that graze America's western plains are well-known examples of herbivores. While insects are the most important pollinators in tropical rain forests, they are not universally beneficial to plants. As herbivores, insects are probably the plant's biggest threat to life.

Of the many important consequences of herbivory, one that has significance for humans is the evolutionary response of both plant and herbivore. Plants have evolved an overwhelming array of defenses against the many herbivores that potentially attack them. Three major types of defense have evolved: structural, chemical, and mutualistic.

Structural defenses include all of the spines and hairs that one knows so well from spiny vines, stinging nettles, and cacti. Such structures certainly need no further explanation. But at a more microscopic level, small hairs, what we might normally regard as fuzz, on the surface of leaves, extra thick cuticle on the stem, and a host of other microscopic equivalents of spines have evolved as a protection against insect herbivores. What seems like fuzz to us is an array of stilettos to a tiny insect.

Only recently have chemical defenses been fully appreciated. While we have known for years that many plants are poisonous, we did not realize that most of those poisons had evolved mainly as a defense against herbivores. Indeed, we now appreciate that most plants, especially those living in tropical rain forests, produce chemicals to protect against the ravages of herbivores—natural insecticides, so to speak.

There is, however, a secondary consequence of this chemical defense. Herbivores themselves evolve. And, just as one can often find a chemical antidote for a poison, herbivores have frequently been able to evolve antidotes for the poisons that plants produce to protect themselves. This process is so common that ecologists have dubbed it the "co-evolutionary arms race." Every time an herbivore evolves a detoxifying mechanism to deal with a plant poison, the plant is subjected to pressure to evolve a new poison, which puts pressure on the herbivore to develop a new detoxifying mechanism. This seems to be a continuously operative process in nature, and has significant consequences for those seeking to engage in agriculture in rain forest environments.

The third form of herbivore defense is mutualism. In a wide variety of cases, plants have evolved the capacity to use other insects to protect themselves from herbivores. The most celebrated case is that of the ant and the acacia plant. Acacia plants produce hollow spines in which stinging ants live. Further, the acacias provide the ants with a self-contained energy and protein source (the acacia produces glands that produce food exclusively for the use of the ant). In return, the ants act as a kind of armed guard for the acacias. They will viciously swarm over and kill any herbivore that makes the mistake of trying to eat the leaves of their host. This phenomenon is quite common and represents the plant taking advantage of the overall structures of the ecosystem. Every herbivore has natural enemies, parasites and predators that eat it. Structures may evolve to attract and co-opt these natural enemies, thus creating a mutualistic relationship between the plant and the predators of its natural enemy—a natural embodiment of the adage, "My enemy's enemy is my friend."

Seed Dispersal

While the problems related to seed dispersal exist all over the world, they are especially important in a tropical forest. Seeds are usually the most energy-rich part of a plant and are thus a prime target for herbivores. The vast majority of energy that humans use is obtained from such seeds as wheat, corn, and rice. If seeds are simply dropped in a bunch at the base of the parent tree, they make an excellent target for the herbivorous insects and mammals that eat them. Consequently, most plant species have evolved mechanisms to disperse their seeds away from the fixed position of the parent plant. In tropical rain forests these mechanisms frequently involve animals, especially mammals and birds.

There is something of a contradiction involved in seed dispersal. While it is generally a good, even necessary, process, seed dispersers also have the potential of being seed predators. Squirrels eating acorns, for example, may very well eat all the acorns produced by a tree, leaving none to produce the future generation of oak trees. To solve this problem, plants have evolved two general methods: separation of seed from the disperser's food reward, and satiation. In the vast majority of cases, plants have evolved attractant structures to entice dispersers to scatter their seeds. Almost all of the fruits we eat are examples of this strategy. A bird that eats a berry digests the pulp of the fruit and passes the seeds in its stool. When a horse eats an apple, the lure of the apple is not the tiny brown seeds within, but the juicy pulp—the horse passes the seeds unharmed. The reward for the animal disperser has been separated from the seed itself.

In a significant number of cases the seed is the attractive structure, for example, oaks and their acorns. Since the disperser, in this case the squirrel, is by definition also a seed predator, a contradiction emerges: how to provide the attraction, yet get the seeds dispersed. This is actually a rather complicated issue and its resolution is only partly understood. It involves a concept called *satiation*. Oak trees tend to have so-called mast years, in which an unusually large number of acorns are produced by all the trees in a population. After three or four years of relatively low production of acorns, in a mast year all the trees in a river basin produce an excessive number of acorns. The consequences are not surprising. After a short supply of acorns for three or four years, the squirrel population has thinned out, and all the squirrels in the river basin are simply not capable of eating the large number of acorns produced. They are satiated. In a mast year the animals are satiated as seed predators and are thus able to act as seed dispersers. In the example at hand, the squirrels continue to gather and bury acorns, but have little motivation to go back, dig up, and eat them. Thus they leave a significant number of acorns to germinate and produce new oak trees. This process of seed-predator satiation is sometimes very important in rain forests, and is almost universal among the dominant trees of the Southeast Asian rain forests.

Gap Dynamics and Other Forms of Disturbance

Old forests typically have old trees, and trees do not live forever. A sudden gust of wind will bring an old tree down, creating a hole in the forest canopy, and bathing the understory with light. What follows is that sun-loving plant species, known as *pioneers*, enter the gap first, followed by secondary species, and eventually a *climax* tree grows up to take the place of the tree which fell. Climax refers to the ultimate stage in this successional sequence. Specific kinds of species are associated with each stage in the sequence, the climax species being the ones that are not further replaced until they die. The process of replacing a fallen tree with a new adult tree takes anywhere from thirty to hundreds of years, depending on the type of forest. The continual process of a tree growing, becoming large, falling to create a gap, and eventually being replaced by another, is thought to be a major force influencing how rain forests are structured, and therefore how they function.[12]

Recent studies suggest that over the last few decades, the turnover rate of these gaps has increased in tropical rain forests.[13] In other words, they form more frequently than in the past. Although the reasons for this increase are not known, it has been suggested that the consequences will be a change in forest structure, and a possible change in function, with an increased predominance of light-demanding plants and the eventual extinction of slow-growing, shade-tolerant species. Plants absorb carbon dioxide and release oxygen. The carbon in the carbon dioxide is incorporated into the tissue of the plants. Trees with harder wood tend to *sequester* more carbon than trees with softer wood. Light-demanding and fast-growing trees generally have softer wood than the shade-tolerant slower-growing ones. Thus, if the structure of the forest changes from one dominated by slow-growing species to fast-growing ones, the forest will change the rate at which it absorbs carbon dioxide from the air. Since carbon dioxide is one of the main greenhouse gases, this change in forest structure may contribute to the increase in global warming.

In the past few years a great deal of attention has been given to changes in rain forests following destructive storms. A large storm may create an exceedingly large light gap in the forest, and the question arises whether post-storm succession is simply a very big light gap, or whether something qualitatively different happens because of the immense size of the damage done by the storm. This is an important question, and while the answer is still elusive, many studies are currently under way. A storm's damage to the forest is similar in many respects (though not all) to damage done by a logging operation. Understanding the natural processes of how the forest responds to a storm gap or a light gap might very well provide insight for designing more ecologically rational methods of forestry than those in current use.

A final point is worth making here. In the past it has been presumed by romantics that tropical rain forests are ancient places, super-stable cathedrals of towering trunks whose age defied human imagination, hardly touched by the hand of *Homo sapiens*, nor ravaged by the vicissitudes of nature. This vision is simply not true. Tropical forests are frequently subjected to tropical storms that periodically knock down almost all the trees, to landslides that remove large sections of vegetation, to naturally occurring fires, and, most importantly in the past several thousand years (at least), to the hunting and agricultural pressure of *Homo sapiens*. Finding a truly "untouched" forest is hardly possible.

This is an important issue. Tropical rain forests can withstand a great amount of physical damage over the long term. They may appear fragile, but we now know they also have a high capacity to restore themselves—perhaps *not resistant* to damaging events, but they are quite *resilient* if given the chance. They inevitably grow back after large storms, after landslides, and after peasant agriculture. The only damage, which may be permanent, results from modern degradations—urbanization and chemically intensive agriculture. A peasant who cuts down a forest to plant corn for a couple of years and then abandons the site does little long-term damage (the forest grows back). But a banana company that physically alters the soil structure, chemically changes the content of the soil, and saturates the ecosystem with pesticides, has a far greater effect. And a piece of land covered with cement will not recuperate as a tropical forest except over a very long period of time. . . .

Soils

Plants get most of their nutrients through their root systems. This means that the soil, where the roots lie, is one important determinant of how well a plant does. In understanding the basics of soils it is appropriate to focus on two related but distinct questions. How does the plant get nutrients out of the soil? And how are nutrients stored in the soil?

How plants get nutrients out of the soil is well understood, largely because of the importance of this topic to the agricultural sciences. Many nutrients occur in the soil as small, charged particles—ions. They are like lint particles with a static-electric charge. The most important nutrients that occur this way are potassium, magnesium, calcium, and one of two forms of nitrogen. All of these have a positive charge, and they are all attached to small clay particles, much like a small magnet attaches to a metal surface. As part of their normal life's activities, plant roots give off positively charged ions (just as we must excrete urine, plants must excrete certain products of their metabolism). Thus, there is a continual gradient of acidity as you move away from the surface of the root (recall that acidity is simply the concentration of positive charges). Because the plant roots give off positive ions, the zone immediately next to the root surface is more acid than the rest of the soil. When the clay particles with the positively charged nutrients attached come near to the plant roots, they encounter this more acid environment. Because the nutrients are now in a changed environment, they change their chemical form and suddenly become available to be absorbed through the root. It is sort of like the magnets attached to the metal surface are displaced by other magnets, metaphorically the small positive-charged ions that are excreted from the roots. And once they are free of the clay particles (once the magnets disengage from the metal surface), they are available to be absorbed into the root of the plant. It is important to note that it is the gradient of acidity that is important. As explained below, the positively charged ions are held fast in the soil at an equilibrium level associated with the acidity. It is the sudden change to a more acid state that makes them available to the plant root.

The way soils store nutrients is also well understood. Two parts of the soil structure are important: the clays, and the organic matter. The clays are exceedingly large chemicals (tiny by absolute standards, but huge as chemical molecules go) whose surface is covered with negative electrostatic charges. Because of their negative charge they attract the positively charged ions in the soil. The greater the abundance of this clay component of the soil, the more positive ions will be attached. Here lies the key point. If the positive ions are not attached to anything, they tend to wash out of the system. Thus, it is extremely important to have clay in the soil to keep nutrients from leaching out of the soil.

Humus, the decomposed organic material of dead plants and animals, functions in a similar way. Very small pieces of humus have negative electrostatic charges on their surface and, like the clay particles, they hold the positively charged ions on their surface. Thus, in terms of plant nutrition and soil fertility, humus acts exactly like the clays, attracting and holding onto positive nutrient ions in the soil, and then releasing them when it comes into contact with the plant roots. But organic matter has an additional use as well. As it decays it releases nutrient ions into the soil. It thus acts as a slow releaser of fertilizer.

Putting together the two concepts of nutrient storage and absorption, it is easy to see the fundamental mechanisms of soil fertility. To the extent that clay particles and humus in the soil have negative charges on their surface, they will tend to take up all the positive charges in the soil, including positively charged nutrient ions. But when one of these clay or humus particles is washed close to the surface of a plant root, a more acid environment is encountered and some of their positive nutrient ions are replaced with positive ions the plant has excreted. The positive nutrient ion is thus freed from the clay particle, and free to be absorbed through the root of the plant. Note how important the acidity gradient is to the whole process. If, when a clay particle moves close to the plant root, it is not induced to give up some of the nutrient ions sticking to its surface, those ions will not be available to the plant. And if there is no gradient (for example, if all of the soil is very acid so that the zone next to the surface of the root is no different), none of those nutrient ions will be available.

That, then, is the general picture of soil fertility and plant nutrition. First, clay particles and humus hang on to the nutrients, preventing them from washing out of the system. Then, when the clay and/or humus particles come within the vicinity of a root surface, they give up the nutrients they are carrying so the plant can absorb them.

Tropical rain forest soils have several characteristics, which make them problematic.[14] First, they are highly acid. This means that the critical acidity gradient between the general soil and the root surface is less dramatic than in other soils. Thus, any crops that farmers try to grow tend to have problems getting the proper nutrients from the soil. Second, rain forest soils typically have the type of clay particles that bear few negative charges on their surfaces and are thus not capable of storing very many nutrient ions. Whatever nutrients may be present, even those from added chemical fertilizer, tend to rapidly leach out of the soil. Third, because of continually high temperature and abundant moisture, the process of decomposition occurs rapidly and the organic matter thus disappears rapidly when the natural forest is taken away. This means that both the source of nutrients and the storage capacity of the soil, consequences of soil organic matter, are very poor when farmers try to grow crops.[15]

The Diversity of Tropical Rain Forests

A fact often not fully appreciated in the popular imagination or literature is that tropical rain forests not only contain a great deal of biodiversity, but there is an enormous diversity amongst kinds of tropical rain forests as well. In a single region one may find distinct combinations of plants and animals on ridgetops as compared to valley bottoms, or on well-drained soils versus humid soils. Indeed, it is the bane of the lumber operator in the American tropics that some patches of forest contain particularly useful species of trees, while other patches contain mainly species that have little market value.

Most important at this level of diversity is the distinction between major groups of forests. . . . The world's major tropical rain forests—in the Americas, Africa, and Southeast Asia—do not operate by universal rules, and indeed, sometimes differences between them are extremely important for the practical problems of forestry and agriculture.

For example, many of the forests of Southeast Asia are dominated by a single family of trees, the *Dipterocarpaceae*. In these forests this family may comprise up to 80 percent of the canopy trees and 40 percent of those in the understory, whereas in Africa there is only a handful of tree species that belong to this family, and in South America, perhaps just one.[16] The *Dipterocarpaceae* family contains tree species that typically have straight trunks, grow to a very large size, and can usually be converted into valuable timber. Because of their generally large size and uniformly straight trunks, they are a timber company's dream. In a single hectare of Southeast Asian rain forest, one might encounter 200 species of trees, 180 of which will be in the family *Dipterocarpaceae*. By comparison a similar plot in America or Africa might also contain 200 species, but they may be members of 150 families, and the most common family might contain only 10 species. Thus, almost any area of a dipterocarp forest can be utilized for cutting, as compared with the American or African tropics where an area must be carefully scouted ahead of time to locate patches of valuable timber.

Furthermore, Southeast Asian forests have a very different physical aspect as compared with American rain forests. The understory vegetation in a Southeast Asian forest is composed mainly of the small trees, seedlings, and saplings which will eventually grow up to become the large trees of the forest. In America, this vegetational stratum is dominated by plants that live only in the understory. This understory is where a wide variety of ornamental plants and other species come from. They never grow very large and live comfortably in a low-light environment such as is found in a rain forest understory, doctor's office, or suburban shopping mall.

Such differences suggest that the details of ecology are also quite discrete from place to place, and the more we learn of rain forests the

clearer it becomes that this is true. It is becoming increasingly difficult
. . . to make generalizations that apply to all tropical rain forests. Professional ecologists rarely refer any longer to "the tropical rain forest," but rather specify whether they are talking about an American, African, or Asian forest.

The Biological Side Summarized

It is useful to understand how a rain forest works, and certainly it will be helpful to comprehend both what happens, and why, when a rain forest is converted to agriculture. . . . Knowledge of these issues will also be constructive as we try to come to grips with the difficulties of developing sustainable logging methods for rain forests. Finally, the political, economic, and social forces that are really behind the destruction of the world's rain forests are made clearer with the help of this background.

By now, hopefully, we have demonstrated that neither of our metaphors is perfectly accurate. Rain forests are not terribly fragile, nor are they especially stable. Rain forests are, however, highly complex and require a great deal of detailed plumbing and wiring and housekeeping—pollination systems, seed dispersal, defenses against herbivores, and proper soil conditions—in order to function properly. Rain forests may even require periodic natural disasters such as storms and landslides, and they are attuned to the recurring formation of light gaps. And while the plants of the rain forest live in an Eden of heat and water, they suffer from a virtually empty pantry of the nutrients they need to survive.

Notes

1. Myers, N. 1980. *The Conservation of Tropical Moist Forests.* Washington, DC: National Academy of Sciences.
2. Whitmore, T. C. 1991. *An Introduction to Tropical Rain Forests.* Oxford: Clarendon Press.
3. World Resources Institute. 1994. *World Resources 94–94.* Oxford: Oxford University Press.
4. Vandermeer, J. H., M. S. Mallona, D. Boucher, K. Yih, and I. Perfecto. 1995. Three years of ingrowth following catastrophic hurricane damage on the Caribbean coast of Nicaragua: evidence in support of the direct regeneration hypothesis. *Journal of Tropical Ecology,* 11(3): 465–471.
5. Janzen, D. H. and T. W. Schoener. 1968. Differences in insect abundance and diversity between wetter and drier sites during a tropical dry season. *Ecology* 49: 96–110.
6. Hölldobler, B. and E. O. Wilson. 1990. *The Ants.* Cambridge, MA: Harvard University Press.
7. Terborgh, J. 1992. *Diversity and the Tropical Rain Forest.* New York: Scientific American Library.
8. Huston, M. 1993. Biological diversity. Soils and economics. *Science* 262: 1676–1680.

9. Werner, E. E. 1992. Individual behavior and higher-order species interactions. *American Naturalist* 140: S5–S32; Schoener, T. W. 1993. On the relative importances of direct versus indirect effects in ecological communities. In H. Kawanabe, J. E. Cohen, and K. Iwasaki (eds.), *Mutualism and Community Organization: Behavioral, Theoretical and Food Web Approaches,* pp. 365–411. Oxford: Oxford University Press.

10. Yih, K., D. Boucher, J. H. Vandermeer, and N. Zamora. 1991. Recovery of the rainforest of southeastern Nicaragua after destruction by Hurricane Joan. *Biotropica* 23: 106–113; Mooney, H. A. and M. Gordon (eds.). 1983. *Disturbance and Ecosystems.* Berlin: Springer-Verlag.

11. Ricklef, R. E. and D. Schluter. 1993. *Species Diversity in Ecological Communities: Historical and Geographical Perspectives.* Chicago: University of Chicago Press.

12. Denslow, J. S. 1987. Tropical rainforest gaps and tree species diversity. *Annual Review of Ecology and Systematics* 18: 431–451.

13. Phillips, O. L. and A. H. Gentry. 1994. Increasing turnover through time in tropical forests. *Science* 263: 954–958.

14. Richter, D. D. and L. I. Babbar. 1991. Soil diversity in the tropics. *Advances in Ecological Research* 321: 315–389.

15. However, if there is a general characteristic that applies to all tropical soils, it is their heterogeneity. Having most of their experience in temperate regions of the world, many soil scientists viewed tropical soils as uniformly acid and infertile. More recent studies have emphasized that this view is incorrect (Sanchez, P. A. 1976. *Properties and Management of Soils in the Tropics.* New York: John Wiley and Sons; Richter, D. D. and L. I. Babbar. 1991. Soil diversity in the tropics. *Advances in Ecological Research* 321: 315–389), that soils vary from highly fertile to highly infertile in the tropics. On the other hand, for most regions of the tropics, agricultural conversion has already discovered the good soils, and the remaining rain forests are generally on very poor acid soils.

16. The species of this family found in South America is a recently described species, which is placed in its own subfamily, but its relationship with the Asian and African dipterocarps is somewhat enigmatic. (Mabberley, D. J. 1992. *Tropical Rain Forest Ecology.* New York: Chapman and Hall)

---

3 José Eustasio Rivera ◆ The Champion of Destruction

José Eustasio Rivera's powerful 1924 novel, La Vorágine *(The Vortex), is today virtually unknown in North America, yet his passionate protest against the exploitation of man and nature in the Amazon rainforest expresses surprisingly contemporary sentiments, however romantic and archaic the language. He talks about intergenerational equity—that overexploitation today defrauds future generations—and about how economic expansion exploits humans and nature, concerns that mainstream social scientists have only recently begun to articulate.*

Rivera is clearly outraged by the degradation of the rubber tappers and the inhumanity of the system of latex extraction that arose during the

From José Rivera, *The Vortex*, trans. Earle K. James (New York: Putnam, 1935), 260–62, 268–72.

great *Amazon rubber boom of the nineteenth and early twentieth centuries. Based on debt peonage that essentially enslaved the rubber tappers,
it mired them in abject poverty and misery while enriching the merchants
and rubber barons who claimed to own vast tracts of rainforest where the
rubber trees grew. The system continued until the 1970s in Brazil, when a
grassroots social movement gained enough political power to free the
rubber tappers from debt bondage (see Selection 18). Rivera foreshadows
the Brazilian rural workers' movement of the late twentieth century.*

    *His portrayal of the tropical rainforest as a vortex that sucks people
into danger and degradation, however, seems an anachronism characteristic of his time and culture. The* Vortex *belongs to a Latin American genre
of* novelas teluricas *(novels of the land) of the early twentieth century in
which the wilderness is seen as barbaric while urban life is regarded as
the essence of civilization. Rivera likens the rainforest to a prison cell
rather than to a cathedral, as Bates did in Selection 1. A member of a
Colombian commission to survey the country's boundary with Venezuela,
Rivera actually experienced many of the dangers and hardships that the
protagonist of the novel suffered. Indeed, Rivera's untimely death in 1928
was attributed to the effects of a tropical disease contracted during his
time in the rainforest.*

No one knows what it is that upsets and confuses us when we travel
through the jungles. Nevertheless, I think I've found the explanation: any of these trees would seem tame, friendly, even smiling in a park,
along a road on a plain, where nobody would bleed it or persecute it; yet
here they are all perverse, or aggressive, or hypnotizing. In these lonely
places, under these shadows, they have their own way of fighting us: something scares us, something makes us shudder, something oppresses us,
and then jungle giddiness turns our head, and we want to flee, and we get
lost—and because of this, thousands of rubber workers never emerge from
the jungle.

"I, too, have felt its evil influence—especially in Yaguanarí."

For the first time I saw the inhuman jungle in all its horror, saw the
pitiless struggle for existence. Deformed trees were held imprisoned by
creepers. Lianas bound them together in a death grip. Stretched from tree
to palm in long elastic curves, like carelessly hung nets, they caught falling leaves, branches, and fruits, held them for years until they sagged and
burst like rotten bags, scattering blind reptiles, rusty salamanders, hairy
spiders and decayed vegetable matter over the underbrush.

Everywhere the matapalo—the pulpy creeper of the forest—sticks its
tentacles on the treetrunks, twisting and strangling them, injecting itself
into them, and fusing with them in a painful metempsychosis. The
bachaqueros vomit forth trillions of devastating ants. These mow down
the mantle of the jungles and return to their tunnels over the wide swaths
they cut, carrying leaves aloft like the banners of an army of extinction.

The comején grub gnaws at the trees like quick-spreading syphilis, boring unseen from within, rotting tissue and pulverizing bark, until the weight of branches that are still living brings the giant crashing to the ground.

Meanwhile, the earth continues its successive renovations: at the foot of the colossus that falls, new germs are budding; pollen is flying in the midst of miasmas; everywhere is the reek of fermentation, steaming shadows, the sopor of death, the enervating process of procreation. Where is that solitude poets sing of? Where are those butterflies like translucent flowers, the magic birds, those singing streams? Poor phantasies of those who know only domesticated retreat!

No cooing nightingales here, no Versaillesian gardens or sentimental vistas! Instead the croaking of dropsical frogs, the tangled misanthropic undergrowth, the stagnant backwaters and swamps. Here the aphrodisiac parasite that covers the ground with dead insects; the disgusting blooms that throb with sensual palpitations, their sticky smell intoxicating as a drug; the malignant liana, the hairs of which blind animals; the pringamosa that irritates the skin; the berry of the curujú, a rainbow-hued globe that holds only a caustic ash; the purging grape; the bitter nut of the corojo palm.

At night, unknown voices, phantasmagoric lights, funereal silences. It is death that passes, giving life. Fruits fall, and on falling give promise of new seed. Leaves come to earth with a faint sighing, to become fertilizer for the roots of the parent tree. Crunching jaws are heard, devouring with the fear of being devoured. Warning whistles, dying wails, beasts belching. And when dawn showers its tragic glory over the jungles, the clamor of survivors again begins: the zoom of the shrieking guan; the wild boar crashing through the underbrush; the laughter of ridiculous monkeys. All for the brief joy of a few more hours of life!

This sadistic and virgin jungle casts premonitions of coming danger over one's spirit. Vegetable life is a sensitive thing, the psychology of which we ignore. In these desolate places only our presentiments understand the language it speaks. Under its influence man's nerves become taut and ready to attack, are ready for treachery and ambush. Our senses confuse their tasks: the eye feels, the back sees, the nose explores, the legs calculate, and the blood cries out: "Flee! Flee!"

And yet, it is civilized man who is the champion of destruction. There is something magnificent in the story of these pirates who enslave their peons, exploit the environment, and struggle with the jungle. Buffeted by misfortune, they leave the anonymity of cities to plunge into the wilderness, seeking a purpose for their sterile life. Delirious from malaria, they loose themselves of their conscience, and adapt themselves to the environment; and with no arms but the rifle and the machete, they suffer the most atrocious needs, while longing for pleasures and plenty. They live exposed to the elements, always ravenous, even naked, for here clothes rot on one's body.

Then some day, on the rock of some river, they build their thatched huts and appoint themselves "masters of the enterprise." Although the jungle is their enemy, they don't know whom to fight; so they fall upon one another and kill and subdue their own kind during intervals in their onslaught on the forests; and at times their trail is like that left by an avalanche. Every year the rubber workers in Colombia destroy millions of trees, while in Venezuela the balatá rubber tree has disappeared. In this way they defraud the coming generations. . . .

Dreams never realized, triumphs that were lost—why do you hover in my memory, as if trying to shame me? See what this visionary has come to: wounding an inert tree, in order to fatten the wealth of those who do not dream; enduring insults and tyranny just for a few crumbs at night-fall!

Slave, do not complain of your fatigue! Prisoner, do not regret your jail! You know nothing of the torture of wandering unfettered in a prison like the jungle, a green vault walled in by immense rivers. You don't know the torment of the shadows, when one may see a glimpse of sunshine on the opposite shore of a river, but a distant bank one can never reach. The chains that gnaw your ankles are more merciful than the leeches in these swamps. The keeper who torments you is not so cruel as these trees, who watch you without ever speaking.

I have three hundred trees to take care of, and it takes me nine days to lacerate them. I have cleaned them of creepers and lianas. I have opened a path toward each of them. On trudging through this army of giants, to fell the ones that don't shed latex, I often find tappers stealing my rubber. We tear at each other with fists and machetes; and the disputed latex is splashed with red. But what does it matter if our veins increase the supply of sap? The overseer demands ten liters a day, and the lash is a usurer that never forgives.

And what if my neighbor dies of fever? I see him stretched out on the leafy mold, shaking himself, trying to rid himself of flies that will not let him die in peace. Tomorrow I shall move away, driven elsewhere by the stench. But I shall steal the latex he gathered. My work will be so much lighter. They'll do the same with me when I die. I who have never stolen, not even to help my parents, will steal when I can for my oppressors.

As I gash the dripping trunk, as I channel it so that its tears may flow into the tin cup, clouds of mosquitoes that protect it suck my blood, and the miasmas of the forests dim my eyes. Thus both the tree and I, suffering, are tearful in the face of death: and both of us struggle until we succumb.

Yet I cannot pity the organism that does not protest. Tremorous branches are not a sign of rebellion that will inspire me with affection. Why doesn't the entire jungle roar out and crush us, like reptiles, in order to punish this vile exploitation? I feel no sadness—only desperation.

I would like to have somebody with whom to conspire! I'd like to start a gigantic battle of the species, die in cataclysmic struggles, see the cosmic forces inverted! If Satan would lead this rebellion. . . .

I have been a rubber worker, I am a rubber worker. And what my hand has done to trees, it can also do to men.

---

4 Betty J. Meggers and Clifford Evans ◆ Environmental Limitations on Culture in the Tropical Forest

Betty Meggers and Clifford Evans's archaeological work has influenced our thinking about the Amazon for decades. Representing a perspective called "environmental determinism," they believed that infertile soils and extensive seasonal flooding placed severe limitations on the size of the human population and the development of advanced material cultures in Amazonia, as set forth in this 1957 article. A new generation of scholars is still debating their conclusions. Many seek to refute their hypotheses about the limitations of the Amazon basin as a home for human beings, and subsequent research has called into question the assumptions that they made about small, nomadic populations in Amazonia.

The geographer William Denevan, for example, using historical accounts from the period of initial European contact, as well as archaeological evidence, estimates a fairly large pre-Columbian population for Amazonia—from five to seven million. Apparently much of this population concentrated along the rivers, leaving sparsely populated areas in the infertile uplands, confirming Meggers and Evans's contention that the latter supported few people. Further research has supported their conclusions about the poverty of the majority of Amazonia's soils. But current theory favors the view that they underestimated the native population's complex adaptations to floodplains and management of the environment of the infertile uplands. Darrell A. Posey's article in Part IV represents a perspective that is gaining ascendancy among modern ethnographers: native peoples, while lacking in material technology, manage their environments with sophisticated methods.

We are familiar with the pattern of culture characteristic of the living tribes of the lowland tropical forest, and have noted some of the ways in which this type of culture is an adaptation to the environment in which it exists. In the present report, it will be shown that seven of the

From Betty J. Meggers and Clifford Evans, *Archaeological Investigations at the Mouth of the Amazon*, Smithsonian Institution Bureau of American Ethnology *Bulletin* 167 (Washington, DC: Smithsonian Institution, 1957): 26–32.

eight archeological Phases identified on Mexiana, Caviana, and Marajó Islands and in the Territory of Amapá fall within the Tropical Forest Pattern. They differ from one another in details of pottery type and decoration, in village size and composition, and in burial customs, but all of these variations come within the range exhibited among living Tropical Forest tribes.

The sites and ceramics of the eighth culture, the Marajoara Phase, are so outstanding that they previously completely overshadowed the less spectacular remains of the earlier archeological horizons on Marajó Island. Their exploitation is so obviously profitable, even in the eyes of the *caboclos* [backwoodsmen], that it is only with difficulty and persistence that one is able to secure information on Ananatuba, Mangueiras, and Formiga Phase sites within the limits of the Marajoara Phase area of distribution. The high degree of technical and artistic competence attained by the Marajoara Phase ceramicists caused early writers to suggest that the makers must have been descended from, or at least have had contact with, Egyptian or Oriental civilizations (Lisle du Dreneuc, 1889, p. 19). This evaluation cannot be given scientific credence today, but the observation on which it is based, namely, that Marajoara Phase culture is considerably more highly developed than other living or extinct cultures in the area, receives the support of modern archeological investigation. The quality and standardization of the ceramics, the differential elaborateness of the burials, and the large earthworks are material indications of a level of social and political organization more comparable to that of Circum-Caribbean and Andean cultures than to Tropical Forest tribal society.

The appearance of this advanced culture on Marajó Island in the midst of a succession of simpler ones throws the contrast between the two levels of development into high relief and raises questions that otherwise might not come to the attention of the archeologist. Why, for example, did none of the other archeological cultures attain, or even begin to reach, such a high level of development? Why did the Marajoara Phase undergo a cultural decline on Marajó Island? Could it have originated elsewhere in the Tropical Forest area?

Seeking answers to these questions requires a study of anthropological theory. Analysis of the forces contributing to the evolution of culture elsewhere has shown that agriculture exercises a dominant role (White, 1949; Childe, 1951). Wherever it has been introduced, there is an almost immediate and revolutionary change in the culture; where it has not penetrated, the culture never advances (except in special situations) beyond a nomadic hunting and gathering level, with undifferentiated social organization and simple technology. Agriculture is not a simple "open sesame" to the unlimited vistas of civilization, however. Its effectiveness as a subsistence base depends on two factors: the potentiality of the environment and the agricultural technology of the culture. The variant combinations of these extant in the world explain and in some cases determine the differences in level of development that can be described (Meggers, 1954).

The principle behind this conclusion can be summarized briefly. A food-gathering type of economy is undependable and time consuming. The return per man-hour of labor expended is small and sufficient only to satisfy immediate needs. The supply of roots, fruits, and seeds is seasonal, and game is unconcentrated. In order to maintain an adequate food supply, constant activity is required by all the able-bodied members of the community, which is limited to a small group typically composed of kin. This type of cultural adjustment, characterized by a minimum of material goods and a minimum of sociopolitical organization, was universal over the world until the commencement of the Neolithic [Period], which is marked by the introduction of domesticated plants and animals. It has survived until the present in scattered environments where agriculture cannot be introduced.

The adoption of agriculture as the basic food source meant that man was able for the first time to devote a good part of his time and attention to other things than the securing of food. As a result, the introduction of agriculture everywhere transformed the typically nomadic life of hunters and gatherers with remarkable rapidity into a new pattern characterized by settled villages and by the acquisition of the ceramic and textile arts. This initial revolution brought little alteration in the social organization— no strong chiefs, social classes, occupational specialization—or in religious concepts or practices. These advances came later and depended upon the increasing productivity of agriculture; in other words, on the deflection of larger amounts of time and effort from food production to be expended instead on culture building.

Where the techniques are absent or the environment prohibits their use and agriculture does not increase in productivity, the culture is arrested temporarily or permanently after the consummation of the first stage of advance. In temperate regions like Europe and North America, the fertility of the soil can be permanently maintained and the yield often increased by scientific crop rotation, fertilization, and similar means. In desert regions like Coastal Peru or in fertile river valleys like that of the Nile, the soil is almost unlimited in its ability to produce abundant crops year after year, which selective plant breeding can augment. But there is no evidence from geographers, soil experts, agronomists, or botanists that such a thing is possible where tropical forest conditions require slash-and-burn agricultural exploitation, and anthropological data add confirmation. No culture deriving its subsistence from slash-and-burn agriculture is able to maintain any of the traits of advanced agricultural societies, such as well-developed leadership, class distinction, occupational specialization, priests, temples or high gods, large and permanent cities and towns, and empires. There are only small, scattered, and semipermanent villages and a relatively simple development of some of the basic technologies, like ceramics, textiles, woodworking, and basketry.

Much speculation has surrounded the promising potentialities of the American Tropics as the garden spot of the world. Observers of the densely populated areas in equatorial Asia have been led to view the Amazon drainage as equally capable of intense exploitation, lacking only in sufficient advertising. Anthropologists, seeing that the Amazon lagged behind tropical regions nearly everywhere else in the world in the level of cultural development, have been inclined to invoke the late start of the American Indians compared with cultures in the Old World, the constant state of hostility and warfare between the Amazon tribes, or simply to leave the question unanswered.

There is abundant evidence, both from geographers and ethnologists, however, that the limited productivity of slash-and-burn agriculture is the true cause. Robert Pendleton (1950, pp. 115–16), a leading authority on tropical land use, has recently put the situation in decisive language:

> In higher latitudes, and particularly in the United States, a widespread opinion prevails that such humid regions as the enormous Amazon basin, now occupied by luxuriant and apparently limitless tropical high forests, must certainly have rich soils, and hence, great potentialities for the production of food, fiber, and other agricultural crops. . . . It is true that certain regions such as those with recently active volcanoes, and those recent alluvial soils in humid equatorial lowlands which are not deeply flooded, do have great crop growing potentialities; they are producing and can continue to produce much from the soil. Nevertheless, on the whole, the soils of the humid equatorial regions have distressingly limited possibilities for plant production. . . . This pessimistic attitude is no longer the result of mere opinion, for in a number of widely scattered regions in the humid low latitudes agricultural scientists have been and still are seriously at work.

The reason for this seeming contradiction in plant productivity is in the differential ability of the crops to utilize the resources of the soil:

> The reason for the rapid decline in productivity is that practically all of the plant nutrients within reach of the roots of the forest trees have been taken up and are in the growing trees. Almost all the plant offal (dead leaves, twigs, fruit, fallen trees, etc.) which falls to the ground is quickly attacked by termites and decay organisms; as a consequence it rapidly disappears. Organic matter cannot persist long on the soil; leaf mold as it is known in the north temperate U. S. does not develop. However, the heartwood logs of certain very durable sorts of trees will last a couple of years or more. The nutrients thus released and washed into the soil by the frequent drenching rains are quickly taken up by the tree roots lying in wait just under the soil surface. All the nutrients within reach of the tree roots are in the vegetation, and are being cycled. When the forest is cut and burned the cycle is broken, the plant nutrients being released in soluble form in the ash. The soil itself is extremely acid, often being pH4. The burning slightly reduces the acidity and supplies

available nutrients for the crop plants which may be planted in the clearing. But before the annual or biennial crop plants can develop extensive root systems sufficient to absorb any considerable proportion of these liberated nutrients, most of the soluble materials will have been washed down deep into the subsoil by the almost daily rains—thus quite out of reach of the roots.

The effects of this leaching process are dramatically reflected in differences in yield from the same field in successive years. [Charles] Wagley (1953, p. 67) reports that the second planting is only about half as productive as that of the first year after clearing. Re-use of the area before it has had sufficient time to return to tall secondary growth results in a less productive harvest than is achieved if the vegetation is allowed to reach this stage before another attempt at cultivation (op. cit., p. 68). Wasteful as it appears to be, slash-and-burn agriculture is the only method of exploitation that is adapted to the major portion of the Amazon area. The adverse conditions of high temperature and humidity, heavy rainfall, and low initial fertility of the soil make short intervals of cultivation separated by long periods of fallow and reforestation the only circumstance under which the long-range pursuit of agricultural return is feasible, given the plants available aboriginally.

In addition to the general poverty of the soil for agricultural purposes, there is a further factor that serves to reduce the utility of the land. This is its topography and elevation. Estimates of the possibilities of tropical agriculture often leave this out of consideration and as a result make the picture appear considerably brighter than it actually is. [Edward] Higbee (1948), for instance, has estimated that the land in a sixty-mile radius around the Maya site of Tikal could feed five hundred thousand people. This calculation is based on the observation that the production from one acre of land will feed one person for two years. After clearing, thirty years of fallow are required for the return of fertility, before reclearing is profitable. Under these conditions, an allotment of fifteen acres per person would insure a permanent food supply. Division of the area within a sixty-mile radius of Tikal into fifteen-acre plots gives Higbee his estimated population of five hundred thousand. However, this method of calculating subsistence potential fails to make allowances for irregularities in the terrain. To be usable for agriculture, the land must be above flood level and have a minimum of slope. In a region where rivers rise from ten to twenty or more feet in the rainy season, a substantial part of the land is submerged for several months each year. Hills often have steep banks and summits too small for a field. Our own estimate of agriculturally usable land in British Guiana, Brazilian Guiana (Territory of Amapá), and on the Islands of Mexiana, Caviana, and Marajó, is that it constitutes about one twenty-fifth of the total dry season extent. Since this is based on traveling over the countryside and along the rivers rather than on a specific survey, and in order to avoid an error on the conservative side, we increased this figure two and one-half times, bringing it to 10 percent of the total land area.

Tropical areas with more favorable conditions for agriculture exist, but Marajó Island is not one of them. On the contrary, its potentiality is rather lower than average. The forested western part, poorly drained even during the dry months, is inundated during the rainy season. The campo dominating the eastern half is also hostile to agriculture. Unlike the fertile plains of temperate regions, the tropical grasslands are even lower in agricultural potential than the forests. It is only with extensive preparation of the soil with fertilizer and by careful nurturing that the modern ranchers succeed in bringing a rare fruit tree to maturity (Lage, 1944, pp. 244–245; Pendleton, 1950, pp. 119–120). Only in the limited area along the southeastern coast can the conditions be said to be all favorable to cultivation. Productivity can be judged on the basis of efforts to establish agricultural colonies on the opposite side of the Baia de Marajó, where the land is part of the same formation as on the Island (Pendleton, 1950, p. 116):

> The peasants who pioneered here soon found that while they could get a good crop of food the first year after cutting and burning the primeval forest and could get a following crop or two of mandioca, no further cropping was worthwhile for them, even though very little labor was needed to cut down and clear the second growth that came in after they abandoned their two or three years' cultivation of crops in the new clearing.

The inescapable effects of reliance on slash-and-burn agriculture have been recorded repeatedly by ethnographers: "The periodic exhaustion of the soil by manioc produces a seminomadic tribal life" among the Cubeo (Goldman, 1948, p. 770); "The Jívaro community is . . . moved at least every 6 years as new farm land is needed" (Steward and Métraux, 1948, p. 621), etc. The pattern of "shifting cultivation" requires that the rest of the culture remain simple enough to retain its mobility, to be capable of ready transferral from place to place, or become extinct as local food resources give out.

Examples of the degeneration or extinction of cultures that had become adjusted to permanently productive agriculture and were attracted or pushed into the tropical forest are also abundant. [Frederick] Johnson (1948, p. 196) summarizes the Central American situation:

> The few colonies which the Meso-Americans sent into the Tropical Forest were mere outposts, some of which succumbed to the environment, while others, probably under environmental influence, adopted the indigenous culture. The colonies which retained their Meso-American features were evidently not established long enough before the Conquest for local environmental and cultural influences to have changed them.

Students of the Andean cultures have commented that even the re-markably organized Inca system was unable to surmount the limitations of the lowland tropics. [Matthew] Stirling notes that "archeological sites . . . in the valleys of the Upano and Namangosa Rivers demonstrate that the material culture of the Jivaros in pre-Columbian times resembled that of the ancient cultures of the highlands much more closely than do present-day survivals" (1938, p. xi; also Steward, 1948, pp. 13–14).

This process of deculturation can be observed in progress in the changes that occurred in the culture of the Marajoara Phase during its habitation of Marajó Island. In this instance we have as complete posses-sion of the facts as we are likely to have for the assessment of the causes of this decline. We have comparative material in the form of four other cultures of the Tropical Forest Pattern that occupied the same area at dif-ferent times. These form a sharp contrast to the Marajoara Phase and emphasize its more advanced character, which can be paralleled only by cultures of the Circum-Caribbean and Sub-Andean levels of development. We have a detailed knowledge of the environment today, and the high probability that in the short time represented by the archeological sequence there was no notable ecological alteration. All of this evidence makes as clear a case as possible for the conclusion that this environment cannot support a culture more advanced than the Tropical Forest Pattern.

If this is true, then the Tropical Forest Pattern represents the maxi-mum development of culture that could have been attained in the area where agricultural exploitation is limited to slash-and-burn. This limita-tion is first and foremost an environmental one, which operates in terms of restricting the subsistence resources, both in quantity and permanence. Some variation exists within the region, and this is correlated with larger or smaller communities, ranging from two or three families to a thousand or more individuals (Tupinambá). The upper limits of this range, how-ever, resemble culturally the lower limits more closely than they do mem-bers of the more advanced Circum-Caribbean and Andean Areas. The cultural development of the Tropical Forest Area cannot be said to have been "arrested" by the advent of the Europeans as it might have been in other parts of the New World; it had already been arrested by the agricul-tural deficiencies of the environment in which it existed.

An understanding of this situation permits a more realistic interpre-tation and evaluation of the past and present cultures at the mouth of the Amazon than would otherwise be possible. The similarities between the archeological Phases and their comparability to living Tropical Forest cultures become the expected components of a total pattern of adaptation to and limitation by a particular type of environment. The deculturation suffered by the Marajoara Phase and its lack of influence on tribes in the nearby area become understandable and explainable. Knowing the limita-tions of the tropical forest for the development of culture makes it possible to conclude that some other part of the South American continent with greater subsistence potential must hold the key to the origin of the Marajoara Phase, and this clue can be pursued and verified by use of the comparative method.

That the ecological situation in the Tropical Forest Area can be so sharply defined is a fortunate and unusual circumstance. In most other types of environment, the limitations and possibilities for cultural development are less readily delimited, and differences in technological achievement, especially in the realm of agriculture, can play an important role in determining the productivity of the subsistence and through it the level to which the culture can attain. Hence the approach employed here may not turn out to be particularly useful to archeologists working in other parts of the New World. This does not argue against making the fullest use of it in the tropical forest, where the data recovered by archeology are so meager that all conceivable methods of analysis and interpretation must be explored.

Literature Cited

Childe, V. Gordon. 1951. *Social Evolution*. London.

Goldman, Irving. 1948. Tribes of the Uaupés-Caquetá Region. In *Handbook of South American Indians, Bureau of American Ethnology Bulletin* 143, vol. 3, pp. 763–798.

Higbee, Edward. 1948. Agriculture in the Maya Homeland. *Geogr. Rev.*, vol. 38, pp. 457–464.

Johnson, Frederick. 1948. The Post-Conquest Ethnology of Central America: An Introduction. In *Handbook of South American Indians, Bureau of American Ethnology Bulletin* 143, vol. 4, pp. 195–198.

Lage, Sandoval. 1944. *Quadros da Amazonia*. Rio de Janeiro.

Lisle du Dreneuc, P. de. 1889. *Nouvelles découvertes d'idoles de l'Amazone*. Paris.

Meggers, Betty J. 1954. Environmental Limitations on the Development of Culture. *Amer. Anthrop.*, vol. 56, pp. 801–824.

Pendleton, Robert L. 1950. Agricultural and Forestry Potentialities of the Tropics. *Agronomy Journ.*, vol. 42, pp. 115–123.

Steward, Julian H. 1948. The Circum-Caribbean Tribes: An Introduction. In *Handbook of South American Indians, Bureau of American Ethnology Bulletin* 143, vol. 4, pp. 1–41. 1949. South American Cultures: An Interpretive Summary. In *Handbook of South American Indians, Bureau of American Ethnology Bulletin* 143, vol. 5, pp. 669–772.

Steward, Julian H., and Métraux, Alfred. 1948. Tribes of the Peruvian and Ecuadorian Montana. In *Handbook of South American Indians, Bureau of American Ethnology Bulletin* 143, vol. 3, pp. 535–656.

Stirling, Matthew W. 1938. Historical and Ethnographical Material on the Jivaro Indians. *Bureau of American Ethnology Bulletin* 117.

Wagley, Charles. 1953. *Amazon Town: A Study of Man in the Tropics.* New York.

White, Leslie. 1949. *The Science of Culture.* New York.

---

5   Katherine Milton ◆ Civilization and Its Discontents

Until recently, outsiders have remained ignorant of the vast storehouse of knowledge contained in the oral traditions, religious rituals, and other nonmaterial aspects of tribal cultures because their peoples are nonliterate and tend to devalue material possessions. Over the past several decades, however, ethnographers have begun to see indigenous cultures from within through the process of participant-observation—by living with these peoples as members of their communities. Westerners have gradually come to appreciate the wisdom encoded in indigenous cultures' adaptation to nature, and as this appreciation has grown, popular perception of native peoples has become more and more romantic.

The increasing awareness of the complex systems of tribal knowledge has led to a belated realization that modernization represents a great threat to the continued existence of these traditional cultures. The environments on which they depend are being destroyed, and new technologies and manufactured goods are changing their ways of life. Representative of the prevailing contemporary ethnographic views on tribal peoples, anthropologist Katherine Milton's 1992 perspective on the Indians of Amazonia derives from her extensive personal experience of living with them in their rainforest homes.

For more than a decade now, I have led a double life. I spend part of my time in the United States, living in an apartment in Berkeley and teaching anthropology classes at the University of California. The rest of my time is spent in the Amazon basin, where I live in the company of recently contacted Indian groups, studying their traditional ecology and features of their tropical forest environment. On returning to the United States after one of these extended stays in the jungle, I always experience culture shock as I strive to regain control of my possessions, which I have totally forgotten about.

Usually my first act is to retrieve my dust-covered car, which has languished for some six to eighteen months in a garage. The battery must be charged, and then I must wash and vacuum the car, fill it with gas, and check out its many parts. Once I am mobile, I rush to a large supermarket to stock up on cleaning supplies and food. My first few days are com-

From Katherine Milton, "Civilization and Its Discontents," *Natural History* 101, no. 3 (March 1992): 36–43. © 1992 by the American Museum of Natural History. Reprinted by permission of *Natural History*.

pletely taken up with chores; there never seems to be a moment when I am not contemplating some type of home repair or new purchase.

And then there is my body. What a job it is to live up to what is expected of the average American. I must visit the dentist—often more than one kind of dentist—to be sure my teeth are performing at top level. The doctor must be seen for a checkup; my eyes must be examined, glasses and contact lenses adjusted, and so on. I begin to wonder how my friends in Berkeley manage to have any free time at all, since I have fewer possessions than they do—I own no television set, no stereo or compact disc player, no video machine, home computer, food chopper, or any number of other items my friends seem to dote on. I don't even own my apartment.

Plunged back into life in Berkeley, I see myself as a slave of material possessions, and I notice that I deeply resent the time and energy required to maintain them. Nothing could be more different from the life I have been leading with hunter-gatherers deep in the rainforests of Brazil, where people have almost no possessions, and those that they do have are made from local forest materials and are entirely biodegradable.

The groups I have visited live far from any cities, towns, or commercial enterprises. They include the Mayoruna and Maku from Amazonas State; the Arara, Parakana, and Arawete from Pará State; and the Guaja from Maranhão State—peoples so remote and little known that few outside their immediate geographic area have heard of them. Often I am one of the first nonindigenous females many members of the group have ever seen. With my pale skin and hair I am a truly terrifying apparition to younger children, who sometimes scream with fear when they first see me.

All these peoples have been recently contacted: only a few months or, at most, years have passed since the Brazilian Indian Bureau (FUNAI) managed to establish a formal relationship with them. Previously, these groups avoided or were strongly hostile to outsiders, but with contact, they have permitted a few Indian Bureau employees to live with them, to assist them, and, at times, to protect them in dealings with other Indian groups or members of the wider Brazilian society. Living with these people has given me the chance to see how even modest changes in their traditional lifeways—the introduction of something as innocent in appearance as a metal cooking pot or ax, a box of matches or some salt—can be the thin edge of a wedge that will gradually alter the behavior and ecological practices of an entire society.

These people typically live in small villages of fewer than a hundred inhabitants, in some cases in groups of only fifteen or twenty. Most practice slash-and-burn agriculture on a small scale, complementing crop foods with wild game and fish, forest fruits and nuts, and occasionally wild honey. For some months life may revolve around the village, but sooner or later every group I have worked with leaves, generally in small parties, and spends weeks or even months traveling through the forest and living on forest products.

Throughout the forest there are paths that the Indians know and have used for generations. They travel mainly when wild forest fruits and nuts are most abundant and game animals are fat, but families or small groups may go on expeditions at other times of year as well. They trek a few miles, make a temporary camp, and then hunt, gather, and eat several meals in the area before moving on to a new site. At certain times of year, many groups relocate to the borders of large rivers, where they obtain turtle eggs or other seasonal river foods.

The accumulation of possessions would be an impediment to this seminomadic life-style. Whenever individuals go on a trek, they carry everything they need. Leaving possessions behind in a thatch-and-pole hut, to be retrieved later, is not an option, since the humid climate and voracious insects would quickly destroy them. Great numbers of insects often live inside Indian dwellings, principally jungle cockroaches that hide in the roof thatch by day but come out by the thousands at night. Indians seem oblivious to them, letting them run about on their bodies and even crawl on the food so long as they are not perched on the next bite.

Granted, these are generally soft-bodied, small jungle cockroaches and not the tough, large roaches of our urban areas, but even so, I found it difficult to adjust to them. My frantic efforts to remove cockroaches from my body and clothes were regarded as strange by my Indian hosts. At one site, I resorted to storing my clothing each night in a heavy plastic bag, which I sealed shut and suspended from a piece of plastic fishing line tied to a roof pole. Otherwise, at night, the roaches covered my shirt and pants so thoroughly that often the fabric could not be seen. Although the roaches would be gone the next morning, they would leave a musty smell; further, just the idea of wearing garments that I had seen coated with cockroaches gave me a squirmy, unclean feeling.

On the forest treks, the women are invariably the most burdened, something Western observers often find difficult to understand or accept. A woman will walk for hours carrying a toddler, a large palm basket containing fifty or more pounds of animal or plant foods, hammocks, a cooking utensil or two, a machete, and the family pets, such as parrots, monkeys, and young puppies. In all the groups I have observed, the women's legs and feet are deformed by the pigeon-toed walk they adopt to give them added traction and stability on the slippery, narrow forest trails. The feet of adult men turn in only slightly, because men usually carry nothing heavier than a bow and arrows (ostensibly to be free to take advantage of any hunting opportunities).

The most important possession the Indians carry with them, however, is knowledge. There is nothing coded in the genome of an Indian concerning how to make a living in a tropical forest—each individual must become a walking bank of information on the forest landscape, its plants and animals, and their habits and uses. This information must be taught anew to the members of each generation, without the benefit of books, manuals, or educational television. Indians have no stores in which to purchase the things they need for survival. Instead, each individual must learn to collect, manufacture, or produce all the things required for his or her entire lifetime.

Because people differ in their talents, the pool of community information and abilities is far greater than its component parts. Individual men and women have their own areas of expertise, as well as their share of general knowledge. Members of the group know whom to consult for special information on hunting practices, the habits of particular game animals, rituals, tool manufacture, crop varieties, and the like.

Tropical-forest Indians talk incessantly, a characteristic I believe reflects the importance of oral transmission of culture. When I lived with the Maku, I slept in a hammock inside a small communal palm shelter. If a Maku awoke in the middle of the night, he usually began to talk or sing in a very loud voice—apparently without any thought that anyone might object to this behavior. It was considered normal, what you do when you wake up in the middle of the night and aren't sleepy. Others learn, as I did, to sleep through it or, if they aren't sleepy, to listen to it. Vocal expression apparently is expected and tolerated in Maku culture, no matter what the hour, an indication to me of how much it is valued.

Unlike our economic system, in which each person typically tries to secure and control as large a share of the available resources as possible, the hunter-gatherer economic system rests on a set of highly formalized expectations regarding cooperation and sharing. This does not mean hunter-gatherers do not compete with one another for prestige, sexual partners, and the like. But individuals do not amass a surplus. For instance, no hunter fortunate enough to kill a large game animal assumes that all this food is his or belongs only to his immediate family.

Quite the reverse is true: among some forest peoples, the hunter cannot eat game he has killed or is restricted to eating only one specific portion of his kill. Game is cut up and distributed according to defined patterns particular to each group and based in large part on kinship and marriage obligations. A hunter may have amazing luck one day, moderate luck on another, and no luck at all on a third. But he can usually expect to eat meat every day because someone bound to him in this system of reciprocity may well make a kill and share the meat.

Despite the way their culture traditionally eschews possessions, forest-living peoples embrace manufactured goods with amazing enthusiasm. They seem to appreciate instantly the efficacy of a steel machete, ax, or cooking pot. It is love at first sight, and the desire to possess such objects is absolute. There are accounts of Indian groups or individuals who have turned their backs on manufactured trade goods, but such people are the exception.

When Cândido Rondon, the founder of the Indian Protection Service in Brazil, began his pacification efforts in the early 1900s, he used trade goods as bait to attract uncontacted Indians. Pots, machetes, axes, and steel knives were hung from trees or laid along trails that Indians frequented. This practice proved so successful that it is still employed (see "Overtures to the Nambiquara," by David Price, *Natural History*, October 1984).

Whether they have been formally contacted or not, forest-living groups in the Amazon Basin are probably well aware of steel tools and metal cooking pots. After all, such goods have been in circulation along trade routes in these regions for centuries, and an Indian does not have to have seen a non-Indian in order to acquire them. However, such manufactured goods are likely to be extremely scarce among uncontacted groups. When the Arara Indians were first approached in 1975, they fled their village to escape the pacification party. Examination of their hastily abandoned dwellings showed that stone tools were still being used, but a few steel fragments were also found.

Since they already appreciate the potential utility of manufactured goods, uncontacted Indians are strongly drawn to the new and abundant items offered to lure them from isolation. Once a group has been drawn into the pacification area, all its members are presented with various trade goods—standard gifts include metal cooking pots, salt, matches, machetes, knives, axes, cloth hammocks, T-shirts, and shorts. Not all members of the group get all of these items, but most get at least two or three of them, and in a family, the cumulative mass of new goods can be considerable.

The Indians initially are overwhelmed with delight—this is the honeymoon period when suddenly, from a position in which one or two old metal implements were shared by the entire group, a new situation prevails in which almost every adult individual has some of these wonderful new items. The honeymoon is short-lived, however. Once the Indians have grown accustomed to these new items, the next step is to teach them that these gifts will not be repeated. The Indians are now told that they must work to earn money or must manufacture goods for trade so that they can purchase new items.

Unable to contemplate returning to life without steel axes, the Indians begin to produce extra arrows or blowguns or hunt additional game or weave baskets beyond what they normally need so that this new surplus can be traded. Time that might, in the past, have been used for other tasks—subsistence activities, ceremonial events, or whatever—is now devoted to production of barter goods. In addition, actual settlement patterns may be altered so that the indigenous group is in closer, more immediate contact with sources of manufactured items. Neither of these things, in itself, is necessarily good or bad, but each does alter traditional behavior.

Thus, the newly contacted forest people are rapidly drawn into the wider economic sphere (even into the international economy: for example, the preferred glass beads for personal adornment come from Czechoslovakia). The intrusion of every item—mirrors, cloth, scissors, rice, machetes, axes, pots, bowls, needles, blankets, even bicycles and radios—not only adds to the pressure on individuals to produce trade goods but also disrupts some facet of traditional production.

Anthropologist Paul Henley, who worked with the Panare, a forest-based people in Venezuela, points out that with the introduction of steel tools, particularly axes, indigenous groups suffer a breakdown in the web of cooperative interdependence. In the past, when stone axes were used, various individuals came together and worked communally to fell trees for a new garden. With the introduction of the steel ax, however, one man can clear a garden by himself. As Henley notes, collaboration is no longer mandatory nor particularly frequent.

Indians often begin to cultivate new crops, such as coffee, that they feel can be traded or sold easily. Another is rice, which the Indian Bureau encourages forest people to plant because, of course, all "real" Brazilians eat rice every day. Rice is an introduced crop both to Brazil and to forest Indians. Traditional crop foods, the successful cultivation of which has been worked out over generations in the forest environment and which are well suited to the soil conditions in particular regions, may become scarce, with the result that the Indian diet becomes unbalanced.

Indians who traditionally plant manioc as a staple crop may be encouraged to increase the size of their fields and plant more manioc, which can then be transformed into farinha, a type of cereal that can be sold in the markets. Larger fields mean more intensive agricultural work and less time to hunt—which also affects the diet. The purchase of a shotgun may temporarily improve hunting returns, but it also tends to eliminate game in the area. In addition, shotgun shells are very expensive in Brazil, costing more than $1 U.S. apiece. Dependence on the shotgun undermines a hunter's skill with traditional hunting weapons, such as blowguns and bows and arrows, as well as the ability required to manufacture them.

Clearing larger areas for fields can also lead to increased risk from diseases such as malaria and leishmaniasis, because cleared areas with standing water of low acidity permit proliferation of disease-bearing mosquitoes and flies. New diseases also appear. Anthropologist-epidemiologist Carlos Coimbra, Jr., for example, has shown that Chagas disease, which is transmitted to humans by trypanosome-carrying assassin bugs, apparently does not yet affect Indian populations in lowland areas of the Amazon basin. Only when Indians cease their seminomadic way of life and begin to live for prolonged periods in the same dwellings can Chagas-carrying bugs adjust their feeding behavior and begin to depend on human hosts rather than small rodents for their blood meals.

The moment manufactured foods begin to intrude on the indigenous diet, health takes a downward turn. The liberal use of table salt (sodium chloride), one of the first things that Indians are given, is probably no more healthful for them than it is for Westerners. Most Indians do not have table salt; they manufacture small quantities of potassium salts by burning certain types of leaves and collecting the ash. Anthropologist Darrell Posey reports that the Kayapo Indians of Brazil make salt ash from various palm species and use each type for specific foods.

Sweets and other foods containing refined sugar (sucrose) are also given to Indians, whose wild fruits, according to research by botanists Irene and Herbert Baker, contain primarily other sugars, such as fructose. Indians find that foods containing sucrose taste exceptionally sweet, and they tend to crave them once sampled. While a strong, sugary taste in the natural environment might signal a rare, rich energy source, the indiscriminate consumption of canned foods, candies, and gums containing large amounts of refined sugar contributes to tooth decay and can lead to obesity and even health problems such as diabetes.

Results of dietary change are often difficult to anticipate. Anthropologist Dennis Werner found that the Mekranoti of central Brazil, who did not make pottery, traditionally roasted most of their food. But the introduction of metal cooking pots allowed them to switch to boiled foods. This, in turn, allowed nursing mothers to provide supplemental foods to their infants at an earlier age. Werner found that the average nursing period in the Mekranoti had dropped steadily from 19.7 months prior to 1955 to 16 months in recent years, which corresponded to the period of steady increase in the use of metal cooking pots in the village.

One of the first things the Indian Bureau doctors generally do after contact is try to protect the Indians from the Western diseases that may be communicated to them during their first prolonged interaction with outsiders. The doctors give them immunizations and may also hand out drugs to prevent or eradicate dangerous malarias. Pregnant women, infants, and preadolescents often receive massive doses of antibiotics. Antibiotics and antimalarial drugs, although helpful in some respects, may also have detrimental effects. For example, individuals exposed to antibiotics in utero or when young generally have teeth that are abnormally dark and discolored. Some drugs are reputed to interfere with fertility among women in recently contacted groups. If this lack of fertility combines with a drop in population size due to deaths from new diseases, a population can fall to a precarious low.

Perhaps the most critical disruption suffered by these groups, however, concerns how detailed information on features of the forest environment is diluted and forgotten. This is the pool of shared knowledge that traditionally has been the bedrock, the economic currency, the patrimony of each of these nontechnological forest societies. Manuel Lizarralde, a doctoral student at the University of California, Berkeley, who has done ethnobotanical work with the Bari of Venezuela, reports that in just a single generation there was a staggering loss of information about the identity of forest trees and their uses.

Despite this tale of disruption, disease, and destruction, many of the indigenous forest cultures are proving to be far more resilient than might be expected. The indigenous peoples remaining today in the Amazon basin are true survivors who have successfully resisted the diseases, explorers, missionaries, soldiers, slave traders, rubber tappers, loggers, gold miners, fur traders, and colonists who have persistently encroached on them during the past five centuries.

Anthropologist Bill Balée, for example, had found that the Ka'apor Indians of Maranhão State, in peaceful contact with outsiders since 1928, still maintain many features of their traditional economy, social organization, and ritual life. He attributes this to the continued integrity of the nuclear family and the persistence of specific ritual duties between husband and wife that prohibit certain foods at different seasons or life stages. Such ritual practices have not only spared red-legged tortoises and other wild resources from being overharvested but have also diffused hunting pressures over a large area, thereby contributing to the persistence of the traditional economy.

Unfortunately, cultural persistence will do indigenous peoples no good if their tropical forest habitat is destroyed. Deforestation is primarily the result of outside influences, such as lumbering, cattle ranching, and colonization, that are permitted by government policies. Some estimates suggest that all remaining tropical forests will be destroyed by the year 2045.

Once the technological roller coaster gets moving, it's hard to jump off or even pause to consider the situation. Some say, so what? We can't all go back to the jungle, we can't all become forest-living Indians. No, we can't. But as I stand in my apartment in Berkeley, listening to my telephone's insistent ring and contemplating my unanswered mail, dusty curtains, dripping faucets, and stacks of newspapers for recycling, I'm not sure we wouldn't be far happier if we could.

---

6 Gerardo Reichel-Dolmatoff ◆ A Well-Adapted Life

Western culture generally conceptualizes the world dualistically by setting society in opposition to "nature." Consequently, Westerners are able

From Gerardo Reichel-Dolmatoff, "A View from the Headwaters," *The Ecologist* 29, no. 4 (July 1999): 277–80. Photographs omitted. Reprinted by permission of *The Ecologist*.

to view nature as a commodity—a source of wealth. It is seen as some-
thing that humans can manage—indeed, that should be "developed"—in
order to improve our standard of living. In contrast, the first inhabitants
of America's tropical rainforests have almost always perceived the world
as based on an inherent interconnectedness between humans and nature.
They do not conceptualize them as separate entities.

This excerpt from an essay in The Ecologist *by Colombian anthro-*
pologist Gerardo Reichel-Dolmatoff gives us a glimpse into the worldview
of the Tukano Indians of northwestern Amazonia, who have developed a
complex cosmology that provides a moral framework for their society.
Shamans (people who learn to communicate with the spirit world) repre-
sent a powerful force in controlling and managing relationships between
members of society, and between people, nature, and the spirit world. The
shaman is responsible for maintaining harmony between all of these ele-
ments. This view of the universe is common among tribal peoples. Selec-
tion 19, by Darrell Posey, offers further insight into the ways in which
indigenous cultural practices are based upon the moral imperative of
maintaining harmony between humans, nature, and the spirit world.

A nd then there is the forest. The forest has different dimensions: it
offers other resources and all of these have their spirit-owners and
therefore require different behavioural norms. Above all, there are the
game animals. Between the hunter and the animals he kills, there exists a
relationship of reciprocity. The spirits of dead or frightened animals take
their revenge by causing illness to the hunter and his family. In fact, the
animals are "hunters" in their own right, in that they "hunt" people with
diseases, accidents and nightmares.

In order to establish and maintain a viable relationship between the
hunter and the hunted, people must observe many dietary and sexual restrictions. The former have two complementary functions: on the one hand
they act as controls, as deterrents to overhunting; on the other hand, they
serve to mask human body odours. The consumption of peppers, for example, or the smoke of burning pitch will make the game animals disregard any human scent while the consumption of fatty or oily substances
"makes the hunter visible" (as the Indians say) by his strong body odour.

To the Indians of the north-west Amazon, the river and the forest are
living organisms, kept alive and fertile by the cosmic energy of the Sun
Father. This father figure is in continuous exchange with our Earth, which
is a female principle. Between the two—solar energy and the Earth's fertility potential—exists a circuit; whatever man subtracts from it for his
sustenance, be it fishing, hunting or harvesting, he must return by saving
energy through personal sacrifice. This principle of "saving" is reflected
in the conscious and planned conservation of natural resources.

Most adult people are quite aware of this principle, but the true power
of planning and decision-making in these ecological matters lies in the

hands of shamans and elders. I have seen shamans carefully measuring out the adequate amount of fish poison to be put in the creek; I have heard them interpret dreams in terms of game conservation, explaining that the frightening appearance in a dream, of a certain animal, was a warning that the species was being over-hunted. Shamans will control the felling of trees, the firing of clearings; they will control house construction, canoe making, the brewing of beer, the processes of daily food preparation, and a great multitude of other activities.

In the evening, the men will sit around their fires and talk, and in these nightly conversations they will refer to the change of seasons, the appearing [*sic*] in the sky, the water level and the current of the rivers and creeks, the animals they have seen and heard, the fruits that are ripening in the fields or in the forest. Every few weeks there will be a slight change in the subject matter of these nightly talks, and the seasonal cycle or rainy or dry months will mark major changes in emphasis. There will be talk of bird migrations and of fish runs; fields must be fired and planted. And night after night people talk while the shamans and elders listen and occasionally ask some questions.

In the shamans' minds, all this information will be organised into structured knowledge which henceforward, for the next few weeks, determines their activities, be they expressed in ritual, in recommending hunting strategies or in arranging social gatherings. For each season of the year, for each distinct shorter time-span, and for each ecosystem, all behavioural norms have to be re-adapted and co-ordinated anew.

And this is why the Indians' knowledge is so vital. The great "energy" potential of soils, plants, game animals and fish has to be redistributed to the cosmic energy circuit by rituals, recitals, myths and admonitions which, in their totality, prescribe a way of life. If observed in their full context, these norms constitute an integrated system. For thousands of years, the Amazon Basin has been inhabited by Indians who knew how to conserve their habitat; we have archaeological evidence for their demographic density and the cultural inventiveness of these peoples.

Of course, I am quite aware of the fact that, occasionally, the Indians have contributed to the destruction and degradation of their lands, especially when acting under the pressure of encroaching mestizo peasants, but as a general rule they have managed their natural environment with ecologically sound land-use planning. But the pressure of outside forces upon the Amazon environment is increasing day by day. In the course of my travels, and of long years of field experience in Colombia, I have seen many irreparable changes in the natural environment brought about by human agency; I have seen the ancient deserts of central Asia and I have seen the rapid expansion of modern deserts on the plains and mountains of Colombia. But no single case has impressed me more than what is happening, and what might be happening, in the Amazon Basin.

In speaking of Colombian Indians, I have mentioned some isolated customs, some animistic beliefs and shamanistic images such as might be described for many aboriginal societies of the tropical rainforest or the Andes. But what I want to emphasise is this: these beliefs and attitudes toward life, these visions of the universe, these hundreds of little things a person does or thinks or avoids, form a highly structured order.

In myth and ritual, in conversation and daily activities, the Indians express deeply felt beliefs. During an Indian's entire life, there is a constant, more or less conscious, interplay between the individual and the way in which he perceives the environment. There are shapes and colours, movements and gestures, sounds and smells; there are different temperatures, different flavours to taste, things to touch, air to breathe. There is the power of the spoken word, the rhythm of music, the bond of kinship. All these manifold sensations, perceptions and feelings are consistently coded and carry specific meanings, the total message of which is life—a well-adapted life.

Every single musical instrument, every single feather in a headdress, every dance-step or body gesture is imbued with a specific meaning. And to these are added dietary restrictions, the rules of food processing, hunting and fishing, the clearing of a field, the firing of a clay vessel or the manufacture of a basket. And then there are dreams and visions, visions induced by the controlled use of hallucinogenic drugs, or by deep meditation; and from these visions, a person awakes with the certainty that what he has seen or heard and felt in that other dimension was true.

The sounds of the river and the forest, at different times of day or night, may be warnings or encouragements; the screech of a parrot, the eyespot pattern on a fish tail, the smell of rotten wood or of an aromatic herb may determine a man's activities and thought for a day or a week. In this manner, the person is continuously exposed to messages which, in all essence, are of a biological nature because they mainly refer to the following rules: to find the right person to marry, to find the right food to eat, and to obtain both in the right way, without upsetting the balance— the energy circuit—that links man to his society and his environment.

How to read the signals the environment is sending out, a person has to learn through myth and ritual, through the long recitals of genealogies, the casting of spells, and, above all, through the nightlong conversations of shamans and elders who are the true suppliers and transmitters of knowledge made wisdom. We should never underestimate this learning process, because it is an exacting mental discipline which eventually enables people to live in nature and with nature, and in society.

Our cosmovision is based upon our science; the Indians' is based upon their knowledge. Of course, we want to continue in our world which, for better or for worse, is our creation. But in order to live in it, here, today, tomorrow and in the future, we need the Indians' knowledge. And here I am referring not only to the practical knowledge of the Indians, to the sort of things a peasant knows. What I am trying to say is that the Indians' way of life reveals to us the possibility of a separate strategy of cultural development; in other words, it presents us with alternatives on an intellectual level and on a philosophical level. We should keep in mind these alternative cognitive models.

The conservation of the Amazon is not a visionary scheme of ecologists and romanticising anthropologists; it is a vital necessity for mankind on a global scale: for the study of biological evolution, the study of soil-plant co-evolution, the study of species diversity; to understand the linguistic, ethnographic, and biological diversity of human societies. We need the Amazon for its enormous human potential, quite apart from its economic or technological promises.

Up to this point, I have been writing this article as a humanist, as an intellectual, as an anthropologist who is profoundly concerned about the future of the Indians and their natural environment. But now I shall begin to write as a rationalist too: as a person who is acutely aware of the realities of our present times, and who knows that the future lies in the hands of the intelligentsia, of the technologists and bureaucrats. It is they who have the power, and according to them the Indians are primitives who have to be integrated; according to them, nature is something that has to be exploited for the benefit of man.

We may know that we need the Indians: we may know that the ruthless exploitation of natural resources has limits; but the leading intelligentsia and their development agencies recognise no limits to their all-embracing technology. We have to be realistic, and accept the fact that the Indian world is on the wane. The Amazon Basin and many, many other, formerly remote, regions of the Third World are being opened to outside influences and to technological development. In some regions this process will be slower and less turbulent than in others: some aboriginal societies will be able to re-adapt, but others will become profoundly modified, and some will perish altogether, biologically, culturally, linguistically. As anthropologists and biologists, we know only too well that these changes are part of the historical scheme of things.

These are disturbing thoughts, to say the least, and I wish I could be more positive when thinking of the future of rainforest Indians and aboriginal peoples in general. But in fifty years, I have seen too many traditions being lost: I have seen entire tribes disappear; I have seen too much misery among gentle, helpless people.

Although I know that the Indians' world is on the wane, I believe that this knowledge does not exempt us from certain obligations. So, here, I shall attempt to suggest a few approaches to these problems: I shall try to make an effort to envisage a better future for the Indians, by suggesting a few personal ideas.

In the first place, I think we should make a combined effort to study the Indians' knowledge of their biotype, taking into account not only our, but above all their, concepts of ecosystems. Every square kilometre of forest contains a library of important biological, cultural and psychological information, and if we study it in the company of the Indians our insights in all these fields will be enormously enriched. The death of an old Indian who never had the chance to share with us his knowledge of the forest and the river is the equivalent of a whole library disappearing. If we undertake this study alone, we will get a mere inventory; but if we work together with the Indians our insights will be greatly enriched by a kind of knowledge which, at present, still lies beyond our experience. For five hundred years we have witnessed, and played along with, the destruction of the Indians; now we are witnessing the destruction of the natural habitat. What are we waiting for?

There can also be no doubt that as anthropologists, biologists and ecologists we possess an enormous amount of information, or practical field experience, and of the many forms of human vulnerability and of the destruction of the natural environment. By transforming this information into practical knowledge, in a manner that would make it understandable and convincing to national leaders and planning agencies, we can influence the process of decision-making; we can convince those in power of the biological and social necessity to conserve these lands; and we can convince them of the dignity and value of our Indian societies.

It is not sufficient to say that what we owe to the Indians is potatoes, maize and quinine. It is not sufficient to retell their myths and tales in florid Portuguese or Spanish or to stage their dances in a pseudo-Indian setting on television. What we must show is the Indians' philosophy of life, their cosmogonic and cosmological schemes, their ethical and aesthetical attitudes. What we must show is their courage of choice, their option of other ways of life, different from ours; the courage and genius of having built their societies, their cultures based upon an astonishing combination of realism and imagery.

II

Explanations for Deforestation in Latin America

The tropical rainforest has become a major arena for the conflicts arising out of the prevailing forms of social and political organization and dominant development strategy in Latin America. This system, based on modernization and the encouragement of rapid economic growth, fuels a stream of people and capital into the ever more remote reaches of the region's rainforests. The moving frontier represents both a continuation and an intensification of the historical processes set in motion by the arrival of the Iberians five hundred years ago.

The economic and political systems established by the Spaniards and Portuguese gave rise to a society of extreme concentration of resources and wealth in the hands of a few, as exemplified by the latifundia system. The latifundia, or great estates, traditionally included a work force tied to the estate by debt to the owner. Selection 7 shows how sugar production exacerbated unequal land tenure and economic status in Cuba during the colonial period. It also reveals the links between technological change, political economy, and deforestation. Contemporary social and environmental relations in Latin America have deep roots.

Another of the legacies of colonialism in Latin America is a tendency for many latifundia to be dedicated to extensive and inefficient cattle raising, a traditional land use that has continued to expand in the last thirty years and has contributed to the destruction of vast areas of tropical rainforest. Selection 10 shows how the post-World War II export beef boom pushed small farmers off their land and forced them to cut and burn rainforests. The expansion of export commodity production has increased landlessness and the number of farmers trying to subsist on minifundia (farms too small to support a family), creating conditions that may result in political instability.

The contemporary approach to development in Latin America has created social conditions that encourage migration to frontier zones, where colonists may come into conflict with existing forest people (often Indians). Selection 8 demonstrates how such trends play out in Chiapas, where the rural poor have become increasingly marginalized, both economically and ecologically. Agricultural modernization during the past two or three decades has caused a decrease in employment opportunities on the latifundia, a "squeezing out" of small independent farms, and the emigration of landless peasants searching for a way to support their families. Even though the economies of Latin America are industrializing, there are not enough industrial jobs to employ all potential workers—especially the minimally educated, such as the rural poor. Added to a high rate of population growth since the 1950s (especially in rural areas), this state of affairs has created a large reserve of un- or underemployed workers that has kept wages low. The resulting poverty and misery are widespread and motivate migration to the frontier.

Government policy encourages this population shift because the settlement of the forested frontier serves the needs of the state in various ways. Powerful politicians generally come from, or are allied with, the landholding class and therefore tend to seek solutions to agrarian problems without having to undertake reforms opposed by the landed elite. Opening up frontier zones to colonization by the landless, usually by building roads, serves two important purposes: it protects the interests of the politically powerful landed elite, and it defuses potential unrest by the poor and landless. In Amazonia, concerns over effective control of remote frontier areas and fears of neighbors' designs on land and resources have led governments to encourage the settlement of the hinterlands by members of the dominant culture, even though the region is already inhabited by indigenous people.

Throughout Latin America, state policy has tended to encourage land speculation and commercial development by the politically well connected. In fact, government subsidies often make up a significant part of the economic return on investments in "developing" rainforest regions (Selection 11). On the other hand, forest people have used various means to resist this alliance of government and business interests, revealing the contested nature of tropical rainforests (Selections 8 and 9). The history of the oil industry in Mexico and Ecuador exemplifies competition for scarce resources on local, national, and global scales (Selection 9).

Crushing foreign debts have forced many Latin American countries to exploit their natural resources—petroleum, gold, iron ore, or tropical hardwoods—in order to earn foreign exchange for debt repayment. Pursuit of economic growth has encouraged the building of large hydroelectric dams to promote industrial development as well as ambitious highway and port construction to facilitate trade. During the 1980s debt crises, structural adjustment programs mandated trade liberalization, which was further expanded during the 1990s with international agreements such as NAFTA. This approach to economic growth has been encouraged by the lending policies of multilateral banks (the World Bank and the Interamerican Development Bank), which historically have supported megaprojects such as the Grande Carajas project in Brazil or Colombia's Plan Pacífico.

Proponents of rainforest conservation face powerful obstacles. Urban populations, often divorced from and unaware of the problems caused by deforestation, have more political power than do rural populations, which are more directly interested in forest issues. In particular, Latin America's elites are often opposed to paying for policies from which they derive little, if any, benefits. On the contrary, forest conservation may be more likely to penalize the elites, who lose potential profits from developing the land, while it benefits others such as indigenous people, rubber tappers, and in some cases peasants. Another obstacle derives from the widespread perception that economic growth and environmental protection are mutually exclusive. These obstacles prevent effective implementation of the conservation programs proposed by environmentalists and supported by scientific research over the past several decades.

In conclusion, a number of social, economic, and political factors contribute to government policies that promote settlement in rainforest regions (Selection 11) and their conversion to other, more "productive" uses (Selection 12). Many observers emphasize one factor over others in their explanations for the causes of deforestation. The selections in Part II are a sample of the various perspectives on tropical deforestation. Taken together, they reveal the complex dynamics involved in forest clearance in Latin America. And an understanding of the various factors is not just an academic exercise; it is a necessary foundation for the formulation of effective policies to control deforestation and environmental degradation. A policy based on simplistic, one-dimensional explanations of deforestation will inevitably fail.

---

7 Manuel Moreno Fraginals ◆
The Death of the Cuban Forests

This excerpt from a book about the role of sugar in Cuba's history provides an early example of the analytical framework that would now be called "political ecology." The author was a Cuban economist trained in the methods of historiography. After ten years of working in market research for multinational enterprises, including the sugar industry, the Revolution challenged him to shift his professional focus. Manuel Moreno

From Manuel Moreno Fraginals, *The Sugarmill: The Socioeconomic Complex of Sugar in Cuba, 1760–1860*, trans. Cedric Belfrage (New York: Monthly Review Press, 1976), 73–77, 168. © 1976 by Monthly Review Press. Reprinted by permission of the Monthly Review Foundation.

Fraginals wrote The Sugarmill *in early postrevolutionary Cuba to provide scholarly support for Marxian ideology.*

Selection 7 shows how powerful interests gained control of colonial economies and established the conditions of inequality that have persisted in modern Latin America. The Sugarmill *also analyzes the linkages between global and local processes. Through meticulous research using primary documents, Moreno clearly reveals the inextricable relationship between the system of production and virtually all other aspects of society and nature. As he explains in the preface to his study of the role of sugar in Cuba's history, "I aim . . . to follow the trails which start with sugar and surface in the founding of a university chair, in a decree on tithes, in a characteristic style of town mansion, or in the dire effects of deforestation and soil erosion." His path leads him into the sometimes hidden conflicts between various stakeholders over timber rights during the great sugar boom of the late eighteenth and early nineteenth centuries in the West Indies.*

In the material excerpted here, the author demonstrates how a "plunder culture" developed with the technological changes that occurred in Cuba during the sugar boom. These allowed the sugar barons to minimize production costs by taking advantage of one of nature's subsidies—the nutrients stored in mature tropical ecosystems.

Up until the end of the eighteenth century, Cubans took pride in their forests. The whole island was a stand of precious wood—mahogany, cedar, ebony, dagame, quebracho—among which soared giant palms. Early chroniclers could not suppress their amazement at our trees in whose shade, they insisted, one could walk from one end of the island to the other. The Laws of the Indies guarded this wealth jealously, taking the socially responsible position that the forests were not the landowner's property since they also belonged to future generations. Before sugar, before tobacco, before cattle, it was precious wood that symbolized the Far Antilles. From Cuban wood were carved the gorgeous ceilings of the Escorial, its still-intact doors and windows, and the incredible mahogany table, the world's largest made from a single piece. Boards from giant Cuban trees made the doors of San Francisco El Grande in Madrid, and Cuban wood abounded in the Royal Palace. Documents tell us that a typical form of English and French piracy was to plunder the forests of the semi-populated island: how much Cuban wood went into English and French palaces we do not know.

The protection of the forests was legally defined in the so-called Cortes de El Rey (Royal Timber Prerogatives) to be found in Law 13, Title 17, Book 4 of the *Recopilación de Indias*. These Cortes were the basis for setting up the Havana shipyard, which in a few years built 128 ships of all types and sent mountains of timber to Spain. The ships, ranging from 120-cannon giants to 30- and 40-cannon frigates, helped defend the Spanish empire; many went to the bottom at Trafalgar, but the exceptional timber used made them twice as durable as European ships. They derived toughness from *sabicú* and *chicharrón* bottoms and lightness from cedar planking.

Large-scale manufacture rang the forest's death-knell. The best sugarmaster of the early nineteenth century left us this crisp sentence: "The sugarmill's need for firewood is alarming—and where are the forests that can meet it?" He was José Ignacio Echegoyen, Arango's technician at La Ninfa, later proprietor of the giant La Asunción mill. Firewood consumption depended on the kettle system. The unit by which it was calculated was the "task," a cubic volume of 3 x 2 x 1 yards. A caballería of forest was estimated to yield about 1,000 tasks. The "Spanish train" consumed one task of firewood for each 5 or 6 arrobas of clayed sugar:* use of the Jamaica train more than doubled the yield, to 13 arrobas per task. We can easily calculate that at the end of the eighteenth century about 500 caballerías of forest were being felled each year to be burned in making sugar, plus many more for building new mills.

With sugar's advance, tree-clearing became a well-paid activity for the small Havana peasantry of the late eighteenth and early nineteenth centuries. They received between 300 and 500 pesos for "cleaning" one caballería. As prices rose over the years, the work became the speciality of teams employed on a piece-work basis. Although slaves were often used for wood cutting, it became more and more a free worker's job as the institution of slavery became bloated. Masters found that their blacks constantly disappeared into the woods and it was hard to catch them.

We must make a clear distinction between ground that was cleared for planting cane and building mills, and forests cut down for firewood. In the first case the method was simple. A machete gang first tackled the reeds and vines, leaving clear spaces around the big trunks. This "chopping" of the undergrowth was followed by the "toppling" of ancient trees. After thirty or forty days came the "burning" of the chopped, now-dry vegetation. If it was a "slash and leave" job, the trunks not consumed by the fire stayed where they had fallen and sugarmill slaves stacked them for use as fuel. If it was a "slash and burn" job, the fires were repeated and the trunks cut small so they would burn completely. When some of the timber remained unburned, it was piled into small bonfires (*fogatas*), a process known as *foguerear*. The most precious woods—ebony, mahogany, quebracho—were generally of great size and took two or three fires to burn.[1]

No one can calculate the extent of sugar's forest depredation. We have suggested that it ran to 500 caballerías a year in the late eighteenth century; by 1809 it was twice as much, and in 1830 sugarmen Andrés de Zayas and José María Dau estimated it at 2,000 caballerías—half for fuel

*Editor's note: 1 caballería = 13.4 hectares (33.16 acres); 1 arroba = 25.36 lbs.

and half burned up to make room for new mills.[2] The figure rose to 4,000 in 1844, at which point the Junta charged with protecting the trees announced that the forest laws had given "happy and satisfactory results."[3]

The right to destroy the forests was one of the sugarmen's great legal victories. The Cortes del Rey were a feudal privilege that was in open contradiction to the interests of large-scale manufacture and were interpreted by the bourgeois-minded sugarocracy as an encroachment on the "universal and sacred right of property." There was a stormy confrontation that took the outward form of a battle between the Junta de Maderas (Timber Board)—a feudal institution controlled by the Navy—and the Real Consulado. While the Junta was defending a privilege that ran counter to productive economic development, many of its arguments were well taken. It was undeniable that if the forests were unreservedly surrendered to the sugarmen's voracity they would disappear. Faced with this cold reality, the Consulado could only argue that Cuban forests were "excessive" and their total liquidation was "impossible, as the natural order of things attests." Meanwhile, Arango was saying that many Havana *hacendados* [estate owners] did not have any forests or that those they had "did not contain a stick of any value." The sugar producers were caught in flagrant contradictions, but here was the confession of the death of the forest at their hands. Their power was decisive and on February 4, 1800, they obtained a Real Cédula, calling for a Consulado study of the possibility of withdrawing Crown timber rights to a distance of 81 miles from Havana. This was, in fact, a green light for free sugar expansion throughout the island's western area.[4]

On August 30, 1805, the sugar bourgeoisie secured the right to dispose of trees on their land with no limitations other than those in certain ordinances, which were never written. The final victory was won in the Spanish parliament: Cuban sugar spokesmen Andrés de Jáuregui and Juan Bernardo O'Gavan obtained the total repeal of all Crown timber privileges in the island. In Havana the Junta de Maderas, led by engineer Diego de la Parra, tried to resist the new legislation and was put to rout. A Real Cédula of August 30, 1815, summarizing the entire forestry code, put the finishing touches to the freedom of the bourgeoisie. The sole qualification was a new junta to study the results of the new forestry laws; its history is both long and short: it held its first meeting in the month of its establishment, May 1816, and its second and last in 1844, twenty-eight years later.

These legal comings and goings developed amid polemics which sometimes became violent. The battle, which appeared to be between the Navy and the Consulado, was in fact between the old feudal superstructure and the new wave of large-scale manufacture. As usual, the *hacendados* left no argument unvoiced in defense of their rights, so that— again, as usual—startlingly cynical documents appear in the record. To cite just one, very representative of the polemical tone: the Consulado, by a Real Orden of October 5, 1795, issued a report on the production of wax. It said that the main obstacle to Cuban beehive development was "the trouble facing beekeepers in the matter of using cedar for their hives"; in order to produce wax and honey, permission to fell trees was requested. Las Casas, the sugar producers' staunch ally, accepted this as valid, but the forestry director, Pedro de Acevedo, replied with firm indignation. It was another pretext, he said, "to annihilate the forests."[5]

The many arguments used in the drawn-out controversy were summed up in a sage observation by Ramón de la Sagra: "At no time has the rational use of forest resources been discussed, only the question of who has the right to fell and raze."[6] As we have seen in other cases, so with forests: the legislation came *a posteriori*. The sugar expansionists ignored the Junta de Maderas, continuing to fell and raze through the great 1792–1802 boom. Throughout the eighteenth century, burning forests were a daily spectacle in the Cuban countryside. The name "Quemados" (burned) appears more than any other in Vives's map of the island, designating a host of places where memories of a forest in flames persisted.[7] Thus the new legislation merely recognized old and irreversible facts. If after its promulgation there was more destruction than ever, this was not due to the newly acquired rights, but to the steady growth of production, progressively claiming more fuel and land. The system resulted by midcentury in the conversion of the Havana area and part of Matanzas into treeless plains. In Cienfuegos, founded in 1819 beside forests "which the world envies," firewood had become a serious problem. The Sagua and San Juan de los Remedios areas presented the same vista of a land without shade.

Not until the disappearance of the trees began affecting production did the sugarocrats begin to worry. Then they changed the kettle system back to the one-fire train, planted more otaheite cane,* and used bagasse as fuel. The more forward-looking ones wrote memos reflecting in part the outlook of the great manufacturing pioneers. The Count de Mopox y Jaruco and José Ricardo O'Farrill talked of replacing the stands of precious wood.[8] Others, thinking not in terms of forests but of firewood, proposed solutions to the fuel problem. José Pizarro y Gardín, for example, suggested extensive planting of royal palms—13,533 to the caballería, yielding "186,636 *pencas* [gigantic palm leaves] and the same number of *yaguas* [leaf sheaths]" annually for fuel.[9] Dau saw the best solution in wild indigo, one and one-half caballerías of which could yield 44,085,760 pounds of brushwood a year; or, if not, *paraíso*-tree plantations would

---

*Otaheite cane was a tall, thick-stalked, fast-maturing cane whose *bagasse* (what remains of the cane after juice extraction) was useful as fuel for sugar trains. However, compared to other varieties it was less drought-tolerant and required more fertile soil.

give almost the same results.[10] Only one man of the time, Sagra, proposed untouchable forest reserves to safeguard the island for future generations. Realizing that this ran counter to the bourgeois concept of property, he made a socialist criticism of what he called "the vices of the economic theory of misconceived liberty" and demanded subordination of that liberty to the public interest.[11]

The death of the forest was also, in part, the long-term death of the island's fabled fertility. This was an old Antillean process with which our sugarocrats were already acquainted. Slave labor involved the use of crude techniques with a low yield. To compensate for manufacturing deficiencies, the highest agricultural yield was sought, but this was in no way the result of rational soil utilization, only of the exceptional richness of recently cleared virgin land. First plantings of a dead forest commonly produced well over 120,000 arrobas of cane per caballería. Annual cane cutting and neglect of the hilling and strawing of shoots lowered the crop of a field which was neither irrigated nor fertilized. When a critical point was reached it was abandoned, another forest was cut, and the fabulous cane production statistics were again repeated.

The Cuban *hacendado* did not invent this barbaric system: it was born with Antillean sugar, a typical product of the plantation. Technicians called it "extensive cultivation," while Liebig and Sagra gave it the more precise name of "plunder culture." The English used the same system in the small islands and were soon left without trees; by 1749 they were calling their once-fertile lands "poor and worn out."[12] French producers, one up on them at the time, were working land that was "fresh and fertile," but a century later a traveler noted that "the inhabitants can't even find roots to feed themselves." It was an exaggerated version of what had happened in Europe, attributed by [Karl] Marx to the insuperable limitations with which private property always confronts the most rational agriculture.[13] On top of all the agricultural and economic motivations for destroying forests came the wars of independence. In the campaign plans drawn up by Generals Concha, Valmaseda, Caballero de Rodas, Ceballo, and Azcárraga, it was estimated that 55 million trees would be felled for the various military arteries and roads.

A fantastic footnote on the contradictions of Cuban sugar production is that in the same years that the island was burning its own timber wealth, it was the top buyer of United States lumber. From the end of the eighteenth century, pine and cypress boards for making sugar boxes were arriving at Havana ports. The lumber trade was one of the United States' best-paying businesses. Imports, without counting contraband, ran between 600,000 and 1,000,000 pesos a year in the first two decades of the nineteenth century. José de Arango called this trade "shameful." He complained about the fate of our forests, "given to the flames or remaining in useless abundance while we empty our pockets for the foreigner's benefit."[14]

The excuse for importing lumber was simple—wood was needed which did not impart smell or taste to the sugar, so cedar and mahogany would not do—but the truth of the matter lay elsewhere. The sugar industry had absorbed the island's free labor and work had been degraded by slavery. This had so raised the wages for cutting and transporting wood that it could more cheaply be brought in from the north. In 1813, Havana had a steam sawmill—the first in Latin America—with no wood to cut. José de Arango did his utmost to convince the *hacendados* that because of its toughness, lightness, odorlessness, and ease in cutting, *jobo* was the ideal wood for sugar boxes. He presented testimonials to this effect by the Marquis de Arcos and the Count de Gibacoa. Little came of it and boxes continued to be made of northern wood.

But not only sugar-box wood was brought from outside: from 1837 on we find contracts for the importation of firewood to run the railroad. The Drake concern promoted the first deal at 14 pesos a cord: George Knight shipped it from New Orleans and sold it at 17 pesos. The cheerful slogan of this business was that "Northern wood gives more flame." Heavy imports of coal began later, reaching 92,000 tons in 1860.[15]

Sugar exterminated the forests. Deaf and blind to history, focusing on the present, the sugarocracy destroyed in years what only centuries could replace—and at the same time destroyed much of the island's fertility by soil erosion and the drying-up of thousands of streams. An extra debit item on the ledger of an irrational system of exploitation based solely on calculations of immediate profit was the resulting Cuban contempt for trees. Yet the poet Pobeda sang in praise of trees, and among other voices heralding the future was that of Sagra, who wrote: "At this stage of maturity, when man is enriched by the conquests of science and illuminated in his endeavors by moral sentiments, he faces the great enterprise of exploiting his planet not merely for his own generation but for those to come. This cannot be done unless individual, ephemeral, and transitory interests are subordinated to the general and eternal interests of all humanity."[16]

Of Cuba's forests, its legendary mahogany, almost nothing remains today. In 1962 one could still see the *palanqueros* at work on the Río Sagua, whose waters flow gently between treeless banks. They drive a long iron-pointed pole into the riverbed until they feel they have struck timber; they dive, secure it, and drag it to the bank. A hard, slow, monotonous job, like the throes of death. Day by day they bring up from the river bottom bits of the trees that sugar cut down. They live off the corpses of the forest. All that remains to them of the ancient wealth is the echo of an old folksong:

> Tomorrow I go to Sagua
> To cut me some boughs
> To make me a house
> On the slopes of Jumagua.[17]

Notes

1. Rodríguez Ferrer, *Naturaleza y civilización de la grandiosa isla de Cuba, 1876–77*, vol. I, pp. 681–765.
2. Zayas, *Ingenios de fabricar azúcar*, p. 33. In *Memorias de la Sociedad Patriótica de La Habana*, May 1837.
3. Sagra, *Cuba en 1860* (1861), p. 69.
4. *Espediente instruido con los antecedentes del recurso dirigido a las Cortes generales y extraordinarias sobre las reservas hechas en la Junta de Maderas del 22 de junio de 1812 por el Ingeniero Don Diego de la Parra contra el decreto que restituye a los particulares el dominio de los arbolados*, Real Consulado, leg. 94, no. 3955.
5. *Espediente sobre cumplimiento de la Real Orden de 5 de octubre último que previene el fomento del cultivo de la cera en esta Isla*, Real Consulado, leg. 92, no. 3927.
6. Sagra, *Cuba en 1860*, p. 67.
7. Study of Cuban toponymy initiated by the Instituto de Geografía de la Academia de Ciencias (in preparation, data supplied by Professor Juan Pérez de la Riva).
8. O'Farrill, *Memoria sobre bosques, Anales de la Real Junta de Fomento y Sociedad Económica de La Habana*, vol. IV (1851), p. 236; Mopox y Jaruco, *Ruina de nuestros preciosos montes, necesidad de reponerlos, Memorias de la Sociedad Económica de Amigos del País* (1843), p. 232.
9. Pizarro y Gardín, *Reposición de los bosques que se consumen anualmente en el combustible de los ingenios, Memorias de la Sociedad Económica de Amigos del País* (1846), p. 373.
10. *Gaceta de La Habana*, March 2, 1848, and March 10, 1848.
11. Sagra, *Cuba en 1860*, Chapter 1.
12. *The State of the Sugar-Trade* (1747).
13. Marx, *Capital*, vol. III.
14. José de Arango, *Jozo, Discurso dirigido al Excmo. Sr. Gobernador y Capitán General, Memorias de la Sociedad Económica de Amigos del País* (1817), pp. 264–273.
15. *Espediente formado para contratar la leña necesaria de las máquinas del camino de hierro*, Real Consulado, leg. 38, no. 1664.
16. These are the final words in Sagra's chapter on forests in *Cuba en 1860*.
17. This is a traditional folksong, transmitted orally, collected by Professor José Sainz Triana of the Universidad Central de Las Villas.

---

8 Philip Howard ◆ The History of
Ecological Marginalization in Chiapas

Philip Howard's meticulously researched historical review demonstrates why scholars of revolutionary movements should pay attention to differ-

From Philip Howard, "The History of Ecological Marginalization in Chiapas," *Environmental History* 3, no. 3 (1998): 357–77. Figures and table omitted. © 1998 by the Forest History Society and the American Society for Environmental History. All rights reserved. Reprinted by permission of Duke University Press.

ent groups' degree of access to natural resources. This advice is true both for historians reconstructing past events and for scholars of contemporary social movements. Howard's work clearly shows that there is a relationship between increasing environmental scarcities and the rise of class struggle and social movements. The events described in Selection 8 are not unique to Chiapas and Mexico; they are representative of political struggle over forested land in many parts of Latin America. For other examples, see selections 9, 10, 17, and 18.

The environmental history of Chiapas reveals the various ways in which local and national elites have controlled state policy, manipulated property rights, and appropriated and managed resources with the result that the rural poor have been ecologically and economically marginalized. In recent years, global (and hemispheric) political economy has also played a role as Mexico's debt crisis prompted economic restructuring that further marginalized campesinos. Globalization continues to intensify economic exploitation of the region—at the expense of poor campesinos and natural ecosystems. The impact of economic exploitation is exacerbated by high rates of population growth in marginal zones such as eastern Chiapas, due both to immigration and to natural increase.

In the hushed morning after San Cristóbal's New Year's celebration in 1994, hundreds of masked troops moved through the empty streets, cutting phone lines, dismantling the local security apparatus, and establishing an alternative political order. The revolutionary Zapatista government lasted only four days in San Cristóbal and other urban centers of the Central Highlands of Chiapas, Mexico. In the following year, the Ejercito Zapatista de Liberación Nacional (EZLN), or Zapatista National Liberation Army, would bring the plight of Chiapan peasants to the attention of other Mexicans, foreign investors, and the international community, challenging anew the legitimacy of the Institutional Revolutionary Party (PRI), the long-standing ruling party of Mexico. While many revolutionary objectives have been attributed to the Zapatistas, the rebels admit that their publicly stated aims mask their most enduring claim against Mexico's authoritarian regime: freedom and relief from the escalating environmental scarcities that have been impoverishing their communities.

By exploring the ecological history shared by the people and natural environment of Chiapas in this century, a better understanding emerges of some of the tangible, proximate sources for the grievances of the EZLN, the group responsible for organizing many of the ecologically marginalized poor of Chiapas into open rebellion. The changing supply and quality of soil and forest resources can be traced through social periods defined by the general principles under which state elites managed resources and manipulated property rights. From the Spanish Conquest until the Mexican Revolution, an almost feudal social order in Chiapas allowed state elites to capture resources as necessary. The revolution sought to stop this practice by redistributing land resources to peasants, but powerful elites in Chiapas still manipulated the resource regime as the competition for resources grew fierce and their supply dwindled. The Mexican debt crisis of the early 1980s prompted an economic restructuring which allowed elites to be more aggressive, resulting in a large population of ecologically marginalized poor, some of whom organized the Zapatista Rebellion in 1994. The ecological marginalization of many Chiapans has been the result of a rising scarcity of land and fuelwood resources, a situation that has grown acute in recent decades.[1]

The setting for this story is the Central Highlands and Eastern Lowlands of Chiapas. The Central Highlands rise some nine hundred meters from the Soconusco Coast on the Pacific Ocean and contain the fertile lands surrounding the Grijalva River. The Highlands encompass two major urban centers, Tuxtla Gutiérrez, the state capital, and San Cristóbal, a former seat of colonial power and now a popular tourist destination. The municipality of Reforma, with its abundant oil and natural gas reserves, also lies in the Central Highlands. The Eastern Lowlands include the Lacandón Rainforest, which is bounded by the Usumacinta River and Guatemala to the east, the heavily deforested area of the Marqués de Comillas to the south, and the increasingly populous area of the Cañadas at the foot of the Highlands. In this frontier region between the Highlands and the Eastern Lowlands, people have experienced the most severe environmental scarcities, and here the EZLN finds its greatest support.

Five groups are particularly important in the story of the Zapatista uprising. The *indígenas* are the native inhabitants of this region of Central America; their common cultural and linguistic traits cross state and municipal territories that have historically tried to contain and manage them. The largest groups of indígenas are the Tzeltzal, the Tzotzil, and the Chol. The EZLN does not represent all peoples of the Eastern Lowlands, but many of the most marginal of those who have colonized the Lacandón Rainforest over the past forty years. The *campesinos* produce their own food or participate in the economy of family or community subsistence by handcrafting small tradables or by working for wages; Spanish is often their first language. Like many of the indígenas, they either practice subsistence farming or raise small crops for purchase by local marketing boards; they often earn income from tourism or from meeting the seasonal demand for labor elsewhere in the state. The majority of campesinos live on public land assigned to their community by the government, though a growing number live without land titles of any kind. Intellectuals, churches, and opposition leaders have helped organize indígenas and campesinos, first by encouraging them to think of their ecological marginalization as an injustice, and then by encouraging them to express dissatisfaction with unfulfilled political promises of state elites. The *latifundistas* are a relatively small group of owners who control vast tracts of private land, such as the great coffee plantations of the Soconusco

Coast. Similarly, the *rancheros* have used state subsidies to accumulate large tracts of grazing land for their cattle herds. Latifundistas, in partnership with rancheros, have withstood federal attempts at political reform and land redistribution for many years by maintaining control over state politics. The *caciques* are political bosses who work for the landowners and government elites. They mobilize community support for the PRI, exact tithes for traditional festivals, and benefit economically from their role in containing opposition.

Ecological fragility does not necessarily make an area ecologically marginal. Rather, the combined ecological quality of fragility and the social assessment of the resource wealth of a place produces such a designation. For example, communities often find tropical farming unsustainable because soils erode quickly or remain fertile for only a few seasons once the natural tropical forest cover is removed. Moreover, if one particular resource is valued by social elites, they may shift access rights in their favor. For example, if a company observes that forest timber is being removed for fuelwood by a rapidly growing community, it may ask the state to deny access to local groups so that the timber can be removed exclusively for the benefit of the company.

Ecological marginalization results from a rapid growth in human population and a degradation in the quality or quantity of natural resources within the context of an inegalitarian resource regime that denies a portion of the population regular access to healthy resources. In response to the rising consumption of local resources, social elites further manipulate this regime to capture the best resources for themselves, often forcing a population to deepen their poverty through migration to ecologically fragile areas unable to support large human communities. These areas are "marginal" because the land is relatively susceptible to rapid degradation by erosion and overuse. It may be fertile and productive in the short term, but this productivity is difficult to maintain for more than a few years.[2]

Because marginalization results from an interaction between ecological trends and social institutions, several components of the environmental history of Chiapas must be followed—deforestation, soil erosion and nutrient loss, human population growth, and the manipulation of the resource regime by powerful elites. Much of this story takes place at the periphery of the Lacandón Rainforest, which at the turn of the century extended from the Eastern Lowlands up to the foothills—an area called Las Cañadas—of the Central Highlands. Throughout the twentieth century, the frontier of the forest receded from the foothills as logging concessions, ranching operations, and farming communities grew. As Neil Harvey notes, "although the ejidos and comunidades agrarias account for approximately half of Mexico's land surface, most of it is rain-fed, undercapitalized and of poor quality." In Chiapas, the government granted these communal land titles at the edge of the Lacandón Rainforest; to this day, the largest remaining tract of tropical rainforest in Mexico is in the Montes Azules Reserve of the Lacandón, an area containing more Mexican mammal species facing extinction than any other reserve, the only Mexican habitats for many of these species, and the most diverse ecosystem in Mexico.[3]

From Conquest to Revolution to Liberalization

The first Spanish explorers to encounter the rainforest of southern Mexico called it the *desierto de los lacandones*. This "wasteland" of over 1.2 million hectares contained precious hardwoods, undiscovered species of plants and animals, and a wealth of mineral resources, not to mention the cultural wealth of the inhabitants. Spanish mercantilism turned these resources into fuel for European prosperity and colonial expansion, though the indígenas fought in countless riots and rebellions to prevent their conversion into chattels. A fascinating history rich with Church politics, colonial atrocities, and indigenous myths and prophecies, these uprisings more often than not had at their core a demand for land resources. "Land hunger propelled the Chamulas [indígenas] forward as much as did their talking stones and living Saints. The *criollos* of San Cristóbal so dominated cultivable land in these high pine mountains that the holdings of Chamulans—much as they still are today—were measured in rows and not hectares."[4] During this time, the class distinctions that still exist began to take shape:

> Within the landscape of haciendas and republics of Indians there stood the cities, the seats of the merchants who supplied both haciendas and mines, of officials who regulated privileges and restrictions, of priests who managed the economy of salvation. From their stores, offices, and churches extended the communal networks which supplied the mines and drew off their ores; the bureaucratic network which regulated life in the hinterland; and the ecclesiastic network which connected parish priests with the hierarchy at the center. In the shadow of palace and cathedral, moreover, there labored the artisans who supplied the affluent with the amenities and luxuries of a baroque colonial world, the army of servants, and the enormous multitude of the urban poor.[5]

Local elites had regularly vacillated on whether to associate their political and economic future with either Mexico or Guatemala, but in 1824 a hesitant decision was made to join Mexico. Logging began in the Lacandón in 1859, with the first large cedars and caobas being felled at the juncture of the Usumacinta and Jacate Rivers, the logs driven down the Usumacinta into Tabasco for shipment to New York, Liverpool, and Calais. By the beginning of the twentieth century, four entrepreneurs had been allowed to purchase all three million acres of forest at the encouragement of Porfirio Díaz's investment-hungry regime. In 1880 three large companies—Bulnes Brothers, Valenzuala & Sons, and Jamet & Sastre—

cornered the world market for mahogany at a high price. Enticed by the potential for profit, other firms began to explore the rivers of Chiapas, and by the end of the nineteenth century, private companies and individuals owned all the shorelines of the Lacantum, Pasión, and Usumacinta rivers, floating fallen trees downriver for processing in foreign ports.[6]

Great private investment opportunities arose in earnest during the *Porfiriato*, the years of Porfirio Díaz's national tenure at the turn of the century. He facilitated the formation of great *latifundios*, private estates varying in size from tens to thousands upon thousands of hectares. By building the nation's rail system, Díaz gave the latifundios access to distant markets and won the loyalty of many established coffee plantation owners on the coast of Chiapas. During this period, large tracts of land were prepared for monocultural production. Indigenous populations were either entrapped as forced laborers or channeled into the new peasant economy at the margins of estates and the frontiers of uncut forest.

The Mexican Revolution arguably saved both the Mayans and the forest from devastation by logging camps. It was a fight for land; by 1910 the latifundistas, who represented 1 percent of the population, controlled 81 percent of the land. After more than a decade of fighting, political leaders slowly began to implement the Mexican Constitution of 1917, with Article 27 guiding the redistribution of Mexican territory into *ejidos, comunidades agrarias*, and private landholdings. The new constitution arose from two desires—to bring political stability to a country that had experienced violence since 1910, and to redistribute land among peasants who had lived without secure access to land resources since the sixteenth century. Its framers firmly established the right of peasants to petition for the legal recognition of title to occupied land, even if the land was formally part of another private holding.[7]

In Chiapas, landholdings could be grouped in four categories. *Ejidos* were areas consisting of individual and communal lands that could not be sold, rented, or used as collateral. Claims could be filed with the state for title to latifundio land that had long been occupied by squatters. *Comunidades agrarias* were areas claimed primarily by indigenous communities from private owners that had encroached on their communities in previous decades. *Private landholdings* were privately held areas restricted to five thousand hectares or less, except in Chiapas, where state legislators extended the limit to eight thousand hectares. In practice, however, the illegal renting of communal land (or "name-lending," the assignment of neighboring land titles to family members and contractors) increased the actual size of some estates well beyond the legal limit. *Official bioreserves* and *national parks* were areas set aside for the conservation of local ecology, often superimposed upon existing land titles.

Land reform and redistribution in Chiapas occurred only where large landowners permitted the practice, primarily because of their dominant role in managing the affairs of the state. The best lands of the state surround the Grijalva Valley, the Soconusco Coast, and parts of the highland close to market transportation routes. These areas experienced relatively little redistribution. The terms of land redistribution favored the original landowners by allowing them to choose which properties to sell and by allowing them to retain any capital investments such as seed, fertilizer, supplies, and farming equipment. Not surprisingly, the land chosen for sale always represented the most marginal area of an estate, and it was often sold to the state at an inflated value.[8]

As late as the 1940s, the population of Chiapas numbered about five hundred thousand, but by the following decade the trickle of migrants into the Eastern Lowlands grew to a steady stream of people coming from other parts of the state, from neighboring states, and from Guatemala:

> The first wave of settlers were, like the "new" Lacandones before them, Chol refugees pushed out of Palenque. They were soon joined by highland Tzotziles, squeezed off the undernourished soils of Chamula. . . . Non-Mayan Indians from Oaxaca, forced off their communal lands by government dams, arrived in the Desert of Ocosingo; indígenas dislodged by the White Guards of southern Veracruz's murderous cattle kings, a regional industry sustained by World Bank credits; landless mestizo farmers from as far away as Guerrero and Michoacán joined the flow in pursuit of a patch on which to grow a little corn.[9]

When migrants arrived, they found the PRI's network of caciques strongest in the Central Highlands and along the Coast, and with the active encouragement of government officials, many moved on to the Eastern Lowlands to build their communities. Excluding in-migration, many communities grew at about 4 percent per year through the middle of the century, an astonishingly high figure at the upper limit of human reproductive capacity.

Demand for timber also increased substantially after World War II, and again entrepreneurial effort was channeled into purchasing land and evading rules established by the Mexican Constitution. For example, by 1949 the American firm Vancouver Plywood had pasted together a territory of six hundred thousand hectares through a system of name-lending between families and contractors. In 1957 and 1961 presidential decrees granted various privileges to logging companies in order to facilitate the removal of precious hardwoods like mahogany, tropical cedar, oak, madrone, and pine. Between 1875 and 1969, the area of prime jungle was reduced from 1,245,000 hectares to 800,000 hectares; much of this was logged with modern machinery in the 1950s and 1960s.[10]

Many migrants came to Chiapas to meet the labor demands of the timber industry, but as communities grew they came into direct competition with state and private logging companies for forest resources. Communities needed fuelwoods for heating and cooking, and they sought to clear trees for pasture and farmland. Logging companies disliked this depletion of forest resources that were not being put to good use as they defined it. "By 1971," writes James Nations, "the individuals who controlled these companies realized that the farm families they had pushed into the Selva Lacandona were clearing and burning the forests before the commercial hardwoods could be extracted." As competition for these resources increased, elite pressure on the state also grew; in 1972, President [Luis] Echeverría granted the small community of Lacandón Maya title to 634,000 hectares of the Lacandón Rainforest, authorized cooperative management of immigration and resource control, and ordered other occupants of the forest to relocate to several larger communities or to move out entirely.[11]

This maneuver facilitated the removal of precious hardwoods by rationalizing forest resources under the control of a single Mayan community from whom logging rights could be easily secured. Only after violent protests were a number of other land titles recognized within the Lacandón Reserve, though the government continued to relocate families into a larger township so that logging could continue unimpeded. Consequently, logging operations expanded in 1974 when the Lacandona Forestal Company and Palenque Triplay Company were granted a concession of 1.3 million hectares of primary, secondary, and fragmented forest, in addition to assistance from public capital. Road construction into the forest increased again following a PEMEX study of the area's oil reserves, and this allowed more access to primary forest growth. The decade of the 1970s saw a total of 440,000 hectares logged from the periphery of the rainforest, the edge of the Usumacinta River and its major tributaries, and the paths followed by roads cleared for the transport of oil exploration equipment.[12]

Most campesinos and indígenas had been forced to settle at the edge of the rainforest by political, population, and ecological pressures elsewhere, and the state's decision to evacuate all but the Lacandón Maya in 1972 radicalized many communities. The order to evacuate was the beginning of an assault—indirect by way of ecological marginalization, direct by way of bribery and murder of opposition leaders—on the lives and livelihoods of the region's migrants. An obvious manipulation of the state resource regime in favor of logging concessions, the decision not only ignored some long-standing land claims but also denied state participation in the settlement schemes of the 1950s and 1960s. The sympathies of many who lived in the Eastern Lowlands turned towards the liberation theology of the Catholic church or the new Protestant missions. These parishes provided a forum for communities to organize in pursuit of land claims and to resist the political entreaties of the PRI.

Logging was not the sole reason for the deforestation of the Eastern Lowlands. Ranching operations expanded rapidly in the early 1970s, particularly at the northern edge of the forest around Palenque; they converted

some 76,000 hectares of forest cover to pasture land. In addition to sur-
rendering trees for fuel, timber, and pasture land, the Lacandón Rainforest
also supplied nutrient-rich soils to the growing population of subsistence
farmers. Accordingly, erosion became both an ecological and a social problem. Erosion occurs when soil is repeatedly tilled and exposed to the energy of wind and rain that would otherwise be absorbed by a more diverse
vegetative cover. Highland areas are particularly vulnerable to the dis-
lodging of soil and fine organic particles. Eroded soils often contain three
times the amount of nutrients found in the soils of larger particles and
stones left behind. Erosion also exposes soil to other forms of degradation by reducing water infiltration and holding capacity, nutrient levels,
soil biota, and depth.[13]

Agricultural production grew significantly during the 1960s, and
Mexico became a net exporter of grains for the first time. In Chiapas, the
beef and coffee sectors led this wave of agricultural growth. Cattle ranching was restricted to a small segment of the state population. Most residents began to participate in the growing economy of cash crops like coffee,
bananas, and cocoa by developing small plots of land at the edge of forest
land. To their dismay, however, the campesinos discovered that the seemingly rich soils of erstwhile rainforests became tired after just a few years
in production. Unable to sustain crops, the land returned only a fraction
of earlier yields with each successive season.

No long-term study of soil erosion in Chiapas exists, but anecdotal
evidence about farming techniques in the Central Highlands reveals the
impact of soil erosion on peasant communities from the 1940s onward.[14]
According to anthropologist George Collier, land abuse occurred throughout the Central Highlands, but the growing population of Chamula (an
area north of San Cristóbal) particularly tested the ecological limits of
highland soils because intense swidden agriculture did not allow soils to
adequately regenerate. The population of the area had grown from 16,010
in 1940 to 26,789 in 1960. Farmers would slash and burn forests to open
fresh fields every few seasons, leaving the exposed and tired soils unused
or relegated to pasture land. Collier describes a process that became familiar in many other parts of the state:

> The water supply in hamlet water holes becomes variable, the soil hav-
> ing lost its capacity to maintain a high water table through the dry win-
> ter season. Heavy summer rains erode the edges of trails that crisscross
> the grasslands, silting in the natural limestone sinks, which alternatively
> flood and dry as mud flats according to the season. Continued
> shepherding takes its toll. Because of constant clipping off at the roots,
> grass gives way to gullies of erosion, which spread out from trails along
> the hillsides. In a matter of years a hill can erode from grazing land to a
> heap of rocks devoid of top and subsoil.[15]

Since Collier's 1975 study, the pattern of declining agricultural production due to environmental scarcities has been replicated, with some variation, in parts of the Eastern Lowlands.

Traditional slash-and-burn practices used to prepare forest soils for subsistence crops of corn, beans, chilies, and coffee were responsible for a significant portion of the deforestation outside of the Lacandón Rainforest. Since the population growth of many campesino communities hovered around 4 percent, these traditional practices proved unsustainable very quickly as the rich but thin topsoil tired from the rigorous production regime. As a result of several decades of rapid population growth and rising agricultural demands, the problem of soil erosion grew most serious in the Highlands; many families chose to move on to the Eastern Lowlands and the frontier of the Lacandón Rainforest in the hope of finding a healthier land that they could call their own.

In 1974 the Chiapan Indigenous Congress complained about injustices in other parts of the state: "We have problems with ranchers who invade our lands. . . . We need land, we don't have enough of it, so we have to rent it, or go away to work. The lands we have been given are infertile. We need to be taught our rights under the Agrarian Laws."[16] Land seizures became common as communities fought to obtain a basis for subsistence living. The creation of a national park around the Lacandón Rainforest in 1978 did not discourage the flood of people from Central and Northern Mexico from making their home at the edge of the forest, even though the legal status of "national park" was supposed to deter further settlement except in designated towns.

As far as the government was concerned, migration to these towns brought relief from the demands of campesinos for land reform and the demands of latifundistas for protection from squatters. The forest became a safety valve for the particularly high pressure of growth in indigenous communities living at the edge of private holdings. As Collier notes, however, "by the 1970s the population density of the Central Highlands of Chiapas had almost negated the benefits of land reform," and those who did farm the Eastern Lowlands found the costs of farming, fertilizers, herbicides, labor, and transportation prohibitive. Populations leaving the Central Highlands of Chiapas settled in the frontier areas of the Lacandón Rainforest, occupying land and coming into conflict with more established communities. Furthermore, once a community had cleared forest lands to which they had no legal title, landowners with political clout could claim the land for their livestock. As populations grew, large landowners were forced to expel squatters, if only to prevent them from petitioning the federal government for land titles. When the federal government mandated land reform and redistribution, its plans were manipulated by powerful elites within the state to further the ecological marginalization of the poor. Legislators exempted certain private properties from redistribution, owners submitted their least productive lands for sale at good prices, and people were relocated to the frontier of the Lacandón and assigned titles there. In short, the PRI and the elites of Chiapas redistributed just enough land to accommodate a growing population within an inegalitarian resource regime.[17]

The cattle industry required land more than labor, and ranchers from the states of Tabasco and Veracruz established large ranches at the northern frontier of the Lacandón Rainforest by clearing new forest or assuming control—through rent or repression—of areas already cleared by the milpa production of migrant communities. Both the World Bank and the Mexican state encouraged peasants to participate in the growing cattle industry during the 1960s and 1970s. Ultimately, these subsidies encouraged large ranchers to manipulate small ranchers into raising calves, by far the riskiest part of cattle ranching, and many families found it more sensible to rent their ejidos illegally for cattle grazing. While the statistics of aggregate sectoral growth may be impressive, by 1983 one hundred thousand peasants were landless, and 30 percent of the communal land titles were actually controlled by latifundistas. By 1970 the population of grazing animals had quadrupled from that of 1950, though 75 percent of the head were on private lands.[18]

Competition for resources grew fierce. Cattle ranchers wanted more pasture lands, plantation owners wanted to maintain their holdings, loggers wanted larger tracts of forest, environmentalists wanted a protected bioreserve, established communities wanted room for expansion, and migrants wanted fuelwood and land for subsistence production. Indígenas and campesinos lost this competition, and many were marginalized to the most ecologically vulnerable part of the state, the frontier of the Lacandón Rainforest. Whenever competition grew into conflict, indígena and campesino migrants suffered the most. Despite growing pressure for serious and comprehensive management by the national government, Mexico's political system contained the problem by fragmenting or co-opting opposition groups.[19]

As peasants found the productivity of their land decreasing in the Eastern Lowlands, they began to sell their labor time as seasonal workers, a commitment that required the migration of men from the Eastern Lowlands to the great latifundios of the Soconusco Coast. By one estimate, the migration of several hundred thousand Chiapan and Guatemalan campesinos and indígenas through the Lacandón destroyed some 11,000 hectares of forest each year. Labor migrants returned to their communities with money and with heightened expectations about the usefulness of commercial fertilizers and herbicides in coaxing another season's growth out of tired rainforest soils. This represented an important step in the proletarianization of peasants, for, as Collier observes, traditional agricultural methods were supplanted by modern techniques or abandoned in favor of small microbusinesses, a trend which made Chiapan peasants highly susceptible to the economic downturns that occurred in the mid-1980s.[20]

From Economic Liberalization to Rebellion

The population of Chiapas grew from 1.5 million in 1970 to 3.2 million in 1990, with an annual growth rate of 3.6 percent; however, the growth rate for the indígena population was 4.6 percent over the same period, with the population growing from 290,000 in 1970 to 710,000 in 1990. This population growth, in combination with migration from Guatemala, created a population of over 300,000 living in one of the most marginal parts of the state, the foothills between the Central Highlands and the Lacandón Rainforest, an area often lacking potable water, electricity, or civil infrastructure. Much of the indígena population lives in the Eastern Lowlands, and rapid growth has increasingly required the use of soil resources from small farmholds. Seasonal labor migration once relieved population pressures on small farmholds, but with the economic downturn of the mid-1980s, this safety valve no longer worked. In addition to the natural growth rate of Chiapan populations, significant numbers of migrants came to the Eastern Lowlands. As many as three hundred thousand Guatemalans moved across the border during the political conflicts of the mid-1980s. Throughout that decade, tens of thousands of people moved into the Eastern Lowlands. With the 1983 eruption of the Chichón volcano in the north and the flooding of land in the Grijalva Basin by massive hydroelectric projects, thousands more were relocated into the Eastern Lowlands by the government of Chiapas.[21]

In the late 1980s, Mexican and international environmental lobbies coordinated their efforts to limit the amount of area cleared annually at the edge of the Lacandón by loggers and peasants. As with other government policies, the limits were unevenly applied, and peasants in the Cañadas found themselves under a more rigorous regime, enforced by caciques, than that governing the growing number of ranchers to the north or the loggers farther east. For example, between 1983 and 1988 another 143,000 hectares were logged. In total, 665,000 hectares of prime, secondary, and fragment forest have been logged since the nineteenth century; with the benefit of modern machinery, 85 percent of this timber has been removed since 1970.[22]

The Lacandón Rainforest was also fragmented by squatter settlements and cattle ranchers, who tripled the amount of pasture land within the forest between 1980 and 1988, usually by taking land that had been slashed and burned clear by farmers. According to the most comprehensive study of the northern frontier of the rainforest, the Lacandón Rainforest was deforested at a rate of 7.7 percent each year between 1974 and 1986. In all, 42 percent of the exposed areas went to pasture land, 42 percent was overtaken by secondary forests, and 6.7 percent was lost to severe soil erosion. Only 3.7 percent remained used for agriculture. The fragmentation of forests by road construction, hydroelectric and oil development projects, logging, and swidden or pastoral agriculture also disrupted the overall integrity of the forest ecosystem.[23]

Throughout the state, 60 percent of the total population and 80 percent of the indigenous population use firewood as their cooking and heating fuel. Lacandón communities use oak, madrone, and cedar for cooking, for firing the kilns that produce ceramic goods, and for the distilleries that produce moonshine. For many communities, supplies of these woods could no longer be found at the edge of their settlements, but only high in the neighboring hills. These special "cloud-forests" (so named because of the unique flora and fauna found only at the crest of hills permanently engulfed by tropical mists) now became the prime target of firewood gatherers.[24]

The pattern of intense swidden agriculture and soil erosion that Collier found in the Central Highlands had spread early in the 1990s because many of the people using these techniques were forced to migrate to the frontier of the Lacandón. Scarcities of healthy land eventually drove thousands from the Central Highlands and Soconusco Coast to the frontier of the Lacandón. Jungle colonizers had habits that differed significantly from those of early occupants, particularly agricultural practices not suited to the tropical ecosystem. They opened up new lands for agriculture and cattle, and by 1993 they were approaching the limits of production. Highland communities continued to grow, with the population of Chamula doubling over the three decades since Collier's original study.[25]

Estimates suggest that the erosion rate of Highland and Lowland soils greatly exceeded seventeen tons per hectare per year during the 1980s. Topsoil loss of three or four tons per hectare per year is considered sustainable, but in many parts of Chiapas the annual rainfall is quite high, and the type of rainfall—torrential, heavy tropical rains coupled with high-speed winds—significantly erodes soils. Given the high slopes of Central Highland farms around the two largest urban centers in Chiapas and the thin topsoil of Eastern Lowland farms supporting rapidly growing communities, wealthy farmers had to use large amounts of fertilizer to temporarily relieve the effects of erosion. But Lowland soils still did not recover in time to support many producers. As Rattan Lal noted, "the drastic erosion-caused productivity decline in soils of the tropics is due partly to harsh climate and partly to low-fertility and poor-quality subsoil. It is because of the low productivity of the exposed subsoil that erosion is considered more severe in the tropics than in the temperate-zone soils." Although no statewide studies exist, a long-term experiment on the hillsides of La Fraylesca and Motozintla found high levels of soil loss— twenty-five tons per hectare per year for maize fields that have been grazed and burned from forests, fifteen tons per hectare per year for fields that were burned but not grazed, and less than three tons per hectare per year for fields that were neither grazed nor burned.[26]

Such soil erosion particularly affected subsistence and small-crop farmers. Neil Harvey noted a drop in the output of milpa production—a 20 percent drop in maize and an 18 percent drop in beans between 1982 and 1987—despite increases in the area of land dedicated to production (20 and 10 percent increases, respectively, over the same period). Much of this expanded production was in the Lacandón, where tropical soils were unsuited for sustainable agriculture once the biomass had been destroyed.[27]

In the years following the 1982 debt crisis, Mexico undertook liberal economic reform by selling off state agencies and removing some market controls, subsidies, and public credits. Restructuring required a speedy capitalization of agriculture from private sources given the cessation of government subsidies for fertilizers, tools, and credits. In Chiapas, the effect of this capitalization was clear. Those with wealth earned outside the agricultural sector could invest in fertilizers, herbicides, tools, and transport services, while those with little or no capital were forced to practice basic subsistence production or to lease their land and labor to wealthier producers.

Government subsidization of fertilizers, tools, and product prices declined because of waning state funds, forcing many farmers out of production or, in the best cases, into their own credit-loaning agencies. Such organizations helped to support subsistence and small agricultural producers who lacked access to government credit, a group that included on average almost 80 percent of all agricultural producers in Chiapas from 1985 to 1989. In 1990 almost 90 percent of agricultural producers had no access to credit. The effect of agricultural subsidies also differed between the regions of Chiapas. The subsidy of maize production, for example, was a palliative in the Central Highlands and Eastern Lowlands, where payments were made through PRI representatives to manage peasant unrest and to secure political support at election time. As part of the state development strategy, hydroelectric energy from the Grijalva River was captured by a system of dams completed in 1986; however, the dams flooded over one hundred thousand hectares of fertile land in the Grijalva basin in subsequent years, forcing tens of thousands of people to relocate into the Eastern Lowlands, commonly in Las Cañadas. The economic

restructuring program faltered around the mid-1980s because of the compounded effects of an oil shock, peso depreciation, rising inflation, and a
stock market crash. President Carlos Salinas de Gortari attempted to re-
organize the national economy, and one component of this "Economic
Solidarity Pact" addressed the agricultural sector by promising to abolish
the protective institution of the ejidos and to phase out most price controls, agricultural subsidies, and marketing boards.[28]

In anticipation of changes to the land tenure system, social elites in
Chiapas began to manipulate the resource regime in their favor. First, the
state governor launched an extensive land redistribution program that gave
more land titles and more hectares of land to campesinos and indígenas in
his six-year term than had been redistributed in the previous thirty years
(consistent with corporatist strategy, however, only 27 of 493 major land
grants went to peasant organizations not allied with the PRI). Second, to
protect private land, particularly property owned by rancheros, the governor issued special *certificados de inafectabilidad* to shelter individual
holdings from the national land reform project. By 1988, 4,714 certificados —95 percent of the total number distributed in the state since 1934—
protected 70 percent of the land used for cattle grazing from agrarian
reform.[29]

By the end of the decade, these changes had also affected the character of coffee production within the state. Most of the best land for coffee
lies along the Soconusco Coast, and this area was controlled by a small
number of large coffee estates (the largest 116 owners controlled 12 percent of the land devoted to coffee production). Farm size drops as one
moves east across the state to land of generally lower quality, and the land
becomes predominantly public and communal rather than private. The
91 percent of coffee growers in Chiapas that own less than five hectares
are mainly located in the Central Highlands and Eastern Lowlands. As of
1990, the distribution of coffee land was significantly more skewed towards the wealthy in Chiapas than in Mexico as a whole. Mexico and
Chiapas have virtually the same percentage of coffee producers with two
hectares or less of land, yet in Chiapas the percentage of coffee growers
with more than fifty hectares is twice as high as that for all of Mexico. By
the beginning of the decade, two-thirds of Mexican latifundios with more
than one hundred hectares operated in Chiapas.[30] The marginal quality of
the land is also evidenced by below-average yields. Average coffee yields
in the Cañadas were under three hundred kilograms per hectare, compared with the state average of over five hundred. Similarly, the average
maize yield for the Cañadas region was about thirteen hundred kilograms
per hectare, while for the state it was over two thousand kilograms.[31]

In 1991 the PRI amended the Mexican Constitution and designed an
Agrarian Law which drastically changed the land tenure system. While

nearly two thousand unresolved land claims—30 percent of those filed in all of Mexico—were for tracts of land in Chiapas, campesino and indígena organizations were not consulted in the design of the new Agrarian Law, which contained the followed modifications:

1. Ejido members were given the legal right to sharecrop or rent their land.

2. Ejido members were given the legal right to purchase, sell, rent, or mortgage the individual plots and communal lands which constitute each ejido land title. If government-endorsed cash crops were grown, private companies of as many as twenty-five individuals could purchase twenty-five times the size of single land permits.

3. Constitutional mechanisms allowing squatters to make land claims were removed.[32]

Ecological problems had long made the rent of ejido land to ranchers necessary, even if illegal, so the change in property rights only legitimized many existing property arrangements. Government representatives promised to resolve the remaining land claims and offered peasants new land in the Lacandón; however, private owners were given a year to sell off excess property that would eventually be scheduled for redistribution, an option that permitted landowners to hold out for higher prices if their land was of marginal quality.

Peasant organizations fought violently with each other in anticipation of granting decisions, trying to isolate radical groups undeserving of political favors from the state. The government distributed parts of bioreserves and meager estate lands that latifundistas were eager to sell, often giving the same piece of land to several competing peasant communities, thus creating patchworks of overlapping land titles like those that currently exist around the Montes Azules Bioreserve in the Eastern Lowlands. Regulations in the Montes Azules Bioreserve were tightened prior to negotiations over the North American Free Trade Agreement (NAFTA), and another 81,000 hectares were reclassified as bioreserve lands. Severe quotas on timber extraction by small producers were also put into effect, and communities were instructed to find other sources of fuel.[33]

A massive backlog of land claims has arisen since the early 1970s, and it still remains unprocessed by the state government. Most often, claimants appealing for legal control were punished and cajoled by caciques and private armies, or by more established communities claiming the same plots of land for themselves. Most of these disputes occurred between communities of ecologically marginalized poor at the frontier of the Lacandón.

Environmental Scarcities, Rising
Grievances, and Conflict in Chiapas

In Chiapas, the best land resources have always been captured by the latifundistas, and even the land reform initiatives for which Mexicans fought during the Revolution were perverted in Chiapas to marginalize a large portion of the campesino and indígena population on ecologically vulnerable lands. In a process often replayed since the Spanish Conquest, these groups settled at the periphery of towns, private estates, ranches, or logging concessions on lands that appeared unclaimed. When the need for land or forest resources grew, those living in desirable areas were evicted; ranchers and plantation owners were particularly interested in land cleared by squatters for their own subsistence agriculture.

In absolute terms, the statewide amount of cultivated land per person increased steadily over much of the twentieth century as new lands, especially forest lands, were opened to cultivation. In the mid-1970s, however, this trend reversed, and a decline in the amount of cultivated land per capita continues. Today, the average endowment for subsistence production is two hectares, compared to twenty hectares for commercial production. Significant regional differences exist, however, between the Coast, the Central Highlands, and the Eastern Lowlands. Great tracts of coffee and maize plantations have existed in the coastal region since before the Revolution, and the demands of a growing population have largely been met by labor opportunities on the latifundios. In contrast, the Central Highlands have a higher population density, particularly in and around San Cristóbal, where the growing population has consumed much of the forest and land resources, significantly changing the local landscape. Even the expansion of municipal boundaries by seven thousand, and later ten thousand, hectares could not meet the local demand for land resources, and the area of worked land increased at the expense of forested areas. As resources became increasingly scarce in this populated area of Chiapas, the poorest subsistence farmers were often forced to give up land and move their families to the Lacandón frontier.[34]

Much of the commentary on the recent rebellion in Chiapas only investigates general grievances, such as dissatisfaction with the electoral system or perceptions of widespread economic injustice. But close study of the ecological history of Chiapas reveals that the process of ecological marginalization also plays a significant causal role. The rioting, protesting, human rights violations, and electoral fraud of the past fifty years have often been over land tenure issues and the manipulation of property rights, factors stemming from and complicated by rapid population growth, soil erosion in the Central Highlands, and deforestation in the Eastern Lowlands. These same processes have hindered economic prosperity because powerful elites marginalized the poor into the areas that were most vulnerable to the cumulative effects of rapid population growth, soil erosion, and deforestation. The adoption of liberal economic reforms forced the PRI to subordinate its patronage commitments to client groups (labor and peasants), commitments that had maintained political stability for sixty years. Within the context of rapid political and economic change at the national level, state elites maintained their dominance by capturing the best state resources and marginalizing the poor to certain areas of the state.

Not surprisingly, violent opposition to state development has arisen over numerous issues in the history of Chiapas, and ecological marginalization is not the only grievance of the modern Zapatista rebels. Many communities, particularly indígena communities, have no electricity, piped water, or drainage systems, and most indígena communities have no such infrastructure at all. A majority of the people in the state have not completed "primary" level education, and they often work for the minimum wage or less (58 percent of the working population of the state and 83 percent of the working indigenous population of the state are employed by the primary sector). These developmental problems have historically plagued many parts of the state; however, only at the edge of the Lacandón have farmers, ranchers, squatters, loggers, and indigenous communities so fiercely competed for natural resources. Incidents of conflict over land and forest resources grew increasingly violent and increasingly frequent after 1972 as the pace of expulsions and intercommunity competition over natural resources quickened. Because of fraud, elections in Chiapas frustrated the ability of a growing portion of the population suffering from environmental marginalization to express their grievances, resulting in ever more political clashes.[35]

The modern Zapatista insurgents would never use the term "ecologically marginalized" to describe the historical condition of their communities, but in the last twenty years many communities in the Central Highlands and Eastern Lowlands have experienced a kind of "cognitive liberation" in which church and opposition leaders redefined social categories of distributive justice and convinced many that their situation of ecological marginalization was ill deserved and intolerable. "It strikes me that what most radicalized our companions were the changes to Article 27," wrote Subcomandante Marcos in 1994. "That was the door that was shut on the Indian people's ability to survive in a legal and peaceful manner. That was the reason they decided to take up arms, so that they could be heard, because they were tired of paying such a high blood tax." The intellectual leadership of figures like Marcos provided followers with an interpretation of the economic, social, and ecological forces that entrapped them and gave them an insurgent consciousness.[36]

This insurgent consciousness also contains crucial ecological content. Since the power base of the EZLN is and has always been intimately tied to local resources and has long lived with inadequate, marginal lands, intellectual leaders explained not only *why* the best lands went to state elites, but also *how* modernization had disconnected the "ecological basis" of indígena culture. The EZLN membership understands the importance of crop rotation, forest health, and ecologically sustainable development better than any state planner. Awareness of their own "ecological marginalization" is evidenced by their constant demand for ecologically healthy land and their staunch refusal to accept land titles in the Montes Azules Bioreserve.[37]

The ecological marginalization of growing populations in Chiapas was a direct result of intentional manipulation of land tenure arrangements by powerful elites within the state and an indirect result of macroeconomic and macropolitical change. These changes were certainly experienced by other communities in the state, but never have such grievances inspired an open insurgency like the one organized by the Zapatistas of the Lacandón frontier. Many people have been left impoverished and dispossessed by a half-century of development under Mexico's system of one-party governance, but understanding the unique history of ecological marginalization is crucial to understanding the modern conflict in Chiapas.

Notes

1. This paper neither recounts the events of the rebellion itself, nor reviews the academic debate over the form of Mexico's evolution as a corporatist state and its current program of economic liberalization, since both of these topics have been exhaustively explored elsewhere. I argue that an important set of Zapatista grievances regarding land distribution is the result of rising resource scarcity and the land reform efforts of the last five decades. While I trace the contemporary principles of land reform back to the Mexican Revolution, I do not take on the task of providing a history of land and property laws back to the Spanish Conquest. For readers interested in that level of detail, I recommend Robert Wasserstrom, *Class and Society in Central Chiapas* (Berkeley: University of California Press, 1983); *White Fathers and Red Souls: Indian-Ladino Relations in Highland Chiapas, 1528–1973* (Cambridge: Harvard University Press, 1977); Ronald Nigh, *Evolutionary Ecology of Maya Agriculture in Highland Chiapas, Mexico* (Palo Alto, Calif.: Stanford University Press, 1975); and especially Antonio García de León, *Resistencia y Utopia* (México, D.F.: Ediciones Era, 1985).

2. See Philip Howard and Tad Homer-Dixon, "Environmental Scarcity and Violent Conflict: The Case of Chiapas, Mexico" (occasional paper, Project on Environment, Population, and Security, University of Toronto, 1996).

3. Neil Harvey, "Playing with Fire: The Implications of Ejido Reform," *Akwe:kon Journal* (1994): 22; Rodrigo Medellín. "Mammal Diversity and Conservation in the Selva Lacandón, Chiapas, Mexico," *Conservation Biology* 8 (1994): 780–99.

4. John Ross, *Rebellion from the Roots* (Monroe, Maine: Common Courage Press, 1995), 67.

5. Eric Wolf, *Peasant Revolutions of the Twentieth Century* (New York: Harper & Row, 1969), 5.

6. "Forest Policies in Chiapas," Public Communication from Felipe Vallagran to Oscar González Rodríguez, Subsecretary of Natural Resources, Secretariat of Environment, 10 May 1995.

7. Ross, *Rebellion from the Roots*, 254: Judith Teichman. "Political Economy of Mexico" (seminar paper, University of Toronto, February 1993).

8. George Collier, *Basta! Land and the Zapatista Rebellion in Chiapas* (Oakland, Calif.: Institute for Food and Development Policy, 1994), 32, fig. 1.3.

9. Ross, *Rebellion from the Roots*, 255–56.

10. Ibid., 255.

11. James Nations, "The Ecology of the Zapatista Revolt," *Cultural Survival Quarterly* (1994): 32.

12. "Forest Policies in Chiapas."

13. O. Mazera et al., *Carbon Emissions from Deforestation in Mexico* (unpublished manuscript, Centro de Ecología, UNAM, México, D.F., 1990); Nigh, *Evolutionary Ecology*, 15. See also David Pimentel et al., "Environmental and Economic Costs of Soil Erosion and Conservation Benefits," *Science*, 24 February 1995, 1117–23.

14. See the chapter on "Soil Erosion in Chamula," in George Collier, *Field of the Tzotzil: The Ecological Bases of Tradition in Highland Chiapas* (Austin: University of Texas Press, 1975).

15. Collier, *Fields of the Tzotzil*, 115.

16. Collier, *Basta!*, 63.

17. Ibid., 111.

18. Peter Rosset and Roger Burbach, "Chiapas and the Crisis of Mexican Agriculture," *Food First Policy Brief* 1 (Oakland, Calif.: Institute for Food and Development Policy, 1994), 6; Ronald Nigh, "Consecuencias de la Colonización Agropecuaria para las Selvas Tropicales del Sureste de México: Implicaciones Regionales y Globales" (working paper, Centro de Investigaciones y Estudios Superiores en Antropología Social del Sureste, 1994), 12.

19. Patricia Gómez Cruz and Christina Maria Kovic, *Con un Pueblo Vivo en Tierra Negada* (San Cristóbal, Chiapas: Centro de Derechos Humanos, 1994); Carlos Heredia and Mary Purcell, *The Polarization of Mexican Society* (México, D.F.: Equipo Pueblo, 1994): Thomas Benjamin, *A Rich Land, A Poor People* (Albuquerque: University of New Mexico Press, 1989); Neil Harvey, "The Difficult Transition: Neoliberalism and Neocorporatism in Mexico," in *Mexico: Dilemmas of Transition,* ed. Neil Harvey (London: Institute for Latin American Studies, 1993); Denise Dresser, *Neopopulist Solutions to Neoliberal Problems: Mexico's National Solidarity Program* (La Jolla, Calif.: Center for U.S.-Mexican Studies, University of California-San Diego, 1991); Judith Adler Hellman, *Mexico in Crisis* (New York: Holmes & Meier, 1988), chap. 5; Wayne Cornelius, Judith Gentleman, and Peter Smith, eds., *Mexico's Alternative Political Futures*, Monograph Series, no. 30 (La Jolla, Calif.: Center for U.S.-Mexican Studies, University of California at San Diego).

20. Alain de Janvry and Raul García, "Rural Poverty and Environmental Degradation in Latin America" (unpublished manuscript, Department of Agricultural and Resource Economics, University of California at Berkeley, 1988), 7; "The Toll of Restructuring on Lives and Communities," in George Collier, *Basta!*.

21. Luis Raul Salvado, *The Other Refugees: A Study of Nonrecognized Guatemalan Refugees in Chiapas, Mexico* (Washington, D.C.: Hemispheric Migration Project, Georgetown University, 1988), 13.

22. "Forest Policies in Chiapas."

23. A. Cuaron, *Conservación de los Primates y sus Habitats en el Sur de México* (master's thesis, Universidad Nacional de Costa Rica, Heredia, 1991), cited in Nigh, *Evolutionary Ecology*, 15; A. Cortez Ortiz, *Estudio Preliminar sobre Deforestación en la Regional Fronteriza del Rio Usumacinta* (Informe Técnico, Instituto Nacional de Estadística, Geografía e Informática, México D.F., 1990), cited in Nigh, *Evolutionary Ecology,* 15.

24. "Maximo Lopez, Firewood Gatherer," *American Forests*, November-December 1988, 38.

25. Dr. Pablo Farias Campero, ECOSUR, private communication with the author, Chiapas, Mexico, May 1995.

26. Howard and Homer-Dixon, "Environmental Scarcities," 11; Rattan Lal, *Soil Erosion in the Tropics* (n.p.: McGraw-Hill, 1990), 4. See also Pimentel, "Environmental and Economic Costs," 1119. For discussions of the soil types in Chiapas, see Maximiliano Huerta Cisneros et al., *Características Generales de la Vegetación y su Utilización en 25 Municipios de Chiapas* (Chiapas, Mexico: Fomento de Corporación de Chiapas, 1986), and María del Carmen Carmona Lara et al., *Ecología: Cambio Estructural en Chiapas: Avances y Perspectivas* (Tuxtla Gutiérrez, Mexico: Universidad Autonoma de Chiapas, 1988); Olaf Erenstein, Centro Internacional de Mejoramiento de Maíz y Trigo, private communication with the author, 30 May 1995.

27. Neil Harvey, "Rural Reforms, Campesino Radicalism, and the Limits to Salinismo," *Transformation of Rural Mexico* 5 (Ejido Reform Research Project, Center for U.S.-Mexican Studies, University of California-San Diego, 1994), 11.

28. Secretaria de Agricultura y Recursos Hidraulicos and Comisión Económica para América Latina y el Caribe, *Primer Informe Nacional sobre Tipologia de Productores del Sector Social* (México, D.F.: Subsecretaria de Política Sectorial y Concertación, 1992), 19; Harvey, "Rural Reforms," 14; Nora Lustig, *Mexico: The Remaking of an Economy* (Washington, D.C.: Brookings Institution, 1992).

29. Rosset and Burbach, "Chiapas and the Crisis of Mexican Agriculture," 8; Harvey, "Rural Reforms," 22.

30. Neil Harvey, "Rural Reforms," 10.

31. A. Carlos Santos, "Development and Conservation of Natural Resources in the Las Cañadas Region of the Lacandona Rainforest," in *Population/Environment Equation: Implications for Security: Third Conference on Environmental Security*, 31 May–4 June 1994.

32. See Alain de Janvry et al., *Mexico's Second Agrarian Reform: Household and Community Responses, 1990–1994* (La Jolla, Calif.: Center for U.S.-Mexican Studies, University of California-San Diego, 1997).

33. Most observers agree that unlike the industrialized states in northern Mexico, the largely agricultural economy of Chiapas is only slowly beginning to feel the specific impact of NAFTA. Economic malaise in Chiapas is more sensibly attributed to the last decade of ecological degradation and economic liberalization, of which NAFTA is only the most recent manifestation.

34. Nigh, "Consecuencias de la Colonización Agropecuaria," 27.

35. Gómez Cruz and Kovic, *Con un Pueblo*.

36. Subcomandante Marcos, *La Jornada*, 7 February 1994.

37. Collier, *Fields of the Tzotzil*; Victor M. Toledo, "The Ecology of Indian Campesinos," *Akwe:kon Journal* (1994): 41–46; and Nations, "The Ecology of the Zapatista Revolt," 31–33.

9 Myrna Santiago ✦ Rejecting Progress in Paradise: Huastecs, the Environment, and the Oil Industry in Veracruz, Mexico, 1900–1935

This selection explores the social and environmental changes that took place on Mexico's Gulf Coast as a result of the oil boom during the early twentieth century. Myrna Santiago uses in-depth historical research on a well-defined period to challenge a widely held assumption that indigenous people are merely the passive "victims of progress" when commodity markets invade and transform their homelands.

The Huastec Indians of northern Veracruz co-existed with tropical rainforests for hundreds of years. Their economy and culture were based on subsistence slash-and-burn farming (in which fields alternated with secondary forest on fallow land) and careful management of communal forests. They limited their participation in the market economy and had long had to defend their ancestral lands from outside forces. Santiago shows the importance of state policy in the continual struggle for access to land and resources. During Porfirio Díaz's regime (1876–1911) the Mexican government pushed hard for modernization and aggressively sought to eliminate communal lands and subsistence farming in order to make the land "productive." Díaz's push for the privatization of landholdings made it difficult for Indians to assert their rights to traditional lands held in communal tenure. All over Latin America, indigenous peoples have lost their traditional homelands when state policy has favored privatization in the name of progress. The Huastecs, however, did not always acquiesce to the loss of their land without attempts to protect their interests—especially in terms of maintaining enough access to agricultural land to preserve their farming way of life. Santiago demonstrates that in at least two key historical periods the Huastecs were able either to influence state land policy or to utilize sympathetic governments to gain legal rights to land. Other selections in this volume explore various aspects of the struggle over land and resources in the course of economic development. (See Selections 8, 10, 17, and 18)

In December 1932, the society pages of the *Los Angeles Herald Express* noted that Countess Estelle Doheny had honored Bishop John J. Cantwell with a banquet where "exotic orchids graced [the] table." Orchids were the former telephone operator's pride; with them, she had won

From Myrna Santiago, "Rejecting Progress in Paradise: Huastecs, the Environment, and the Oil Industry in Veracruz, Mexico, 1900–1935," *Environmental History* 3, no. 2 (1998): 169–88. Map omitted. © 1998 by the Forest History Society and the American Society for Environmental History. All rights reserved. Reprinted by permission of Duke University Press.

the sweepstakes at the Pasadena Flower Show the previous year. Not native to southern California, Mrs. Doheny's orchids bloomed inside a custom-made "glass-and-steel conservatory" that she had erected in the backyard of her Spanish Gothic mansion. The flowers had travelled to Los Angeles from the Mexican tropical forests that still covered northern Veracruz when Edward L. Doheny began investing in oil there in 1900. By 1931, however, the companies had exhausted the oil mantles, abandoned the "fields," and, by most popular accounts, destroyed the forest and left its "Indian" inhabitants as steeped in poverty as they were before the industry arrived.[1]

Despite these popular notions, the details of what took place at the local level during the "golden years" of oil production in northern Veracruz, from 1908 to 1921, and during the aftermath, from 1921 to 1935, remain largely unexplored. To date, most scholarly work focuses on the diplomatic and political aspects of Mexican petroleum, sparked by President Lázaro Cárdenas's 1938 decree expropriating the British and American companies operating in the country. A number of questions still await full investigation. What did the oil country look like? Who lived there? How did local residents navigate through the abrupt series of transformations that oil extraction inevitably engendered? What happened to them and their surroundings when the oil stopped flowing? Categorical statements at this early stage in the historiography of local oil production are premature, but a careful reading of the available sources does allow for a preliminary analysis of the social and environmental changes that transpired in northern Veracruz as a result of oil exploitation between 1900 and 1935.[2]

The interaction between the oil companies and the native population of northern Veracruz, the Huastecs, had a longer and more complex history than previous studies have suggested. Their relationship followed a historical trajectory that included a rapid acceleration in the decades-old struggle to appropriate indigenous land holdings; an unprecedented and massive, yet ultimately temporary, incorporation of native males into the labor force; and a return to subsistence agriculture in a degraded environment when the wells ran dry.

Even if the period of oil extraction "passed by like a summer storm, leaving very little and building even less," as Carlos González Salas argues, the indigenous people of northern Veracruz were not merely leaves caught in the wind. At each turning point in the turbulent process of oil extraction, indigenous men and women either resisted oil companies or attempted to reap temporary rewards in the form of royalties or wages. Ultimately, the Huastecs rejected the only lasting opportunity the industry offered—proletarianization. When exploration and new drilling in their region ended in the second half of 1921, the Huastecs did not follow the industry to blacker pastures. Abandoning agriculture to become part of the nascent Mexican industrial working class was not an option that they exercised, unlike thousands of other peasants. Instead, they organized during the late 1920s to press a sympathetic state government for collective land grants (*ejidos*) in their attempt to maintain an agricultural way of life and to protect the land from further degradation.[3]

Why did the native population apparently reject progress in "paradise"? While any answer is sheer speculation, given that the Huastecs left no written record of their impressions of the oil industry, it seems that the monetary benefits offered by the industry could not offset the price of "progress." The Huastecs apparently decided that they could best reproduce themselves and their culture through subsistence farming.

The state of Veracruz rests like a half moon on the shores of the Gulf of Mexico. Geographers, economists, anthropologists, and historians have traditionally divided it into three regions or zones: north, central, and south. The northern area included four *cantones* (the political territorial unit used until 1921)—Ozuluama, Tantoyuca, Tuxpan, and Papantla—and extended approximately three hundred kilometers, from the Tamesí River on the north to the Cazones River in the south. Oil deposits occurred throughout this northern region, bubbling to the surface in sticky black pools that the locals called *chapopoteras*. An area known as the *Huasteca* included only the first three political divisions.[4] As late as 1900, the land inhabited by the Huastecs for several centuries remained covered by an awe-inspiring tropical forest.[5] Finding specific information on the exact composition of this "jungle" poses a curious challenge, however. Most period sources adopted "a narrative of paradise," to borrow a phrase from historian Candace Slater. Visitors as diverse as ornithologist Frank M. Chapman, travel guide author Thomas Philip Terry, and *Saturday Evening Post* journalist Carl W. Ackerman described the *Huasteca* as an "Eden."[6]

Allegorical descriptions only raise an obvious question: What kind of an ecosystem existed in heaven? As botanist Arturo Gómez-Pompa admitted, the naming and classifying of "jungles" has been varied and sometimes inadequate, an understandable frustration given that classification systems evolve over time. The characterization of Veracruz's vegetation made by José Ramírez in 1899, for instance, bears little resemblance to the one made by Peter G. Murphy and Ariel Lugo in 1986. While Ramírez described northern Veracruz as a "region of tropical forest . . . perfectly characterized but not profoundly so," Murphy and Lugo classified the world's current tropical areas as 42 percent dry, 33 percent moist, and 25 percent wet/rainforest, depending on annual rainfall. Rainfall figures for northern Veracruz in the last century are not easy to find, but several observers noted that the difference between the "rainy" and "dry" seasons was a matter of degree. Doheny's complaint about "the apparently incessant rains" might not have been much of an exaggeration. As novelist Jack London wrote about Tampico in 1914, "rain falls every month of the year, the 'rainy season' merely connoting the period of excessive rain."[7] Based on rain patterns and surviving tree species, botanist Jerzy Rzedowski argued in the mid-1980s that "until the last century" the moist/rainforest of Veracruz extended from Ozuluama to Chiapas. Even if generally correct, this does not mean that the nineteenth-century forest was "pristine" or "untouched by the hand of man," as the Edenic narratives would have it. The northern Veracruz forest, in fact, had a long history of change at the hands of the Huastecs who had inhabited it for centuries.[8]

The Huastecs, who call themselves Teenek, are related to the Maya of Yucatán. Since pre-Hispanic times, they have been settled in the region named for them, in what later became the intersection of three Mexican states: San Luis Potosí, Hidalgo, and Veracruz.[9] Government officials and other observers further divided the region into three areas: *huasteca potosina, huasteca hidalguense,* and *huasteca veracruzana.* The Huastecs probably did not recognize such discrete divisions of their territory, but they are useful demarcations because oil development took place only in the *huasteca veracruzana.* Although archaeological evidence points to a Huastec presence in modern Tamaulipas state, by 1900 few Huastec speakers could be found in northernmost Ozuhuama *cantón,* between the Tamesí and the Pánuco Rivers. Census figures show that their population remained below twenty-five thousand adults well into the twentieth century.[10]

Before oil development began, the entire Huastec family apparently participated in the enterprise of survival, using all the resources available to them. To a casual observer like geologist Charles Hamilton, such expert use of the environment made them appear "self-sufficient" because "what they [couldn't] grow they [could] pluck wild from the forest." In reality, their daily routine combined both market behavior and subsistence practices. The Huastecs relied on the market economy and intrepid vendor-translators like Serapio Lorenzana to provide them with goods such as soap, salt, needles, scissors, and machetes. Since at least the mid-nineteenth century, Huastec men also cultivated sugarcane in small quantities as a cash crop, and women kept small orchards and beehives near their conical, thatched-roof dwellings, selling fruit or honey for money on market days. By the late nineteenth century, a significant number of men and boys also worked for money on the encroaching *haciendas,* further strengthening their links to the market economy. Despite this emerging cash nexus, the Huastecs' primary economic activity remained the growing of corn for subsistence in a communally owned forest.[11]

The Huastecs, like peasants the world over, practiced slash-and-burn agriculture, a method appropriate for the poor, fragile soils of the tropical forest. This approach could sustain life for many generations, so long as the forest population remained small; indeed, the Huastecs apparently lived and reproduced their culture in northern Veracruz for centuries using this method. Men worked collectively to chop and burn patches of forest, transforming the environment without destroying their habitat. Anthropologists calculated that the typical size of one family's clearing was 1.5 hectares (3.6 acres), a unit known as a *destajo*. An American shopping for land for a tropical plantation in Tuxpan in 1896 noted that natives only cultivated a field for "a couple of years," after which they felled another patch of forest, allowing the previous one to lay fallow in order to recover its fertility. That cycle apparently accounts for the large areas of rainforest that observers encountered in the early twentieth century, as well as the smaller forests that might have represented a second generation of trees and plants growing in fallow cornfields.[12]

For the dictator and modernizer of Mexico, Porfirio Díaz, subsistence agriculture in a region as exuberantly green as the *Huasteca* meant wasted market potential. Anxious to bring capitalist development and material progress to Mexico, Díaz and his positivist inner circle envisioned changing such "obviously" fertile land into a "productive" enterprise—a plantation. Advertising the "Agricultural Possibilities in Tropical Mexico" in respectable magazines like *National Geographic*, Díaz embarked on a campaign to attract international capital. For the Huastecs, these plans and policies meant a continuation of the long war to maintain access to their land.[13]

From the mid-nineteenth century on, the Liberals in power had pressed hard to dismantle all forms of communal property in favor of private ownership. According to the Liberal creed, only individual ownership of land and production for market—either on small holdings or on extensive *haciendas*—generated wealth and brought progress. The communal and seemingly isolationist ways of Indians, according to this logic, were atavistic, retarding the arrival of modernity in Mexico and requiring eradication. The Huastecs thought otherwise. Throughout the first half of the nineteenth century, they took up arms to protest Liberal legislation aimed at destroying communal property. The tide of history worked against them, however. Not squeamish about eliminating rebellious Indians who stood in the way of progress, Díaz intensified the campaign to sell Indian lands once he came to power.[14]

While it did not stop modernization efforts, Indian resistance did force a compromise. The Veracruz land reform of 1874 authorized municipalities to divide land into "large lots of collective (but not communal) ownership" in areas where division into individual lots proved impossible due to the "conflicts that could be generated." This created a form of land tenure known as the *condueñazgo* (coproprietorship). While the *condueñazgo* did not stop the sale of Indian land, it represented a temporary victory for communities facing total dispossession.[15]

The *condueñazgo* was a modified version of private property, with land owned collectively by heads of household who could not sell the tract. Individuals, however, could "alienate" their rights to usage and ownership (*el derecho a usufructo* and *la acción de copropiedad*) to another party. In theory, the land would be partitioned into lots for each *condueño*, but in practice the co-owners seldom assigned themselves specific plots, and Huastec-controlled forest continued to exist and produce corn without fences or markers of any kind. Those who lost their lands stayed on their small *ranchos*, living on what were now private *haciendas*, paying rent to the new landowners, typically cattle ranchers. Many men, including *condueños*, worked part time for the *haciendas* to supplement family production or to cover the rent. When the news spread in 1900 that Mexico possessed significant oil deposits, the loss of land proceeded swiftly. The alienation provision in the *condueñazgo* law allowed voracious oil companies to control millions of acres of tropical forest in ways that could not be resisted by force of arms.[16]

Soon after the discovery of the precious crude deposits, oil baron Edward L. Doheny unleashed a truly unprecedented land grab on the Gulf coast. Immediately upon his arrival in 1900, Doheny borrowed money from a Mexican bank and bought two enormous tracts of land—the *haciendas* of Tulillo and Chapacao—on the banks of the Pánuco River in northern Veracruz. Together, they comprised 448,000 acres, acquired for the hefty sum of $150,000 (U.S.). In 1906, Doheny organized the Huasteca Petroleum Company while continuing to acquire land throughout the region. By 1917, his "jungle kingdom" totaled over 600,000 acres. Following closely in Doheny's footsteps was Weetman Pearson, an English engineer who had enjoyed a successful career in Mexico. In 1901, while waiting for a train connection at Laredo, Texas, Pearson wired his man in southern Veracruz to "secure an option not only on oil land, but all land for miles around." Five years later, he reported owning "about 600,000 acres of land in the oil country and hav[ing] royalty leases for 200,000 or 300,000 acres." His land holdings spread over the entire Gulf coast, from a site in Tampico for a refinery to marshes and swamps in northern and southern Veracruz, Tabasco, and Chiapas.[17]

While some tracts were unusually large, many were small plots acquired through deals with *condueños*, particularly in the *Huasteca*. To buy or lease land from poor Indian peasants, the companies hired "agents" who freely resorted to extralegal means to pressure household heads to sign on the dotted line. The Mexican literature on the subject brims with well-documented examples of swindles, testimony to the cunning and cruelty of such agents. They faked romance to obtain an illiterate woman's signature, murdered men in line for an inheritance, discovered "long lost heirs" to disputed land, and, as a last resort, burned Indians out of their homes. While violence or the threat of violence certainly motivated peasants to sell or lease their property, a number of native men and women managed to negotiate with the companies with a modicum of success, or at least with enough savvy to gain some advantage from tragic circumstances not of their making. If the native communities of northern Veracruz suffered a defeat in their confrontation with oil over the long term, they nevertheless remained active agents throughout the conflict.[18]

The stories of José Anacleto Morelos and Eufrosina Flores illustrate the maneuvering the Huastecs engaged in to maintain their way of life (or in Flores's case, to provide for the next generation). Anacleto Morelos was a Huastec *condueño* in Zacamixtle, in the middle of the *Huasteca*. In 1901, he arranged to purchase eighty-nine acres of forest property in Amatlán (known as Lot 113) from Antonio Zamora, who unfortunately died before the deal was finalized. Anacleto Morelos then closed the transaction with Zamora's heirs. Eleven years later, an agent for El Aguila, Weetman Pearson's company, leased the subsoil from Anacleto Morelos at the unusually high rate of 5 percent of future gross oil production (a possible indication of Anacleto Morelos's negotiating skills). In 1917, El Aguila replaced this percentage scheme with a straight 2.5 cents per barrel. The company began drilling the following year, ultimately producing several million dollars' worth of oil from one well in 1919. After striking salt water in 1920, El Aguila abandoned the lot, paying only 10 percent of the royalties due and returning the land to Anacleto Morelos.[19]

In 1929, a company known as La Comercial challenged the original deal between Anacleto Morelos and El Aguila. General manager José Domingo Lavin argued that Anacleto Morelos was not the rightful owner of Lot 113 because Antonio Zamora had died without leaving a will; thus, Zamora's heirs were not authorized to sell the lot in the first place. Furthermore, La Comercial claimed to have found the rightful owner, one Agustín Hermas Martínez, the son of Concepción Zamora, Zamora's "natural daughter." Martínez, not surprisingly, had sold the rights to Lot 113 to La Comercial. When government officials ratified this concession, Anacleto Morelos sued La Comercial to establish his property rights; undoubtedly, he received legal counsel from El Aguila, which had reason to support his claims—La Comercial had sued El Aguila for twenty million pesos in back royalties. On October 15, 1933, a Mexico City court ruled in favor of both Anacleto Morelos and El Aguila.[20]

Despite the court's ruling, La Comercial again attacked Anacleto Morelos by initiating eviction proceedings against him in 1933. Anacleto Morelos responded by selling the lot to El Aguila in July of that year for ten thousand pesos, 2.5 cents per barrel of oil produced, and a promise that he could remain on the land. The following year, an appellate court overturned the lower court's decision, a decision appealed by El Aguila without success. El Aguila eventually settled out of court for twelve million pesos. While the documents do not mention if Anacleto Morelos was evicted, the record clearly demonstrates that he had learned to navigate through the treacherous legal terrain to keep his property for as long as possible.[21]

Eufrosina Flores, an "Indian" from Cerro Azul, also exhibited skill and creativity in negotiating with an oil company, albeit at an extremely high emotional cost. Her father, Ignacio Flores, was a *condueño* on the future site of what Edward L. Doheny called "the world's greatest oil well," Cerro Azul No. 4. When Ignacio died in 1902, Eufrosina's legal guardian leased her father's plot to a Frenchman for five hundred pesos per year; the Frenchman, in turn, transferred his rights to Doheny in 1906 for $87,800 in Mexican gold. By that time, Eufrosina had married Hilario Jacinto. To confirm his lease, Doheny arranged for Jacinto to cosign the contract with Eufrosina, offering the young couple what must have seemed an impressive sum: twenty-five thousand pesos in cash, with a promise of sixteen thousand more in the future. When Doheny's company, La Huasteca, decided to buy the couple out in 1911, Jacinto hired a lawyer and transferred the subsoil rights to his sister, María Luisa (the third clause in their contract stated that Jacinto had undertaken such action because agents of La Huasteca had "threatened" him). Unfortunately, for reasons unknown, Jacinto's lawyer proved dilatory in filing the new contract, and in June 1911, Jacinto died of knife wounds inflicted by Otilio López in a bar fight. Rumors later circulated that the company had arranged for Jacinto's murder.[22]

Six months after Jacinto's death, Eufrosina sold her rights to La Huasteca for a stunning five hundred thousand pesos, suggesting a high degree of negotiating ability on her part. Having lost her husband, she understood that her children's future depended upon the Cerro Azul property; she knew she could not work the land alone, and she knew that directly confronting the company could prove lethal. Thus, selling her subsoil rights for the highest possible price and moving away apparently seemed the most realistic course of action, as well as the best guarantor of her children's safety. Ironically, when La Huasteca invited Eufrosina to visit Doheny's hometown of Los Angeles, she decided to migrate there with her children and the remainder of her fortune.[23]

Although Eufrosina Flores and Anacleto Morelos received only minor sums in comparison to the profits realized by El Aguila and La Huasteca, neither fits the stereotype of the passive Indian victim so often found in the literature. On the contrary, both individuals showed the resolve and perseverance necessary for grappling with—and prevailing over—powerful, ruthless, and resourceful enemies. Further research into the negotiations that often took place between oil companies and indigenous landowners would show, no doubt, that the abilities and strategies of Eufrosina Flores and Anacleto Morelos were not rare. Their will to act, even in the face of certain failure given the power of the oil companies, revealed itself at each stage in the process of oil development.

Having amassed millions of acres of tropical forest by 1906, the oil companies prepared to commence drilling in earnest. The native population faced a new set of choices. They could migrate inland toward the mountains of the Sierra Madre Oriental and avoid any further clashes with oilmen, agents, lawyers, and thugs, or they could stay on the land, pay rent to the companies, and continue planting corn until their particular "field" was put into production. Both strategies had their adherents.[24]

The latter option brought the most rapid change, as the Huastecs witnessed the transformation of their isolated *ranchos* into bustling "oil camps." Rapidly outnumbered by newcomers, the Huastecs watched as the forest became a "panorama of misery, filth, [and] lack of hygiene," an overcrowded town where men worked hard twelve hours a day, then played hard the rest of the time. Improvised *cantinas* and brothels rose up amidst the derricks at least as quickly as workers' barracks. Furthermore, the companies severely curtailed the Huastecs' freedom of mobility, along with all camp dwellers, workers, or travellers. Roads leading to and from oil camps became company property, and no one could walk or ride on them without the express written permission of the camp's foreign superintendent. Guards posted at checkpoints along the road demanded passes before anyone could continue the journey.[25]

In 1908, a well exploded at San Diego de la Mar, a few miles inland from the Tamiahua Lagoon, confirming the suspicion that Mexico was a world-class oil producer. On July 4, according to geologist Charles Hamilton, "the gas [from the well] created fissures in the ground" and a huge hole began to form. "Soon the hole began to crater—drilling rig, derrick, pumps and boilers, all disappeared," swallowed by the earth. According to eyewitnesses, a black column shot over one hundred feet into the air, then turned into a heavy and sticky rain as the wind carried it off into the distance. With the vegetation around the well dripping black, the gases and petroleum that had spilled on the ground caught fire, producing an explosion of enormous magnitude. Unprepared for a discovery on this scale, the camp's American superintendent had not ordered his Mexican laborers to dig out earthen reservoirs deep or large enough to contain the hemorrhage of oil. The crude began to form rivers that slowly crept toward the Carbajal River. The oil—"six inches deep"—subsequently flowed down the river into the marshes that surrounded the Tamiahua Lagoon, finally entering the lagoon itself near its southern edge three months later. Eventually, tens of thousands of barrels of crude flowed out of the lagoon into the Gulf of Mexico.[26]

This event, unprecedented in Mexican history, made a deep impression on the population for miles around. The explosion, the shaking, the heat, the flaming trees, the rivers of fire undulating toward the lagoon— all left witnesses in awe of nature's power. A government inspector referred to the burning well as an "enraged Cyclops," a "roaring volcano," a "monster vomiting from its blackened crater." Locals watched birds fall out of the sky, victims of the toxic gases expelled from the well. Fish by the thousands appeared belly up on lake waters. The paint on homes in Tantoyuca, Tuxpan, and Ozuluama turned black, as did silverware in places like Papantla, seventy miles to the south. The fire's glow painted the evening skies red in the port of Tampico, sixty miles to the north, and "ships at sea a hundred miles off could see the plumes of fire," according to geologist Everett Lee DeGolyer.[27]

For people native to the *Huasteca*, the "Dos Bocas" blowout seemed even more ominous, for it represented an extreme danger to life and a long-term threat to the environment. The well was located in the small agricultural community of Tantima, whose population of 6,774 in 1900 included mestizo peasants and ranchers, Huastec speakers (27 percent), and Nahuatl speakers (3 percent). The peasant Indian and mestizo families would never forget the panic that swept their community. Gonzalo Bada Ramírez was six years old when the well exploded; he remembered his mother and grandmother running from their house when the expansive shock wave hit the village. His uncle picked him up and carried him away on horseback. Along the way, he saw "people getting out, some on foot, some running, some barefooted, some did not even get a chance to take a shirt with them." It remains unclear how many workers died in the actual explosion (perhaps less than ten), but many died in the attempt to suffocate the fire.[28]

By all accounts, the native population around Dos Bocas refused to work in the camp. As a general rule, the few indigenous men who had worked in petroleum-related activities had done so as guides, leading geologists and their mestizo helpers to the oil leaks that occurred naturally at numerous locations deep in the tropical forest; their role in locating these seepages led some observers to credit the indigenes with the discovery of oil in Mexico. But the Dos Bocas conflagration entailed an altogether different kind of participation, one unpopular with native men used to agricultural labor. Weetman Pearson, the legal owner of the well, required laborers to work at a frenzied pace digging dams and trenches to contain the burning oil, dumping gravel on the fiery column, and knocking down trees to prevent the spread of fire into the forest. According to Juan Palacios, a Mexican government official on the scene, the "crass" locals refused the high wages offered to them and fled, forcing the Mexican army to deploy its special forces, the *zapadores*, to fight the fire. Over four hundred soldiers participated in the effort, pledging to fight the walls of fire to their death, if necessary. An unknown number of soldiers did perish in the effort, but to no avail. Only nature could extinguish the flames.[29]

The Dos Bocas well burned from July 4 to August 30, 1908, when the fuel finally exhausted itself. According to Mexican officials, ground zero became a dangerous hole over three hundred feet in diameter. Cattle and men who wandered too close to the site died, suffocated by sulphurous clouds that could trap the unwary after a sudden change in wind direction. One public health official travelled to the town of Tamiahua in October to investigate an alarming and rare outbreak of "pinkeye." To the doctor's surprise, the eighty afflicted persons did not have the infectious eye disease; rather, they suffered from exposure to the poisonous gases exuded by the crater. The *nortes*, or Gulf winds, had carried the gases into town. As the doctor reported, "one can feel very clearly that the atmosphere is impregnated with noxious and irritant substances and when the wind blows in [this] direction, the nauseating smell of rotting eggs is intolerable. I felt my eyes, my nose, and even my throat burning."[30]

Even after the fire burned out, various rumors about the well continued to circulate among the native population of the *Huasteca*, fanning their fears of the oil industry (for example, people argued that no one could come close without risking death, that the well might explode again, or that a volcano was actually being born on the spot).[31] Of course, the bleakness was real enough. In 1913, Charles Hamilton found that the crater spread over forty acres and that "the potent hydrogen sulphide gas had killed everything. What had been a lush *monte* was now a gaunt specter of dead trees. The air stunk with the smell of rotten eggs. There was no sign or sound of animal, bird, or insect life. Nothing stirred in the breeze. The silence was appalling. It was eerie and frightening."[32] But local rumors ballooned to include tales of "many" who died after being "gassed," including "the poor *indígenas* [who] died like flies."[33]

Such rumors, when combined with the reality of local devastation, made the recruitment of workers difficult for the company.[34] Thus, when the next blowout occurred, Weetman Pearson resorted to forced labor. In December 1910, two years after Dos Bocas, the Potrero del Llano No. 4 well "came in like a raging monster" in Temapache, a predominantly mestizo community bordering on two largely Indian towns: the Nahuátl stronghold of Tepetzintla on the south, and the Huastec community of Tancoco on the north. According to his biographer, Pearson had learned how to recruit "Mexican Indians [with] the reputation for being sullen, suspicious, violent and difficult to handle." He seized upon a traditional *hacendado* practice: all able-bodied men from neighboring communities under the control of sympathetic political or military officers were required to work in gangs for food, with all wages withheld until the work was finished. Geologist Everett Lee DeGolyer even helped organize "chow lines" that fed the "pressed-in-to-service help" daily rations of "mostly bean-filled *tacos*" spooned from "huge pots." With federal authority firmly behind him, Pearson could count on Huastec and Nahua laborers to control the well.[35]

Native workers successfully brought the well under control in March 1911, but three years later the indigenes would again experience the power of Potrero del Llano No. 4. On August 14, 1914, lightning ignited the gas escaping from cracks in the well. "All the available workmen, to the number of 3,000, were immediately mobilized and armed with shovels," wrote Arthur B. Clifford, the fire expert on the scene. Upon arriving at the scene, Francisco Solís Cabrera, a fire fighter and former oil worker, found "nothing but little Indians [*puros inditos*]" working in hellish conditions.[36]

This experience and the continuing exploitation encouraged native radicalization. In late 1914, the entire Mexican work force in the area organized itself and staged what Clifford labeled a "strike." For eight days, "about fifty white men had to take the duties of 3,000 natives," who had set up "the Mexican equivalent of pickets" demanding an increase in pay and other benefits. At the end of the week, they won both and returned to work.[37]

Within weeks of this triumph, indigenous men faced another critical dilemma. One of the subcontractors working at Potrero del Llano, Manuel Peláez, quit in December 1914 to take up arms against the revolutionary faction led by Venustiano Carranza. Carranza's followers had taken over the governments of Veracruz and Tamaulipas in the civil war that ensued after the fall of Porfirio Díaz and the assassination of his successor, Francisco Madero. With the conflict now in the *Huasteca*, local men had to decide whether to continue working on the blazing No. 4 well or to join the revolution with Peláez. The native population of the *Huasteca* had certainly accumulated enough grudges against landowners, company lawyers, and oil company "recruiters" to make armed struggle attractive once again. Peláez, moreover, was not a stranger to the indigenes. He was a native son, born and raised in the *Huasteca* to a wealthy and powerful family. Had he been capable of articulating the deeply felt grievances of the Huastecs, or even the Nahuas, he might have convinced them to choose his cause over oil work. Instead, he turned to more coercive tactics to raise a fighting force.[38]

Peláez actively recruited in Potrero del Llano, with mixed results. He "invited" Francisco Solís Cabrera to join the revolutionaries, for example, but Solís Cabrera politely refused. Seventeen other men accepted the offer, however, and along with them Peláez obtained what he called a "loan" from El Aguila, Weetman Pearson's oil company. To increase the number of recruits, Peláez and the *hacendados* he represented exercised their authority over local mestizos and neighboring Huastec men (the Nahuas joined the *carrancistas*). Initially, all peons working on Peláez's own properties, on estates belonging to his family, and on the *haciendas* of his associates were "incorporated" into his army, in what amounted to an involuntary draft. As the years passed, Peláez established himself as the strongman in the *Huasteca* (a position he held until 1920); he eventually attracted enough followers to dispense with such coercive measures.[39]

Peláez's favoritism toward landowners may have discouraged greater Huastec participation in his army. By his own admission, Peláez personally sympathized with Félix Díaz, the nephew of Porfirio Díaz and a leading antirevolutionary figure, and he rebelled to protect fellow landowners living off oil royalties from tax-levying *carrancistas* in control of the government in Veracruz. That did not mean, however, that the Huastecs joined other armies. On the contrary, according to anthropologists, the Huastecs avoided all factions, some families even fleeing "into the high mountains" to escape the fighting.[40]

Opting out of alliances with revolutionaries, the Huastecs took a second look at oil work. Rather than continue as fire fighters, they apparently decided to take advantage of the presence of foreign capital by working for the oil industry, with conditions imposed on the type of work they would perform. They were able to negotiate a niche for themselves because world conditions created new opportunities. World War I raged in Europe, making the oil pools in the Huastecs' backyard an essential commodity for the English fleet. The demand for manpower created opportunities for native men already working on *haciendas* to supplement subsistence farming; moreover, Huastec men understood that one peso per day in an oil camp was preferable to 35 cents per day on a *hacienda*. Soon, throughout the *Huasteca, hacendados* complained to authorities about the scarcity of labor created by the demand for oil workers. No peasant wanted to work for less than oil industry wages.[41]

According to former oil workers, the indigenes preferred working on construction projects, particularly the building of thatched-roof dormitories (*galleras*, or "chicken coops"). The logic was eminently agrarian. Building dormitories was task work, paid for as it was completed rather than with daily or weekly wages. It did not require any new skills since the Huastecs made their own homes in the same fashion. Even those who did not speak Spanish could chop palm, bamboo, and other trees and weave them into dwellings. Such work did not interfere with agricultural cycles and could be finished quickly by men working in teams, another traditional practice used by the Huastecs to clear plots or erect community buildings.[42]

The urgent manpower needs of companies and their practice of hiring as many local inhabitants as possible to perform the menial labor necessary in the infrastructure stage of oil extraction made other types of task work (*destajo*) available to Huastec men and boys. Such projects included leveling acres of forest for housing and derricks, chopping down trees for roads and railways, shoveling out trenches for pipeline, digging giant holes for the storage of extracted oil, and any other work that required physical exertion alone. Although the written record contains few traces of Huastecs among the least-skilled laborers, a Mexican engineer employed by the oil companies in Zacamixtle noted that "all the peons who cleared paths [through the tropical forest] were aborigines, Huastecs who spoke no Spanish." Bada Ramírez, the oil worker who fled Dos Bocas

as a child, recalled that he had worked in the San Jerónimo field in Tantima alongside twenty-five to thirty other boys, "many of them indigenes."
The advantages of *destajo* work were the same as those for building
dormitories. Time and again, the oil companies noted that the men came
"when they wish[ed] and [left] when their private occupations call[ed]
them."[43]

Their peasant background and limited knowledge of Spanish guaran-
teed that the Huastecs would occupy the lowest level of a labor hierarchy
organized by nationality and ethnicity. As was customary among all foreign interests in Mexico, foreign nationals occupied the top of the hierarchy, mestizo skilled artisans dominated the middle, and a mass of migrant
peasants undergoing proletarianization occupied the bottom. Huastecs
most likely belonged to this last group. They were day laborers like the
rest of the peasants, but with a crucial difference—the Huastecs had not
come looking for work, work had come looking for them. Although they
worked harder than ever before, the bosses demanded more energy than
the Huastecs were capable of or were willing to exert (one Englishman
claimed that their output "was only about 25% of that of the British").
The rationalized and intense labor necessary to open an oil field apparently did not interest the Huastecs enough to lure them into industrial
labor on a permanent basis.[44]

Oil fever ended as abruptly as it started. In the second half of 1921,
more than twelve years after the Huastecs had sold or leased their properties to the oil industry in northern Veracruz, the oil business peaked and
began its rapid descent. A number of factors coalesced to reverse Mexico's
meteoric rise to second place in the world's oil production hierarchy. World
War I had ended, along with the military demand for large quantities of
oil. Several companies had discovered oil deposits in Venezuela and transferred their skilled crews south; moreover, a major dispute between the
companies and the Mexican revolutionary government over taxes and the
terms of concessions led the oilmen to shut down production in many
fields. Finally, frenzied exploitation of the oil mantles facilitated the intrusion of salt water into the fields, ruining productive wells and reducing the need for labor.[45]

The oil "bust" drove thousands of workers out of the *Huasteca*. Cara-
vans of men and their families walked to Tampico, begging for food in
the streets while they waited for free government railroad passes back to
their places of origin. Hundreds of others wandered to the Pánuco fields
west of Tampico, hoping to find jobs in Cacalilao, Tulillo, and other former
haciendas where the companies were building the infrastructure for a new
cycle of production. The remaining productive wells of the *Huasteca* required no more than skeleton crews; less than a dozen men could guard
the pumps that kept the crude flowing out of the area via pipeline. Despite their poverty, the Huastecs remained behind, waiting for an oppor-

tunity to reclaim what was left of "paradise" rather than following the migrant oil trail.[46]

With the end of large-scale extraction, the Huastecs stood poised to inherit large areas of deforested land blanketed in oil, polluted streams and river beds, diminished oyster beds and shrimping areas, and irreparably damaged hunting grounds. They expressed their discontent to the secretary of the interior, Plutarco Elías Calles, in 1921. On a tour through the *Huasteca*, the future president acknowledged to a reporter from the Mexico City *Excélsior* that the indigenes had "complained" to him about the oil companies. He concluded that the companies had "ruined" the land with oil spills. Prominent local figures like José Luis Melgarejo Vivanco vividly imagined the indigenes' lament—"the Mayans, startled, must have said: *mani, mani;* everything is gone; desolation remained."[47]

Jeremiads aside, the Huastecs took advantage of sympathetic state governors and new legislation to organize and petition for communal lands (*ejidos*). In the mid-to-late 1920s, Huastec men and women, like thousands of other peasants throughout Veracruz, joined local agrarian leagues to claim their ancestral lands from *hacendados* and oil companies. In Tantoyuca, for example, seventy-three Huastec men formed the Sociedad Cooperativa de Campesinos in July 1925, even though only twenty-nine knew how to sign their names, and many required a translator to explain the state's labyrinthine agrarian reform bureaucracy. In San Antonio Chinampa, a major "field" in 1921, thirty men formed the Unión de Campesinos Agricultores in January 1929. In their petitions, native and mestizo peasants alike denounced the landowners who had abandoned agriculture altogether, instead "hoping . . . to sell [their land] for several hundred thousand pesos to oil companies." The Huastecs of Tamalín also expressed dismay at the deforestation in the former oil field of La Trinidad. More articulate mestizo petitioners explained to the Agrarian Commission that they were "peasants in origin," but were "accidentally living off company work." In their request, they expressed their desire to return to agricultural work if the state would grant their petition for parts of a Peláez *hacienda* in Llano Grande. A similar rejection of proletarianization informed Huastec petitions; by the early 1930s, they had successfully petitioned for land in Tierra Amarilla, Zacamixtle, and Cerro Azul.[48]

The Huastecs clung stubbornly to their despoiled homelands. In doing so, they not only reclaimed historical property rights, but also helped prevent further degradation of the environment. Eventually, rain would wash spilled oil from the land, and river currents would carry the pollution elsewhere. Though the tall trees would never grow again, the fragile soils left behind might still support subsistence agriculture, and fallow cycles might allow for regeneration of the sturdiest tropical plants. Without actually calling it a defense of the rainforest, the Huastecs did just that in protecting their agricultural practices and economy.[49]

What the Huastecs thought about notions of progress at the beginning of the twentieth century is impossible to ascertain, but their reactions to oil are somewhat clearer. Always active participants in the history of their region, they made a reluctant accommodation with oil extraction once open resistance became futile. Despite the violence inflicted by the companies, the Huastecs held out for the highest price they could obtain when selling land. They initially resisted joining the labor force, working as fire fighters only under duress; then they again accommodated, negotiating a space in the industry that would not disturb their agricultural activities. In the aftermath of massive oil extraction, they organized to reclaim the land and its ancient uses. While they sometimes succeeded in gaining control over their ancestral territory, no visitor would ever again describe the *Huasteca* as a "paradise."

Notes

1. "Clippings from the *Los Angeles Herald Express*," December 1932, Doheny Collection, University of Southern California: Kevin Starr, *Material Dreams: Southern California through the 1920s* (Oxford: Oxford University Press, 1990), 126; Jorge Garcia Granados, *Los veneros del diablo* (Mexico City: PEMEX, 1988); Gabriel Antonio Menéndez, *Doheny el cruel: episodios de la sangrienta lucha por el petróleo mexicano* (Mexico City: Ediciones "Bolsa Mexicana del Libro," 1958); José Domingo Lavin, *Petróleo: pasado, presente y futuro de una industria mexicana* (Mexico City: EDAPSA, 1950); Antonio Rodríguez, *El rescate del petróleo: epopeya de un pueblo* (Mexico City: Ediciones "El Caballito," 1975); Xavier Villegas Mora, *Petróleo, sangre y justicia* (Mexico City: Editorial Relámpagos, 1939); Javier Santos Llorente, *Episodios petroleros* (Mexico City: PEMEX, 1988); José López Portillo y Weber, *El petróleo de Veracruz* (Mexico City: Editorial Libros de México, 1976); Dan LaBotz, *Edward L. Doheny: Petroleum, Power, and Politics in the United States and Mexico* (New York: Praeger, 1991); Verna Carleton Millan, *Mexico Reborn* (Cambridge, Mass.: The Riverside Press, 1939).

2. Lorenzo Meyer, *México y los Estados Unidos en el conflicto petrolero, 1917–1942* (Mexico City: El Colegio de México, 1972); Leopoldo Alafita Méndez, Mirna Benítez Juárez, and Alberto Olvera Rivera, *Historia gráfica de la industria petrolera y sus trabajadores, 1900–1938* (Xalapa: Universidad Veracruzana, 1988); Javier Santos Llorente, Manuel Uribe Cruz, Mirna Alicia Benítez Juárez, Rodolfo Zavala, Alberto Olvera Rivera, *El petróleo en Veracruz* (Mexico City: PEMEX, 1988); Lourdes Celis Salgado, *La industria petrolera en México: una crónica*, vol. 1 (Mexico City: PEMEX, 1988); Jonathan Brown and Alan Knight, eds., *The Mexican Petroleum Industry in the Twentieth Century* (Austin: University of California Press, 1992); Jonathan Brown, *Oil and Revolution in Mexico* (Berkeley: University of California Press, 1993).

3. Carlos González Salas, *Tampico: crónicas de una ciudad* (Tampico: Ediciones Contraste, 1977), 136. All translations from the Spanish are mine.

4. Hisakichi Hisazumi, "Informe preliminar acerca de la geología petrolera de la zona comprendida entre los ríos de Tuxpan y Misantla, en los estados de Puebla y Veracruz," *Anales* of the *Instituto Geológico de México* 3 (1929): 3–48; William T. Sanders, "The Anthropogeography of Central Veracruz," *Revista Mexicana de Estudios Antropológicos* 13 (1952–1953): 28–29; Rebeca de Gortari, "Petróleo

y clase obrera en Veracruz, 1920–1935," in *Memoria del primer coloquio regional de historia obrera* (Veracruz: Centro de Estudios Históricos del Movimiento Obrero Mexicano, 1977), 286–88; Carlos Basauri, *La población indígena de México: etnografía*, vol. 2 (Mexico City: Secretaría de Educación Pública, 1940), 57–79.

5. PanAmerican Petroleum and Transport Company, *Mexican Petroleum* (New York: PanAmerican Petroleum and Transport Company, 1922), 16–17.

6. Candace Slater, "Amazonia as Edenic Narrative," in *Uncommon Ground: Toward Reinventing Nature*, ed. William Cronon (New York: W. W. Norton and Co., 1995), 114–31; Frank M. Chapman, "A Naturalist's Journey Around Veracruz and Tampico," *National Geographic*, May 1914, 533–57; Thomas Philip Terry, *Terry's Guide to Mexico* (Boston: Houghton Mifflin Company, 1923), 50; Carl W. Ackerman, *Mexico's Dilemma* (New York: George H. Doran Company, 1918), 83.

7. Arturo Gómez-Pompa, *Ecología de la vegetación del Estado de Veracruz* (Mexico City: Editorial Continental, 1977), 45; José Ramírez, *La vegetación de México* (Mexico City: Oficina Tipográfica de la Secretaría de Fomento, 1899), 64; Peter G. Murphy and Ariel E. Lugo, "Ecology of Tropical Dry Forest," *Annual Review of Ecology and Systematics* 16 (1986): 67–88, esp. 72–73, 76; William T. Sanders, *The Lowland Huasteca Archeological Survey and Excavation: 1957 Field Season*, University of Missouri Monographs in Anthropology, no. 4 (Columbia: University of Missouri Press, 1978), 7; PanAmerican Petroleum, *Mexican Petroleum*, 17; Jack London, "Our Adventures in Tampico," *Collier's*, 27 June 1914, 5.

8. Jerzy Rzedowski, *Vegetación de México* (Mexico City: Editorial Limusa, 1986), 155–56, 160; Terry, *Terry's Guide to Mexico*, 48.

9. Janis B. Alcorn, *Huastec Mayan Ethnobotany* (Austin: University of Texas Press, 1984); Ludka de Gortari Krauss and Jesús Ruvalcaba Mercado, eds., *La huasteca: vida y milagros*, Cuadernos de la Casa Chata, no. 173 (Mexico City: Centro de Investigaciones y Estudios Superiores en Antropología Social, 1990); Eva Grossner Lerner, *Los Teenek de San Luis Potosí: lengua y contexto* (Mexico City: Instituto Nacional de Antropología e Historia, 1991); Jesús Ruvalcaba and Graciela Alcalá, eds., *Huasteca*, 3 vols. (Mexico City: SEP/CIESAS, 1993); Marcelo Alejandre, "Noticia de lengua huasteca," *Boletín* of the *Sociedad Mexicana de Geografía y Estadística, segunda época* 2 (1870): 733–90; Marcelo Alejandre, *Cartilla Huasteca* (Mexico City: Oficina Tipográfica de la Secretaría de Fomento, 1889); Serapio D. Lorenzana, *Un intérprete huasteco* (Mexico City: Oficina Tipográfica de la Secretaria de Fomento, 1896); Frederick Starr, *Notes Upon the Ethnography of Southern Mexico*, reprinted from vol. 9 of the *Proceedings of Davenport Academy of Sciences* (Putnam Memorial Publication Fund, 1902), 16; Walter Staub, "Some Data About the Pre-Hispanic and the Now Living Huastec Indians," *El México Antiguo* 1 (1919): 52; Rudolf Schuller, "La posición etnológica y linguística de los Huaxteca," and "Notes on the Huaxteca Indians of San Luis Potosí, México," in *El México Antiguo* 2 (1924–1927): 130–40; Luis Antonio González Bonilla, "Los Huastecos," *Revista Mexicana de Sociología* 1 (1939): 28–58; Benito Coquet, *Ensayo histórico-político sobre los habitantes indígenas de Veracruz* (Xalapa, 1939); Walter Krickeberg, *Etnología de América*, trans. Pedro Hendrich (1922; reprint, Mexico City: Fondo de Cultura Económica, 1946); "Huastecos, Totonacos y sus vecinos," special issue, *Revista Mexicana de Estudios Antropológicos* 13 (1952–1953); Lina Odena, *Totonacos y Huastecos* (Mexico City: Museo Nacional de Antropología, INAH-SEP, 1968); Guillermo Bonfil Batalla, "Notas etnográficas de la región huasteca, México," *Anales de Antropología* 6 (1969): 130–48; William T. Sanders, "Cultural Ecology and Settlement

Patterns of the Gulf Coast," *Handbook of Middle American Indians: Archeology of Northern Mesoamerica*, vol. 11, pt. 2, ed. Gordon F. Ekholm and Ignacio Bernal (Austin: University of Texas Press, 1971); Guy Streser-Pean, "Ancient Sources on the Huasteca," *Handbook of Middle American Indians: Archeology of Northern Mesoamerica*, vol. 11, pt. 2, ed. Gordon F. Ekholm and Ignacio Bernal (Austin: University of Texas Press, 1971); Charles Hamilton, *Early Day Oil Tales of Mexico* (Houston: Gulf Publishing Company, 1966); Leon Tinkle, *Mr. De: A Biography of Everett Lee DeGolyer* (Boston: Little Brown, and Company, 1970); Percy Norman Furber, *I Took Chances: From Windjammer to Jets* (Leicester, England: Edgar Backus, 1954); Ezequiel Ordoñez, *El petróleo en México: Bosquejo histórico* (Mexico City: Empresa Editorial de Ingeniería y Arquitectura, 1932).

10. González Bonilla. "Los Huastecos," 38; Schuller, "Notes," 131–32.

11. Hamilton, *Early Day Oil Tales*, 18; Lorenzana, *Un intérprete huasteco*, 1–3; Staub, "Some Data," 54: Gonzalez Bonilla, "Los Huastecos," 42, 88; Odena, *Totonacas y Huastecos*, 16; Schuller, "La posición etnológica," 143; Krickeberg, *Etnología*, 272; David Robles Saldaña, interview by Leif Adleson, Ciudad Madero, Tamaulipas, 12 March 1975, PHO/4/39 INAH, Proyecto de Historia Oral, Archivo de la Palabra, Instituto Nacional de Antropología e Historia [hereafter PHO].

12. Alcorn, *Huastec Mayan Ethnobotany*, 50; E. O. Wilson, ed., *Biodiversity* (Washington, D.C.: National Academy Press, 1988), passim; Henry H. Harper, *A Journey in Southeastern Mexico: Narrative of Experiences, and Observations on Agricultural and Industrial Conditions* (Boston: The DeVinne Press, 1910), 81; Sanders, "Cultural Ecology," 546–47.

13. Pehr Olsson-Seffer, "Agricultural Possibilities in Tropical Mexico," *National Geographic*, December 1910, 1023–35.

14. Leticia Reina, *Las rebeliones campesinas en México, 1819–1906* (Mexico City: Siglo XXI, 1980), 325–59.

15. José Velasco Toro, "La política desamortizadora y sus efectos en la región de Papantla, Veracruz," *La Palabra y el Hombre* 72 (1989): 145–47.

16. Valasco Toro, "La Política desamortizadora," 147; Ordoñez, *El petróleo*, 42–44; Alcorn, *Huastec Mayan Ethnobotany*; 43; Hamilton, *Early Day Oil Tales*, 44.

17. Joaquin Meade, *La huasteca veracruzana*, vol. 1 (Mexico City: Editorial Citlaltépetl, 1963), 136, 142; Testimony of Edward L. Doheny, Senate Committee on Foreign Relations, *Investigation of Mexican Affairs*, vol. 2, 66th Cong., 1st sess. (1920), 209–11; José Santos Llorente, "Los gobernadores," *El petróleo en Veracruz* (Mexico City: PEMEX, 1988), 35–36; *El Mundo*, 6 March 1938, 1; *Boletín del Petróleo* 3 (1917): 215; Frederic R. Kellogg, *The Case of the American Oil Companies in the Controversy with Mexico* (New York: Association of Producers of Petroleum in Mexico, 1927), 2; Kevin Starr, *Material Dreams*, 125; J. A. Spender, *Weetman Pearson, First Viscount Cowdray, 1856–1927* (London: Cassell and Company, Ltd., 1930), 149–50, 152, 179, 188–89.

18. García Granados, *Los veneros del diablo*, passim; Santos Llorente, *Episodios petroleros*, 50–52, 73–77, 86; Apolo García Herrera, *Memorias de un trabajador petrolero* (Mexico City, 1965), 46. José Domingo Lavín was an engineer intimately involved in lawsuits over disputed land, and he was not above devising his own schemes. See *The Amatlán Suit: Commercial Petrol Co. vs. Mexican Eagle Oil Co.: Texts of Statements* (Mexican Eagle Oil, 1934). A number of oral histories refer to the burning of Zacamixtle. See Gonzalo Ruíz Carrillo, interview by Leif Adleson, Tampico, Tamaulipas, 11–12 March 1975, PHO/4/38 INAH, PHO.

19. "Escritura de división y partición de Zacamixtle," 18 November 1898, Departamento del Petróleo, Caja 9, Expediente 38, 040/60, Archivo General de la Nación, Mexico City [hereafter AGN]; *The Amatlán Suit*, 6, 11–12, 20; Campañía Mexicana de Petróleo El Aguila, *Frente a los ataques de que esta siendo*

objeto por la explotación que hizo del lote 113 de Amatlán (Mexico City: Compañía Mexicana de Petróleo El Aguila, 1930), 4, 7, 9, 40; R. A. Basso, *En las garras del buitre* (Tampico, 1935), 4–9.

20. *The Amatlán Suit*, 13–15; Compañía Mexicana de Petróleo El Aguila, *Frente a los ataques*, 7; Lavín, *El Petróleo*, 125; Richard O'Connor, *The Oil Barons: Men of Greed and Grandeur* (Boston: Little, Brown and Company, 1971), 157–58; Frank C. Hanighen, *The Secret War* (New York: The John Day Company, 1934), 22.

21. The Commercial Petroleum Company, *First General Report of the Suit-at-Law Against the Mexican Eagle Petroleum Company* (Mexico City: The Commercial Petroleum Company, 1934), 1; Basso, *En las garras del buitre*, 10–14; Meyer, *México y los Estados Unidos*, 292; Josephus Daniels to the Secretaary of State, 2 May 1936, File 812.6363/2896, Roll 126, RG 59, National Archives, Washington, D.C.

22. Letter from Margarito Velázquez, n.d., Departamento del Petróleo, Caja 7, Expediente 20, 032(02)/55, AGN; Mexican Petroleum Company of Delaware, *Cerro Azul No. 4: World's Greatest Oil Well* (New York: The DeVinne Press, 1916?); Santos Llorente, "Los gobernadores," 30–32; García Granados, *Los veneros del diablo*, 75–76, 77–78; Santos Llorente, *Episodios petroleros*, 50–51.

23. García Granados, *Los veneros del diablo*, 82–84, 86; Santos Llorente, *Episodios petroleros*, 71.

24. Staub, "Some Data," 54. Examples of native communities paying rent to oil companies can be found in the "Concessions" section of *La Gaceta Oficial* (Veracruz), 22 July 1922; 19 December 1922; and 31 July 1923.

25. Ordoñez, *El petróleo en México*, 93, 94–95; Lavín, *El petróleo*, 142.

26. Hamilton, *Early Day Oil Tales*, 74; Juan D. Villarello, "El pozo de petróleo de 'Dos Bocas,' " *Boletín del Instituto Geológico de México* 3 (1909): 17–21.

27. Juan Palacios, "Memoria sobre el incendio del pozo de petróleo de 'Dos bocas,'" *Boletín del Sociedad Mexicana de Geografía y Estadística, quinta época* 3 (1908): 10; Tinkle, *Mr. De*, 18; Furber, *I Took Chances*, 185.

28. Dirección General de Estadística, *Censo general de la República Mexicana verificado el 28 de Octubre de 1900* (Mexico City: Oficina Tipográfica de la Secretaría de Fomento, 1904); Gonzalo Bada Ramírez, interview by Leif Adleson, Tampico, Tamaulipas, 30 September 1978, PHO/4/91 INAH, PHO.

29. Hamilton, *Early Day Oil Tales*, 47; Furber, *I Took Chances*, 114; Ordoñez, *El petróleo*, 56; Palacios, "Memoria," 1.

30. "Conjunctivitis," report from Dr. Cantonal, October 1908, Gobernación files, Section on Salubridad, Enfermedades y Medicinas, Box 2, No 77, Letter C, Veracruz State Archive, Xalapa, Veracruz [hereafter VSA].

31. Villarello, "El pozo," 22.

32. Hamilton, *Early Day Oil Tales*, 76.

33. Santos Llorente, *Episodios petroleros*, 49.

34. Villarello, "El pozo," 23.

35. Estadística, *Censo General*, 1900; Desmond Young, *Member for Mexico: A Biography of Weetman Pearson, First Viscount Cowdray* (London: Cassell and Company, Ltd., 1966), 106; Tinkle, *Mr. De*, 42, 44–46, 55.

36. Arthur B. Clifford, "Extinguishing an Oil-Well Fire in Mexico, and the Part Played Therein by Self-Contained Breathing-Apparatus," *Transactions of the Institution of Mining Engineers* 63 (1921): 3; Francisco Solís Cabrera, interview by Leif Adleson, Tampico, Tamaulipas, 7 and 18 September 1976, PHO/4/56 INAH, PHO; A. E. Chambers, "Potrero No. 4: A History of One of Mexico's Earliest and Largest Wells," *Journal of the Institution of Petroleum Technologists* 9 (1923): 148.

37. Clifford, "Extinguishing an Oil-Well Fire," 8; Chambers, "Potrero No. 4," 149–50.

38. Menéndez, *Doheny el cruel*, 82–84; Chambers, "Potrero No. 4," 152; *Boletín del Petróleo* 22 (1926): 205. Manuel Peláez is a controversial figure in the history of Mexican oil and the Revolution. With varying degrees of passion or scholarship, most authors portray him as a local *caudillo*, or chieftan, who transformed his troops into the private army of the oil companies. See Villegas Mora, *Petróleo*, 31–32; Ackerman, *Mexico's Dilemma*, 74–79, 86; Lavín, *Petróleo*, 124; Heather Fowler Salamini, *Agrarian Radicalism in Veracruz, 1920–1938* (Lincoln: University of Nebraska Press, 1978), 173; Menéndez, *Doheny el cruel*, 76–94; Meyer, *México y los Estados Unidos*, 99–103; Rodríguez, *El rescate del petróleo*, 41–43; Alma Yolanda Guerrero Miller, *Cuesta Abajo: declinación de tres caciques huastecos revolucionarios: Cedillo, Santos y Peláez* (Mexico City: Grupo Editorial Miguel Angel Porrúa, 1991), 72–93. By contrast, Jonathan Brown attempts to prove that Peláez was a rebel with his own agenda who forced the companies to pay him. See *Oil and Revolution in Mexico*.

39. Meyer, *México y los Estados Unidos*, 59, 89–90; Solís Cabrera, interview; Rodríguez, *El rescate del petróleo*, 42–43; Testimony of Michael A. Spellacy, Senate Committee on Foreign Relations, *Investigations of Mexican Affairs*, vols. 1–2, 66th Cong., 1st sess. (1920), 943; El Aguila to the Secretaria de Guerra y Marina, 23 August 1918, Departmento del Trabajo, Caja 7, Expediente 37, 039(02)/12, AGN; Guerrero Miller, *Cuesta abajo*, 79; Report from the Topographer, 30 July 1933, Comisión Local Agraria, Expediente 887, Ranchería Tierra Amarilla, Municipio Temapache, VSA.

40. Menéndez, *Doheny el cruel*, 88; Guerrero Miller, *Cuesta abajo*, 77; Grosser-Lerner, *Los Teenek*, 16; Staub, "Some Data," 54; Linda Hall and Don M. Coerver, "Oil and the Mexican Revolution: The Southwestern Connection," *Americas* 41 (1984): 234.

41. *Boletín del Petróleo* 5 (1918): 453; Ticiano Jiménez, *Veracruz: en las huelgas y en el hambre!, 1920–1924* (Veracruz, 1925?), 70.

42. Gonzalo Bada Ramírez, interview.

43. PanAmerican Petroleum, *Mexican Petroleum*, 21; Manuel Mesa Andraca, *Relatos autobiográficos: con las compañías petroleras, mi vinculación con la reforma agraria* (Mexico City: Editorial Nuestro Tiempo, S.A., 1981), 49; Bada Ramírez, interview; Guerrero Miller, *Cuesta abajo*, 76: "Cuestionario," 1921, Departamento del Trabajo, Caja 326, Expediente 2, AGN; "Informe," 18 November 1921, Departamento del Trabajo, Caja 326, Expediente 3, AGN.

44. Spender, *Weetman Pearson*, 116.

45. Jonathan Brown, "Why Foreign Oil Companies Shifted Their Production from Mexico to Venezuela During the 1920s," *American Historical Review* 90 (1985): 362–85; Chargé in Mexico to the Secretary of State, 21 January 1920, *Papers Relating to the Foreign Relations of the United States*, 1920, vol. 3 (Washington, D.C.: GPO, 1936), 202; L. G. Huntley and Stirling Huntley, "Mexican Oil fields," *Mining and Metallurgy* 177 (1921): 28–30; Meyer, *México y los Estados Unidos*, 189–92.

46. *Excélsior* (Mexico City), 11 March 1921, 1; 5 July 1921, 1.

47. Ibid., 12 June 1921, 1; 6 July 1921, 1; José Luis Melgarejo Vivanco, *Tamiahua: una historia Huaxteca* (Jalapa: Ediciones Punto y Aparte, 1981), 15.

48. "Sociedad Cooperativa de Campesinos de Galera, Tantoyuca," Junta Central de Conciliación y Arbitraje (Veracruz), Caja 48, Expediente n/n, 1925, VSA; "Unión de Campesinos Agricultores," Junta Central de Conciliación y Arbitraje (Veracruz), Caja 84, Expediente n/n, 1929, VSA; Letter to Agrarian Commission, Comisión Agraria Mixta, Expediente 1954, Municipio Tamalín, VSA;

Comisión Local Agraria, Expediente 887, Ranchería Tierra Amarilla, Municipio Temapache, VSA; Comisión Agraria Mixta, Expediente 1809, Zacamixtle, Tancoco, VSA; García Granados, *Los veneros del diablo*, 95–96; *La Gaceta Oficial* (Veracruz), Comisión Agraria Section, 9 September 1922; 30 November 1922; 18 April 1929; 29 October 1931.

49. On the slow regeneration of tropical forests, see A. Gómez-Pompa and B. Ludlow Wiechers, "Regeneración de los ecosistemas tropicales y subtropicales," in *Regeneración de selvas altas en Veracruz, México*, ed. A. Gómez-Pompa et al. (Mexico City: Compañía Editorial Continental, 1976), 11–24. On the relationship between the *ejido* and the tropical rainforest, see V. M. Toledo, "El ejido y la selva tropical húmeda: una contradicción ecológica y social," in *Regeneración de selvas altas en Veracruz, México*, ed. A. Gómez-Pompa et al. (Mexico City: Compañía Editorial Continental, 1976), 641–67.

---

10 Daniel Faber ◆ Revolution in the Rainforest

The roots of deforestation in Central America, according to Daniel Faber, can be traced to decades of development policies that have favored expanding the production of export commodities over farming to meet the basic needs of the people of the region. The export beef boom, along with chemical-intensive cotton production, proved to be the most socially and ecologically destructive activity of the post-World War II period. This approach to development, augmented by new export commodities, continues to enjoy the support of local oligarchs, international lending agencies, and the U.S. government despite growing opposition by proponents of sustainable development. As capitalist production for export expands into the remaining forested zones, land hunger and poverty increase among the poor majority. Thus, both social and environmental problems can be seen as outcomes of the dominant development paradigm in Central America. Selections 8, 9, 11 and 17 show how this approach to development plays out in other Latin American countries.

> The creation of the first guerrilla detachment in the Guatemalan jungle was one of the richest and most rewarding revolutionary experiences for our organization.
>
> —*Mario Payeras*[1]

Ten-year-old Tomás León lives at the edge of the rainforest on the eastern slopes of a Central American country. Six months after he was

From Daniel Faber, "Revolution in the Rainforest," in *Environment under Fire: Imperialism and the Ecological Crisis in Central America* (New York: Monthly Review Press, 1993), 117–46, 262–68. Map and tables omitted. © 1993 by Daniel Faber. Reprinted by permission of the Monthly Review Foundation.

born, his family was forced by their own government from the fertile interior highlands they had farmed for generations. Government officials insisted that prosperity lay just down the new road built to the agricultural frontier. The León family joined a government-sponsored rainforest colonization project and received more land than they'd ever had before. However, three years after clearing trees to plant crops, the Leóns were forced to move deeper into the forest, this time by a cattle rancher who mysteriously produced titles to the land they worked. The Leóns were evicted a third time three years later.

Today, Tomás and his mother farm the new family plot while his father earns a dollar a day on the nearby cattle *hacienda*. Despite their hard work, the family often goes hungry. The forest animals Tomás and his father hunt grow scarcer each year. Although young and illiterate, Tomás understands that his family has lived with injustice for far too long.[2]

The story of Tomás León is a microcosm of Central America's social and ecological crisis. There are hundreds of thousands of families like the Leóns throughout the region. Their continued political domination and economic exploitation by local oligarchs and allied foreign powers, namely the United States, has brought about widespread poverty and environmental destruction—problems that have produced revolutionary movements and civil war in much of the isthmus in recent decades.

The magnitude of this crisis is reflected most dramatically in the destruction of Central America's tropical forests. In 1960, woodlands blanketed nearly 60 percent of the region. Today, less than one-third of the original forests remain standing; the rest have vanished. Even more devastating is the felling of Central America's (broad-leafed) lowland and lower montane rainforests, one of the richest reserves of biological diversity found anywhere in the world, which has proceeded at a rate between 1,351 and 1,545 square miles a year over the last decade. Although slowing, if current deforestation rates continue, most of the remaining rainforests could be completely destroyed within the next twenty years, except for small remnants in parks and preserves.[3]

The loss of genetic material is astounding. For instance, in Costa Rica, a country the size of West Virginia but home to 5 to 7 percent of the world's known species, there are over 8,000 plant species and 758 bird species—620 of which are residents—a greater variety than that found in all of North America above the Tropic of Cancer. Although only 1,803 acres in size, the La Selva Reserve alone contains 320 tree species, 42 fish, 394 birds, 104 mammals (including 62 bats), 76 reptiles, 46 amphibians, and 143 butterflies—a diversity of species equal to about half that of the entire state of California.[4] For the last ten years, an area of jungle the size of the La Selva Reserve has been destroyed every six hours in Costa Rica. In fact, more than two-thirds of the country's tropical forests have disappeared since 1950; less than 4,418 square miles remain, largely on the

Cordillera de Talamanca and Cordillera Central mountain ranges, and in the northeast. Prior to colonization, over 99 percent of Costa Rica was originally forested.[5] Since about 15 percent of some 1,500 trees inventoried in Costa Rica's forests were evaluated as having potential for cancer treatment, their destruction represents an incalculable loss for both present and future generations of humanity.

Occupying only 6 percent of the Earth's surface (it used to be 12 percent), rainforests are home to 80 percent of the world's vegetation and half of the Earth's living species, up to four million life form varieties. Half of the world's medicines originate from tropical forests, including aspirin, quinine, digitalis, cyclosporin, and vincristine, which has been highly successful in the treatment of leukemia in children.[6]

In the fall of 1991 an agreement was reached between the National Biodiversity Institute of Costa Rica, a private, nonprofit organization promoting the preservation of the country's richest biological resources, and Merck & Company, Inc., the world's largest pharmaceutical company. This agreement was the first time a major drug manufacturer collaborated directly with a tropical country to hunt the rainforests for new medicines ("chemical prospecting"), providing economic incentives to preserve biodiversity.[7]

The roots of deforestation can be traced to decades of development policies that have favored the expanded production of traditional and nontraditional capitalist agricultural exports over the sustainable use of natural resources for meeting the needs of the Central American people. Along with chemical-intensive cotton production, the production of beef cattle has proved to be the most important, as well as the most socially and ecologically destructive, commodity for promoting the diversification, modernization, and expansion of capitalist export agriculture in the region since World War II.

This approach to development continues to enjoy the active support of local oligarchs and military officers with the assistance of the United States government and international lending agencies, increasingly rolling back huge areas of *selva* for cattle and concentrating the richest lands and resources under the control of the capitalist export sector. It has also condemned the majority of small farmers to a life of brutal poverty and hardship. Therefore, to understand the current social and ecological crisis it is necessary to look at the expansion of the capitalist export sector, in particular the cattle stampede into the rich tropical forests of Central America.

Deforestation and the Cattle Stampede

Export beef production first began along the western territories of Central America in the late 1950s and early 1960s. The financial capital and technical assistance necessary to develop the cattle industry came from United States government agencies and international financial institutions, principally the World Bank, Inter-American Development Bank (IADB), U.S. Agency for International Development (USAID), and Central American Bank for Economic Integration (CABEI).

Most of the funding for cattle and export agriculture was provided by the Inter-American Development Bank. The IADB invested some $3.037 billion in Latin American agriculture between 1961 and 1978, 22 percent of their total distribution of loans.[8] The World Bank provided massive financial support, spending $154 million on the livestock industry in Central America and the Caribbean in its first two decades of development lending, some 56 percent of its total direct commitments to agriculture. During the 1960s, more than one-fourth of the private loans made to agriculture also went to cattle production, converting it from a system of hoarding to an instrument of capitalist production for money profit.[9]

In fact, all of the agricultural credit provided by the International Development Association (IDA, a division of the World Bank) in the Western Hemisphere between 1961 and 1970 went for livestock improvement. In addition to the credit provided by the IDA, loans to the cattle industry by the International Bank for Reconstruction and Development (IBRD) between 1961 and 1965 comprised 28 percent of its total agricultural allocations made to Latin America and 51 percent from 1966 to 1970.[10]

As was the case with cotton and other export crops, the flood of development assistance gave Central American governments the financial tools for creating the appropriate ecological and communal (or infrastructural) conditions for export beef production. This was first accomplished through improving the quality of existing pasture in the Pacific coastal lowlands, ensuring suitable feedstock for the dry season, and reconstructing the "biological character" of the cattle herds.

One of the primary barriers to the export of Central American cattle was the poor quality of the criollo stock, a breed inherited from the Spanish colonists. Slow maturation rates and relatively modest weight gains were serious obstacles. To be competitive in the world market, ranchers required breeds that would maximize the rate of quality beef formation in the shortest amount of time. Santa Gertrudis, purebred Brahman, Zebu, and other new breeds of beefier, faster-maturing cattle, more resistant to disease and the environmental conditions of the tropics, were imported to replace and upgrade the inferior quality of the existing stock.[11]

Commodities and techniques for improving the health of the herds were also purchased and adopted, including vaccines, medicines, and vitamin supplements for combating diseases, such as leptospirosis, and parasites like screwworms, vampire bats, and ticks (which transmit protozoal diseases like anaplasmosis and paraplasmosis). In Costa Rica, animal medicines were the third-largest imported agricultural input during the mid-1970s, behind only pesticides and fertilizers.[12]

The "biological character" of the existing landscape was also reconstructed. A number of high-yielding African grasses were imported to replace the unproductive varieties native to Central America.[13] Combined with the increased use of chemical fertilizers, pesticides, wells, and irrigation, the productivity of pasture grasses jumped significantly, particularly on those ranches that fattened cattle for slaughter. Pasture improvements also raised land values and required fencing the once-open fields and forests as a means for securing title as capitalist private property.

Before these improvements, cattle expended great amounts of energy roaming vast areas of unfenced and unimproved pastures. This traditional pasturing technique produced malnutrition, insect infestation, disease, and infertility in the cattle, thereby lowering the rate of beef formation and increasing gristle content.[14]

Finally, the influx of foreign capital financed construction of an elaborate system of highways, feeder roads, and bridges leading to the Pacific ports, as well as the truck fleets, packing plants, warehouses, and facilities necessary to efficiently transport and process this beef for the world market. By 1960, ships laden with frozen beef for the U.S. fast-food hamburger and pet food industries sailed from Guatemala every five days.[15]

With these investments, the modernization and expansion of export cattle production caused massive deforestation in the Pacific coastal lowlands and coincided with the development of large-scale cotton and sugar estates. Cattle proved to be a very effective and highly flexible instrument for wealthy land speculators since herds could be moved from titled to untitled areas and sold (along with the "newly developed" land) when market conditions were most favorable (unlike agricultural crops, which were fixed investments that had to be harvested and sold in a specific period of time). This process also accelerated deforestation and habitat destruction, since stripping the land of its tree cover, or "land improvements," demonstrated not only de facto ownership but also expanded the pasture area for growing herds.

In some areas, cattle ranching was the dominant force behind the destruction of dry and moist tropical forests along the Pacific coast. A tropical dry forest formation is characterized by a low, semi-deciduous canopy of trees, usually twenty to thirty meters tall with short, stout trunks and large spreading crowns. Tropical moist forests are usually taller, multistratal, semi-deciduous, or evergreen forests.[16]

In Escuintla, Guatemala, a mere 12 percent of the land was in pasture while 48 percent stood forested in the early 1950s. By 1964, Escuintla had emerged as the country's largest cattle-raising department, holding one-fifth of the nation's herd. Some 42 percent of the land was in pastures of imported pangola and other African grasses. Only a paltry 16 percent of the area remained forested.[17]

Cattle ranching was particularly expanded in the Pacific lowlands of Honduras and Costa Rica because cotton production assumed much less importance there in comparison to the rest of the region. The western department of Choluteca developed into Honduras's largest cattle raising department by the early 1970s, for instance, with one-tenth of the nation's herd.[18]

In the northern Pacific province of Guanacaste in Costa Rica, wealthy ranchers utilized discriminatory state banking policies, land laws, and tax credits to double their pasture acreage from 765,621 acres in 1963 to 1,468,027 acres in 1973, forcing 22.12 percent of all small peasant farmers to leave the province. Of the more than 701,000 acres of new pastures of jaragua grass developed in the province, 587,860 acres (or 82 percent) went to farms of 247 acres or more in size.

The displacement of peasants by increased land values (and rents) and discriminatory state policies resulted in the decline of every food crop except rice.[19] By 1974, 65 percent of Guanacaste was in pasture, its rich forests slashed from 34 percent to a mere 13 percent in a decade.[20] Similar processes also occurred in the neighboring provinces of Puntarenas and Alajuela.

Today, only a few patches of Costa Rica's original woodlands of guayacan, amarillo, granadilla, madrone, and other trees remain, typically in the most inaccessible areas of the Pacific lowlands and surrounding mountains. These remaining forests have lost some of their regenerative capacity, not only because of the small size of the remnants, but also because of the decline, and even local extinction, of animal populations that have co-evolved mutualistic relationships with the wild plant species.[21]

Once home to an abundance of North American birds, such as the broad-winged hawk, stripe-headed sparrow, American wideon, great blue heron, and the solitary sandpiper, these provinces now support herds of cattle. Peccaries, agoutis, pacas, coatimundis, jaguars, pumas, ocelots, foxes, tapirs, caimans, crocodiles, scarlet macaws, parrots, great curassows, and other animals found in the forest have been either eliminated or greatly reduced. White-tailed deer and howler monkeys are still present in areas with some remnant forest and secondary growth, but in reduced numbers. Coatimundis, collared peccaries, agoutis, pacas, and tapirs are still found in some forested areas, generally near streams, although the last two have become very scarce. The big cats are becoming exceedingly rare and are probably extinct in most of lowland Guanacaste, except in parks and reserves. The harpy eagle and hookbilled kite, the latter almost exclusively restricted to dry forest habitats, are both almost completely gone. Only a few generalists such as rabbits, coyotes, squirrels, armadillos, and iguanas have adapted to the open grassland monoculture.[22]

Revolution and Repression, Life and Death in the Rainforests

As "development" of the narrow Pacific coastal plains was completed during the course of the 1960s, Central America's landed oligarchs and bankers turned their attention to the vast wilderness areas and peasant communities in the rugged eastern territories. They soon realized that large profits could be garnered from the conversion of these less-accessible zones (previously immune to capitalist export agriculture) into extensive cattle ranches.

Beef cattle take four to six years before they reach the most profitable slaughtering weight of 400 to 450 kilograms (880 to 1,000 pounds). This maturation rate for cattle grazing on more marginal lands, particularly in nutrient-poor rainforest areas, requires the creation of extensive cattle ranches for moving herds to new pastures as older pastures degrade over time, and therefore contributes to deforestation. Unlike more geographically specific commodities such as cotton and coffee, cattle were less restricted and could be raised wherever pasture grasses would grow. In fact, the longer rainy season in the region's interior, particularly in the lower montane and lowland rainforests of the Caribbean slope, offered the possible year-round growth of pasture grasses. Mature cattle from the enlarged herds in the wetter interior zones could then be culled and sold to the more modern ranches on the Pacific coast to be fattened for slaughter and exported.[23]

Fueled by increased financing from bilateral and multilateral lending agencies, Central America's large cattle ranchers moved quickly to realize the profit potential, expanding toward the rolling mountains and valleys of the interior. Through the economic processes of land speculation, higher rents, legal trickery, and land titling from "sympathetic" government officials, these cattle ranchers displaced tens of thousands of peasant families from lands they had traditionally farmed for generations. In areas where peasant communities organized against eviction, government repression, including U.S.-sponsored military counterinsurgency operations, was used to expropriate their farmland.

In the interior department of Olancho, Honduras, a series of peasant massacres by the army and private security forces in coordination with the National Federation of Farmers and Cattlemen (FENAGH) and sectors of the business establishment were carried out in the 1960s and 1970s. The aim of the repression was to attack leading organizers in Olancho's peasant movement who were resisting the expansion of cattle ranches onto their farmland and adjacent forests. By the 1970s, Olancho had the fastest growing cattle herd in the country. Nearly half of Olancho's farmland was untitled national land occupied by peasants. Ironically, many of these peasants were displaced migrants from the Pacific coastal region of Choluteca. Thus, peasant and export sector conflicts along the Pacific coast in the 1960s were displaced into the interior during the 1970s.[24]

The use of repression to "capitalize nature" was even more widespread in Nicaragua. In the mountainous northern department of Matagalpa, the country's leading producer of corn and beans in the early 1960s, most of the farmland was worked by peasants without title. By the mid-1960s, the area emerged as the country's most important cattle-producing department, as President [Anastasio] Somoza's feared National Guard evicted families from their traditional plots of land. In 1963, 30 percent of Matagalpa was in forest, compared to only 5 percent in 1976. Pastures, on the other hand, increased from 39 percent to 94 percent of the farm area over the same period.[25]

Conflicts between small family farmers and large cattle ranchers intensified. By 1967, the rural guerrilla movement, the Sandinista National Liberation Front (FSLN), emerged with the support of the peasantry to combat the capitalization of Matagalpa.[26] The Somoza dictatorship quickly declared the area a counterinsurgency zone and, with U.S. assistance, launched a brutal campaign of repression that devastated the guerrilla movement (including the killing of thirteen senior members of the FSLN leadership). Those families resisting eviction from then on were routinely arrested, tortured, killed, or imprisoned in the nearby Zelaya concentration camp.[27]

Spurred by the militarization of the countryside, as well as government colonization projects and road-building programs, ranches quickly spread eastward into the country's lower montane and southeastern Caribbean lowland rainforests, particularly along the boundaries of the Rama road.[28] Cattle ranching destroyed more than 386 square miles of Nicaragua's broad-leaved and coniferous forests annually during the 1970s, the highest level of any country in Central America. Pasture lands expanded to blanket 10,000 square miles by 1978, compared to 6,602 square miles in 1961.[29]

By this time, Nicaragua possessed the largest cattle herd in all of Central America and had become the United States' number one Latin American beef supplier. Beef exports from Nicaragua jumped from $6.7 million in 1965 to $26.6 million in 1970.[30] Officers of Somoza's Guardia and local magistrates took advantage of the repression to establish their own ranches. The Somoza family itself utilized its control of the country's military apparatus to appropriate a lion's share of the profits from the cattle export boom.

By 1979, land holdings belonging to Somoza and his associates expanded to more than two million acres, more than half of which was extensive ranchland.[31] Six Miami meatpacking plants and the largest slaughterhouse in Central America, all owned by Somoza, were key ingredients in this recipe for rainforest destruction.[32]

Perhaps the most brutal repression occurred in Guatemala. Between 1950 and 1964, the departments of Zacapa, Izabal, and Chiquimula experienced heavy deforestation and peasant displacement by large cattle ranchers. During this period, pasture acreage tripled in Izabal and nearly doubled for Zacapa. Deforestation was particularly severe along a road running eastward from Guatemala City through the richly forested Motagua River Valley to Puerto Barrios and Matías de Gálvez, major beef ports on the Caribbean.[33]

Discontent quickly ripened into rebellion at the edge of the rainforests. By the mid-1960s, as in Matagalpa, Nicaragua, a guerrilla organization emerged. Rebel Armed Forces (FAR) formed widespread alliances with desperately poor peasant villagers in Zacapa and Izabal to resist the appropriation of their land. (In March 1965, these two rebel fronts split into two separate revolutionary organizations.)[34]

In 1966, at the urging of the U.S. State Department, the Guatemalan government declared these eastern districts a counterinsurgency zone, launching a series of merciless attacks on peasant communities to break the resistance. U.S.-supplied and -piloted helicopter gunships, T-33 fighter jets, and B-26 "invader" bombers armed with napalm and heavy bombs assisted the Guatemalan army in the carnage, killing some 6,000 to 10,000 people between 1966 and 1968.[35]

The "success" of these military campaigns quickly opened up the farms and rainforests found on the "agricultural frontier" to huge cattle ranches owned by landed oligarchs, local and national government officials, military officers, and paramilitary personnel. The U.S.-trained commander of the counterinsurgency, Colonel Carlos Arana, known as "the Butcher of Zacapa," became one of the largest ranchers in northeast Guatemala and later president of the military government.[36] The political career of Colonel Arana is indicative of the manner in which Guatemala's military officers and government officials have promoted rainforest destruction as a means for acquiring large cattle ranches and assuming [*sic*] their own personal fortunes.[37]

By the mid-1970s, the cattle stampede had spread to the pristine rainforests in the Mayan Indian departments of Alta Verapaz, El Quiché, Huehuetenango, and northwest Izabal (also known as the Northern Transversal Strip). The Guatemalan government was particularly anxious to "develop" the tropical evergreen seasonal forests in the immense northern department of El Petén, an area comprising about one-third of the country. The Petén included upland forests of mahogany, Spanish cedar, ceiba, and zapote.[38]

An extension of Mexico's oil-bearing Chiapas rainforest, the discovery of nickel, oil, and the enormous hydroelectric potential in the Petén wilderness and other northern departments further increased the pressure to open up the region to foreign capital. This sparked an intensified wave of violence and state terror against church-backed peasant cooperatives and traditional Indian communities. By 1973, the $250-million Mineral Explorations and Exploitations (Exmibal) nickel mining and processing operation was conceded in the department of Alta Verapaz. By 1978, seven international oil companies had received concessions in northern Guatemala.[39]

As the decade progressed, the receding edge of the tropical rainforest became the setting for growing peasant resistance to encroachment by large cattle ranchers and multinational resource companies. Another revolutionary organization, the Guerrilla Army of the Poor (Ejército Guerrillero de los Pobres, EGP), was born in this period. After a series of spectacular attacks by the EGP in northern El Quiché, the army launched massive counterinsurgency operations designed to "clear" the Transversal Strip of its small farmer inhabitants, including the massacre of more than 100 Kekchí Indians in the town of Panzós in 1978.[40] This massacre is considered a turning point that resulted in an upsurge of grassroots resistance by the Mayan Indians who make up more than half of the country's 8.7 million people. Entire Indian villages joined the popular movement or the armed resistance waging revolution in the rainforest.[41]

Despite the armed resistance, military officers, government officials, and landed elites continued to destroy rainforests. General Romeo Lucas García, who was in charge of the counterinsurgency operations in the Northern Transversal Strip before he became president of the country in 1987, acquired a number of ranches and timber properties on the strip ranging from 81,000 acres to 135,000 acres. This stretch became known as "the Zone of the Generals."[42] Other members of this cattle-military-industrial complex acquired properties, including the defense minister General Otto Spiegler Noriega, General Carlos Arana Osorio, and President Kjell Laugerud.[43]

Today, the army contributes directly to the deforestation of the Petén by building roads, clearing areas up to 300 yards on either side to prevent guerrilla ambushes, and opening up the jungle to further logging, cattle ranching, and colonization by landless peasants. The National Agency for the Economic Promotion and Development of the Petén and its temporary successor, the Comisión Liquidador, are operated by the Guatemalan Armed Forces and as such have been largely immune to government oversight as they continue to grant huge logging concessions in the Petén.[44] In fact, a 1983 USAID-financed study claimed that 60 percent of the Department of Alta Verapaz is owned by the army, and army land holdings are rapidly growing in the Petén as well.

It is widely suspected that government officials at the highest levels receive substantial bribes for granting illegal logging concessions, even in designated "protected areas." Archaeologists report that loggers enter the parks surrounding the archaeological sites to cut trees. According to one scholar working in the area, it is not unusual for loggers with a license for cutting a maximum of 2,000 board feet to cut two to four times that amount as the authorities look the other way.[45]

Park boundaries are also ignored by multinational corporations, such as Basic Resources International, Ltd. (BRI), a Canadian-backed company based in the Bahamas, which owns a concession in the northwestern part of the Petén, formerly belonging to Texaco. One active oil well, called Xan1, which suffered a major spill in 1989, operates on the boundary of the 174-square-mile Laguna del Tigre reserve, an area of pristine wetlands, grasslands, and subtropical semi-humid forest, and numerous endangered species. Additional wells are planned for the reserve's interior and will likely further increase land values and speculative deforestation. In 1989, Exxon planned exploratory oil drilling in the rainforests surrounding Ceibal, one of the country's most prestigious archaeological sites. Fortunately, Guatemala's environmental movement has successfully blocked Exxon's plans, at least for now.[46]

Mining and logging operations also take a toll. In 1977, Exmibal constructed a $220-million plant capable of producing 28 million pounds of nickel annually on the shore of the huge Lake Izabal. Partly owned by the Hanna Mining Company of Cleveland, along with Guatemala's military government, the plant employed fewer than 500 Guatemalans at between $2.50 and $7.50 *a day*, while its strip-mining operation and tailings waste irreversibly damaged the fragile environment around Lake Izabal. It finally shut down in 1981 under the weight of low world prices for nickel and high energy costs.[47]

To pay off a growing $490-million foreign debt, the Guatemala government has considered reopening a pulp processing mill in the small town of El Rancho. Called "CELGUSA," the pulp plant was built in the 1970s with obsolete and environmentally contaminating technology and caused extensive damage before closing in 1986. Its reopening threatens to deforest an estimated 17,290 acres of coniferous highland forests per year and would release dioxins and other toxic chemicals into one of Guatemala's most important sources of water, the Rio Motagua. According to some environmentalists, the ecological damage caused by the original mill has exceeded the amount of the debt, and a reopening would further decimate the country's woodlands.[48]

Another environmental threat facing the Petén rainforests and peasant communities is a drug eradication program, using U.S. pilots and planes to spray lethal herbicides on allegedly burgeoning fields of opium and marijuana. The U.S. Drug Enforcement Agency has carried out the program, working with Guatemala's military intelligence division, the G-2, which is notoriously connected with the death squads operating in the country.

Human deaths, deformed children, ulcerations of the mouth and throat from drinking sprayed water sources, increased infant mortality, deaths of entire cattle herds and vegetable crops, as well as scores of endangered quetzals and other species, and the widespread defoliation of the Petén have all been reported as a result of the campaign over the last five years. Although the DEA claims to be using only the herbicide Roundup (glyphosate), most of these effects cannot be attributed to this chemical but are instead reportedly consistent with much more lethal chemicals such as paraquat, 2,3,5-T, and 2,4-D.[49] Many environmentalists argue that the sprayings are also concentrated in areas of guerrilla activity in the Petén, San Marcos, and Huehuetenango, and are part of a military counter-insurgency program to decimate the growing revolution in the rainforest.

Poverty, Deforestation, and the Hamburger Connection

Central American peasants displaced by the stampede of cattle ranchers, loggers, land speculators, and multinational corporations face a number of options in addition to armed resistance. Tens of thousands of families are moving into the region's rapidly growing cities in search of wage jobs in factories or on nearby agricultural export estates harvesting cotton, sugar, or coffee.

Others settle on the steep slopes of the volcanoes and hillsides along the Pacific slope, clearing them of trees and other protective vegetation to plant food crops. Most of the deforested hillsides are inappropriate for agriculture and soon develop severe problems with erosion and fertility loss, flash flooding, and decreased productivity. Tens of thousands more are joining the urban informal service sector to look for incomes as street vendors, household servants, and any other tasks that offer the hope of survival.

The end results of cattle expansion therefore include the overcoming of potentially severe seasonal wage-labor shortages through the marginal-ization of the rural peasantry. It also creates a large army of desperately poor workers residing in the city *barrios*. In this sense, the cattle boom has been (and continues to be) a safeguard for the economic viability of capitalist export-agriculture and industry along the Pacific coast.[50]

Many displaced peasants escape their landless condition by moving east in advance of the cattle stampede into the tropical rainforests of the interior. Often utilizing agricultural methods ill suited to the rainforest ecosystem, migrating peasants clear and burn the forest vegetation to plant subsistence crops such as corn, beans, rice, and manioc, as well as small-scale cash crops such as coffee, chiles, bananas, and cacao.[51] However, rainforest soils planted in crops are typically thin and poor; the nutrients normally stored and protected by the jungle canopy quickly leach out when exposed to the hard rains and burning tropical sun, and eventually the soil turns to brick. Denied access to critical financial and social services and technological inputs necessary to protect the land and improve their lives, [these peasants find that their] crops soon begin to fail after a few short years. Yet, as biologist James J. Parsons points out, "enduring countless hardships and difficult living conditions on an isolated and malaria-infested fringe" is often the only available means to ensure survival for the family which clears the forest and plants in its ashes.[52]

As invasive weeds and noxious insects take over the degraded soils, these families become forced to abandon or sell their plots to a second wave of land speculators and cattle ranchers. Many others simply have their farms appropriated by the military or paramilitary personnel acting on behalf of wealthy ranchers and government officials. In areas where government repression is less overt, cattle ranchers employ wage workers to slash and burn the trees and brush and plant pasture grasses. Many landowners rent forested parcels of land or *rozas* to subsistence farmers, who in exchange will clear the trees and grow food crops for a year or two, just long enough for the stumps to rot. After this time, they will be evicted and the land seeded for pasture. New forest parcels are rented, and the process will be renewed once more.[53]

In numerous instances, peasant families follow roads into the forests created by extensive logging operations, particularly in Honduras, Guatemala, and Costa Rica. The Honduran government's Forestry Development Corporation (COHDEFOR) has cleared large areas of tropical forest in the northern provinces, contributing to the destruction of over 4.94 million acres of Honduran forests since 1960. In addition, commercial loggers clear an estimated 123,500 to 148,200 acres of pine forests annually.[54]

Despite its potentially high economic value, however, most processes of small farmer displacement and land speculation usually waste the felled timber. Up to three-fourths of it is burned on the ground. For instance, an estimated $320-million worth of cut hardwood is burned or left to rot each year by land speculators and migrating campesinos.[55] The burnings create heavy influxes of ash and organic matter in local waterways, depressing oxygen levels and causing recurring fish kills, such as on the western shore of majestic Lake Izabal in Guatemala.[56] These patterns are repeated time and again. Peasants move ever deeper into the rainforests, only to eventually lose their farms to the cattle stampede. In effect, Central America's impoverished peasantry are mere pawns in a general's game, serving as an effective vehicle for clearing the rainforests, free of charge, for wealthy ranchers.[57]

As part of this larger process, destruction of Central America's tropical rainforest is further exacerbated by government-sponsored peasant colonization projects. More often than not, these projects only reinforce structures that benefit the capitalist export sector (particularly ranchers) and foreign capital at the expense of the region's majorities and environment.[58] Often called "land reforms," these resettlement projects are designed to serve as an outlet for potentially explosive social tensions caused by land-tenure conflicts and urban overcrowding elsewhere in the region. In many cases, however, these conflicts often reappear between colonizing peasants and ranchers on the agricultural frontier. Peasant colonists often refuse to move on when cattle ranchers are ready to take over their land, precipitating violent confrontations.

Such was the case in Honduras in 1975, when a cattle rancher was implicated in a grisly multiple murder of priests and peasant activists organizing against eviction. Recently, in Costa Rica, campesinos have reclaimed abandoned cattle lands, causing conflict between large ranchers and peasant families.[59]

Peasant colonization and destruction of rainforest as an alternative to comprehensive agrarian and economic reforms are often promoted by the United States. For instance, in response to the growing insurgency during the 1960s in Matagalpa, Nicaragua, the U.S. Agency for International Development and the Inter-American Development Bank provided an $80-million loan to the Somoza dictatorship for small-farmer colonization and road projects into the jungles of Zelaya, causing massive deforestation of the area.[60] Under the Nicaraguan Agrarian Institute (Instituto Agrario de Nicaragua, IAN) and, later, the Campesino Welfare Institute (Instituto de Bienestar Campesino, INVIERNO), a total of sixty-three colonies involving 2,651 families relocated from the Pacific coastal plain were established on the Atlantic coast and agricultural frontier by the mid-1970s.[61]

Pushed from behind by the cattle stampede, many displaced peasants deforested and settled land traditionally belonging to the Miskito, Sumu, and Rama Indians of Nicaragua's Costa de Miskitos, resulting in clashes between the two cultures.[62] In fact, throughout Central America the common woodlands and ways of life of other indigenous Indian communities—including the Kekchí and Chorti of Guatemala, the Paya and Miskito of Honduras, the Talamanquenos of Costa Rica, and the Kuna and Chocó of Panama—continue to be threatened by expanding cattle ranchers and displaced farmer colonists.[63]

Under Somoza, peasant rainforest colonization and other "surface" reforms in the Pacific highlands of Carazo and central highlands of Matagalpa and Jinotega failed to stem the deepening poverty of the Nicaraguan people and therefore halt the growing social unrest and FSLN guerrilla activity in the countryside. In response, Somoza imposed a news blackout and state of siege in 1975, ordering the National Guard to carry out extensive "search and destroy" missions, which, with U.S. support, included the use of napalm, defoliants, and indiscriminate bombing of rural communities. As part of this state of siege, estimated to have killed some 3,000 people in thirty-three months of generalized terror, thousands of families saw their huts burned out and crops destroyed, their women raped and brutalized, their fathers and sons tortured—actions that invigorated the Sandinista-led revolutionary movement which overthrew the Somoza dictatorship on July 19, 1979.[64]

These actions were repeated in Guatemala's tropical rainforests of the Petén and other northern departments during the same period. Already spontaneously colonized in some areas by isolated peasant families engaging in primitive forms of shifting agriculture, the government sought to further develop these pristine rainforests by employing displaced small farmers through road-building programs and "official" colonization projects as a means for relieving land conflicts occurring in other parts of the country, particularly the eastern ranching districts.[65]

For instance, in 1976 the National Institute for Agrarian Transformation (INTA) utilized $5.6 million in USAID money to have some 5,000 families join a cooperative colonization project of former highland peasants from Huehuetenango in the Ixcán region of the Transversal de Norte development zone. However, as characteristic of the prevailing land tenure system in the rest of the country, these settlers were placed on the more marginal lands and provided little capital assistance. The better lands were distributed to large cattle ranchers. As the nutrient-poor soils of the Petén lost their fertility during the course of the 1970s, ever larger numbers of small corn farmers lost the land they had worked so hard to clear and cultivate to the expanding cattle latifundia. As a consequence, the 1976 harvest of 1.5 million quintales of maize fell to slightly over 500,000 in 1978.[66]

These injustices sparked a guerrilla operation by the EGP, which in June 1976 killed landowner Luis Reina, "the Tiger of Ixcán"—virtual lord of the large, newly acquired tracts of land in the area. In retaliation, the army systematically murdered cooperative leaders in the Ixcán area in operations the following month. As social unrest in the rainforest grew with the discovery of oil and conversion of land to large cattle [ranches], the army eventually launched a wave of terror in the late 1970s against peasant communities and cooperatives, further fueling the growing revolution in the rainforest.[67]

Spurred by the "first wave" of peasant colonization, deforestation and the expansion of Central America's cattle industry was further accelerated by the large market in the United States for imported beef. In what is often referred to as "the hamburger connection," exports of deboned, frozen beef from Central America feed the burgeoning fast-food hamburger joints, pet food industries, and processed and frozen food sections in U.S. supermarkets.

During the 1970s, as the U.S. fast-food industry grew 20 percent a year (2.5 times faster than the restaurant industry overall), the United States was the world's biggest importer of beef. It imported about 132 pounds per average citizen, accounting for about one-third of all international trade, compared to less than eighty-eight pounds of beef per citizen in 1960.[68] Deboned frozen beef quickly emerged as Central America's most dynamic export commodity, with a 400 percent increase in trade between 1961 and 1974 alone.[69] As a result, during the height of the cattle boom between 1970 and 1980, an area of tropical forests larger than Belgium was annihilated.[70]

By 1980, Central American beef exports to the United States skyrocketed to over $290 million annually, constituting 15 percent of the total U.S. beef imports (compared to only $9 million in beef exports, or 5 percent of U.S. total imports in the early 1960s). U.S. per capita beef consumption had risen to 117 pounds a year, a figure twice the yearly average for Western Europe. Exports rose from 20,000 tons a year in 1955 to almost 150,000 tons twenty years later, as 90 percent of total Central American exports went to the U.S. market.[71] According to the U.S. Department of Agriculture, from 1981 to 1992 Central America exported over 612,760 tons of beef to the United States.

Ironically, the cattle stampede and destruction of Central America's rainforests has resulted in declining beef consumption and growing hunger among the majority of Central Americans. Since the capitalist export sector monopolizes the best land, the rural poor cannot grow enough food to survive or afford to buy beef. In Costa Rica, where only 2,000 ranchers control more than half of all agricultural land in the country, beef production doubled between 1959 and 1973, while per capita beef consumption dropped from thirty to nineteen pounds over the same period.[72] Even in prerevolutionary Nicaragua, which became the only country in Central America with more head of cattle than people, per capita beef consumption declined during the 1970s.[73] As part of this general "protein flight," a typical house cat in the United States now consumes more beef than the average Central American peasant.[74]

Central American beef exporters enjoy a number of competitive advantages in comparison to domestic producers in the U.S. market. In particular, North American ranchers suffer higher costs because of the need to supply feed grain to cattle during the winter, as well as higher land prices (rents) and labor costs. Central America's most important cost advantages over the United States lie primarily in the cheaper cost of equivalent areas of ranchland and freedom from the costs of corn and hay feed during the winter months. About 60 percent of U.S.-produced beef is fed grain, hay, corn, straw, and other roughage. These competitive advantages are rooted in the massive conversion of tropical rainforests into extensive pastures. In fact, Central American beef costs one-fourth of the amount needed to produce grass-fed beef in the United States.[75]

The rapid expansion of hamburger joints and the pet and frozen food industries has created a market niche for the cheaper, leaner, grass-fed beef from Central America over the more expensive, redder cuts of U.S. grain-fattened beef. (The red, well-marbled meat of grain-fed cattle is graded by the U.S. Department of Agriculture as prime or choice cuts used for steaks, roasts, and other more expensive meats.) It is estimated that imports of cheaper Central American beef reduce the price of hamburger by about five cents a pound in the United States. For instance, the average price of imported Central American beef was $0.67 per pound in 1978, compared to $1.50 for U.S.-produced beef. Some U.S. officials have claimed that beef imports have done more to hold down food price inflation than any other single government initiative.[76]

Central American beef exporters also enjoy competitive advantages in the U.S. import market in comparison to South American countries, which are restricted by the presence of hoof-and-mouth disease. All beef produced south of the Panama Canal is banned for export into the United States unless it is pre-cooked, which imposes a prohibitive cost.

In recent years, beef exports have declined because of regional military conflicts, growing protectionism, and falling prices, as well as declining per capita beef consumption by the increasingly health-conscious U.S. market. Between 1960 and 1980, beef production doubled and exports tripled in Costa Rica, Guatemala, Honduras, and Nicaragua. Since then, however, beef exports to the United States have steadily declined, forcing the region's producers to scramble for new markets. Total beef exports declined from 162,000 metric tons (40 percent of total production) in 1979 to 61,000 tons (19 percent of total production) in 1985; total beef production dropped from 400,000 tons to 318,000 tons. In 1991, the United States imported only 46,231 tons of Central American beef, a substantial decline from the 1970s.[77]

Despite this decline in beef exports, deforestation has continued apace. Regionwide, an estimated 4,208 square miles of Central America's tropical forests and woodlands are destroyed each year. In 1961, 116,301 square miles of tropical forests and woodlands blanketed 57 percent of the region's total area. Today, only 52,340 square miles remain to cover 26 percent of the total area, representing the destruction of over 63,960 square miles of forest in a mere thirty years.

The impact on the landscape has been enormous. The isthmus of Central America is being ecologically transformed into one great stock ranch. Once traveling through hundreds of miles of dense woodlands in the 1950s, the entire paved length of the Pan American Highway (including its 3,700-meter summit in Costa Rica) is now surrounded by croplands and *repasto*, planted pastures of aggressive African grasses such as guinea, pará, molasses, jaragua, pangola, and African star.

In 1955, some 4.7 million head of cattle grazed on 8.5 million acres of pasture. Twenty years later, over 10 million cattle occupied 20 million acres, an area exceeding that of all other agricultural land combined. Without the importation of the more palatable, productive, and aggressive colonizing varieties of African grasses, the enormous expansion of export-beef production would not have been possible.[78] The massive "Africanization" of Central America's forests and fields—the conversion of over 25 percent of its entire land mass into permanent pasture, more land than that used for all other agricultural commodities combined—is considered to be the most dramatic socially created ecological transformation in the region's history.[79]

Countless numbers of unique animal, plant, and insect species found nowhere else in the world will soon be lost forever, along with the habitat for many migratory bird species that make Central America their winter home. For instance, the rapidly dwindling forests of Panama lie in the path of three of the four major bird migration routes between North and South America and support 800 bird species, more than the number found in the United States and Canada combined.

At least twenty-four major species of wildlife are now threatened with extinction in Honduras and Guatemala, including jaguars, pumas, river otters, manatees, tapirs, ocelots, giant anteaters, crested eagles, and other large animals (particularly mammals), which require expansive areas of primary tropical forest to survive.[80] These genetic storehouses are for all practical purposes nonrenewable, since certain lowland rainforest ecosystems require a successional process of 1,000 years after large-scale clearing before a full primary status can be achieved once again—if ever. The destruction of these unique and wonderful ecosystems represents, in Norman Myers's words, "one of the greatest biological debacles to occur on the face of the Earth."[81]

Costa Rica is symptomatic of the crisis. Although it possesses the most extensive park system in Central America, covering some 22 percent (or 4,417 square miles) of the country, Costa Rica also has the highest national deforestation rate (6.6 percent) of any country in Latin America, including Brazil and Ecuador.[82] Often touted as a model of conservation for the Third World, the Costa Rican government is finding itself increasingly unable and unwilling to reconcile the intensifying conflict that pits environmental protection and growing inequality against a debt-ridden economy dependent upon the export of cheap renewable and nonrenewable resources.

Numerous species of flora and fauna, particularly larger mammals, are dependent on these relatively small islands of preservation in a sea of ecological devastation. But their survival requires much larger territories than the rapidly dwindling forests remaining in the country's parks and protected areas in immediate danger of extinction. All species of cat and monkey are endangered, a condition aggravated by illegal commercial hunting. Also among the country's sixteen officially endangered animal species are the tapir, manatee, two highland squirrels, and the giant ant-eater. Eleven species of birds are also endangered, including seven birds of prey.[83]

Most of Costa Rica's parks are not even adequately maintained, but menaced by encroaching cattle ranchers and growing numbers of displaced peasants who move into protected areas to begin farming and/or mining. Over the last decade, United Brands and other producers switched from banana production on some of their plantations to the more profitable but less labor-intensive palm oil. Thousands of unemployed banana workers have since traveled into the tropical forests of Corcovado National Park to mine gold and poach wildlife, resulting in deforestation, habitat destruction, siltation, and soil erosion.[84]

The Failure of Deforestation for Development

Development on the agricultural frontier through the destruction of tropical rainforests has proved to be an economic and ecological disaster in Central America. Unlike the rich volcanic soils found in the highland and Pacific coastal regions, which can support intensive cattle ranching indefinitely given the proper care, the soils underlying the Caribbean rainforests are mostly poor, their nutrients leached by millions of years of torrential rains. Rather than residing in the shallow and poorly drained soils underneath the ground, about 90 percent of the ecosystem's nutrients exist in the biomass which makes up the living canopy of plants and the thin layer of humus above the ground.

In the words of Douglas Shane, "some sixty million years of evolution have enabled the flora of the tropical forest to perfect methods of capturing and storing essential nutrients such as nitrogen, calcium, potassium and phosphorus before they are flushed into ubiquitous river systems."[85] Once this protective canopy is cut and burned, rainforest soils lose the ability to replenish nutrients, which quickly leach beyond the shallow root zones of newly planted pasture grasses and food crops. The natural biomass that sustains the maintenance of nutrients in the ecosystem is quickly reduced to a low biomass with little storage capacity.

Nearly 9,000 of the more than 22,400 families to have received land under the Honduran agrarian reform over the last thirteen years have been forced to abandon their plots.[86] Soils with high clay contents common to Central America's rainforest zones are particularly vulnerable, as noted above, literally turning into brick once exposed to compaction by grazing cattle, torrential rains, and the blazing sun. Other soils high in acid eventually kill pasture grasses in a few short years, giving birth to noxious weeds and insect pests. The neurotoxins emitted by these poisonous weeds accumulate in the grazing cattle, often resulting in their death. James J. Parsons notes: "Unless carefully managed, and usually fertilized, both planted and natural grasses become sparse or woody with overgrowth, trampling, compaction, and declining soil fertility."[87]

What was once an oasis of jungle life is quickly reduced to a weed-infested wasteland. As the soil degrades, large ranchers clear new areas for pasture, exacerbating destruction of the jungle and displacement of small farmers. Ranchers then typically raise one head of cattle per 2.5 acres during the first seven years of production, but as the soil again deteriorates over the following five to ten years some twelve to seventeen acres of land are needed for each head of cattle. New areas are deforested once again. Grazing still occurs on older pastures until it is no longer productive, at which point it is abandoned. (In some areas, the poor condition of pastures and animal health, high operating costs, and low prices have combined to wipe out any potential profits for the cattle ranchers. Many would not survive economically without alternative sources of income.)[88]

By then the damage to the land is usually permanent. Unlike peasant-based agriculture, which allows for the regeneration of secondary forest growth after the land is abandoned, the use of African pasture grasses and overgrazing deters the secondary rejuvenation of the jungle, obstructing the processes by which nature "heals itself."[89]

One of the most serious long-term environmental impacts of overgrazing in both the Pacific and Caribbean lowlands is soil compaction (or hardening of the ground). In turn, this problem impedes drainage and reduces soil permeability, resulting in more rapid water runoff, accelerated wind and water erosion of the soil, and eventual gully formation, particularly in hillier terrains. Already over 17 percent of Costa Rica is severely eroded and 24 percent moderately eroded. Soil losses, 80 percent of which are caused by overgrazing on degraded pasture lands, reaches an astounding 680 million tons a year, choking waterways with sediment and causing millions of dollars in damage to hydroelectric facilities, which provide over 80 percent of the nation's electricity. Erosion rates are particularly severe on pasture lands in wetter forest zones, averaging an incredible 162 to 324 metric tons per acre annually. Virtually every major watershed in the country is seriously degraded.[90]

In the once-vast rainforests of the Petén in Guatemala, which have lost over five million cubic meters of wood since 1969, annual soil losses on degraded pasture lands is between 1,813 and 2,849 metric tons per square mile.[91] Such massive erosion leads to great fluctuations in the water table (including drought stress in the dry season and flooding in the rainy season), as rapid runoff from the compacted lands allows smaller amounts of moisture to be absorbed into the ground, disrupting the nutri-ent recycling systems of the soil.[92] Considerable soil erosion and sedi-mentation has already damaged the Motagua, Sarstún, and Polochic rivers and watersheds surrounding Lake Izabal, Guatemala's largest lake.[93]

The widespread destruction of forests for cattle ranching is also re-sulting in regional climatic changes. A pristine rainforest canopy acts as a protective umbrella, breaking the force of torrential downpours and recy-cling the moisture throughout the ecosystem. But with the clearing of the forest, water-recycling systems are destroyed. Daytime temperatures rise on the converted savannas, decreasing relative humidity and precipitation levels while increasing the rate of transpiration.[94] As a result, the grass-lands and surrounding forests suffer from increased drought stress.[95]

In fact, regional rainfall is declining as much as one-third of an inch annually, reflecting marked alterations in the climate.[96] In central Panama, deforestation has reduced the average annual rainfall some 17 inches over the last fifty years.[97] When it does rain, the water rushes off the barren slopes to cause downstream flooding, soil erosion, and siltation of water-ways.[98]

Localized climatic changes also occur with the cooler nighttime and warmer daytime temperatures radiated by deforested lands. According to a USAID report, almost 40 percent of Nicaragua's landscape is affected by significant changes in climate, hydrology, soil conditions, and bio-logical complexity.[99] How the so-called "greenhouse effect" and global climate are affected by the destruction of Central America's forest, and in particular by the release of carbon dioxide from burning forests and meth-ane gases from cattle wastes, remains unknown.[100]

Conclusion

Despite the growing ecological and social crisis posed by the destruction of Central America's tropical rainforests, the region's ruling classes are showing little interest in exploring more sustainable and socially just modes of production. Tropical rainforests are indeed a rich environment for effi-ciently and sustainably growing food—as various indigenous populations have demonstrated in practice. The Lacandón Maya's traditional system of rainforest agriculture produces almost 5,200 pounds of shelled corn and 4,000 pounds of root and vegetable crops per acre annually (com-pared to only 9 pounds of beef per acre under current capitalist forms of land use). The Lacandones produce these yields for five to seven con-secutive years before the forest plot is allowed to recover for five to ten years under a system of agroforestry that conserves and regenerates the rainforest biome.[101]

The wasteful exploitation of rainforests, and the misery of small farm-ers who live at their edge, could be ended through the implementation of "sustainable agrarian reform measures" based on the replacement of cereals, roots, and grasses with alternative diversified tree-crops or multistoried forms of agriculture.[102] Another option would be to redistribute prime farmland in the capitalist export sector to the rural poor majorities of Central America, as was done in revolutionary Nicaragua during the 1980s. This not only reduced hunger and poverty in that country, but also greatly diminished peasant migration to the tropical rainforest.[103]

In either case, meaningful agrarian and economic reform offers the best hope of ending deforestation and bringing a more equitable, ecologically sustainable mode of life to the people of Central America. But due to the threat that these alternative measures pose to the economic wealth and political power of landed oligarchs and the agrarian bourgeoisie, the governments they control are unwilling to promote these more sustainable production systems. Their solution to growing ecological degradation is to keep destroying more tropical rainforests through the forces of repression, and in the process reproducing the social and ecological crisis endemic to the rest of the region.

Time is running out. The remaining jungle will be lost forever, unless major political and economic changes which present viable alternatives to the destruction of tropical rainforests soon take place. This must include the implementation of genuine and comprehensive agrarian reform designed to eliminate the impoverishment of the peasantry. With peaceful avenues to democratic change currently blocked by militarization and U.S. foreign policy, it may be that the only hope for an end to the destruction is the revolutionary struggle being waged in the rainforests of Central America.

Notes

1. Active in the Guerrilla Army of the Poor in Guatemala, Payeras is the author of numerous works on ecology, short stories, poetry, and children's literature. The citation is from Mario Payeras, *Days of the Jungle: The Testimony of a Guatemalan Guerrillero, 1972–1976* (New York: Monthly Review Press, 1983), p. 19.

2. The story of the León family, a composite of Costa Rican peasants, is taken from Daniel Faber, with Joshua Karliner and Robert Rice, *Central America: Roots of Environmental Destruction*, Green Paper no. 3 (San Francisco: Environmental Project on Central America, 1986), p. 1. It is based on the personal experiences of the authors.

3. For a comprehensive discussion, see James Nations and H. Jeffrey Leonard, "Grounds of Conflict in Central America," pp. 78–81, in Andrew Maguire and Janet Welsh Brown (eds.), *Bordering on Trouble: Resources and Politics in Latin America* (Bethesda, MD: Adler and Adler, 1986); James Nations and Daniel Komer, "Rainforests and the Hamburger Society," *Environment*, April 1983, p. 12; and Joshua Karliner, "Central America's Other War," *World Policy Journal*, Fall 1989, pp. 787–810.

4. See Norman Myers, "The Hamburger Connection: How Central America's Forests Become North America's Hamburgers," *Ambio* 10, no. 1 (1981): 6.

5. See USAID-Costa Rica I, *Country Environmental Profile: A Field Study*, Prepared for USAID by Gary Hartshorn et al. (San José: Tropical Science Center, 1982), pp. 3–28; and Food and Agriculture Organization of the United Nations, *Production*, vol. 42, Statistics Series no. 88 (1988).

6. See Norman Myers, *The Primary Source: Tropical Forests and Our Future* (New York: W. W. Norton, 1984), p. 142.

7. See Steven Lyons, "Research Pact May Help Rain Forests Pay For Their Keep," *Boston Globe*, 4 November 1991, pp. 25–27.

8. See Douglas Shane, *Hoofprints on the Forest: Cattle Ranching and the Destruction of Latin America's Tropical Forests* (Philadelphia: Institute for the Study of Human Issues, 1986), p. 38.

9. For an excellent discussion of this process, see Robert Williams, *Export Agriculture and the Crisis in Central America* (Chapel Hill: University of North Carolina Press, 1986), p. 223.

10. The World Bank is composed of three major institutions: (1) the International Bank for Reconstruction and Development (IBRD); (2) the International Development Association (IDA); and (3) the International Finance Corporation (IFC). See J. Edward Taylor, "Peripheral Capitalism and Rural-Urban Migration: A Study of Population Movements in Costa Rica," *Latin American Perspectives* 7, no. 2–3 (Spring–Summer 1980): 82.

11. For a discussion, see Williams, *Export Agriculture*, p. 78.

12. Ibid., p. 223.

13. See James J. Parsons, "Forest to Pasture: Development or Destruction?," *Revista de Biología Tropical* 24 (1976): 130.

14. Williams, *Export Agriculture*, p. 80.

15. Nations and Komer, "Rainforests and the Hamburger Society."

16. For a further elaboration, see USAID-Costa Rica I, *Country Environmental Profile*, p. 26.

17. Williams, *Export Agriculture*, p. 26.

18. For an analysis of subsistence production and export beef production in Choluteca, see Billie R. DeWalt, "Microcosmic and Macrocosmic Processes of Agrarian Change in Southern Honduras: The Cattle Are Eating the Forests," pp. 165–86, in Billie DeWalt and Pertti J. Pelto (eds.), *Micro and Macro Levels of Analysis in Anthropology: Issues in Theory and Research* (Boulder: Westview Press, 1985).

19. See Taylor, "Peripheral Capitalism," pp. 83–86.

20. Guanacaste contains a little under 38 percent of Costa Rica's pasture land and about 37 percent of the nation's cattle. See Susan E. Place, "Ecological and Social Consequences of Export Beef Production in Guanacaste Province, Costa Rica" (Ph.D. diss., University of California, Los Angeles, 1981), pp. 68–90; and Williams, *Export Agriculture*, p. 113.

21. See Place, "Ecological and Social Consequences," pp. 124–31, 145–87.

22. Ibid., pp. 29–187. For a discussion of ecological protection and restoration efforts in Guanacaste, see Tensie Whelan, "Rebuilding a Tropical Forest," *Environmental Action*, November-December 1987, pp. 15–17.

23. See Shane, *Hoofprints*, p. 19; Elbert E. Miller, "The Raising and Marketing of Beef in Central America and Panama," *Journal of Tropical Geography* (Singapore), no. 41 (1975): 68; and Williams, *Export Agriculture*, p. 106.

24. Williams, *Export Agriculture*, pp. 126–27.

25. Ibid., pp. 129–34.

26. See George Black, *Triumph of the People: The Sandinista Revolution in Nicaragua* (London: Zed Press, 1981), pp. 78–82.

27. Williams, *Export Agriculture*, p. 129.

28. The northeastern region of Nicaragua's Caribbean lowlands is dominated by lowland wet forests. See USAID-Nicaragua I, *Environmental Profile of Nicaragua* (Tucson: Arid Lands Information Center, University of Arizona, 1981), pp. 34–37.

29. See Nations and Leonard, "Grounds of Conflict," pp. 55–100.

30. See Parsons, "Forest to Pasture," p. 124; and James D. Nations and Daniel I. Komer, "Tropical Rainforests in Post-Revolution Nicaragua," unpublished manuscript (Austin: Center for Human Ecology, 1983b), p. 11.

31. Williams, *Export Agriculture*, p. 106.

32. Nations and Komer, "Tropical Rainforests," p. 8.

33. Williams, *Export Agriculture*, p. 135.

34. See Jim Handy, *Gift of the Devil: A History of Guatemala* (Boston: South End Press, 1984), p. 323.

35. According to then vice-president Clemente Marroquin Rojas, American pilots flew napalm attacks on suspected guerrilla strongholds from a U.S. airbase in Panama. See ibid., pp. 218–33; and Williams, *Export Agriculture*, pp. 134–38.

36. Ibid.; and Handy, *Gift of the Devil*, pp. 218–22.

37. For a discussion, see James Painter, *Guatemala: False Hope, False Freedom* (London: Latin America Bureau, 1987), pp. 47–57.

38. See USAID-Guatemala I, *Draft Environmental Profile of Guatemala* (Athens: Institute of Ecology, University of Georgia, 1981), p. 5.

39. Williams, *Export Agriculture*, pp. 141–42.

40. See Michael McClintock, *The American Connection: State Terror and Popular Resistance in Guatemala*, vol. 2 (London: Zed Press, 1985), pp. 132–36.

41. See also Rigoberta Menchú, *I, Rigoberta Menchú: An Indian Woman in Guatemala*, edited by Elizabeth Burgos-Debray (London: Verso Books, 1984); and George Black, *Garrison Guatemala* (London: Zed Books, 1984).

42. Williams, *Export Agriculture*, p. 143.

43. McClintock, *The American Connection*, vol. 2, p. 136.

44. See Florence Gardner, with Yaakov Garb and Marta Williams, *Guatemala: A Political Ecology*, Green Paper no. 5 (San Francisco: Environmental Project on Central America, 1990), pp. 9, 12.

45. Ibid.

46. Ibid.

47. Handy, *Gift of the Devil*, pp. 219–20.

48. Gardner, Garb, and Williams, *Guatemala*, p. 7; and Guatemala News and Information Bureau, "CELGUSA: An Environmental Disaster in the Making," *Report on Guatemala* (Oakland: GNIB, Spring 1990).

49. See Karen Parker, *Fumigation Programs in Guatemala* (San Francisco: Association of Humanitarian Lawyers, 1989); and Gardner et al., *Guatemala*, p. 13.

50. See Daniel Faber, "Imperialism, Revolution, and the Ecological Crisis of Central America," *Latin American Perspectives* 19, no. 1 (Winter 1992): 17–44.

51. Nations and Komer, "Tropical Rainforests," pp. 13–14.

52. Parsons, "Forest to Pasture," p. 122.

53. For descriptions of this process, see Jefferson Boyer, "Agrarian Capitalism and Peasant Praxis in Southern Honduras" (Ph.D. diss., University of North Carolina, Chapel Hill, 1983); and Nations and Komer, "Rainforests and the Hamburger Society," pp. 13–14; Parsons, "Forest to Pasture," p. 122; and Williams, *Export Agriculture*, p. 114.

54. See USAID-Honduras II, *Country Environmental Profile: A Field Study*, prepared by Paul Campanella et al. (McLean, VA: JRB Associates, 1982), pp. 61–76.

55. Nations and Leonard, "Grounds of Conflict," pp. 78–81.

56. USAID-Guatemala I, *Draft Environmental Profile*, pp. 17–18.

57. Nations and Komer, "Rainforests and the Hamburger Society," p. 14.

58. For example, see Paul D. Lopes, "The Agrarian Crisis in Modern Guatemala" (Master's thesis, University of Wisconsin, Madison, 1986), pp. 68–77.

59. Faber, Karliner, and Rice, *Roots of Environmental Destruction*, p. 3.

60. Nations and Komer, "Tropical Rainforests," p. 10.

61. See Laura Enríquez, *Harvesting Change: Labor and Agrarian Reform in Nicaragua, 1979–1990* (Chapel Hill: University of North Carolina Press, 1991), pp. 50–51.

62. Nations and Leonard, "Grounds of Conflict," p. 61.

63. See James Nations and Daniel Komer, "Indians, Immigrants and Beef Exports: Deforestation in Central America," *Cultural Survival Quarterly* 6, no. 2 (Spring 1982): 12.

64. For an excellent discussion of this account, see Enríquez, *Harvesting Change*, pp. 51–53; and Black, *Triumph of the People*, p. 89.

65. See Nancy Peckenham, "Land Settlement in the Petén," *Latin American Perspectives* 7 (Spring–Summer 1980): 169–77; and John L. Fielder, "Commentary on Land Settlement in the Petén: Response to Nancy Peckenham," *Latin American Perspectives* 10, no. 1 (Winter 1983): 120–23.

66. For an excellent discussion, see Handy, *Gift of the Devil*, pp. 213–18.

67. For an excellent discussion, see McClintock, vol. 2, pp. 324–44.

68. See Myers, "The Hamburger Connection," p. 4; and Myers and Tucker, "Deforestation in Central America: Spanish Legacy and North American Consumers," *Environmental Review*, Spring 1987, p. 66.

69. Nations and Leonard, "Grounds of Conflict," 72.

70. See Jeffrey Leonard, *Natural Resources and Economic Development in Central America: A Regional Environmental Profile* (New Brunswick, NJ: Transaction Books, 1987), p. 7.

71. Myers and Tucker, "Deforestation," p. 31; and Williams, *Export Agriculture*, p. 99.

72. Myers and Tucker, "Deforestation," p. 65.

73. Parsons, "Forest to Pasture," p. 124; and Nations and Komer, "Tropical Rainforests," p. 11.

74. Nations and Komer, "Rainforests and the Hamburger Society."

75. Shane, *Hoofprints*, p. 91; Williams, *Export Agriculture*, pp. 84–100; and Robert H. Holden, "Central America Is Growing More Beef and Eating Less, as the Hamburger Connection Widens," *Multinational Monitor*, October 1981, p. 17.

76. Nations and Komer, "Rainforests," p. 18. See also Shane, *Hoofprints*, pp. 91–93; and Myers, "The Hamburger Connection," p. 4.

77. Shane, *Hoofprints*, p. 77; Myers and Tucker, "Deforestation," p. 67; and U.S. Department of Agriculture, *U.S. Agricultural Imports—Period: Jan. 1990– Dec. 1991* (17 June 1992), p. 001.

78. Parsons, "Forest to Pasture," pp. 121–31; and Williams, *Export Agriculture*, p. 113.

79. Leonard, *Natural Resources and Economic Development*, p. 99.

80. There are at least 112 species of mammals, over 700 birds, and 196 reptiles and amphibians in Honduras. See USAID-Honduras II, *Country Environmental*

Profile, pp. 141–44; USAID-Guatemala I, *Draft Environmental Profile*, pp. 10–11; and James Nations and Daniel Komer, *Conservation in Guatemala*, unpublished manuscript (Austin: Center for Human Ecology, 1984), p. 31.

81. Myers, "The Hamburger Connection," pp. 3–8.

82. See Steven A. Sader and Armond T. Joyce, "Deforestation Rates and Trends in Costa Rica, 1940 to 1983," *Biotrópica* 20, no. 1 (1988), p. 14.

83. See USAID-Costa Rica I, *Country Environmental Profile*, pp. 42–50.

84. See Al Buchanan, "Costa Rica's Wild West," *Sierra* (July/August 1985). For a discussion of national parks and wildlife conservation in Central America, see Faber, Karliner, and Rice, *Roots of Environmental Destruction*, pp. 3–5.

85. Shane, *Hoofprints*, p. 11.

86. See Charles D. Brockett, *Land, Power, and Poverty: Agrarian Transformation and Political Conflict in Central America* (Boston: Unwin Hyman, 1988), pp. 133–34.

87. For an elaboration, see Parsons, "Forest to Pasture," p. 127.

88. Nations and Leonard, "Grounds of Conflict," pp. 73–74.

89. Williams, *Export Agriculture*, 73.

90. USAID-Costa Rica I, *Country Environmental Profile*, pp. 6–64.

91. USAID-Guatemala I, *Draft Environmental Profile*, pp. 6–64.

92. See Rexford Daubenmire, "Some Ecological Consequences of Converting Forest to Savanna in Northwestern Costa Rica," *Tropical Ecology* 13, no. 1 (1972): 40; Charles F. Bennett, "Human Influences on the Zoogeography of Panama," *Ibero-Americana* 51 (Berkeley: University of California Press, 1968), cited in Place, "Ecological and Social Consequences," pp. 101–16.

93. See USAID-Guatemala I, *Draft Environmental Profile*, pp. 17–18.

94. Nations and Leonard, "Grounds of Conflict," pp. 73–74; and Adrian Forsyth and Ken Miyata, *Tropical Nature: Life and Death in the Rain Forests of Central and South America* (New York: Charles Scribner's Sons, 1984), pp. 7–15.

95. Place, "Ecological and Social Consequences," p. 97.

96. Nations and Leonard, "Grounds of Conflict," pp. 80–81.

97. See John Lee and Ronald Taylor, "Ravage in the Rain Forests," *U.S. News & World Report*, 31 March 1986.

98. Leonard and Nations, "Grounds of Conflict," pp. 80–81.

99. USAID-Nicaragua I, *Environmental Profile*, p. 61.

100. See Charles Hall, R. P. Detwiler, Philip Bogdonoff, and Sheila Underhill, "Land Use Change and Carbon Exchange in the Tropics: I. Detailed Estimates for Costa Rica, Panama, Peru, and Bolivia," *Environmental Management* 9, no. 4 (1985): 313–34.

101. See James D. Nations, "Bearing Witness: The Lacandón Maya's Traditional Culture Survives in the Images of Gertrude Blom," *Natural History* 94, no. 3 (March 1985); and Nations and Komer, "Rainforests and the Hamburger Society," p. 15.

102. Parsons, "Forest to Pasture," pp. 127–28. For a highly sophisticated investigation of alternative systems of sustainable commercial development of rainforest ecosystems, see Joseph Tosi and Robert Voertman, "Some Environmental Factors in the Economic Development of the Tropics," *Economic Geography* 40, no. 3 (July 1964): 189–205.

103. See Joseph Collins with Frances Moore Lappé, Nick Allen, and Paul Rice, *Nicaragua: What Difference Could a Revolution Make?*, 2nd ed. (San Francisco: Institute for Food and Development Policy, 1985); and Joshua Karliner and Daniel Faber, *Nicaragua: An Environmental Perspective*, Green Paper no. 1 (San Francisco: Environmental Project on Central America, 1986).

11 José A. Lutzenberger ◆
Who Is Destroying the Amazon Rainforest?

*José A. Lutzenberger is a prominent Brazilian environmentalist. In the
years since 1987, when his article was published in* The Ecologist, *the
environmental movement has gained strength in Brazil, truly coming of
age in 1990 when President Collor de Mello named Lutzenberger to head
the newly created National Secretariat of the Environment. Following
Lutzenberger's lead, Brazilian environmentalists have begun to challenge
their government's conceptualization of "development," which is presented
in Selection 12.*

*In this article, Lutzenberger outlines how the Brazilian state's drive
for capital accumulation and power underlies the current approach to
developing the Amazon. The state has allied itself with large corporations—both multinational and Brazilian—to accomplish its program. This
technocratic view of "progress," Lutzenberger asserts, is destroying the
ecology of the Amazon and the societies and people who have adapted to
living sustainably in the rainforest. He concludes that it is not peasants
who are ultimately responsible for the destruction of the rainforest; they
are, in fact, victims of an economic and political system that drives them
to the Amazon frontier where they are forced to destroy the forest.
Lutzenberger identifies the fundamental assumptions of Brazil's development strategy as the major cause of deforestation and environmental degradation in Amazonia.*

W̶e are witnessing today in Brazil and in much of Latin America the
biggest holocaust in the history of life. Never in the course of 3,500
million years, since the first stirrings of life on this planet, has there been
such a wholesale, accelerated, violent and irreversible demolition of all
living systems as today. We have passed the point where we only des-
ecrate this or that scenic landscape, this or that ecosystem. We are now in
the process of demolishing whole biomes. Now we are getting ready to
finish off the last large, more or less intact, and contiguous jungle on
Earth, the Hylaea, or tropical rainforest in Amazonia.

This systematic destruction is being carried out in the name of "progress." The Brazilian government, the military dictatorship which set itself up in 1964, set a course for "development" at any cost. Its definition
of development is a technocratic one—an economic model geared to fast

From José A. Lutzenberger, "Who Is Destroying the Amazon Rainforest?"
The Ecologist 17, no. 4/5 (July–November 1987): 155–60. Photographs omitted.
Reprinted by permission of *The Ecologist*.

industrialization, where the highest aim is megatechnological concentration and a cash crop agriculture, with vast monocultures, to feed industry and the export market.

The Role of Multinationals

Large-scale devastation of the tropical rainforest and its surrounding transitional forests takes several forms. At one extreme we have gigantic projects. Multinational or Brazilian corporations or powerful individuals go to Amazonia to make large sums of money. Among them are such giants as Anderson Clayton, Goodyear, Volkswagen, Nixdorf Computer, Nestlé, Liquigás, Borden, Kennecott Copper, and the American multibillionaire Daniel Ludwig, or even farmers' cooperatives from the south of Brazil, such as Cotrijui. This is a very small fraction of the list which runs into hundreds. These organizations set up enormous projects—cattle ranches, paper mills, single species monocultures of exotic trees for pulp, immense rice plantations, sugarcane plantations for the "gasahol" program, timber mills, and mining operations.

More often than not, these operations are financed with state subsidies—tax rebates. That is why they are extremely wasteful and can accept scandalously low rates of productivity. On the extensive cattle ranches, the production of meat hardly reaches fifty kilograms per hectare per year, and it rapidly declines after a couple of years as the soils are leached of the scarce nutrients remaining after deforestation. The grasses and legumes sowed for pasture give way to scrub unpalatable to cattle. The scrub is then kept down with heavy machinery, annual burning, or herbicides. This contributes still more to the destruction of the soil and to still lower production. In northern Europe, on organic farms not using imported feed, meat production is closer to six hundred kilograms per hectare per year plus between four thousand and six thousand liters of milk per hectare. No milk is produced on the Amazonian cattle ranches. We must remind ourselves that the intact forest, obliterated to give way to pasture, can produce at least ten times as much food in the form of tropical fruit, game, and fish. Every single adult Brazil nut tree left standing can produce hundreds of kilos of precious food; every pupunha [pejibaye] palm tree or many of the innumerable other species of palm trees occurring in the forest can produce dozens of kilos of food, feed, and construction material. For the inhabitants of the forest there also is no shortage of firewood, a problem that is becoming extremely serious in other parts of the world.

A devastating social effect of those schemes is that they employ an average of one worker per two thousand cattle, that is, one person on at least three thousand hectares! The same area of forest could easily feed and house several hundred people if left intact. The traditional life-style of the Indian, the *caboclo* [backwoodsman], and the *seringueiro* (rubber tapper) is also much more pleasant, easy, independent, and secure than the life-style of the ranch worker. The irony is that the little meat produced is meat for export. The Amazonian *caboclo* wisely says, "Where cattle move in, we move out; cattle mean hunger." The only beneficiaries are the corporations who do not even spend money in the areas they devastate. But they keep saying that they are in the business of feeding starving humanity.

The social devastation caused by the other schemes—the extensive monoculture of trees, open-pit mining, gigantic dams, timber mills, logging on an industrial scale, commercial fishing for export—are just as bad. They are all geared to the enrichment of the powerful groups outside the region. There is no concern for the needs of the local population, much less for their life-style and culture. The local people are uprooted, marginalized, and alienated, and they go either to the slums or escape even deeper into the jungle, as long as there is jungle. The Indians are already reaching the end of the line.

The Brazilian government is now selling off whole mountains, as in the Carajás Project (see *The Ecologist*, vol. 17, no. 2/3). Recently the minister of planning boasted of having received the first down payment of a few hundred million dollars from Japan for ore to be mined in the Carajás mountains. What will future generations say?

Colonization Schemes

At the other extreme we have large-scale demolition of the forest by small settlers, but this is also due to outside forces. The State of Rondônia, in the west of Brazilian Amazonia, about the size of Great Britain, is being systematically cleared by settlers at a rate that, if continued, will leave it without forest within but a few years. The small settlers are more efficient destroyers of the forest than the big companies, who usually abide by the law that requires them to leave half the forest intact. The settler cannot stop; he must go on clearing until nothing is left. Rondônia was chosen as an escape valve. Brazil's colonization agency, Instituto Nacional de Colonizaçao e Reforma Agraria (INCRA), circulates whole-page ads showing aerial views of forest being cleared by settlers. The legend says, "Brazil is making the largest agrarian reform in the world." But these settlement schemes are conceived precisely in order not to have to face agrarian reform in other regions. The settlers come from the northeast where landlords have always prevented a healthy peasant culture from developing and from the south, where soybean monoculture, producing feed for the cows that produce the "butter mountain" of the [European] Common Market, also drives thousands of people off their land. Farther north, in central Brazil, the gasahol program is also displacing masses of people.

The migrants from the south often form the third wave of migration in a century. German and Italian immigrants came to the old colonies in Rio Grande do Sul and Santa Catarina in the last century. Their descendants first moved to the Uruguay river valley [in southeast Brazil]. In the 1950s, they moved to West Paraná, then on to southern Mato Grosso. The frequency of migration waves is becoming shorter. Some families are now moving for the second time. They will probably not stay long in Rondônia.

Hundreds of migrants arrive in Rondônia every day in addition to those unhappy people, much more numerous, who can only escape to the slums of the big cities. Some of the migrants try to settle on their own. They simply move to jungle areas as they become accessible through the new penetration roads that are constantly being opened by the road authorities. If they are lucky, they eventually get title to the land they settle on. For this they have to prove that they have made "improvements" on it. INCRA accepts as improvement the clearing of forest. Hence every settler cuts down as much forest as he can, often much more than the area he can cultivate. Some clear hundreds or thousands of hectares. Many of the settlers go from one clearing to another. As soon as they get title or sufficient proof of property, they sell to the bigger estates and move on. We have met settlers who make a living out of such land speculation.

More generally, not so much in Rondônia, but in other remote regions of Brazil, the wild settler is soon displaced by someone who comes with "legal" title to enormous tracts of land. The settler is then considered a squatter and driven off by the *jagunço* or hired gunman. No records are kept of the names and numbers of those who disappear.

Where the migrants settle legally, they end up in the settlement schemes of INCRA. These schemes are another example of the total disregard for the Amazonian landscape and its people. The division of the land is conceived on the drawing board. A checkerboard-like pattern is imposed on the land without the slightest concern whatever for topography, steep slopes, rock outcroppings, little rivers or brooks, much less ecosystems—a concept that does not exist in the heads of INCRA planners. The lots are 250 meters by 1,000 meters or 500 meters by 2,000 meters or even 4,000 meters. Thus, the farmer actually gets a long strip of land. In some cases his strip cuts across the same waterway several times as it meanders through the forest. He will have to build several bridges. Another farmer may have no access whatever to water, or his land may cut across two steep slopes with two high plateaus and some lowland in between or vice versa. Inevitably he will cut down the forest on the slope. The soil will be eroded away after the first harvest, if there is a first harvest. Even the areas officially left as forest reserves are marked on the map as geometric shapes, somewhere in a corner of the project, without reference to landscape. There is absolutely no provision for the preservation of these areas. The INCRA people say it is the responsibility of the

Instituto Brasileiro de Desenvolvimento Florestal (IBDF)—the forestry agency; IBDF says it has no means to take care of the reserves. In no time they are destroyed by illegal settlers. It often seems as if the whole scheme is deliberately set up so as to guarantee maximum devastation.

The farmers are left to themselves. There is no agricultural extension service worthy of the name. Government extension agencies promote cash crops, and the credit system is geared to monoculture. Most credit plans include a certain percentage of the money for pesticides and chemical fertilizer, regardless of need. Cash crop monoculture is controlled by specialized agencies such as CEPLAC for cocoa, IBC for coffee, and SUDHEVEA for rubber tree plantations. Each agency insists on pure monoculture. Where farmers, out of their own wisdom, make mixed stands of coffee, cocoa, rubber, and citrus trees, the agencies threaten to cut credit unless the farmers turn to pure monoculture of the respective crop. But practice has shown that mixed stands make for healthier plants, require less or no pesticides, and produce more on a more sustainable basis.

Socially, too, the settlement schemes are very disruptive. First, they help to prevent the necessary reforms in the regions where the migrants come from; second, they destroy the existing social fabric in the settlement areas; and third, the new settlers soon run into serious trouble when their soils become degraded and there is no more virgin forest to move into. We have seen settlers on soil so poor that even in the ashes of the clearing, their harvests were not enough for survival.

Local Indians are pitilessly liquidated, the survivors being driven even deeper into the remaining jungle, until they meet colonists advancing in the other direction. Moreover, the rainforest Indians are extremely vulnerable to Western diseases, such as the common cold, measles, and venereal disease. As soon as a tribe makes contact with the "civilized" invaders, they face lethal epidemics. Often as many as 90 percent of a group die within a few years. For the few survivors, it is the end of their culture. It is sad to see the total demoralization of the so-called civilized Indian.

The disappearance of the rainforest Indian cultures is perhaps one of the greatest tragedies of our time. The rainforest Indian is a true ecologist. He knows the forest as no modern ecologist can possibly know it. He reveres it. Yet we are exterminating the Indians before we can even learn from them. Our indecent life-style seems to be trying to make sure that, when it collapses, there will be no alternative life-styles left to take its place.

Traditional Industries Destroyed

The new settlements also displace the *caboclo* and the *seringueiro*. The *caboclo*, the successor of the Indian, is usually of mixed stock, white and Indian, sometimes Negro. He lives in the forest, surviving on shifting agriculture and as a hunter/gatherer. His life-style is quite compatible with the survival of the forest, as long as his population does not increase too much. But we are still very far from that. He has no reverence for the forest and its animal life but he keeps much of Indian wisdom.

There is also the small logger. His life-style is compatible with the survival of the rainforest. He logs only on the floodplains from where he can take his logs out when the water is high, making rafts for transportation to small lumber mills. Felling is selective with little harm to other trees. The floodplains represent the only really fertile soils in the rainforest, being fertilized every year by the annual flood. . . . Trees grow fast on the floodplains. Old loggers often resume logging where they started in their youth. In twenty to thirty years enormous trees grow back, of a size it would take two centuries to grow in Europe.

Where the big multinational logging companies or the large timber companies from the south of Brazil move in, the situation is quite different. They do not limit their activities to the floodplains but operate mostly on the highlands, where soils are extremely poor and regeneration is therefore much more difficult. They also use heavy machinery, causing tremendous degradation, often destroying the whole ecosystem. They are required by law to "reforest." But reforestation consists only of commercial monocultures. This reforestation is often done by specialized companies. The law does not require reforestation to be made in the place where the forest was logged; it is often done somewhere else, even thousands of kilometers away. The reforestation companies often destroy natural ecosystems, other forests, for their plantations. This is so because it is easier to get large tracts of contiguous land in the remaining wilderness areas. The "reforested" area is also almost always much smaller than the area of forest destroyed by logging. There is no supervision and bribing is easy.

Local fishermen, who until recently provided 60 percent of Amazonia's protein, are also being driven off by commercial fishing boats. It is often said . . . that the Amazon can feed the world with fish protein. That is another illusion. There is enough fish for a growing local population but not for a large-scale export business. The Amazonian rivers are incredibly rich in fish. There are more than one thousand different species. Many have not even been classified by zoologists. But there is very little primary production [growth of aquatic plants] in most of the Amazonian rivers. Fish life is mostly dependent on the forest, especially the forest on the floodplains. Many species feed on fruit or forest residues only during the high-water season when they leave the river bed and spread out into the plain. The rest of the year they live off their fat reserves. The destruction of the floodplain forests and of the forests along the smaller waterways in the highlands contributes directly to the diminution of water fauna. Even today there is overfishing. Some important species such as the pirarucu and the tambaqui are nearing extinction and the manatee is very close to extinction. Commercial fishing is also extremely wasteful. It is now common practice for fishing boats to throw overboard whole loads of commercially less valuable fish when they hit upon a school of more valuable species. The commercial fishing fleets have autonomy over thousands of kilometers. In many areas the local population already complains that it is becoming difficult to catch the fish it needs.

Finally, there is the *seringueiro*, or rubber tapper. Like the Indian, he has no sense of land ownership but he has a sense of territory! Each *seringueiro* has his *estrada* or road. He may walk as much as thirty kilometers a day collecting the latex. Today he is no more the slave laborer he was in the past. His transistor radio informs him of the rubber price in São Paulo or Chicago. He makes between five and seven hundred dollars a month, as much as a metal worker in São Paulo, but he has no expenses. He derives most of his food from the forest and the river. He also has no transportation costs. Yet the colonization programs are displacing the *seringueiro*, too. Another life-style compatible with the forest is being destroyed.

Brazil imports two-thirds of its natural rubber consumption of approximately ninety thousand tons a year. By helping the *seringueiro* and by increasing the density of the rubber trees in the forest, which has already been proved possible by some small private enterprises, Brazil could easily have enough natural rubber for export. The monocultures of rubber trees that are now being promoted by the government will probably not last long. The experiment carried out in the 1930s by Ford was a failure. In monoculture the rubber tree is subject to all kinds of pest attacks.

The rubber tapper's income comes not only from rubber; he also collects Brazil nuts. He would be the ideal forest guard, requiring no pay from the government; and although in the past he contributed to the slaughter of the Indians, today, in many areas, rubber tappers and Indians have learned to live together in harmony. . . .

The federal government sees no difficulties in granting the rich title to tens of thousands or even hundreds of thousands of hectares, but it hardly ever gives useful tracts of land to the small operator. I visited one big project in Rondônia; it belonged to a firm that grew powerful in the south by devastating Araucaria forests. Some twenty thousand hectares were being put to pasture and an area much bigger was being logged. On this project, the company closed the road via which the *seringueiro*s not affected by the project used to bring out their rubber and forced them to sell all the rubber to the company at prices far below market prices.

The life-style of Indians, *caboclos*, and *seringueiro*s is compatible with the survival of the forest. Their life-style could easily be improved socially and ecologically by teaching them better cropping and collecting or fishing methods, storage methods, and hygiene. Almost nothing is being done in that direction, even though some very interesting research work already carried out at the Amazonian research agency (INPA) has shown how permaculture with palm trees, breadfruit, and others can produce up to ten times as much food per acre as the shifting agriculture now practiced by the *caboclo* and *seringueiro*. But official philosophy sees only backwardness in subsistence farming, even if it makes people happier. There is also no concern whatever for sustainability.

Poor Not to Blame

In Rondônia it is very easy to see how devastation, even when it is committed by small farmers, is always caused by the shortsightedness and greed of the powerful. The settlements now demolishing the forest in Rondônia are part of a classical colonialist structure of dependence and export. In the new towns of Rondônia, growing like mushrooms, it is almost impossible to find locally produced articles in the shops. Everything, even the broiler or the salad in the restaurant, comes from the industrial south. While enormous quantities of wood go up in smoke or rot in the fields, people cook with bottled gas brought in by truck over 2,500 kilometers. Local power stations also burn petroleum that comes by truck after crossing the ocean on its way from the Persian Gulf. Where the Madeira River passes the capital of Rondônia, Pôrto Velho, one can see thousands of tons of wood, logs, branches, whole trees, floating downriver. No attempt is made to use that wood. When a region has to import everything it consumes, it must pay with exports. Hence the agricultural policy of promoting only cash crops.

While unsustainable forms of agriculture are destroying the tropical rainforest in Rondônia, the regions in the south, from where many of the migrants come, are also being raped. Soybean monoculture to feed cows in the [European] Common Market, rather than people in Brazil, is causing erosion on a scale never seen before. All the rivers are dark brown or red with clay and silt. Monoculture is also destroying what is left of peasant culture. These soils could support a sustainable form of highly productive and diversified agriculture. Now food production in the former peasant regions is going down drastically. In the more mountainous areas of Santa Catarina, farmers plant corn on steep slopes, at enormous costs in terms of erosion, in order to rear chickens for export to Saudi Arabia. The farmers themselves often buy their food in the supermarket, the eggs and vegetables being imported from São Paulo.

If the methods of organic farming were promoted on the good, fertile soils in the south, the northeast, and in central Brazil, and only in those areas already cleared, without touching remaining wilderness, this would dramatically increase productivity with less pollution and erosion. Migration could cease, and could even be reversed. . . . A small step in the direction of organic soil management would immediately lead to dramatic increases in production with equally significant increases in employment.

Brazil need not give up its present exports and could still produce more food. We already have a few examples of farms attesting to that.

Amazonia should be left to the Amazonians. The growth of capital and power at the expense of the ecology and the people of Amazonia is classical imperialism. It makes no difference whether the benefits accrue to powers from overseas or from other parts of Brazil.

Brazil's politics toward Amazonia must change. And they must change within this decade—or it will be too late!

---

12 Tadeu Valadares ◆
Deforestation: A Brazilian Perspective

Tadeu Valadares, a Brazilian diplomat, expresses his government's perspective on the role of the Amazon rainforest in the nation's development. In this 1991 essay he does not question the desirability of developing the rainforest but instead focuses on how to develop rational policies for the use of the region's resources. Valadares admits that the government, especially during the military dictatorship, made mistakes in its management of the Amazon rainforest. He points out, however, that the Nossa Natureza ("Our Nature") program announced by the Sarney government in 1988 offers a plan for incorporating the Amazon into the national economy without destroying the region's ecosystems. He claims that Brazil's new environmental program has benefited from past mistakes—especially those of today's industrialized developed countries (such as the United States), whose predatory actions during their own economic take-off seriously degraded the environment.

With the implementation of this and other environmental laws, the Brazilian government is attempting to bridge the gap between theory and practice. Coming in response to criticism by foreign as well as domestic environmentalists and development experts, Nossa Natureza represents a new recognition of the legitimate concerns and rights of various previously neglected groups of forest dwellers, as well as the need to maintain environmental health. It fails to address, however, some important factors in the destruction of the tropical rainforest, such as road building and large dam projects. The government's environmental policy also reveals how sensitive Brazil (like most Latin American countries) is about the issue of national sovereignty. Its distrust and resentment of attempts

From Tadeu Valadares, "Deforestation: A Brazilian Perspective," in *Economic Development and Environmental Protection in Latin America*, ed. Joseph S. Tulchin and Andrew I. Rudman (Boulder: Lynne Rienner Publishers, 1991), 55–59. © 1991 by the Woodrow Wilson International Center for Scholars. Reprinted by permission of Lynne Rienner Publishers.

by foreigners to dictate how to develop the Amazon is revealed clearly in Valadares's closing remarks: "All other governments and international organizations must recognize that the Brazilian Amazon is first and foremost Brazilian."

In order to tackle the subject of deforestation in a rational and unemotional way, we must take into consideration a few preliminary facts. In a sense these facts are interconnected with the deplorable phenomenon of uncontrolled and illegal burning of forested areas in the Brazilian Amazon. First, in order to conduct a fair analysis of the problem, the sheer magnitude of the Legal Amazon must be acknowledged. This huge region comprises 60 percent of Brazil—approximately 5 million square kilometers. The area covered by the humid forest comprises only slightly more than half of this total, 2.8 million square kilometers. Recognition of the geographical extension of this continent within a continent helps one immediately understand the relevance of the Amazon for Brazil. The Amazon basin has an undeniable strategic significance for Brazil's national development. The integration of the Amazon basin into the national political economy is a goal shared by all informed citizens. Thus, how to mix the resources of the Amazon with other facets of the Brazilian economy is a topic of lively discussion. What is agreed upon by all, however, is that Brazil will be truly developed only if rational policies conducive to the optimum use of the resources offered by our tropical forest are devised and implemented immediately.

Approximately eighteen million people live within the boundaries of this gigantic area. This figure includes eight hundred thousand *garimpeiros* (mineral diggers) and less than two hundred thousand Indians. The inhabitants of the Legal Amazon are the manifestation of a larger historical process of population growth that gained momentum in the last two decades. In 1970 the Amazonian population was only 3.6 million; by 1980 the population had reached 7.6 million. The region is still experiencing rapid growth, as significant waves of migrants from other areas of Brazil are attracted there. From a demographic viewpoint, however, the region may be considered underpopulated.

The region's economy is characterized by all of the economic and social indicators usually associated with acute underdevelopment. Aside from a fragile urban economy based largely on trade, services, administrative activities, and fledgling industries, the mainstay of Amazonian economic growth continues to be agriculture, cattle raising, mining, and, to a much lesser degree, extractive industries. It is interesting to note that between 1970 and 1985 the number of rural properties increased by 91 percent and the number of cattle herds more than doubled.

The rural economy is characterized by a mix of large and small properties. Smallholders usually practice some kind of subsistence agriculture using a primitive technique, the *coivaras*, which consists of burning trees and secondary vegetation (*capoeiras*) in order to prepare the soil for agricultural use. Although this is a source of deforestation, the *coivaras* have only a minor impact on the deforestation problem. Ignacio Rangel, one of Brazil's most respected economists, affirms: "Much of the most terrible devastation we have observed, especially in the Amazon, is not the smallholders' responsibility. It is the result of actions undertaken by large capitalist entrepreneurs." But Rangel emphasizes that the aggressive pattern of behavior displayed by some large agricultural enterprises may change over time as a result of technological progress and applied scientific expertise. On the other hand, the impoverished small producer lacks the financial resources that would enable him to use mechanical equipment and employ modern agronomic techniques and is therefore bound to continue using primitive techniques that invariably affect the environment in a negative way.

The uncontrolled and illegal burning of the forest is a most serious problem. The Brazilian government, civil society, and an absolute majority of public opinion are highly sensitive to the menace created by this vandalism. The indiscriminate burning of the forest irreversibly destroys one of our largest sources of future wealth and potentially endangers the ecological balance of the entire region. Government figures reveal that 200,000 square kilometers of the Legal Amazon were burned in 1987 and 120,000 square kilometers were burned in 1988. The government intends to reduce this to 60,000 square kilometers through new policies, recently enacted legislation, and innovative administrative measures.

How much of the forest has already been destroyed? Some say 12 percent; others say 7 percent. The Brazilian government indicates that the deforested area probably comprises 5 percent of the Legal Amazon. The underlying meaning of these figures is the bleak reality that an enormous area of tropical rainforest is already gone and an irreplaceable amount of wealth, life, and beauty has disappeared. Additionally, this unreasonable havoc produces nearly 4 percent of the carbon dioxide contributing to the greenhouse effect that threatens global ecology. In this context, however, it is important to remember that 85 percent of the greenhouse effect is directly produced by the unbridled consumption of fossil fuels in the advanced industrialized countries.

The Brazilian government's concern with the national environment predates the current situation in which so much of the national and international media is paying close attention to the Amazon. In fact, during the 1930s the first examples of what would today be called "environmental legislation" were adopted in Brazil. The adoption of a water code and mining code, the creation of the National Department of Public Works and Sanitation, and the establishment of the first national park all occurred under [President Getúlio] Vargas at that time.

During the long military cycle that began in 1964 and lasted until 1985, additional important legislative and administrative measures were undertaken. These included a forest code, established in 1965, a 1967 law on the protection of wildlife, the integration of environmental concerns in the theory and practice of public planning, the creation of a special secretariat on environment in 1973, and the establishment of a national policy on environment in 1981. The measures demonstrate the willingness of Brazilians to address environmental issues irrespective of the character of the dominant political regime.

Nonetheless, it is also true that the environment has never received as extensive or systematic an analysis as the one undertaken by the Sarney administration. At the end of the military regime, the authoritarian model of centralized decision making resulted in an unsuccessful attempt to develop the Amazon, which in turn created an economic disruption compounded by aggressive ecological side effects. In the process of transition from authoritarianism to democracy, the Constituent Assembly drafted a new bill of rights. The final text was adopted in October 1988, and one of its most daring innovations is a new chapter that establishes the guidelines for state and society on environmental issues. Article 225 declares that the environment is a common heritage of the Brazilian people and entrusts government and society with the duty to defend and preserve it for present and future generations. Yet the unavoidable gap that exists between theory and practice, constitutional clauses and everyday life, is well known. In order to bridge this gap, President [José] Sarney launched a new environmental offensive.

On October 12, 1988, the "Our Nature" program was presented to the Brazilian people as a new landmark on the long road in pursuit of the ancient dream of incorporating the Amazon into the national economy. This is to be accomplished without the destruction of the Amazonian ecosystem, with deep awareness of past mistakes, and with a critical evaluation of the predatory models followed by today's industrialized countries when they were in the take-off stage of economic development. The main goals of the program are: (1) to halt predatory actions against the environment and renewable natural resources; (2) to create an environmental protection system for all of Brazil and specifically for the Amazon; (3) to promote environmental education and public consciousness regarding conservation of the Amazonian environment; (4) to regulate the settlement and exploitation of the Legal Amazon based on territorial planning; and (5) to protect Indian communities, the population living along the rivers, and those involved in sustained exploitation of natural resources.

This long-term effort has already produced a change in policy orientation. The government has created new forests. The Institute on the Environment was created to centralize government action concerning ecological issues, forestry exploitation, fishing, and the protection of ecological systems. A new concept of economic and social development for the Amazon is being designed, allowing for the fact that only 17 percent of the region is effectively suited for economic exploitation and that a new philosophy is needed to combine the ongoing flux of settlers with the economic and ecological potential of the area. We have recognized the need to accelerate agrarian reform in other parts of Brazil in order to diminish the waves of migrants who continue to enter the region. At the same time, Brasília adopted a new policy of giving priority to settlements in the central and western regions, ecologically less fragile than the Amazon.

The government has suspended all fiscal incentives and official credits for livestock and agricultural projects, and also prohibited exportation of timber "in natura." In the coming years the government will make a systematic effort to define areas of permanent preservation and to select microregions particularly appropriate for a range of economic activities. The government will also do whatever is necessary to enforce the law establishing 50 percent of each rural property as a protected site ("legal reserve") in forested areas. By 1995 reforestation is expected to provide 100 percent of wood consumption for all large steel projects like Grande Carajás as an additional means of protecting the rainforest. Protection of the rainforest also entails the establishment of fire prevention and extinction systems, which will be a priority of the "Our Nature" program.

The Brazilian government and civil society have clearly expressed their willingness to cooperate with other countries, international organizations, and interested institutions. In a world that is still, unfortunately, ruled by power politics and in an international arena where hegemonic behavior is an undeniable aspect of superpower strategy, the administration sets only one precondition: in order to be able to cooperate with the Brazilian government in the search for solutions to global environmental problems, all other governments and international organizations must recognize that the Brazilian Amazon is first and foremost Brazilian. When this basic fact is acknowledged by our eventual companions on the road toward an environmentally safer world, the Brazilian people are quite sure that Brazil and the international community will be able to advance the intertwined causes of economic development and sound environmental policies.

III

Why Save the Rainforest?

"Save the Rainforest" has become a rallying cry of environmentalists around the world, resulting in a high level of visibility for forest activists, especially since the Earth Summit in Rio de Janeiro in 1992. Media coverage of the issue, however, rarely includes discussion of the many underlying factors involved in rainforest destruction. This volume provides an overview of some of the most important causes of deforestation in Latin America as well as arguments for conservation. The arguments for saving the remaining rainforest tend to focus on one of several categories: ecological, economic, and cultural or ethical, although these are ultimately interrelated. The selections in Part III offer a sample of some of the more prominent arguments for tropical forest conservation. Its proponents have recently begun to take a more holistic approach, as evidenced by the prominent role of "Save the Rainforest" groups in the anti-globalization demonstrations that accompanied meetings of the World Trade Organization, World Bank, and International Monetary Fund in 1999 and 2000.

Tropical rainforests, in common with other wild ecosystems, involve a number of ecological functions that underpin our economies and sustain our lives. Referred to by some scholars as environmental services or subsidies, these processes include regulation of climate and water cycles, protection of the soil, and provision of materials that humans need for housing, fuel, and various economic activities. Tropical rainforests have many unique ecological characteristics such as the rapid cycling of nutrients to aid survival of plants in acidic infertile soils and extremely high species diversity—with many species having tiny populations patchily distributed, and many strange and wonderful relationships between different species. These characteristics make conservation of tropical rainforests a critical environmental issue. Selection 2 (in Part I of this volume) gives some background on the ecological processes of tropical rainforests.

We have come to realize that destruction of neotropical forests has the potential to affect North American environments by precipitating climatic shifts or by decreasing migrant bird populations. Many birds that breed in North America overwinter in the tropical forests of Latin America

(Selection 13). Declines in the populations of these birds, therefore, might have substantial impacts on our ecosystems—in the control of insect populations, for example. Moreover, we now know that in the Amazon a number of fish species depend on the fruits of rainforest trees as a food source during the flood season and that deforestation may adversely affect the Amazon fishery, an important source of high-quality protein for the region's inhabitants. Conversely, a serious decline in certain fish populations could affect the seed dispersal capability of various tree species particularly critical to the reestablishment of the forest in cleared areas. In fact, the biological diversity of tropical forests is so complex and poorly understood that we do not know how removing a particular species will affect the whole system (Selection 2). Modification of the forest, therefore, must be undertaken with great care so as not to destabilize the entire forest ecosystem.

The economic implications of ecological factors must also be considered. In addition to environmental services, tropical rainforests produce materials that can be turned into commodities in the world market. Selection 17 discusses a variety of land uses in southern Mexico, many of which destroy both the forest and the indigenous people who have traditionally lived there. As these people fight for the forest they also fight to preserve their culture. Studies have shown that the economic value of renewable products (such as oils, resins, nuts, and fruits) produced per hectare of wild rainforest can be greater than that produced by cattle ranches or monocultural plantations of equal size. Many tropical plants contain pharmacologically active substances of unknown potential, so that every plant that becomes extinct represents a possible loss to pharmaceutical companies and to future generations (Selection 16). Preservation of the genetic diversity of the wild progenitors of our crop plants is essential to the breeding or genetic engineering of new varieties (Selection 15). And, finally, nature tourism—ecotourism—based on the presence of wild tropical forests may generate more income in the long run for Latin American countries than the destruction of forests and the one-time exploitation of their resources. (Ecotourism is discussed in Part IV.)

A number of arguments for saving the tropical rainforest center on its human inhabitants or on the actual or theoretical relationship between humans and nature. Some are practical considerations, such as preserving tribal peoples' knowledge and wisdom about the rainforest accumulated during the hundreds or thousands of years they have coexisted with it (Selections 6, 16, and 19). The knowledge of native healers, for instance, could increase the efficiency of Westerners' search for new pharmaceuticals. Unfortunately, Native Americans' intimate knowledge of the forest and its useful properties is being lost rapidly as habitat destruction and acculturation lead to the demise of tribal cultures.

Deforestation also raises ethical questions. Increasingly, destruction of the tropical rainforest is seen as a human-rights violation against the tribal peoples who require intact forest for their physical and cultural survival. To indigenous people the tropical rainforest is not only the source of material benefits, but it is also the foundation on which their cultures are built, the resting place of their ancestors, the home of their deities. Their culture and environment are inextricably intertwined as parts of a single system. From this perspective, destruction of the tropical rainforest amounts to ethnocide. (In addition, some Westerners, such as Deep Ecologists, extend our system of ethics to include nonhuman species, arguing that all living things have an intrinsic right to exist. In their view, human beings have no right to drive other species to extinction simply because they have the technological capability to do so.)

Other scientific and anthropocentric reasons are raised for preserving natural ecosystems. If large enough, wild ecosystems constitute natural laboratories for evolution and for future scientific research and training of scientists. In addition, most humans seem to have a psychological need for wild places, both for spiritual renewal and as a respite from the stresses of our modern lifestyle. The rapidly growing visitorship to national parks, both in the United States and abroad, attests to our powerful need for nature. And finally, a long history of failed attempts to settle and exploit tropical rainforest regions such as the Amazon should cause us to approach such development with caution. Taken together, the selections in Part III provide a cautionary tale that should inform and influence planning for the future of the remaining rainforests of Latin America.

---

13 John Terborgh ◆
A Glimpse at Some Tropical Habitats

By 1980 over one-half of the total area of Central America and the Greater Antilles had been cleared of forest. Because two-thirds of the breeding pairs of North American woodland birds migrate to the Neotropics for the winter, the past decade witnessed a surge of interest in the consequences of tropical deforestation for the survival of these birds. It is clear that habitat destruction—both in North and Latin America—is a threat to the survival of species that inhabit forests. Some people believe that the ex-

From John Terborgh, "A Glimpse at Some Tropical Habitats," in *Where Have All the Birds Gone?* (Princeton: Princeton University Press, 1989), 157–66. © 1989 by Princeton University Press. Reprinted by permission of Princeton University Press.

*tinction of birds due to habitat destruction is a warning of a similar fate,
farther down the road, for other species—including our own.*

This reading, excerpted from Where Have All the Birds Gone? *(1989)
by ornithologist John Terborgh, sets forth convincingly the current threat
to birds posed by the widespread destruction of their habitats. Terborgh
argues for preservation of all the habitats (including mature tropical forests) necessary to protect the full diversity of birdlife. He argues against
accepting the fallacy of equivalency of species, which some scientists
immersed in their bird counts tend to do. He reminds us of the great variety of forest types in the American tropics and that each is home to a
different assemblage of bird species, both resident and migrant. Destruction of these forests will inevitably lead to extinction of some forest species, even if the overall number of birds remains the same (which is
doubtful). Animal species that require forest for their survival cannot just
move to another place; they must have an environment that meets their
physical and behavioral requirements. In the tropics this is particularly
important because many species have very narrow requirements and cannot easily adapt to other conditions. Some birds, although physically able
to fly, will not cross a cleared area only one hundred meters wide—the
open space creates an absolute barrier to them. Scientists are concerned
that forest clearance will lead to massive extinction of not only bird species but of many other types of plants and animals as well. We do not
know the full significance of this problem and are therefore taking a large
risk by destroying vast areas of forest.*

To the uninitiated, the word *tropics* often carries the connotation of
steamy jungles teeming with malevolent pests and awash with debili-
tating fevers. In reality, tropical landscapes are as varied, and often as
beautiful, as any one sees in the temperate regions. The vegetation may
be lush and dense, but so may it be in some temperate environments. Perhaps it is the palms, vines, and epiphytes that create the exotic flavor of
tropical vegetation. But once the novelty of these unfamiliar plant forms
has worn off, tropical habitats can be seen to be as distinct and varied as
those in the observer's homeland. The word *jungle* then ceases to have
any meaning, just as it has no place in the botanical lexicon.

The environments in which North American migrants spend the winter are at least as varied as those in which they breed. Chilly mountaintops
in Mexico, limestone scrub in the Antilles, the vast grasslands or llanos
of Venezuela and Colombia, mangroves in Panama, cloud forests on the
slopes of the Andes, the forbidding thorny fastness of the Paraguayan
chaco, even Tierra del Fuego—all provide a retreat for one species or
another.

A visitor viewing migrants for the first time in one of these environments would find both the expected and the unexpected. He or she would
be reassured to note that most species choose winter homes that bear some
obvious resemblance to their summer habitats. Louisiana waterthrushes

course along clear pebbly streams, yellow-throated warblers creep around pine boughs, willow flycatchers sally from willowlike plants along rivers, and dickcissels throng to the grasslands and ricefields of the llanos. But a visitor would also find some disconcerting exceptions, such as indigo buntings in flocks of hundreds along Yucatán roadsides; eastern kingbirds, also in large flocks, feeding on avocadolike fruits in the canopy of the Amazonian rainforest; and chimney swifts darting over the Peruvian coastal desert.

There is another surprise when one finds species in seemingly incongruous combinations. A rainforest in the Dominican Republic, for example, might have Cape May warblers and gray-cheeked thrushes from the boreal forest; black-throated blue warblers and redstarts from the Appalachians; and parula and worm-eating warblers from the eastern lowlands. There is nothing sacrosanct about the "communities" of species we find breeding together, for they recombine in many ways during the months they are beyond our purview.

It is also surprising to find so many species together. Rich eastern deciduous forests commonly harbor four to six warbler species, but perhaps due to the geographical congestion of the wintering grounds, one may find eight, ten, or even (in western Mexico) fifteen warbler species in a single homogeneous habitat (Hutto, 1980). We now see that not only are the populations of individual species geographically concentrated in the winter, but the species may also be crowded into communities of extraordinarily high diversity. Once we realize this, we can appreciate that many tropical habitats, from a conservation standpoint, are even more precious than our own. . . .

We have seen that migrants pass the winter in a diverse array of environments—high and low, wet and dry, both north and south of the equator. As time goes on, many of these natural vegetation formations are being transformed by relentless economic pressures.

The magnificent pine and fir forests of the Mexican cordilleras are being felled to build houses in the crowded cities, and the once extensive evergreen forests of Mexico's Caribbean lowlands have been reduced to mere fragments to provide pasture for an ever-expanding market for beef. Lowland dry forests in Guatemala are being cleared for cotton growing and to raise winter crops, such as melons, for the North American market. Much of the natural vegetation of Cuba and the Dominican Republic has been replaced with sugarcane fields. In Jamaica, Guatemala, Panama, and other countries, coffee growing to supply export markets has drastically reduced the amount of mid-montane forest available to migrants. Lowland rainforests in Honduras, Panama, and Ecuador are being replaced with banana plantations, again for export to richer countries in the north. African oil palms are changing the landscape in Costa Rica, Ecuador, and elsewhere. Mid-elevation cloud forest has been discovered to offer a propitious climate for dairy farming in Costa Rica, Colombia, and Ecuador. And in the future there looms the truly grim prospect that many of these countries will have to devote major portions of their national territories to biomass plantations for alcohol production to reduce the cost of petroleum imports, as Brazil is already doing. When this happens, what will become of the migrants?

Not all of them will disappear, that is certain. Some species seem to benefit from disturbance; others, to varying degrees, adapt to it; and still others, we hope a minority, will decline in proportion to the disappearance of primary habitats. If we are not to blunder blindly into this future, we should make an effort to establish which species can adapt to disturbance and which cannot. Only then can we begin to define priorities.

Winter travelers in the New World tropics commonly remark on the conspicuous abundance of migrants in early successional habitats, such as gardens, hedgerows, brushy pastures, and young second growth (Karr, 1976; Terborgh, 1980). Observations of this type have led at least one author (Monroe, 1970) to the sanguine conclusion that "opening up" the tropical forest could even lead to an increase in the capacity of the landscape to harbor overwintering migrants. If this were true, we could all rest comfortably and leave the tropical countries to cope with their own conservation problems.

But an impressionistic assessment, even if correct, should not be taken at face value without probing its implicit assumptions. Among the hidden assumptions, two are particularly crucial: first, that migrants in general would benefit; and second, that the new "habitats" generated by deforestation would be more conducive to migrants than the original forest. We shall see that neither of these projections is valid. To illustrate the point, let us proceed with . . . concrete examples.

In 1985 I surveyed migrants in the Quijos Valley of Ecuador. It is magnificent terrain on the eastern slopes of the Andes. Lush cloud forests sweep down from misty, unseen heights to roaring whitewater torrents in deep canyons below. It is the land of cock-of-the-rock and quetzal, breathtaking in its scale and beauty, but formidable of access.

The Ecuadorean government has recently completed a road down the valley to service a pipeline carrying oil from its eastern fields. When I was there in early 1985, the road was carrying a steady flow of settlers into the region, and scattered openings were beginning to punctuate the forested vistas. It is at this incipient stage in the modification of an erstwhile wilderness that one has the best opportunity to make "before" and "after" comparisons.

A representative area of natural forest contained a dazzling array of bird species, far too many to discover and enumerate in the span of a brief sojourn. Migrants were present in addition to the myriad residents, but in the verdant gloom of the cloud forest, birds of any kind were frustratingly difficult to find. It took me most of three days to accumulate an adequate sample of sightings, a hard-won goal in the brief bursts of sunlight between showers.

Yet my perseverance was rewarded. Migrants represented 16 percent of the tally. The species present were olive-sided flycatcher, Swainson's thrush, blackburnian, caerulean, golden-winged, and Canada warblers, redstart, and summer tanager—a set of birds with real class.

A few miles farther along the road, I found a narrow footpath that led sharply down a slope into one of the newly established clearings that are beginning to dot the landscape. Venturing forth, I was pleased to find that the peasant owner of this plot was cheerful and accommodating, and that his dogs were not prohibitively aggressive.

On a slope that was somewhat gentler than the rest, he was preparing pasture for a nascent herd of Brahman cattle. The forest had been cut and burned less than two years before, as one was reminded by the many charred snags that projected incongruously from the lush grass. Here, in the "after" setting, birds were conspicuous. They flew up from the edge of the path and sallied out from the many naked snags. Migrants seemed plentiful too, but *which* migrants? Not one of the species I had seen in the nearby cloud forest was in that pasture.

The total diversity of species was drastically diminished, to a mere 15 or 20 from the 150 or more that had inhabited the original forest. Gone were the colorful cocks-of-the-rock, tanagers, trogons, and hummingbirds. Flycatchers and seedeaters took their places in the pasture. As for migrants, the proportion remained about the same—18 percent—but there was only one species, the western wood pewee, instead of eight. Apparently the rough-hewn opening on the mountainside provided good conditions for hawking flying prey, for pewees were there by the dozen, sallying out from the sun-bleached branches of forest ghosts.

The lesson to be drawn from this example is a general one. When natural habitats are modified to serve human purposes, they lose the structural complexity and botanical richness that are required to maintain highly diverse bird communities. It may indeed be true that the *proportion* of migrants is unaffected by clearing the primary forest, but the total number of birds, and certainly their diversity, is bound to decline. That the birds are more conspicuous only creates a seductive illusion. . . .

"Opening up" the tropical forest does not automatically benefit migrants. The contrary impressions of earlier authors, although accurately reflecting their observations, were concerned more with quantity than quality. Disturbed habitats in some regions do support higher densities of migrants than undisturbed primary vegetation, but it is seldom true outside of lowland Amazonia that disturbed habitats support more species (Fitzpatrick et al., in press). Furthermore, it has recently been pointed out that past comparisons of migrants in primary forest versus second growth, many of which were conducted with mist nets set on the ground, neglected the forest canopy. Now that special attention has been given to the canopy it has also been found to harbor considerable numbers of migrants (Greenberg, 1981; Loiselle, 1987).

The take-home message one derives from this is that disturbance nearly always leads to simplified communities. This was especially evident in the Ecuadorean cattle pasture, but was also apparent in the comparison of abandoned Yucatán milpas [crop fields] to regenerating forest. . . . True, one might retort, but in a slash-and-burn rotation system most of the land is fallow. If the cycle length is twenty years, then perhaps only 5 to 10 percent of the landscape is under cultivation at any time. The remaining 90 to 95 percent is undergoing succession and remains as suitable habitat for a wide range of migrants.

Although this argument might literally be true, it overlooks some important facts. First, as we have seen, the migrant species that use early successional vegetation are not the same as those that inhabit primary forest. The argument assumes the equivalency of all migrants, an assumption that many would be reluctant to accept. Second, slash-and-burn agriculture is on the way out and soon will be as obsolete as the shocks of corn that used to add an autumnal flavor to the landscape in my youth. In the ever more crowded world we live in, intensive, rather than extensive, agricultural practices are, of necessity, the current trend. Any realistic model of the future is therefore better represented by the Ecuadorean cattle pasture than by the abandoned milpas in Mexico. This future does not bode well for migrants, even if they are only catbirds and yellowthroats.

Literature Cited

Fitzpatrick, J. W., S. K. Robinson, and J. Terborgh. In press. "Distribution and Abundance of North Temperate Migrants in the Amazon Basin and Eastern Andes." *Biotrópica*.

Greenberg, R. 1981. "The Abundance and Seasonality of Forest Canopy Birds on Barro Colorado Island, Panama." *Biotrópica* 12:241–51.

Hutto, R. L. 1980. "Winter Habitat Distribution of Migrant Land Birds in Western Mexico, with Specific Reference to Small Foliage-gleaning Insectivores." In Keast and Morton 1980, pp. 181–204.

Karr, J. H. 1976. "On the Relative Abundance of Migrants from the North Temperate Zone in Tropical Habitats." *Wilson Bulletin* 88:433–58.

Keast, A., and E. S. Morton, eds. 1980. *Migrant Birds in the Neotropics: Ecology, Behavior, Distribution, and Conservation.* Washington, DC: Smithsonian Institution Press.

Loiselle, B. A. 1987. "Migrant Abundance in a Costa Rican Lowland Forest Canopy." *Journal of Tropical Ecology* 3:163–68.

Monroe, B. L., Jr. 1970. "Effects of Habitat Changes on Population Levels of the Avifauna in Honduras." In *The Avifauna of Latin America*, edited by H. K. Buechner and J. H. Buechner, *Smithsonian Contributions to Zoology* 26:38–41.

Terborgh, J. W. 1980. "The Conservation Status of Neotropical Migrants: Present and Future." In Keast and Morton 1980, pp. 21–30.

---

14 David R. Francis ◆ Natural Resource Losses Reduce Costa Rican GNP Gains

Environmentalists have long been concerned about the way economists ignore the environmental consequences of economic activity such as deforestation, dismissing them as "externalities." In recent years the field of environmental economics has developed, and its focus is on the environmental aspects of our economy, especially the costs of our current system of production and consumption. Our present accounting system measures only the economic growth that results from the exploitation of natural resources, while the costs of resource degradation, including pollution, are not considered as such. (Actually, to the extent that we must pay for pollution abatement or the restoration of degraded habitats, environmental degradation actually increases the gross national product [GNP] because we count the jobs and production created but do not subtract the costs involved, especially the ones levied on future generations.)

In this article, originally published in 1991 in The Christian Science Monitor, *David R. Francis summarizes the results of a study of the Costa Rican economy by Robert Repetto, an environmental economist. Repetto found that forest clearance and subsequent agricultural practices have caused a depreciation in the value of Costa Rica's forest resources and soils on the order of 5 percent of GNP per year for the past twenty years. This translates into a 25 to 30 percent reduction in potential economic growth in that country. Studies such as Repetto's are causing some economists to call for a revision in the way GNP is calculated, to factor in the costs of environmental degradation. If this were done, under some circumstances it would make more economic sense to preserve the rainforest than to convert it to other uses.*

Between 1970 and 1989, national output in the Central American republic of Costa Rica grew at an average annual rate of 4.6 percent. To economists, that's handsome progress. It beats the high 2.5 percent annual growth in Costa Rica's population and thus raised living standards.

But to economist Robert Repetto there's a serious flaw in those numbers. They don't take account of the destruction of natural resources in this tropical democracy.

In a report of the World Resources Institute (WRI) in Washington and the Tropical Science Center in San José, Costa Rica, Mr. Repetto and several other authors note that Costa Rica's conventional national accounts record timber output, fish harvest, and crop production as income but ignore the costs of deforestation, overfishing, and soil erosion. Natural resource assets worth more than one year's gross national product (about $4.1 billion in 1984 U.S. dollars) vanished without a trace in those two decades, the study calculates.

"A nation's depletion of its natural resources—consumption of national capital—can . . . masquerade as growth for decades, even though it will clearly reduce income prospects from resource sectors in the future," notes James Gustave Speth, president of WRI. "Just as ignoring the deterioration of man-made assets skews economic assessments, so does overlooking the degradation of natural assets."

Idea Gains Favor

This idea of taking account of resource depletion in the measurements of a nation's economy is "catching on," Dr. Repetto says. Developing countries such as Mexico, El Salvador, Chile, Brazil, the Philippines, Indonesia, Malaysia, and India have been studying the issue. China, switching from the old communist measure of "net material product" to the broader Western system of national accounting, has also examined measures of resource depletion.

Among industrial nations, Norway, Germany, the Netherlands, Canada, and Australia are looking into the issue. France has a "patrimony" account that attempts to include natural resource factors. In the United States, Congress appropriated funds two years ago for a study by the Bureau of Economic Analysis in the Commerce Department.

Repetto would like the United Nations' Statistical Commission, which is in the process of revising the UN system of national accounts (SNA), the standard-bearer for measuring economic development in countries around the world, to include measures of changes in natural resource assets.

"The current UN system of national accounts is a cover-up for the environmental degradation that's occurring," he states. "There is a dangerous asymmetry in the way economic performance is analyzed that validates the notion that rapid economic growth can be achieved and sustained by exploiting the environment. The UN's national income accounting framework is a relic of the 1930s when raw materials were cheap and few economists could foresee environmental threats."

The study suggests that the UN should announce at the June 1992 meeting in Brazil of the UN Conference on Environment and Development that "this distortion in the treatment of natural resources will be removed in the ongoing revisions to the SNA."

The Brazil conference follows the 1987 report of the World Commission on Environment and Development, which called for "sustainable development" that meets the current generation's needs without depriving future generations by drawing down productive assets.

Potential Growth Cut 30 Percent

In Costa Rica, the study used remote sensing and satellite imaging, detailed field studies, scientific samplings, and Geographic Information Systems methodologies and mapping to measure natural resource losses. They found that the depreciation in the value of Costa Rica's forests, soils, and fisheries averaged 5 percent of GNP per year over the twenty years of the study or one-third of gross capital formation. This means a 25 to 30 percent reduction in potential economic growth. Net capital formation was in effect overestimated by at least 40 percent.

---

15 Norman Myers ◆ A Cornucopia of Foods

In this chapter from The Primary Source *(1984), Norman Myers discusses the importance of the tropical rainforest as a powerhouse of evolution and a source of genetic material (germplasm) for the improvement of existing crop plants or the breeding of new ones. Because of the extremely high biodiversity of the tropical rainforest and the tendency of its species toward patchy distributions, its widespread clearance will inevitably result in the extinction of certain gene pools. As the population of a plant or animal species shrinks, it loses some of its genes, even if the species itself continues to exist. This ultimately reduces the flexibility of the species to adapt to changing conditions and reduces the opportunity of future generations of humans to benefit from presently unknown but potentially useful properties of wild plants and animals. Many scientists believe that this subtle erosion of the genetic diversity of life on Earth is one of the greatest threats posed by the destruction of the tropical rainforest.*

Our daily wake-up cup of coffee owes its far-past origin, and its currently acceptable price, to tropical forests. Perhaps we shall shortly sweeten that cup of coffee with a natural sweetener that contains next to no calories; if so, the plant from which the sweetener is prepared will almost certainly come from tropical forests. At breakfast, we may well enjoy a slice of papaya, a banana, a mango, an avocado, or any of at least two dozen fruits that derive from tropical forests. As a measure of our daily delight in these tasty offerings of tropical forests, a typical citizen of North America and Western Europe consumes about 10 kilograms per year of bananas; worldwide, people eat their way through 40 million tons of bananas each year, plus 13 million tons of mangoes, and about 1.5 million tons each of papaya and avocado. We can assert much the same about many other items that turn up in our daily diets, right through to the late-evening cup of hot chocolate.

Of course, these items do not come to us directly from tropical forests. They come from plantations. But as is the case with many established crops around the world, tropical fruits, plus beverages such as coffee and drinking chocolate, cannot keep on flourishing without season-by-season infusions of new genetic material from their wild relatives, among other sources of "support germplasm."[1] However much we may suppose that a banana plantation remains superbly productive because the farmer throws masses of fertilizer and pesticides at it, the key lies rather with its genetic underpinnings. Indeed, all modern crops, being the refined products of selective breeding, constantly require new genetic material in order to maintain and even expand their productivity, to enhance their nutritive content, to improve their taste (or to restore it), and to resist emergent types of diseases and pests, as well as environmental stresses such as cold and drought.

During the past several decades, genetic resources from tropical forests have saved a number of important crops, including cocoa, banana, and coffee. Wild germplasm for cocoa is found in the species' native habitats in western Amazonia and in relict patches of forest in the Pacific coast zone of Ecuador—where one particular variety of the cocoa plant has now been reduced to just a few surviving individuals in the 1.8 square-kilometer biological reserve at Rio Palenque. It is a type of cocoa with better taste and other virtues than almost all other gene pools of wild cocoa.[2] Another example is the sugarcane crop. During the mid-1920s, sugarcane growers in the Deep South of the United States ran into trouble from a mosaic virus transmitted by aphids, which brought the crop crashing from over 180,000 tons per year to only 43,000 tons. Fortunately, mosaic-tolerant varieties of sugarcane were found in a wild species that grows in secondary forests of Java, saving the U.S. sugarcane industry from bankruptcy.[3] Since that time, further wild types of sugarcane have supplied resistance to red rot, gummosis, and other pathogens that plague sugarcane growers.

More recently, coffee growers faced a major setback in 1970 when a rust disease appeared in southern Brazil. This was no ordinary type of disease. It revealed at least thirty different races and types. The rust soon spread to Central America, threatening the economies of several countries where coffee exports are the premier source of foreign exchange, earning a total of $3 billion a year. Coffee growers tried conventional methods of fighting the rust, principally by spraying of fungicides. But the cost ran to $200 per hectare, more than many farmers could afford. Again, it was crop geneticists who saved the day. A rust-resistant strain became available from germplasm collected in forests of Ethiopia—the original source of genetic variability for coffee. Even though at least four fifths of Ethiopia's original forests have been eliminated, and the rest are facing imminent threat, germplasm collectors reached the wild gene reservoirs in time—whereupon coffee growers in Latin America were saved from catastrophe, and coffee drinkers around the world were saved from the one-dollar cup of coffee.[4] Even health addicts benefit from wild sources of coffee germplasm. A new variety of wild coffee, containing not a trace of caffeine, has been discovered in such tiny patches of forest as still survive in the Comoro Islands off eastern Africa.

Significant as these instances have been, the most remarkable contributions from wild germplasm almost certainly lie ahead of us, provided we safeguard the wild gene reservoirs in time. An illustration of the wild gene support yet to come involves the recent discovery, in a small patch of montane forest in south-central Mexico, of a weedy-looking form of wild teosinte, the closest relative of corn.[5] Curiously enough, this proved to be the first perennial type of teosinte with the same chromosome makeup as corn, allowing it to be crossbred with conventional, that is, annual, varieties of corn. A hybrid strain might eventually eliminate the heavy year-by-year costs of ploughing and sowing, since the crop would spring up by itself with every new season, just like daffodils. The wild corn also offers resistance to several diseases, including at least four out of eight major viruses and mycoplasmas that are more than troublesome to corn growers and to corn consumers worldwide.[6] Corn appears not only in cornflakes and popcorn, but in preserves, salad dressing, catsup, soft drinks, beer, and bourbon. Moreover, since the wild species has been discovered at elevations between 2,500 and 3,250 meters, where its cool mountainous habitats are often damp, it may well thrive in wet soils that have hitherto been beyond the survival capacities of conventional corn. The wild species could thus expand the cultivation range of corn by as much as one tenth, or many millions of hectares. Overall benefits for the global corn industry could eventually be measured in billions of dollars per year.[7]

Entirely New Foods

Tropical forests not only support modern agriculture through their genetic contributions to established crops, they offer hosts of opportunities
for entirely new crops, in the form of foods that we may scarcely have
thought about thus far. Unaware as we may be, forest plants of the humid
tropics have supplied us with many staple foods, including cereals such
as rice and millet; pulses such as peanut and mung bean; roots and tubers
such as yam and taro; and other well-known items such as cassava and
pineapple, to name but the leading foods.[8] But the fact that these crops
are so widely grown does not necessarily mean that they are the best crops.
We can argue that today's crops are accidents of history. While we may
well believe that rice and other staple products of the tropical forest zone—
together with wheat, potatoes, and two dozen other basic foods from other
parts of the world—are eaten by the great majority of humankind each
day on the grounds that they constitute the world's best food plants, we
actually grow these plants because it turned out they were suited to cultivation by Neolithic man. The plants that were selected as most appropriate 10,000 years ago still supply virtually all items on our meal tables
today. Many new crops could be awaiting our attention, capable of becoming front-rank crops in many lands if they were given a chance.

As an example of a plant with unusual promise, let us look at the
winged bean, a plant from the forests of New Guinea.[9] Because of the
shape of its pods, it is also known as the four-angled bean and the aspara-
gus pea; and it has long been known to forest tribes of its native New
Guinea as a crop with outstanding nutritional content. The vinelike plant
contains far more protein than occurs in potatoes, cassava, and several
other crops that serve as principal sources of food to many millions of
people each day in the tropics. The winged bean offers nutritional value
equivalent to the soybean, with 40 percent protein and 17 percent edible
oil, plus vitamins and other nutrients. It is not to be decried as a poor
man's crop, a vegetable to be dismissed as a second-rate product for third-
rate communities. Its capacity to match the soybean's nutritional value
might remind us that the United States used to produce only scattered
patches of soybean for at least one century before the plant was finally
upgraded to a widespread crop. Today the soybean is the principal protein
crop in the world, flourishing in dozens of temperate-zone countries. Could
not a similar prospect be in store for the winged bean, scheduled to become the long-sought "soybean of the tropics"? The bean has received a
crash program of development and improvement during the last few years,
until it now helps enhance human diets in more than fifty countries of the
developing tropics.

Probably fruits offer the greatest promise for new foods. Temperate-
zone forests have yielded only about 20 major fruits, whereas tropical

forests feature at least 250 fruits that please human palates in their millions, and many more are enjoyed locally. In New Guinea alone, 251 tree species bear edible fruits, most of them consumed, at one time or another, by local communities—yet a mere 43 have become established as cultivated crops, and only about one dozen reach the marketplace, indicating the scope for future development.[10] There could well be 2,500 fruit species in tropical forests for human consumption—and of these, perhaps 250 are widespread, 50 are well known, and 15 rank as major commercial species.[11]

To get an idea of what these fruits might consist of, let us look at a couple that deserve to become as widely established as bananas and mangoes. First, the pummelo, a citrus fruit that appears splendidly suited to the warm, moist areas of the lowland tropics. Virtually all other citrus fruits require subtropical environments, with cool, damp winters followed by warm, drier summers. But the pummelo thrives in year-round warmth and moisture. Native to Southeast Asia, it prefers lowland areas, and it can even prosper in shoreline soils, revealing a high tolerance for saline conditions—a trait that would allow it to be grown in brackish, marshy areas. The pummelo is the largest of the citrus fruits, larger even than a grapefruit. As a measure of our global appetite for citrus fruits, we eat 55 million tons per year, and a U.S. citizen consumes an average of ten kilograms per year, probably enjoying the sharp flavor of oranges and so forth virtually every day. Second, a fruit from tropical America, the soursop. A large fleshy fruit that can weigh four kilograms or more, with a white juicy interior, the soursop's smell is akin to that of a pineapple, but its taste is a striking mixture of musky and acidic flavors. The fruit can be eaten raw, or it can be pulped for use in ice cream and soft drinks.

Similar accounts could be presented, without further field research, for many dozens of other tropical fruits; for instance, the mangosteen of Malaysia, described as "perhaps the world's best-tasting fruit."[12] So when we visit the fruit section of our local supermarket and marvel, as we rightly may during certain seasons of the year, at the bountiful variety of fruits shipped in from the tropics, let us reflect that these represent but a tiny fraction of the array that we could enjoy if botanists and agriculturists were to exploit the far greater variety of fruit trees available in tropical forests—and that steadily decline toward extinction before the axe and the chainsaw.

As for vegetables, we find that nutritious leaves and other greenery of tropical forests are equally diverse. At least 1,650 plants of tropical forests offer vegetablelike materials of various sorts.[13] Having looked at tropical forest fruits in some detail, we shall not linger with an instance-by-instance account of vegetables—except to note a distinctive way of deriving high-quality food from forest greenery, in the form of leaf protein.[14] This type of food is not yet something that we can purchase in cans in our local supermarket, yet it could become, in just a few more years, a significant factor in our diets—and even more importantly, a common item among protein-deficient areas of the world. Through a process that is sometimes known as green-crop fractionation, plant leaves and stems can be ruptured to release juices and saps that contain several proteins, also sugars, salts, lipids, and vitamins. The process is relatively simple. Leaves are passed through a pulper; the juice is drained and then heated to 70–80 degrees Fahrenheit, causing the protein to coagulate, whereupon it can be separated by means of a filter press. The protein material, dark green and cheeselike in appearance, is mixed with established foods as a protein reinforcer.

A key question is, Which plants best lend themselves to supply of protein through this technique, that is, which offer the greatest quantity of best-quality protein in their tissues, which grow fastest, which best tolerate less-than-ideal conditions, and so forth? Thus far, scientists have been inclined to focus on a series of legumes, with a protein content between 12 and 36 percent. Given present technology for green-crop fractionation, we can generate leaf protein from legumes at a cost of only one fifth as much as soybean protein, and one seventeenth as much as protein in the form of milk or meat. Via experimental projects, protein of this sort has been extracted from alfalfa, clover, oats, spinach, Chinese cabbage, water hyacinth, and numerous grasses. Now that we know that green-crop fractionation can be applied to a wide variety of leafy plants, the challenge is to find the most suitable candidates. Plainly, the best bet for investigators lies with the zone that features almost as many plant forms as in all the rest of the Earth.

Natural Sweeteners

In the wake of the cyclamate and saccharin controversies, there is urgent need for an alternative non-nutritive sweetening agent, that is, one that does not add calories to our diet and centimeters to our waistlines. Although sweetness is only one of four basic tastes of humans, it commands far more attention than all the others combined—to the detriment of our health and our appearance, since a single cola drink contains as many calories, in the form of sugar, as half a kilogram of potatoes. We must break ourselves of our sugar habit, since we already consume far too much —100 million tons worldwide each year, or almost twenty kilograms for each global citizen. The average American consumes at least forty-five kilograms of sugar per year, making it a key factor in overweight problems and associated diseases such as heart disorders and tooth decay.

Many plant pigments, such as carotenoids in sweet-tasting fruits, attract birds, insects, and other herbivores. Almost certainly, then, they are not toxic to mammals, including humans. The problem with the natural sweeteners of fruits that we consume is that they are nutritive sugars—glucose, fructose, and sucrose—and we already consume far more of them than is good for us. Fortunately, we are finding that a few natural sweeteners in fruits are made up of protein compounds; and these materials, identified only during the last ten years, make up an entirely new class of natural sweeteners.[15] They are all 1,000 times sweeter than sucrose, and at least 300 times sweeter than saccharin.

A leading example of a source of protein sweeteners is the so-called miracle fruit *Synsepalum dulcificum*, a berry from West African forests. It causes sour foods to taste splendidly sweet, as anyone can tell by merely chewing on a berry at the same time he or she is eating lemons, limes, rhubarb, or grapefruit. Another fruit from West Africa's forests, known as the serendipity berry, *Dioscoreophyllum cumminsii*, has a sweetness 3,000 times greater than that of sucrose. The red, grapelike berry derives its curious name from an occasion in 1965 when an American scientist, Dr. George Inglett, was exploring West African forests for sweet fruits. Coming across the plant by chance, he was surprised to find that its berries tasted so sweet; he had gotten no indication from scientific reports.

Still more important than these two is a third fruit from the forests of West Africa. The katemfe, *Thaumatococcus danielli*, contains two sweet-tasting proteins, thaumatin I and II, both of which are 1,600 times sweeter than sucrose. Thaumatin is now widely marketed by the noted sugar corporation in Great Britain, Tate and Lyle Limited, under the trade name Talin. It is becoming strongly established in Japan, where it is used as a sweetener in such diverse products as candies, chewing gum, salad dressing, coffee drinks, soups, jellies, pickles, frozen desserts, fish and meat products, and table-top sachets. It should soon become available in the United States after surviving tests by the Food and Drug Administration.

Control of Agricultural Pests

Tropical forests can further support agriculture by supplying materials to help keep down the many insect pests that account for the loss of 40 percent of all food grown around the world each year. A sound way to control insect pests is to exploit chemicals from plants that have developed mechanisms to resist insects. The finest source of such plants lies with tropical forests and their exceptional variety of plant forms that have co-evolved in equilibrium with associated insects.[16] Tropical forest plants constitute a vast storehouse of chemical substances for defense against insects—not only biocompounds that serve as insect repellants and toxicants, but feeding deterrents of various sorts, inhibitors of insect growth and development, and the like. Since multitudes of plants and insects have evolved symbiotic relationships within their tropical forest ecosystems, we can surmise that there must be many other insect-resisting substances available in the forests, not only of the types listed, but of novel and unrecognized forms as well.

Moreover, all these compounds are biodegradable. This means that they do not accumulate in organisms and thus do not contribute to the environmental problems associated with synthetic chemical insecticides. Perhaps most important of all, they generally cause little, if any, harm to higher animals such as birds and mammals, including humans.

By way of illustration, let us note two main categories of toxic compounds—the pyrethrins, from chrysanthemum-type plants, and the rotenoids, from roots of tropical forest legumes. Rotenoids are the more widely distributed, known to occur in the roots and seeds of at least sixty-seven plant species found across Amazonia and Southeast Asia. Especially important as a source of rotenoids is the *Derris* group of woody climbing plants in Southeast Asia; their roots contain powerful toxins that have long been used by forest tribes as fish poisons. So powerful are these root compounds, that one part of plant to three hundred thousand parts of water is sufficient to kill fish. It was the use of these rotenoids as fish poisons that enabled their toxic characteristics to be identified by Western scientists, and today a series of *Derris*-based insecticides are used in the form of plant sprays for field crops, and as dips and dusting powders for livestock.

In the American tropics, a major agricultural pest consists of leaf-cutting ants. These ants make their living by stripping leaves from plants, including crop plants. Fortunately, at least one species of tropical forest tree produces a chemical compound that actively repels the ant—thus opening up the prospect that the compound could be used to produce an insect repellant. Better still, of course, would be to identify the genes that enable the tree to produce its own internal insect repellant, and then to splice the chemical-generating genes into certain of our food crops. The same approach could apply to many other plant-produced materials, for example, the anti-feedant compound found in bark extracts of forest trees in Papua New Guinea.[17]

But while a gene-splicing strategy will represent by far the most efficient way to use anti-insect compounds produced by plants, the strategy will depend on the greatest possible stocks of genetic variability among wild plants. As the burgeoning industry of genetic engineering reaches a stage where inter-species crosses become not only possible but relatively straightforward, the industry will seek a maximum array of plants with insect-repelling and insect-killing capacity (as they will seek other prized traits, such as resistance to diseases, saline soils, drought, etc.).

At the same time, we should bear in mind that insect pests include variations that can multiply in numbers to overcome plant defenses in as little as ten years, sometimes a mere three years. Hence there is all the greater need to derive further genetic combinations of plants to enable farmers to "stay ahead of the game"—otherwise, they will start to encounter increasing numbers of immune insect strains.

Not all anti-insect defenses in plants are chemicals that make the insect feel sick to its stomach, or worse. A number of chemicals cause insects to moult at the wrong phase of their life cycle; or they inhibit the growth of an infant insect into an adult, leaving it as a perpetual juvenile of harmless scope; or they suppress the reproductive mechanisms of insects; or they make life more than difficult for insects in dozens of other ways.

Pest Control through Natural Enemies

Yet another weapon for the farmer to mobilize against insect pests lies with natural enemies. Certain insect species in the wild operate as predators or parasites to hold down the numbers of their host species—and it is precisely these hosts that frequently proliferate to become pests in agriculture. Predators and parasites attack the eggs, larvae, pupae, and adults of their target species.[18] Since many predators and parasites are highly specific in their choice of prey, they are inclined to target only certain species without doing damage to others. By contrast, the broad-scale use of persistent toxic chemicals tends to kill off far more insects than is necessary.

In any case, many insect pests are growing resistant to chemical insecticides. Among certain species, as few as fifteen generations are needed to build up resistance. According to the Food and Agriculture Organization of the United Nations, more than three hundred species of insects, mites, and ticks throughout the world are known to have become resistant to one or more pesticides, and dozens more are suspected of becoming resistant. In the United States, entomologists in the Department of Agriculture estimate that approximately seven hundred insect species do significant damage to crops within the continental limits (not counting Hawaii, where the problem is still more acute); the loss is calculated at $5 billion per year. Of these seven hundred insect species, around half have developed resistance to at least one pesticide, some to two or more. American farmers apply four hundred thousand tons of chemical insecticides to their crops each year, ten times as much as in 1950, yet they lose twice as much food to insects. Hence the rationale for the natural enemies strategy. The track record of this approach is encouraging. Entomologists have recorded at least 250 cases of pest control accomplished through the introduction of predators and parasites that attack troublesome species. For example, citrus growers in Florida have been able to save their industry $40 million each year through a onetime outlay of $35,000 in 1973 for the introduction from the tropics of parasitic insects that attack citrus-tree pests.[19]

Furthermore, natural enemies can be used against another form of pest, weed plants. In the United States, alligator weed has proved a notorious and costly problem for rivers and lakes, irrigation canals, waterways for boats, etc. No herbicide proved equal to the task. Fortunately, a solution has been found in the form of a flea beetle from South American forests, which regards the alligator weed as its preferred host.[20] Another prominent weed in the United States, as elsewhere in the world, is the water hyacinth; a mere ten plants can multiply to six hundred thousand in just eight months, forming a carpet a quarter of a hectare in size, and a carpet thick enough for a person to walk across. A promising response to the water hyacinth problem lies with herbivorous insects from tropical forests of South America.[21]

The economics of the natural enemies strategy are often highly positive. Across-the-board performance indicates that there is an average of a thirty-dollar return for each dollar expended on importation of beneficial organisms (in contrast to the 4:1 benefit-to-cost ratio for chemical pesticides). In California alone, during the period 1928–1979, a series of natural-enemy projects has reduced crop losses to insects, and has reduced the need for pesticidal chemicals, for savings worth just short of $1 billion (at 1979 prices).[22]

At least 250 insect pests in the United States, accounting for around one half of all crop losses to insects, are species of foreign origin. It is precisely against these imported pests that alien introductions of natural enemies offer the greatest promise.[23] According to preliminary estimates by the U.S. Department of Agriculture, a full 1,000 species of foreign organisms—not only insects, but also mites and pathogens—could be profitably introduced into the United States, at a cost of less than $40 million over a period of twenty years. Much potential is available in the form of, for example, wasps that act as parasites or predators, notably the chalcid wasps, among others that are numerous in tropical forests. At least as much potential appears to lie with the ichneumonid or braconid wasps, and with certain groups of beetles. To date, American pest experts have called on the services of natural enemies from abroad to overcome many dozens of foreign insect pests: the best times still lie ahead.

Forest Animals for Food

Thus far, this chapter has emphasized tropical forest plants that are new sources of food. Let us now take a look at animals.[24]

Within the forests of the Thailand-Kampuchea border lives a secretive, cowlike creature with resplendent horns: the kouprey. A bull kouprey sports horns that are longer and wider than those of any other living wild cattle except the buffalo; a female's are lyre-shaped, corkscrewing upward in a manner akin to those of the lesser kudu in Africa. The kouprey is believed to have been one of the wild ancestors of the humped zebu cattle of southern Asia, which means that further crossbreeding between the two bovids could boost cattle raising throughout the entire region. In particular, the kouprey appears immune to rinderpest, a widespread disease that is fatal to cattle. Regrettably, the kouprey's very survival is doubtful, due to military activity in its habitats during the past several decades. Perhaps only a few individuals remain.

Other wild bovids of Southeast Asia's forests could likewise help cattle husbandry, notably the so-called dwarf water buffaloes, more correctly termed the seladang, the tamarau, and the anoa. But as with the kouprey, the numbers of all these wild cattle have been severely reduced through human disruption of the forest ecosystems. In addition, the forests of Southeast Asia support the babirusa, a distant relative of the pig that seems to be a rudimentary ruminant and, through its distinctive approach to the challenge of converting rough forage into good meat, could upgrade some of the half-billion pigs around the world.

When speculating on the potential contributions of these wild creatures to modern livestock, let us bear in mind that the ancestral stock of the domesticated water buffalo includes the wild *Bubalis arnee* of southern Asia; that among the progenitors of Indian cattle is the gaur, *Bos gaurus*; and that livestock people in Indonesia already use a hybrid animal, known as the madura—a cross between conventional cattle and the banteng, *Bos banteng*.

As for birds, we might reflect, the next time we enjoy a chicken supper, that this most numerous bird on Earth, numbering at least five billion, originated from a pheasantlike creature of India's forests, known as the red jungle fowl, together with some genetic support from the guinea fowl of West Africa.

Wild Meat

In a number of tropical forest countries, wild meat counts as an important item in people's diets.[25] In Nigeria, for example, where the forest cover has been reduced by at least 90 percent, local people still derive a renewable harvest of almost 100,000 tons of good, solid meat per year from animals including grass-cutters (giant rats), small antelopes including bushbuck and duiker, and sundry monkeys. Four people out of five enjoy game meat as a regular item in the cooking pot. On average, it constitutes one fifth of all animal protein of whatever sort for people in Nigeria's forest zone. In Zaire it rises to almost 27 percent, and in Cameroon, Ivory Coast, and Liberia, to a massive 70 percent.

Wild meat comes not only from mammals. In Amazonia, seven species of river turtles could, if properly managed, become sustainable sources of high-grade meat.[26] Turtles feed readily on aquatic plants of all sorts and conditions; they survive temporary food shortages at the end of the dry season without adverse effects; they have low metabolic rates, so they do not become nearly so hungry as warm-blooded creatures; and they appear to need far less living space than higher vertebrates. According to some theoretical calculations, a one-hectare lake of turtles could produce well over two tons of meat each year, in contrast to the fifty kilograms of beef that could come from one hectare of average cattle pasture in the humid tropics. Other creatures of South American forests provide abundant meat, notably the tapir, agouti, and paca (rodents of Amazonia), plus peccaries (wild pigs), monkeys, and other mammals, and also snakes and lizards. In two separate areas of Peru's sector of Amazonia, people living outside townships depend on wild meat for 80 to 85 percent of their animal protein.

To date, the offtake of wildlife in Amazonia has tended to range from next to no harvest at all, to severe over-exploitation. If, however, a controlled-cropping system were to be mounted, the result could be encouraging, according to some preliminary figures worked out by Dr. Angel Paucar, of the Wildlife Division in Ecuador, and Dr. Alfred L. Gardner, of the U.S. Fish and Wildlife Service.[27] Their calculations represent no more than a tentative and speculative attempt to illuminate a situation that remains almost entirely unexplored. So the numbers represent best-judgment guesstimates—no more and no less.

In Ecuador's sector of Amazonia, local people have long taken a self-renewing harvest of wildlife products, partly in the form of meat for consumption and partly in the form of skins and hides for export. In some localities the offtake has been excessive in the case of certain species. But by and large, wildlife has proved itself to be a strongly renewable resource, given the low levels of exploitation to which it has generally been subjected. So few people live in this part of Amazonia, that only a moderate harvest can make a sizable contribution. As much as 85 percent of animal protein consumed by local people comes from wild animals, notably peccaries, deer, tapirs, pacas, and agoutis, among some forty species of mammals in all. A sustainable harvest of wild meat can, according to Paucar and Gardner, amount to 240 kilograms per square kilometer, with a market value of about $1.8 per kilogram, or a total of almost $440 overall. (Were the harvest to be systematized, and expanded to include birds, turtles, and fish, the minimum potential value could be increased as much as ten times.) Furthermore, since almost one third of Amazonian Ecuador consists of swamps and rivers, there is plenty of scope for harvest of caimans, at least two per hectare per year. A caiman measuring 1.5 meters in length is worth $145. Thus one square kilometer of such habitats could yield $14,550 per year for hides alone, rising to $16,370 when we include meat from the caimans. In addition, each square kilometer of forest can renewably produce twenty primates each year for biomedical research, an individual being worth between $200 and $300. So a sustainable harvest of wild primates could generate a minimum of $4,000 per year. Many readers may object to the prospect of using wild primates to foster human health. In the past, the wild primate stocks have almost invariably been overexploited, sometimes critically so. But if this crucial factor can be taken care of, need any objection remain, particularly when a sustainable harvest of primates helps to promote the survival of their forest habitats?

This all means that a forest tract of five hundred square kilometers could, under scientific management, produce a self-renewing crop of wild-life with a potential value of at least $10 million per year, or slightly more than $200 per hectare. These revenues are to be contrasted with a return from commercial logging of only a little over $150 per hectare—and hardwood timber . . . tends to be harvested as a once-and-for-all product, leaving little prospect that a further harvest can be taken within several decades at least.

In conclusion, then, we can accept that tropical forests, while making significant contributions to modern agriculture already, play only a trifling part in the life of the farmer compared with what they could supply. Were we to undertake a systematic exploration and selective extraction of whatever "agricultural" materials are available from tropical forests, we could surely look for a steady stream of new products. Were this chapter to be rewritten in the year 2000, who can guess at the host of exotic articles that it might enumerate? The problem surely does not lie with tropical forests themselves, with their extreme abundance of resources waiting to be brought into the mainstream of our lives. Rather, the deficiency lies with our imaginations: we constantly fail to grasp the scale of potential products from tropical forests that could enrich our lives.

Notes

1. P. Carlson, editor, 1980, *Biology of Crop Productivity*, Academic Press, New York; J. R. Harlan, 1975, *Crops and Man*, American Society of Agronomy, Madison, Wisconsin; N. Myers, 1983, *A Wealth of Wild Species*, Westview Press, Boulder, Colorado; M. L. Oldfield, 1981, Tropical Deforestation and Genetic Resources Conservation, *Studies in Third World Societies*, 14:277–346.

2. A. H. Gentry, 1982, Patterns of Neotropical Plant Species Diversity, in M. K. Hecht, B. Wallace, and G. T. Prance, editors, *Evolutionary Biology*, 15:1–84.

3. J. R. Harlan, 1975, *Crops and Man*.

4. F. P. Ferwerda, 1976, Coffees, in N. W. Simmons, editor, *Evolution of Crop Plants*, 252–60, Longman, New York.

5. H. H. Iltis, J. F. Doebley, R. M. Guzman, and B. Pazy, 1979, *Zea diploperennis* (Gramineae), a New Teosinte from Mexico, *Science*, 203:186–88.

6. L. R. Nault and W. R. Findley, 1981, Primitive Relative Offers New Traits for Corn Improvement, *Ohio Report* 66(6):90–92.

7. A. C. Fisher, 1982, *Economic Analysis and the Extinction of Species*, Department of Agriculture and Resource Economics, University of California at Berkeley; N. Myers, 1983, *A Wealth*.

8. M. Chai, E. Soepadmo, and H. S. Yong, editors, 1979, Proceedings of Workshop on Genetic Resources of Plants, Animals and Microorganisms in Malaysia, *Malaysian Applied Biology, Special Issue* 8(1); M. A. Rifai, editor, 1979, *ASEAN Grain Legumes*, Central Research Institute of Agriculture, Bogor, Indonesia; J. T. Williams, C. H. Lamoureux, and N. Wulijarni-Soetjipto, editors, 1975, *Southeast Asian Plant Genetic Resources*, BIOTROP, Bogor, Indonesia.

9. National Academy of Sciences, 1975, *The Winged Bean: A High Protein Crop for the Tropics*, National Academy of Sciences, Washington, DC.

10. K. Jong, editor, 1979, *Biological Aspects of Plant Genetic Resource Conservation in Southeast Asia*, Institute of Southeast Asian Biology, University of Aberdeen, Scotland, UK.

11. S. Nagy and P. E. Shaw, editors, 1980, *Tropical and Subtropical Fruits*, AVI Publishing Company, Westport, Connecticut; J. A. Samson, 1980, *Tropical Fruits*, Longman, New York; and for several illustrative examples, see National Academy of Sciences, 1975, *Underexploited Tropical Plants with Promising Economic Value*, National Academy of Sciences, Washington, DC.

12. National Academy of Sciences, 1979, *Tropical Legumes: Resources for the Future*, National Academy of Sciences, Washington, DC.

13. G. A. C. Herklots, 1972, *Vegetables in Southeast Asia*, George Allen and Unwin, London, UK; F. W. Martin and R. M. Ruberte, 1979, *Edible Leaves of the Tropics*, Institute of Tropical Agriculture, Mayagüez, Puerto Rico; J. J. Ochse, 1977, *Vegetables of the Dutch East Indies*, A. Asher and Company Publishers Ltd., Amsterdam, Netherlands; J. C. Okafor, 1980, Edible Indigenous Woody Plants in the Rural Economy of the Nigerian Zone, *Forest Ecology and Management* 1:235–47; H. A. P. C. Oomen and G. J. H. Grubben, 1977, Tropical Leaf Vegetables in Human Nutrition, in *Communication* 69:24–41, 51–55, Department of Agricultural Research, Koninklijk Instituut voor de Tropen, Amsterdam, Netherlands; and R. L. Villareal and R. T. Opena, 1976, The Wild Vegetables of Southeast Asia, *American Horticulturalist* 55(3):1–4.

14. J. A. Duke, 1981, *The Gene Revolution*, Office of Technology Assessment, U.S. Congress, Washington, DC; N. Mohan and G. P. Srivastava, 1980, Studies on the Extractability and Chemical Composition of Leaf Proteins from Certain Trees, *Journal of Food Science and Technology* 18:48–50; N. W. Pirie, editor, 1975, *Food Protein Sources*, Cambridge University Press, London, UK.

15. J. A. Duke, 1983, *Ecological Amplitudes of Crops Used as Sweeteners*, Plant Genetics and Germplasm Institute, Agricultural Research Service, Beltsville, Maryland; J. D. Higginbotham, 1979, Protein Sweeteners, in C. A. M. Hough, K. J. Parker, and A. J. Vletof, editors, *Developments in Sweeteners*, Applied Science Publishers, London, UK; G. E. Inglett, 1981, Sweeteners—A Review, *Food Technology*, March 1981, 37–41.

16. L. E. Gilbert and P. H. Raven, editors, 1975, *Coevolution of Animals and Plants*, revised edition, University of Texas Press, Austin, Texas; D. H. Janzen, 1975, *Ecology of Plants in the Tropics*, Arnold, London, UK.; R. L. Metcalfe, 1977, Plant Derivatives for Insect Control, in R. S. Seigler, editor, *Crop Resources*: 165–78, Academic Press, New York.

17. W. Kraus et al., 1980, New Insect Antifeedants from *Toona* Species (*Meliaceae*), in *Proceedings of Fourth Asian Symposium on Medicinal Plants and Species*: 127–35, Government of Thailand in Conjunction with UNESCO and Faculty of Science, Mahidol University, Bangkok, Thailand.

18. S. W. T. Batra, 1982, Biological Control in Agroecosystems, *Science* 215:135–39; C. P. Clausen, editor, 1978, *Introduced Parasites and Predators of Arthropod Pests and Weeds: A World Review*, Agricultural Research Service of U.S. Department of Agriculture, Washington, DC; C. B. Huffaker, 1980, Use of Predators and Parasitoids in Biological Control, in R. C. Staples and R. J. Kuhr, editors, *Linking Research to Crop Production*: 173–98, Plenum Publishing, New York; J. S. Marsden, G. E. Martin, D. J. Parham, T. J. Ridsdill-Smith, and B. G. Johnston, 1980, *Returns on Australian Agricultural Research*, Division of Entomology, Commonwealth Scientific and Industrial Research Organization, Canberra, Australia; R. I. Sailer, 1981, Progress Report on Importation of Natural Enemies of Insect Pests in the U.S.A., in J. R. Coulson, editor, *Use of Beneficial Organisms in the Control of Crop Pests*: 20–26, Entomological Society of America, College Park, Maryland; R. Van den Bosch, P. S. Messenger, and A. P. Gutierrez, 1982, *An Introduction to Biological Control*, Plenum Publishing, New York.

19. V. L. Delucchi, editor, 1976, *Studies in Biological Control*, Cambridge University Press, Cambridge, UK.

20. D. M. Maddox, L. A. Andres, R. D. Hennessey, R. D. Blackburn, and N. R. Spencer, 1971, Insects to Control Alligatorweed, *BioScience* 21:985–91.

21. National Academy of Sciences, 1976, *Making Aquatic Weeds Useful*, National Academy of Sciences, Washington, DC.

22. C. B. Huffaker, 1980, Use of Predators; R. Van den Bosch et al., 1982, *Introduction to Biological Control*.

23. R. I. Sailer, 1981, Progress Report.

24. M. L. Oldfield, 1981, *The Value of the Conservation of Genetic Resources*, Department of Agriculture, University of Texas, Austin, Texas; N. D. Vietmeyer, 1983, *Little-Known Asian Animals with a Promising Economic Future*, National Academy Press, Washington, DC.

25. S. S. Ajayi, 1979, *Utilization of Forest Wildlife in West Africa*, Food and Agriculture Organization, Rome, Italy; A. DeVos, 1977, Game as Food, *Unasylva* 29:2–12; W. Krostitz, 1979, The New International Market for Game Meat, *Unasylva* 31(123):32–36; J. B. Sale, 1983, *The Importance and Values of Wild Plants and Animals in Africa*, International Union for Conservation of Nature and Natural Resources, Gland, Switzerland.

26. R. A. Mittermeier, 1978, South America's River Turtles: Saving Them by Use, *Oryx* 14(3):222–30.

27. A. Paucar and A. L. Gardner, 1981, *Establishment of a Scientific Research Station in the Yasuni National Park of the Republic of Ecuador*, National Zoo, Washington, DC.

---

16 Mark Plotkin ◆ An Earthly Paradise Regained

Shamans (native healers), with their knowledge of how to make use of the tropical rainforest without destroying it, hold the keys to unlocking the pharmacological potential of rainforest flora. Unfortunately, both forests

From Mark Plotkin, "An Earthly Paradise Regained," *Américas* 46, no. 1 (January/February 1994): 14–19. Photographs omitted. Reprinted by permission of *Américas*, a bimonthly magazine published by the General Secretariat of the Organization of American States in English and Spanish.

and shamans are disappearing at an accelerating rate, and with them dies a wealth of possible cures for a variety of ills. In this 1994 article, ethnobotanist Mark Plotkin makes a strong argument for the preservation of the tropical rainforest and for the protection of the tribal peoples who live there. Plotkin and a number of other researchers have begun to challenge the dominant Western perception of tribal peoples as ignorant, backward, and in need of our help. These scholars suggest that perhaps we have more to learn from indigenous peoples than vice versa. (See also Selections 5, 6, and 19.) One of the currently debated issues that Plotkin leaves unaddressed is the question of intellectual property rights. Who owns genetic resources? And what share of the proceeds of commercial development should go to the cultures that first recognized the curative properties of a wild species? See selection 21 for more on these issues.

The Wayanas, a rain-forest people living in southeastern Suriname, believe that each of us has the potential to be a shaman, yet we all have an invisible blindfold over our eyes. The process of becoming a shaman entails removing this blindfold, thus allowing us to see into, and begin to communicate with, the spirit world. This is expected of every Wayana healer. A single Wayana medicine man may know and use over one hundred different plant species for healing purposes.

As an ethnobotanist with Conservation International, a Washington-based environmental organization, I have been studying how the Wayanas, among other indigenous peoples, use tropical plants for medicinal and other uses. Rain-forest plants are now providing Western science with myriad novel compounds that show promise as antiviral agents. For example, Shaman Pharmaceuticals, a small firm in northern California, focuses its research on plants used medicinally by rain-forest peoples. Only three years after the firm was established, it has developed compounds that seem to be effective against two viruses (RSV and acyclovir-resistant herpes) in human clinical trials. And the National Cancer Institute has expanded its effort to find and screen new plant compounds against the AIDS virus.

Nowhere is plant research more promising than in the country of Suriname. Formerly known as Dutch Guiana and inhabited by fewer people than Oklahoma City, this small country is nonetheless home to the most intriguing cultural mixture found on the South American continent. Suriname can be considered a microcosm of the tropical world since it harbors thriving cultures of the American tropics (the Amerindians), the African tropics (the Maroons), and the Asian tropics (Hindustanis, Javanese, and Chinese). Each group maintains its own cultural identity and, for the most part, its own ethnopharmacopeia, or knowledge and use of local medicinal plants.

For the ethnobotanist, the most interesting group is the Amerindians, especially those of the far south who have only had sustained contact with the outside world for less than two decades. Three tribes—the Tiriós, Wayanas, and Akuriyos—are still very much a part of the forest ecosystem, relying on ambient vegetation for most of their material needs.

The Tiriós, who live along the Sipaliwini River in the southwest and the Boven Tapanahoni River in the southeast, probably have the largest known ethnopharmacopeia in Suriname—ranging in size from between three hundred and five hundred species of flowering plants. These Indians are particularly skilled at healing deep fungal infections of the skin, a malady whose cure often eludes Western medicine. On numerous occasions I myself have been successfully treated for this problem by Tirió medicine men (known locally as *piais*). Unfortunately, however, contact with the outside world has taken a serious toll on traditional healing practices: The young do not learn and the elderly do not live forever. With Western medicine proving so effective against introduced diseases, younger members of the tribe have started to believe that the Tirió ethnopharmacopeia is some antiquated phenomenon whose passing should not be mourned. During the past five years, several of the most powerful shamans have died without having the chance to pass their knowledge on to a student. Fortunately, three years ago Conservation International initiated a program with the Tiriós of the southwest both to document the remaining information and to pass it on, in textbook form, to the younger generation.

In the southeastern portion of the country live the Wayanas and the Akuriyos. The Wayanas are found from the Boven Tapanahoni River (where they overlap with the Tiriós in the village of Tepoe), east of the Lawa River (which forms the border), and then into French Guiana. Because missionary activity is strictly forbidden among the Wayanas in French Guiana, and since members of the tribe regularly cross back and forth from Suriname to French Guiana, shamanism continues to thrive.

The ethnopharmacopeia of the Akuriyos is the least known and in some ways the most interesting. They are a hunter-gatherer tribe who, when they were first contacted, did not know how to make fire: They carried it with them from campsite to campsite since they had no fixed villages. The major cause of mortality among adult males was attacks by jaguars because, unlike the other tribes, they hunted alone and without dogs. Their total reliance on the forest for material goods has given the Akuriyos the most detailed knowledge of forest plants. (The Tiriós and Wayanas obtained a few trade goods from more acculturated rain-forest peoples for over fifty years.) However, missionaries and government officials have encouraged the Akuriyos to give up their nomadic lifestyle and settle in Tirió villages, where many of the men have taken Tirió wives and their children have begun speaking Tirió. The future for the Akuriyos as a distinct cultural entity is, at best, uncertain.

Several of the local plants are used by all three tribes and, in some cases, they are employed for the same purpose. For example, a tea of the leaves of *Renealmia*, a common ginger, is used to treat the symptoms due to coughs and colds. (The ancient Chinese used what is now commercial ginger to treat the same ailments.) Such patterns of commonality of usage—where different peoples use the same or closely related species— often indicates that there is indeed a phytochemical reason for the employment of these plants. This is in fact the case with these species since most gingers are rich in essential oils that when taken in a tea can relieve flulike symptoms.

Another plant valued for medicinal purposes is a species of *Geissospermum*, which is made into a tea. While the Tiriós take it for malarial fevers, the Akuriyos rub it on ant stings. One report that I unearthed while working in the Harvard Herbarium about a decade ago was that the Waiwai tribe from neighboring Guyana once used the bark to make *balauitu*, an arrow poison. The study of arrow poisons, also known as curare, is one of the most fascinating aspects of ethnobotany. An arrow poison used by tribes of the western Amazon features a liana of the moonseed family as its major component. The same alkaloid that gives the plant its lethal punch—D-tubocurarine chloride—is extracted from this plant and used in abdominal surgery as a muscle relaxant. Ironically, we cannot synthesize this compound in the lab, but must continue to rely on extraction of the chemical from the lianas, which are found only in the western Amazon.

As far as we know, all the curare made by the Amerindians in Suriname are manufactured from lianas of the genus *Strychnos*. Although it was originally believed that only one species of this genus was employed, the Tiriós recently showed me a "new" species that they also used, previously unreported in the scientific literature as an arrow-poison plant.

Yet these species of *Strychnos* are by no means the most famous members of this genus used medicinally by forest-dwelling people in Suriname: That honor belongs to a species used by African-American peoples living in the central portion of the country. These people, known as Maroons, are the descendants of African slaves who were brought to Suriname in the eighteenth and nineteenth centuries. Some of them escaped into the interior, where they created tribal societies much like those they had been part of in Africa. The Maroons formed themselves into five tribes, whose skill at conducting guerrilla warfare was legendary. The Dutch were never able to defeat them.

The Maroons seem to have an ethnopharmacopeia quite distinct from that of the Amerindians of the interior, even though their medicinal plants, unlike those of the Tiriós, have never been extensively documented. One of the most potent and well-known plants used by the Maroons is *kwasi-bita*, which is employed as a treatment for fevers and stomach ailments. The method of administration is, as far as I know, unique in lowland South America: The medicine man carves a cup from the wood of the *kwasi-bita* tree. When a patient is in need of treatment, a bit of rum is poured into the cup; the alcohol, which draws the medicinal compound out of the wood, is then ingested by the sick person.

The Maroons' form of *Strychnos* is locally called *doubredwa*. The bark of this liana, after being soaked in rum, is reputed to be a powerful male aphrodisiac. A local entrepreneur has started a cottage industry based on this plant, marketing a tea of the bark under the brand name "Pick Big" tea. The marketing slogan claims that this tea is "the ultimate tea for two."

Few of the plants used by the Wayanas, the Tiriós, or the Akuriyos have been extensively examined in laboratories to see what type of useful compounds they may contain for other cultures. How ancient is the knowledge of their healing plants—knowledge that has been transmitted orally from generation to generation? Although it is difficult if not impossible to date oral traditions with certainty, the Tiriós relate a story about their ancestors crossing a land so cold that they had to wrap themselves in the skins of animals. The Tiriós live in the northeast Amazon, where there is no cold weather, and traditionally they wear a *kamisa*, a cotton breech-cloth. This tale seems to be the tribal recollection of crossing the Bering Strait fifty thousand years ago!

Today, sadly, rain-forest peoples and plants the world over are endangered—as is our ability to learn their secrets. Several years ago Doel Soejarto, a colleague from the University of Illinois, was collecting rain-forest plants in Asia to be tested by the United States National Cancer Institute for anticancer and anti-HIV compounds. He received a cable from the laboratory in Washington, stating that extracts made from the bark of a *Calophyllum* tree knocked HIV-1 right out of the test tube. He was ordered to find more trees of that particular species and send back additional samples of the bark as soon as possible. Responding to this request, he found the trees, collected the bark, and mailed it back to the States. A few days later, he received another cable, which noted that the specimens he had sent did not contain the compound that had proved so effective against HIV-1 in the lab. Knowing that trees are like people—even the same species may harbor a different "blood chemistry"—he decided to return to the original trees and collect more of the same bark. Unfortunately, this proved impossible; when he arrived at the original site he found the area deforested.

Although this compound, known as Calanolide A, was not a cure for AIDS, it was useful in the lab for combating the virus and, hopefully, teaching us about improving our methods of fighting this disease. The search is on to find this compound from other trees of this species or other closely related species. Similar chemicals have been located and are being tested, but the original compound has not been found again in nature.

Like the extinction of species, lost knowledge is tragic—an irreversible impoverishment of our planet. The challenge for ethnobotanists today is not just to document this vanishing resource but also to sustain it. And all of us must foster conditions that will allow rain-forest cultures to maintain—and regain—their rightful place on Earth.

---

17 Wendy Call ◆ Mexico's Highway to Hell

The author of Selection 17 works for Grassroots International, a nongovernmental organization that supports indigenous rights and sustainable development abroad. The subtitle of the piece, "Native Peoples Fight for Sustainable Development," illustrates the now widely acknowledged relationship between cultural identity, the environment, and the economy and also alludes to the contested nature of economic development. Wendy Call emphasizes the human costs of mainstream approaches to economic development as exemplified by the Program to Spur Development in the Isthmus of Tehuantepec.

The Trans-Isthmus Project and local responses to it demonstrate how economic globalization introduces new technology to a region, thereby linking the global and the local. Globalization, as this project shows, may encourage central government planning and ignore local participation in the development of the rainforest frontier. This issue also reveals the importance of scale. In contrast to the large, complex development projects proposed by the agents of modernization, local grassroots proposals emphasize "green development"—small-scale, locally owned and controlled economic activities such as family farming and cottage industries (including logging). The tension between large, centrally planned development and local land rights, small businesses, environmental health, and cultural identity is also explored in Selections 8 and 9.

Call asks a key question: "Whose land is it, anyway?" Secure land tenure remains a burning issue to rural people in Latin America for economic, environmental, and cultural reasons. It is inextricably linked to cultural identity, not only for indigenous peoples but also for other forest peoples such as the blacks in northwestern Colombia and the rubber tappers in Brazil.

From Wendy Call, "Mexico's Highway to Hell: Native Peoples Fight for Sustainable Development," *Dollars and Sense* (July/August 1998): 28–31. Reprinted by permission of *Dollars and Sense*.

The road from the dusty Mexican town of Matías Romero into the mountain village of San Juan Guichicovi is little more than ruts and rocks in August, late in the rainy season. As our truck crests the final hill, the thick forest suddenly opens to reveal a sea of people. Hundreds are gathered behind large banners and a brass band at the edge of town. As the band begins another tune, the colorful group begins to march.

Moments before the brass band reaches its destination—the village community center—the impossibly hot afternoon cracks open. The air, just moments before motionless and heavy with water, becomes a searing wind. A few fat drops gather into a wave of cool water as we dash madly to the shelter of the community center. We reach shelter just as the drops become a deluge. There we are greeted warmly by young women in long, slim skirts, high heels, and T-shirts proclaiming, "The Isthmus Is Our Own: A National Forum."

This gathering is one of four held simultaneously in four towns of Mexico's Isthmus of Tehuantepec during August of last year [1997]. Hundreds of indigenous community members from throughout the isthmus— the sliver of land where the southern states of Oaxaca, Chiapas, Tabasco, and Veracruz come together—are gathering in Guichicovi to discuss their collective future. A half-dozen languages mingle in the rising steam from the rain. The residents of Guichicovi, who are from the Zapotec and Mixe native nations, welcome fellow Mixes and Zapotecs, as well as Chinantecos, Chontales, Huaves, Popolucas, and Zoques. Nations with a history of conflict have come together to deal with a common threat.

That threat is the "Trans-Isthmus Project," a proposal from the Mexican government to connect the Atlantic and Pacific Oceans with a "multimodal" freight corridor of rail and road across the Isthmus of Tehuantepec. Those gathered in Guichicovi fear that their strong regional culture—as well as their local economy and ecology—are at risk because of the government's plan to develop an alternative to the overburdened Panama Canal. Already, most of the children of the Zoque nation speak Spanish more fluently than Zoque. So many outsiders have moved in that the Zoques are now a minority on their own lands. The scene at "The Isthmus Is Our Own" roundtable in Guichicovi demonstrates a dual existence. While the steaming tamales that are served for dinner and the women's clothing (ornately embroidered *huipiles*) are traditional, it is clear that the "modern" world has arrived in Guichicovi; the presentations are mostly in Spanish and focus on economic globalization.

The regional union of indigenous communities, the debtors' alliance El Barzón, and a group of indigenous timber workers called "The Isthmus Is Our Own" forum to plot a strategy of resistance to the latest threat to the traditional way of life. This is not a new battle. "Hernan Cortes, the chief conqueror [in 1519], . . . understood the importance of the region and promoted to the Spanish crown a commercial trans-isthmus route, which, as time has passed, has become the dream of all the 'modernizers' of Mexican society," notes prominent environmentalist Alejandro Toledo, a forum participant.

Indeed, three centuries after Cortés's arrival, greedy eyes again focused on the Isthmus of Tehuantepec. The U.S. government first planned to connect the Atlantic and Pacific Oceans across Mexico. At that time, the Mexican government refused to host the canal. The continent was cut in half farther south with the Panama Canal, after the United States helped carve a new nation out of Colombia's northern isthmus.

The new Trans-Isthmus Project proposes a land bridge, not a canal. It requires expanding, improving, and contracting out the operation of the railroad now bisecting the isthmus. The plan, euphemistically titled the "Program to Spur Development in the Isthmus of Tehuantepec," also involves a new superhighway cutting through the region and the redevelopment of the Gulf of Mexico port of Coatzacoalcos and the Pacific port of Salina Cruz. That is only the beginning.

"There are 150 projects," explains Felipe Ochoa, head of Ochoa and Associates, the Mexico City engineering consultants who authored the government's plan for the Trans-Isthmus Project. "We are looking for projects that can 'trigger' development. The forestry, agroindustry, petrochemical industries [are] examples." His proposal includes twenty-four petrochemical facilities, a dozen shrimp farms, two oil refineries, and nearly a half-dozen industrial parks for *maquiladoras*.

Oil development should nicely attract the interest of foreign companies just as the government plans to sell off PEMEX (Petróleos Mexicanos), which has been under government control for fifty-eight years. The Isthmus of Tehuantepec produces 90 percent of Mexico's crude oil, and petroleum sales account for 36 percent to 40 percent of Mexico's federal revenue. Mexican technocrats argued PEMEX should be sold off to raise money to reduce the national debt, but popular resistance forced the government to back off a bit. Now it plans to sell off many of PEMEX's petrochemical facilities while retaining a 51 percent stake in the industry. Although the Mexican constitution protects public ownership of the oil industry, technocrats are now arguing that the provision covers only *gasoline* refineries, not other petrochemical facilities.

The Mexican oil industry already has made the isthmus home to some of the most polluted sites in the country. With the Trans-Isthmus Project, isthmus residents can look forward to increased industrial pollution from the new factories and the destruction of coastal lands—critical breeding grounds for marine life—as they are turned into shrimp farms.

While all this is troublesome enough, residents of the forest communities are especially worried about nearly 400 square miles of eucalyptus plantations mentioned in Ochoa's document. While the proposal gives few details, project opponents assert that virgin rainforest in Zoque territory will be cleared and seeded for this purpose. These forests make Mexico one of the most biologically diverse countries in the world. Eucalyptus monoculture would threaten this by destroying habitat for many plant and animal species, some of which are found nowhere else in the world. When asked about criticism of the eucalyptus plantations, the plan's author, Ochoa, concedes, "Ecologically, they have a point."

Whose land is it, anyway? The Zoques are one of Mexico's largest indigenous landholders. Together, the residents of the two major Zoque municipalities communally control more than 2,300 square miles of land. Its breathtaking diversity includes fertile, lowland plains as well as rugged peaks rising almost 8,000 feet above sea level, blanketed in nearly impenetrable rainforest. Their holdings include one of the largest stands of pristine rainforest left in Mesoamerica, called *Chimalapas* by the Zoques, or "gourd full of gold." Three hundred years ago they were forced to offer just that—25,000 gold coins—to the Spanish colonizers to buy back their ancestral lands.

Yet the 1967 executive decree that recognized Zoque control of their communal lands was never formally ratified by the Mexican government. More recently, NAFTA nullified the section of the Mexican constitution that supported communal holdings by limiting private land ownership. The Mexican government also has a long, sorry history of ignoring its land grants to indigenous groups, and there is little reason to hope it will act differently this time, with oil and timber money at stake. The land grab may be even harder to stop because the states of Oaxaca and Chiapas each deeded portions of the Chimalapas near their common border to different indigenous groups, sowing conflict among them.

Carlos Beas, head of the Union of Indigenous Communities in the Northern Zone of the Isthmus and organizer of the Guichicovi gathering, fears that community resistance to the land grab may also lose out to petty corruption. He explains, "The government has invested a lot of resources in controlling these communities"; in other words, it buys off many local government officials. "Now, the representatives follow the government's policies in return for money."

Much like the Zapatistas, the rebels in neighboring Chiapas, the hundreds gathered in Guichicovi know what will happen if they lose their lands. They conclude their meeting with a public statement asserting, "With the development of an industrial corridor, we see glimmers of the 'proletarianization' of the farmers and the indigenous people. We will lose our dignity. Without land, we will become factory boys, simple workers with miserable wages and inferior jobs."

"Mexican policymakers publicly recognized in 1992 that their agricultural and trade policies would reduce the rural percentage of Mexico's population from 26 percent to 16 percent in less than one decade," notes political scientist Jonathan Fox of the University of California at Santa Cruz. The Trans-Isthmus Project is part of this grand scheme.

From the government's vantage point, nearly half of the communities in the isthmus live in a state of "very high marginalization," meaning that more than half of the population is illiterate and less than half of the homes have electricity and running water. In the Chimalapas, most of the residents still earn their living from subsistence agriculture: corn, beans, and other cultivated crops grown for family consumption. Fifty years ago, coffee cultivation began to move some communities into the cash economy. Cedar and mahogany harvesting, along with cattle ranching, are growing in importance. With the recent crash of the coffee market, many residents in the southern Chimalapas turned to drug trafficking.

The government anticipates the Trans-Isthmus Project will create only 11,000 to 12,000 jobs, meager bait indeed given the potential displacement of people from small-scale agriculture. These precious jobs are also wildly expensive. In a country where the most a worker would earn at minimum wage is under $3.50 a day, various projections estimate an investment of $160,000 to $190,000 for each job created. By comparison, in the first year after NAFTA was implemented, the average cost of a job created by foreign investment in Mexico was about $27,000 in 1994 dollars.

These numbers demonstrate that the Trans-Isthmus Project is not a jobs program, says Beas, but an investment program. "I think that the Mexican government, which is in cahoots with the big corporations, is in a race to get the inter-oceanic corridor," he notes. Indeed, with the transfer of the Panama Canal from U.S. government to local control in 1999, every country from Mexico to Colombia is hoping to cash in on transcontinental traffic. "Studies show that 80 percent of the commerce moving between Asia, Europe, and America crosses in containers via U.S. railroads, and only 20 percent crosses through Panama," Beas explains. "But this 20 percent is a good slice." Combined with businesses' uncertainty over how Panama will manage the canal, along with the increasing trade they expect if the economic integration of the Americas goes as planned for 2005, interest in an alternative is rising.

Colombia has proposed digging its own canal just south of the Panamanian border. Honduras and El Salvador want to collaborate on a railroad network between the two oceans, while Guatemala announced plans to update its own decrepit rail system. Costa Rica's legislature proposed a similar rail link six years ago, but has hardly mentioned the plan since. The Nicaraguan government proposed a system of "dry canals" to link the rivers and lakes between the coasts. This proposal, enthusiastically promoted by an international team of public relations consultants, received the most press in the United States. In an abrupt about-face, however, the Nicaraguans scrapped their plan in late February, citing environmental concerns. With this shift, the Mexican government's proposal may well become the front-runner.

Over the past two years, news of the Trans-Isthmus Project has filled the Mexican media. Newspapers have linked dozens of U.S. corporations— engineering contractors like Bechtel Power Corporation, freight movers including Eagle Marie and Stevedoring Services, and an alphabet soup of railroad operators from the Anacostia & Pacific to Wisconsin Central— with the proposed development. So far, nongovernmental organizations have traced several hundred million pesos' worth—that's tens of millions of dollars' worth—of investment promises from Mexican and foreign companies.

For now, though, the primary boosters of the Trans-Isthmus Project are Mexican technocrats—especially the Secretary of Communications and Transport, Carlos Ruiz Sancristan, and the governors of Oaxaca and Veracruz. Ochoa expresses confidence in spite of lurking questions: What about the forbidding landscape of the isthmus, the instability of the Mexican economy, and the low-intensity war being waged in the state of Chiapas? What about local opposition and the continued wariness of private investors? "We are going ahead," Ochoa asserts. He has been working on plans for a transit corridor across the Isthmus of Tehuantepec for twenty years and insists that the project's time has come. Given the pending free trade zone of the Americas, he may well be right.

Still, Ochoa admits there are "groups that feel they will not benefit" from the Trans-Isthmus Project. Some of these groups counter that this is because they have been excluded from the planning process. "We say no," insists Marina Meneses Velázquez of the Ecological Forum of Juchitán, the regional capital of the isthmus. "We say no because it is unsustainable. We say no because it does not consider our point of view." The government's unwillingness to consult isthmus residents has sparked skepticism in unexpected places, including the Juchitán Chamber of Commerce. In Mexico City last fall, a coalition of senators from all the major political parties joined forces to criticize the "vicious and corrupt" policies of the government agency responsible for the plan.

Now the opponents need a counterproposal, one that guides what one resident attending the San Juan Guichicovi gathering says must be "a green development, not one made of concrete." To chart a course for this "green development," communities are holding a series of local gatherings this summer in villages throughout the isthmus. The ideas floated so far are diverse and even divergent; they range from developing sustainable agriculture and organic coffee cultivation to promoting Mexican-owned small industry and small-scale timber harvesting. The central element of the vision will almost certainly be secure land tenure, something the people of the Chimalapas and other indigenous communities have sought for more than five hundred years.

Delfino Juárez Toledo, a longtime activist from the Mixe nation, concludes that being true to their own native heritage is a prerequisite of any successful development in the isthmus. "If we deny that we are Huaves, Zoques, Nahua-Popolucas, Chontales, Chinantecos, or Zapotecos, then we are already ruined."

IV

Prospects for Development: Alternative Futures for Latin America's Tropical Rainforests

At present, a great debate rages over what to do with the remaining rainforests of Latin America. The failures of past attempts to exploit the resources of regions such as Amazonia, as well as the growing political power and sophistication of groups seeking to preserve the tropical rainforest, have encouraged nontraditional approaches to developing these regions. Selections in previous sections of this book examine the problems associated with colonization along frontier roads and large-scale undertakings such as Mexico's Trans-Isthmus Project and oil production in Veracruz. The selections in Part IV explore some of the alternative approaches to developing tropical rainforest regions. Most represent attempts to find a path to "sustainable development."

Sustainable development is itself a contested subject, with different meanings to different groups of people. As used in this book, however, it refers to economic development based on sustained-yield use of renewable resources, broad-based community participation throughout the process, and an equitable distribution of the wealth created by development. In other words, it has both environmental and social components. The success of sustainable development is measured not by economic growth alone, but by actual improvements in the quality of people's lives—namely, environmental health as well as improved family incomes or access to the resources necessary to meet basic needs.

In tropical rainforest regions, sustainable development will entail preservation of some mature forest while encouraging ecologically sound local exploitation and management of other forested areas. Inevitably, some areas will be converted to other uses entirely. The challenge is to identify the appropriate mix of land uses for Latin America's remaining tropical rainforest regions. Natural and social scientists can provide information about the probable environmental and human consequences of alternative land uses in specific zones. The actual land use that materializes, however, will undoubtedly result from political struggles over rights to rainforest resources. Chico Mendes (Selection 18) gives an insider's view of the political aspects of development in the Brazilian Amazon.

Selection 24 offers another perspective on political aspects of forest conservation as it describes the role of environmentalists in creating national parks in Costa Rica. This story reflects the most traditional way of protecting natural areas—through the establishment of national parks. Many Latin American nations have created national parks, but their ensuing problems reveal the difficulties associated with uncritical adoption of models of conservation from developed countries such as the United States. As long as the economic and social pressures that fuel deforestation persist in Latin America, and public support for national parks is weak or absent, the boundaries of these parks will not be respected. Furthermore, when the inhabitants of designated areas are ignored during park planning, as they often are, they will continue to use the resources of the park in order to meet their basic survival needs, as they have for generations. Tiny, underfunded agencies cannot protect the integrity of national parks under these circumstances. The result has been the creation of "paper parks"—ones drawn on maps but receiving little real protection or development. Selection 24 shows how Costa Rica has struggled to overcome these challenges and has largely succeeded in creating an internationally acclaimed system of national parks and protected areas.

Protection of some national parks and other reserves has been engineered by means of debt-for-nature swaps in a few Latin American countries (including Costa Rica). The debt-swap concept is widely seen as a model for funding conservation projects in the Third World while simultaneously helping indebted countries improve their economic situation. This new approach to conservation of nature and debt reduction is critiqued in Selection 23.

Increasingly, Westerners are becoming aware that indigenous people hold the key to preservation of "natural" ecosystems. After all, they have been co-existing with their environments for many generations. Selection 19 demonstrates how the Mêbêngôkre Indians of the Brazilian Amazon increase biodiversity by altering and managing ecosystems through an integrated system of beliefs and practices. Recognizing that many indigenous groups actively manage ecosystems in this way, it is increasingly difficult to continue thinking of the rainforest as "natural." And there is now widespread acknowledgment of the importance of preserving tribal homelands and protecting the rights of their inhabitants.

The tropical rainforest can provide the foundation for ecotourism. Tourism is a dynamic sector of the world economy, and nature-based tourism is one of its fastest-growing segments. By 1990 in Costa Rica, for example, tourism had surpassed coffee exports as the number-one foreign exchange earner. There is considerable controversy on this topic, however. Proponents argue that tourism attracted by intact tropical rainforest can provide good economic returns year after year, not just the one-time windfall from current methods of timber cutting and cattle production. But critics point out that tourism revenues are notoriously volatile and only a small percentage remains in destination areas. Selection 25 discusses the problematic nature of ecotourism in Costa Rica. Selection 26 describes a small-scale, grassroots approach to sustainable forest-based development, including ecotourism, pioneered by residents of the Maya Biosphere Reserve in Guatemala.

Another approach is to preserve forests as extractive reserves for the exploitation of renewable commodities on a sustained-yield basis. Such renewable forest products include latex (rubber), Brazil nuts, and babaçu (palms) in Amazonia (Selection 18). Extractive reserves, as proposed by Mendes and others, represent a way for traditional forest people to continue living in—and making a living from—the tropical rainforest. Along these lines, using the forest as a source of genetic material or pharmacologically active chemicals represents another alternative for simultaneously preserving mature forest and producing income (Selection 20). On the other hand, Selection 21 raises questions about this aspect of conservation by exploring some of the ethical questions involved in appropriating the accumulated knowledge of tribal peoples without crediting or paying royalties to them. Critics, however, point out that these approaches have limited possibilities for preserving large expanses of Amazonian forest. They support only a relatively sparse population, and not all areas of forest have adequate densities of exploitable resources. Proponents respond that densities of economically valuable species can be increased, and that there are probably as yet undiscovered resources in the forest that could be the foundation of future extractive economies. Furthermore, a system of extractive reserves could form just one part of a multi-approach model of forest conservation that also includes national parks, autonomous Indian lands, and national forests used for sustained-yield forestry.

Although timber generally has not been extracted in a sustainable way in the past, it could be in the future, given the economic and political will to encourage sustained-yield methods. In recent decades, ecologists and foresters have been exploring new forestry systems for the tropics. John Browder (Selection 22) offers an overview of various options for managing production in tropical forests that were previously considered unmanageable because of their complexity.

At present, a number of innovative and promising alternatives for developing tropical rainforest regions are emerging from both research and practical experience. The political struggles of traditionally marginalized groups such as Indians and rubber tappers have focused the world's attention on the social aspects of what has generally been considered an environmental issue. The empowerment of the poor and dispossessed that has resulted from their struggle over rights to the tropical rainforest has led to powerful critiques of the traditional approach to development and has generated many of the innovative alternatives presented in Part IV.

18   Chico Mendes ◆ Fight for
the Forest: Building Bridges

Chico Mendes was an internationally renowned leader in the struggle of forest people against powerful Brazilian landowners over access to tropical forest resources. He was born in 1944 into a rubber tapper's family in Xapuri, in the state of Acre, near Brazil's border with Bolivia, and went to work tapping rubber at age nine. He never had the opportunity to attend school and did not learn to read until adulthood, when a Brazilian activist settled in Xapuri after fleeing Bolivian authorities who sought to stop his organizing of the peasants in their country. The activist taught Mendes not only literacy but also raised his consciousness about social justice and political action. Rubber tappers traditionally lived under virtual slavery, bound by debt to a seringalista *(owner of a tract of rubber-producing forest). Mendes joined the growing rural trade union movement, which, in the 1970s, had some success in breaking the hold that* seringalistas *had over the rubber tappers.*

During this period, however, a new threat to the rubber tappers arose: the expansion of cattle ranches. As seringalistas *sold off their holdings, the land frequently was purchased by cattle ranchers. They proceeded to clear the forest and replace it with pasture for their herds. Obviously the rubber tappers would lose their livelihoods if cattle ranching continued to expand. As the resistance movement by rubber tappers gained strength, so did the violence of the tactics employed by the cattle ranchers. A number of rural union leaders and other activists have been killed in this struggle. Chico Mendes joined their ranks in December 1988— number ninety in that year's catalog of murdered rural workers and their supporters.*

These excerpts from his own writings, published in 1989, describe the link between the economic interests of forest people and the preservation of the Amazon rainforest. Mendes proposes the establishment of extractive reserves as the mechanism for preserving both the forest and the livelihoods of the people who live there. He indicates the economic potential of an Amazon economy based on the extraction of renewable re-

From Chico Mendes, "Fight for the Forest: Building Bridges," in Chico Mendes (with Tony Gross), *Fight for the Forest: Chico Mendes in His Own Words* (London: Latin American Bureau, 1989), chap. 3. Reprinted by permission of the Latin American Bureau.

sources on a sustainable basis. Finally, he points out that the alliance forged between rubber tappers and Indians in the rural unions and trade associations has greatly strengthened the grass-roots movement to save the Amazon rainforest. Now the traditional animosity between these groups has given way to the need to join forces in the battle for their livelihoods and, in many cases, their lives.

We realized that in order to guarantee the future of the Amazon we had to find a way to preserve the forest while at the same time developing the region's economy.

So what were our thoughts originally? We accepted that the Amazon could not be turned into some kind of sanctuary that nobody could touch. On the other hand, we knew it was important to stop the deforestation that is threatening the Amazon and all human life on the planet. We felt our alternative should involve preserving the forest, but it should also include a plan to develop the economy. So we came up with the idea of extractive reserves.

What do we mean by an extractive reserve? We mean the land is under public ownership but the rubber tappers and other workers that live on that land should have the right to live and work there. I say "other workers" because there are not only rubber tappers in the forest. In our area, rubber tappers also harvest Brazil nuts, but in other parts of the Amazon there are people who earn a living solely from harvesting, while there are others who harvest babaçu and jute.*

So what are we really after? Despite the threats, we're fighting for better marketing and price guarantees for rubber. We want better marketing policies and better working conditions for those harvesting nuts. But there is an infinite number of natural resources in the forest, so we also want the government to encourage the industrialization and marketing of other forest products that it has always ignored in the past.

There are other questions to be considered. A sustainable fishing industry could be developed, exploiting the resource in a rational way. The enormous variety of plants with medicinal properties in this forest could prove very important to the country, if only some research was done. The universities, not only in Acre, but throughout Brazil, should spend time researching the Amazon region. I believe if this happened, and if the government took it all seriously, then in ten years the Amazon region could be very rich and have an important role in the national economy. . . .

*Babaçu refers to either of two palm species, *Orbignya martiana* and *O. oleifera*, whose fruit and leaves have a number of uses, both commercially and for subsistence. Jute is a fiber crop.—Ed.

Where did we get the idea of setting up the CNS [National Council of Rubber Tappers]? We discovered there is something called the National Rubber Council, which represents the interests of landowners and businessmen but not the interests of the rubber tappers. So we thought, why not create an organization as a counterweight to all that bureaucracy and try to stop the government from messing the rubber tappers about? The First National Congress set up the CNS and elected a provisional executive committee.

The CNS is not meant to be a kind of parallel trade union, replacing the Xapuri Rural Workers' Union, for example. It is just an organization for rubber tappers. The growth of the trade unions was very important for us, but other agricultural workers including day laborers and so on are also members of the same union. Other kinds of agricultural workers have been seen as having particular needs and interests, but not rubber tappers; it's as though we were something that existed only in the past. So one of the reasons for creating the CNS was to recognize the rubber tappers as a particular group of workers fighting for a very important objective—the defense of the Amazon forest. The idea went down very well.

We also wanted to seek out the leaders of the Indian peoples in Acre and discuss how to unite our resistance movements, especially since Indians and rubber tappers have been at odds with each other for centuries. In Acre the leaders of the rubber tappers and the Indian peoples met and concluded that neither of us was to blame for this. The real culprits were the rubber estate owners, the bankers, and all the other powerful interest groups that had exploited us both.

People understood this very quickly, and from the beginning of 1986 the alliance of the peoples of the forest got stronger and stronger. Our links with the Indians have grown even further this year. For example, a meeting of the Tarauacá rubber tappers was attended by two hundred Indians, and six of them were elected to the Tarauacá Rubber Tappers' Commission. Indians are now beginning to participate in the CNS organizing commissions. In Cruzeiro do Sul about two hundred Indians are active in the movement, and this year they have even joined in our *empates* [mass occupations of forest slated for clearing in order to stop the loggers from cutting the trees].

Our proposals are now not just ours alone; they are put forward together by Indians and rubber tappers. Our fight is the fight of all the peoples of the forest.

When the minister of agriculture met a joint commission of Indians and rubber tappers in his office, he was really taken aback. "What's going on?" he said. "Indians and rubber tappers have been fighting each other since the last century! Why is it that today you come here together?"

We told him that things had changed, and this meant that the fight to defend the Amazon was stronger. People really took notice of that.

19 Darrell A. Posey ◆ Alternatives to Forest Destruction: Lessons from the Mêbêngôkre Indians

Recent research has shown that indigenous peoples manage forest resources in a complex and sustainable way based on extensive knowledge of their local flora and fauna. Modern land-use practices in Amazonia are inherently unsustainable, and in destroying Indian societies they are destroying a vital source of information as to how people can live in and enrich, rather than destroy, the forest. Darrell Posey claims here, in a 1989 essay, that indigenous knowledge of the environment and how to manage it successfully deserves to be seen as a major intellectual contribution to humanity. Research by Posey, Mark Plotkin (Selection 16), Katherine Milton (Selection 5), and other ethnoscientists is beginning to change the way in which Westerners perceive the remaining tribal peoples of Latin America and elsewhere.

Indians in Brazil have historically been considered, at best, as "relatively incapable" human beings who must be "protected" as wards of the federal government. The Brazilian Indian Foundation (Fundaçao Nacional do Indio—FUNAI) serves as the official organ responsible for Indian affairs. Under past national constitutions, FUNAI was considered the only legal institution that could represent or defend native peoples. Land demarcation, sales of mineral and timber rights, judicial proceedings, even labor contracts and agricultural sales could only legally be conducted by FUNAI officials.

Claims of corruption within FUNAI have now swollen to a level equal to accusations against its predecessor, Sociedade para Proteçao do Indio (SPI), which was disbanded due to its scandalous activities, in 1967. A former president of FUNAI, Romero Jucá Filho, has been charged with involvement in the illegal sale of gold and timber rights on Indian lands. This did not stop him, however, from being named acting governor of the Federal Territory of Roraima, where some of Brazil's richest mineral and natural reserves are located—mostly in indigenous reserves.[1]

As Carneiro da Cunha points out, "The Indian question today is centered around disputes over mineral and natural resources on Indian soils and sub-soils." Native peoples, by virtue of their low numbers (approximately 1 percent of the Brazilian population) and cultural, social, and political differences, are markedly disadvantaged in the battle against the powerful forces of international capitalism behind those who seek to exploit these resources.

From Darrell A. Posey, "Alternatives to Forest Destruction: Lessons from the Mebengokre Indians," *The Ecologist* 19, no. 6 (November–December 1989): 241–44. Reprinted by permission of *The Ecologist*.

Maintaining Stereotypes

Much of the general strategy of the exploiters of Indian lands depends upon the maintenance of traditional stereotypes of "primitive" Indians. In a country where paternalism is as much a part of the national fabric as *carnaval*, it has been all too easy to mask attempts to thwart native independence movements with rhetoric about "helping" Indians to make decisions about "what is best for them." Rarely have Indian leaders been heard, because, it is said, they could not possibly know enough about the white man's society to make good judgments.

It is equally important for those who wish to exploit Indian lands—especially in Amazonia, which is the refuge of over half of Brazil's remaining aborigines—to say that such lands are unproductive and/or unoccupied. The whole of the Amazon basin is considered empty—one great frontier where only a few "primitive" Indians and "cultureless" *caboclos* (peasants) struggle to survive. As Carneiro da Cunha notes: "Indian lands are . . . treated as 'no-man's-land': always considered as the first option for mining, hydroelectric projects, land reform, and development projects in general." This strategy has been relatively easy to maintain over the years because of the inability of native peoples and *caboclos* to organize in a dominant society where minority rights have never been considered an issue.

The Human Tragedy

The destruction of Amazonia is a human as much as an ecological tragedy. *Caboclos*, with few exceptions, are ignored in Amazonian studies as though they were devoid of any culture whatsoever. Expelled from their lands as squatters (*posseiros*), they are forced into poverty and dependency in sprawling slums (*favelas*) where they pay the price of "development."

Indians reflect clearly the tragic human costs of Amazonian development.[2] Brazilian Indian populations have declined from approximately eight million, at the time of the first European contact, to less than two hundred thousand today. Eighty-seven Indian groups have become extinct during this century in Brazil alone.[3] With the decimation of each indigenous group, the world loses thousands of years of accumulated knowledge of adaptation to tropical ecosystems. Such precious information is overlooked without the least consideration: the rapid pace of economic development cannot be halted even long enough to take note of what it is about to destroy.

Indian cultures offer a rich and untapped source of information on the natural resources of the Amazonian basin.[4] Recognition of the value of indigenous knowledge by our civilization would permit Indians to be seen as major intellectual contributors to humanity, rather than mere exotic footnotes to the pages of history books. This recognition could provide an "ideological bridge" through which Indians can prosper with the dignity they need and the respect they deserve.

The Mêbêngôkre and the Kayapó Project

The Kayapó Indians once inhabited a territory the size of France between the Araguaia and Tocantins rivers in eastern Amazonia. Today they live on a five-million-acre proposed reserve that includes a variety of tropical ecosystems, ranging from high forests to vast grasslands. All groups within the Kayapó nation call themselves the Mêbêngôkre ("people of the water's source") and speak a language of the Je family of languages.

The knowledge of the Mêbêngôkre Indians is an integrated system of beliefs and practices. Much generally shared information is to be found in a Mêbêngôkre village, in addition to the specialized knowledge held by a few. There are specialists in soils, plants, animals, crops, medicines, and rituals. Each and every Mêbêngôkre believes that he or she has the ability to survive alone in the forest for an indefinite time. Such a belief engenders a strong sense of personal security and is interwoven into daily life.

Forest Islands

The creation of forest "islands" (*apete*) in tropical savannas demonstrates to what extent the Mêbêngôkre can alter and manage ecosystems to increase biological diversity. Such ecological engineering requires detailed knowledge of soil fertility, microclimatic variations, and species' niches, as well as the interrelationships among species which are introduced into these human-made communities. The succcessful *apete* results not only from knowledge of immediate soil and biological properties, but also from the long-term relationships that develop as these forest "islands" become established and increase in density and height. Because numerous plants are cultivated to attract game animals, the *apete* can be viewed as both agroforestry plots and hunting reserves.[5]

The Mêbêngôkre frequently speak of *ômbiqwa-ô-toro* plants, or those plants which are "good friends" or "good neighbors" to one another. The Indians are aware of some species combinations that develop more vigorously when planted together. Such synergistic groups often include dozens of plant species, require complex cultivation patterns, and are characterized in terms of "plant energy." Thus, a Mêbêngôkre garden is created by careful combinations of different "plant energies," just as an artist blends colors to produce a work of art. Planting practices based on plant energies can be compared with ecological principles which allow us to understand, from the viewpoint of Western science, the underlying logic of Mêbêngôkre management.

Mêbêngôkre techniques of long-term management of forest savannas, with regard to both floral and faunal resources, represent an alternative to the destructive development models offered by timber extraction, agro-forestry, agriculture, and cattle ranching. Native animal and plant species can be utilized, while being conserved, if indigenous integrated management principles are adopted.[6] Mêbêngôkre understanding of forest growth also holds useful lessons for those studying the restoration of degraded forest ecosystems.

Ethnopedology: Indian Understanding of Soils

The Mêbêngôkre have a sophisticated understanding of soils, which are classified according to horizontal and vertical distinctions based on texture, color, drainage qualities, friability, and stratification. Soil qualities are frequently related to indicator plant species that allow Indians to predict the flora and fauna associated with specific soil types, each of which is managed differently according to its individual characteristics.

The Indians modify local soils by using different types of ground cover such as vegetation, logs, leaves, straw, and bark to influence soil moisture, shading, and temperature. Holes are sometimes filled with organic matter, refuse, and ash to produce highly concentrated pockets of rich soil. Old banana leaves, stalks, rice straw, and other organic matter are piled (and sometimes burned) in selected parts of fields to create additional local variations.

The Mêbêngôkre have dozens of types of plant ash, each of which is said to have certain qualities preferred by specific cultivars. Plant ash is an important component in all aspects of indigenous agriculture.

The well-known *terra preta dos indios*, the soils formed through Indian occupation, are extremely rich and are distributed throughout Amazonia, but little is known of their formation as they have been considered to be the results of historical practices that are no longer followed. There are, however, numerous Indian groups like the Mêbêngôkre that continue to manage soils to improve fertility and productivity.[7]

The study of indigenous uses of ground cover, mulch, organic matter, and ash could lead to the development of modern agricultural systems in Amazonia that succeed in improving, rather than degrading, soils.[8]

Ethnozoology

Indians are astute observers of many aspects of animal behavior: mating, nesting, feeding, hunting, predator-prey relationships, diurnal and nocturnal habits, etc. They teach these lessons to their children partly through the rearing of pets in the village, and also by encouraging children to learn the behavior patterns and feeding habits of different animal species that are considered to have their own "personalities." Like other tribes, the Mêbêngôkre conscientiously study animal anatomy, giving special attention to the stomach contents of game animals.

A precise knowledge of insect behavior is utilized by the Mêbêngôkre in the control of agricultural pests. For example, nests of ants of the genus *Azteca* are deliberately placed by the Indians in gardens and on fruit trees which are infested with leaf-cutter ants (*Atta* sp.). According to the Mêbêngôkre, the Azteca ants have an odor which repels the leaf-cutter ants. In the same manner, the Indians cultivate several plants which have extra-floral nectar glands, often on the leaves or stems, which attract predatory ants to serve as "bodyguards" for the plant. Several species of predacious wasps nest preferentially under the leaves of banana trees which Indians plant to form a living wall around their fields. Thus, knowledge of insect behavior is an important aspect in the manipulation of the natural biological control of agricultural pests.[9]

Ethnomedicine and Ethnopharmacology

One of the most productive areas of ethnobiological research is ethnopharmacology. Plants used medicinally by native peoples are a prime source of useful drugs for the pharmacological industry. Intensive study of indigenous plant and animal preparations and their administration can enrich conventional medical knowledge. Data on the parts of the plants which are used in medicines, the ecological preferences of these plants, the seasonal cycle of their flowering and fruiting, and the soils in which they grow are important since these factors influence the amounts of pharmacologically active ingredients in the harvested plants.[10]

Not only can ethnopharmacological studies contribute to the discovery of unknown drugs, but they also reveal new sources of known pharmaceuticals. This is especially important for countries like Brazil, where imported medicines are exorbitant in cost.

Ethnopharmacology should be coupled with ethnomedicine to be truly effective. For example, Elisabetsky and Posey have suggested how research into two Mêbêngôkre folk disease categories can advance knowledge of symptoms that complicate diarrhoea and dysentery—the major killers in the humid tropics.[11] The Mêbêngôkre classify over 150 types of diarrhoea/dysentery, each of which is treated with specific medicines. Ethnopharmacologists and physicians frequently forget that disease categories are, like all phenomena, socially classified and not universal: folk categories, as in the Mêbêngôkre case, are often more elaborate and detailed than their Western counterparts.

Ethnoagriculture and Agroforestry

Research into indigenous agriculture has resulted in valuable information on pest control without costly chemical sprays and additives. The use of natural predators, insecticides, and fertilizers makes indigenous agriculture both inexpensive and energy efficient. Intercropping of cultivars appears to be another key factor in natural control, as does the extensive use of "trap crops" within and at the margins of plots. "Natural corridors" maintained between Mêbêngôkre fields serve as biological reserves that maintain species diversity while facilitating the re-establishment of plants and animals during forest regeneration.

When applying the restrictive term "agriculture" to Mêbêngôkre management of domesticated and semidomesticated plants, one must consider that indigenous agriculture begins with a forest opening into which useful species are introduced and ends with a mature forest of concentrated resources, including game animals. The cycle is repeated when the old-field forests become too high and dense for efficient production and are cleared again.

The Mêbêngôkre also practice long-term management strategies to maximize firewood production using a number of techniques, including seasonal cutting schedules, pruning, vertical extraction preferences, limb and trunk size choices, maturation decisions, and drying capabilities.

There is an urgent need in Amazonia for the implementation of integrated agricultural and forest management, which would include both plant and animal resources and not be destructive to the local environment. Indigenous systems, like those of the Mêbêngôkre, have functioned successfully for millennia and offer many ideas for the successful implementation of diversified and sustainable agricultural and forestry practices.

Myths and Ecological Concepts

A knowledge of complex ecological interrelationships is sometimes expressed in the highly codified and symbolic forms of myth and ritual. These can only be understood when one lives and participates in an Indian society for some length of time.

The Mêbêngôkre recognize two mythological entities that illustrate how beliefs can function as ecological concepts. One is *Bepkororoti*, which is the spirit of an ancient shaman unjustly killed by fellow tribesmen while seeking his hereditary share of tapir meat after a hunt. His spirit now manifests itself in the form of rain, lightning, and dangerous storms, which can kill people or destroy crops. He becomes angry when people do not share, and fear of his vengeance compels the Mêbêngôkre to be generous. To placate *Bepkororoti*, Indians cater to his fondness for honey by leaving behind a portion of honey, pollen, and brood in raided hives. As a result, some species of stingless bees return to disturbed hives and re-establish colonies. The belief in *Bepkororoti* thus serves to preserve bee colonies and ensure continued honey production.

The *mry-kàák* is an entity that takes the form of an electric eel-like animal, twenty or more meters in length, that lives in deep pools of water. It is the most feared of all creatures, since it can kill with its powerful electric shock from a distance of five hundred meters or more. It is thought to subsist on minnows; and, whenever the Mêbêngôkre see schools of spawning fish or minnows, they stay clear of the area for fear of the *mry-kàák*. This practice serves to protect the minnows, which are the basic element of the aquatic foodweb of the river.

An Ideological Bridge between Peoples

Mêbêngôkre ecological adaptations and agricultural methods offer new models for resource management of the Amazon without incurring the wholesale destruction which characterizes present development policies. If indigenous experience were taken seriously and incorporated into research and development programs, then the Indians would be recognized for what they truly are: a diligent, intelligent, and practical people who have adapted successfully to their Amazon environment over thousands of years. It is imperative that Indians and their respective systems of ecological management be protected so that they can develop according to their own social and cultural rules which we, in our ignorance, have only just begun to appreciate and understand.

Notes

1. *Survival International News* 22, 1988, 6.
2. Davis, S., *Victims of the Miracle: Development and the Indians of Brazil*, Cambridge University Press, 1977.
3. Ribeiro, D., *Os indios e a civilizaçao*, Ed. Civilizaçao Brasileira, 1970.
4. Posey, D. A., "Indigenous Knowledge and Development: An Ideological Bridge to the Future," *Ciência e Cultura* 35, 7, 1983, 877–94.
5. Anderson, A. and Posey, D., "Reflorestamento indígena," *Ciência Hoje* 6, 31, 1987, 44–51.
6. Posey, D. A., "Indigenous Management of Tropical Forest Ecosystems: The Case of the Kayapó Indians of the Brazilian Amazon," *Agroforestry Systems* 3, 1985, 139–58.
7. Hecht, S. B. and Posey, D. A., "Management and Classification of Soils by the Kayapó Indians of Gorotire," in Posey, D. and Balée, W., eds., *Resource Management by Caboclos and Indians in Amazonia*, New York Botanical Gardens, New York, 1987.
8. Kerr, W. E. and Posey, D. A., "Nova informaçao sobre a agricultura dos Kayapó," *Interciência* 9, 6, 1984, 392–400.
9. Overall, W. L. and Posey, D. A., "Uso de formigas *Azteca* para controle biológico de pragas agricolas entre os indios Kayapó," *Rev. Brasil. Zool.*, 1987.

10. Elisabetsky, E. and Posey, D. A., "Pesquisa etnofarmacológica e recursos naturais no trópico úmido: o caso dos indios Kayapó e suas implicaçoes para a ciencia médica," *Primeiro Simpósio sobre os Trópicos Umidos*, Belém, Embrapa, 1987.

11. Elisabetsky, E. and Posey, D. A., "Etnofarmacologia dos indios Kayapó do Gorotire," *Rev. Brasil. Zool.*, 1987.

20 William Booth ◆ U.S. Drug Firm Signs Up to Farm Tropical Forests

As described here by William Booth in the Washington Post, *in September 1991 a landmark agreement regarding the rights to commercial exploitation of tropical rainforest organisms was reached between a pharmaceutical company (Merck) and a Costa Rican parastatal organization, the National Institute of Biodiversity (INBio). Costa Rica has already earned an international reputation for its national park system, and this agreement enhances its reputation as a leader in conservation among Third World nations. In fact, this agreement is regarded as a model for conservation-based economic development strategies. The Costa Rican government officially launched INBio in 1989, its task being to inventory and catalog the country's enormous biological wealth. INBio's mission was furthered by its agreement with Merck to "prospect" for possible pharmaceuticals in Costa Rica's forests, thereby encouraging forest preservation.*

In what is said to be the first deal of its kind, the world's largest pharmaceutical company announced yesterday it will pay a Costa Rican conservation organization $1 million for the right to screen plants, microbes, and insects gathered in the forests for their possible use as drugs.

The agreement between Merck & Co. and the National Institute of Biodiversity of Costa Rica promises to help the Central American country protect its natural resources by finding new ways to exploit the forests without destroying them.

Cornell University biologist Thomas Eisner, who helped broker the deal, calls the arrangement "chemical prospecting" in which biologists and others would comb the tropical forests for plants and animals that might be made into useful products, such as drugs.

As an example, Eisner suggested that a leaf on the forest floor covered with mold might be the source of a new antibiotic, or a plant untouched by insects might contain a good repellant.

In the deal, local people who live around Costa Rica's twelve thousand square kilometers of protected lands are being trained and paid to gather plants and other materials, which are collected and cataloged by the biodiversity institute, a nonprofit scientific organization.

Merck would then be sent any promising organisms for screening. If a product became a marketable drug—something Merck scientists say is a long shot—the Costa Ricans would be given a share of the royalties, which would be earmarked for conservation.

This is not the first time Merck has pursued natural substances as a source of drugs. Indeed, the pharmaceutical industry was originally based on the use of natural compounds, mostly derived from medicinal herbs. Many drugs still in use were discovered first as natural substances.

Merck already markets four drugs made from soil organisms. A substance called Mevacor, for instance, is made from a microbe dug up in Spain and is used to control high cholesterol. Merck sold $735 million worth of Mevacor in 1990.

While Merck scientists say they are skeptical the forests will ever be the "virtual cornucopia of drugs" that some environmentalists have suggested, they say it is worth a look.

"You read papers today, all those medicines they say are supposed to be in the rainforests," said Georg Albers-Schönberg, head of the natural products chemistry branch at Merck. "I feel some skepticism. But I say, 'Why not give it a try?' Let's try."

Albers-Schönberg said that while plants and insects are difficult to work with as potential drugs, the pharmaceutical industry is now more willing to explore natural substances. Merck also has a deal with the New York Botanical Gardens, whose botanists send promising plants to Merck, which has agreed to share royalties with the country of origin if a marketable drug is developed.

When Merck researchers get an interesting plant from Costa Rica or elsewhere, they grind it up and produce an extract that is then tested for activity against certain enzymes or specific receptors on cells associated with human or animal disease.

If the extract shows activity, the scientists can synthesize batches of the compound. In almost all cases, the forests would not be harvested for more of the plant.

"It's a very productive way to preserve the great biological diversity of land we have, our great greenhouses," said Anna Sittenfeld, a microbiologist and head of science programs at the Costa Rican institute.

"These types of agreements will help us preserve our natural areas by increasing opportunities for people who are living around them. We can hire more people, create jobs. Maybe one day a drug company can move and develop their drugs here," said Sittenfeld. "It also helps people here in Costa Rica understand that the forests are important, not just for land, grazing, and trees, but for drugs and medicines."

---

21 A. B. Cunningham ◆
Indigenous Knowledge and Biodiversity

As the concept of preserving the rainforest for its genetic diversity and pharmacological potential becomes more widely accepted, so does the need to acknowledge and reward people who can tell us how to access that potential. A. B. Cunningham suggests that ethnobiologists and non-governmental organizations (NGOs) ought to serve as intermediaries between tribal peoples and commercial interests, facilitating equitable agreements regarding the distribution of profits from commodities with natural ingredients whose properties were discovered by indigenous peoples. The biodiversity convention signed at the 1992 Earth Summit in Rio de Janeiro declares that countries serving as repositories of genetic material used by the biomedical industry should be rewarded for the use of their resources. This lofty declaration, however, has proven difficult to put into practice. Among other things, it does not indicate what benefit indigenous people should derive from their knowledge of the healing properties of plants.

This selection is an overview of the ethical and practical issues involved in the capture and distribution of benefits from the centuries of accumulated knowledge held by traditional healers (shamans) and other keepers of tribal wisdom. It originally appeared in a special issue of Cultural Survival Quarterly *on the topic of intellectual property rights (or "The Politics of Ownership," as the issue was subtitled). Cultural Survival is an NGO that supports projects designed to help indigenous peoples physically and culturally survive the rapid changes brought about by development. It has been in the forefront of thought and action regarding the issues of both intellectual property and ancestral (land) property rights of tribal peoples.*

The developing world is home to the bulk of the world's genetic diversity and customary knowledge of plant uses. The developed world, with its growing sophistication in biochemistry, genetic engineering, and biotechnology, holds the means to develop such resources. With cultural and environmental changes, however, both biodiversity and customary knowledge are being lost at an increasingly rapid rate. The race for this wealth of information has begun.

From A. B. Cunningham, "Indigenous Knowledge and Biodiversity," *Cultural Survival Quarterly* 15, no. 3 (Summer 1991): 4–8. Reprinted by permission of *Cultural Survival Quarterly*.

Ethnobiologists, economic botanists, and anthropologists work on the cusp of traditional and urban-industrial culture, recording indigenous knowledge accumulated over many generations, knowledge that is often the key to particular active ingredients within plants. In many cases, it can only be obtained from specialists (herbalists, diviners, beekeepers, master fishermen) after the researcher has established credibility with the society and a position of trust with the specialist. But how far does this trust extend?

In general, people with the richest customary knowledge have the least formal education. They also have the least bargaining power in urban-industrial society—particularly hunter-gatherers, whose traditional knowledge is disappearing most rapidly. Ethnobiologists and anthropologists play an essential role in preventing this tragedy, not only for its own sake but for its utilitarian value to a much wider sector of society as a key to new drugs, insecticides, and other industrial products. Researchers working with traditional specialists are not only in a relationship built on trust, but they are also at the "sharp end" of urban-industrial society, gathering data and publishing it. Should a community's knowledge be made public freely or at a price? Many traditional healers in southern Africa feel that this knowledge should certainly not be available to the public; even within their own societies, much of this knowledge is kept private through ritual and taboo. Many traditional healers recognize the value of their knowledge and want part of the benefits arising from its use—and why not?

Industrial Parallels

If a private company in our urban-industrial society accumulates unique and useful knowledge through trial and error, it patents that knowledge and receives a percentage of the profits from its use. For more than a century ethnobotanists have been recording customary knowledge, much of which relates to medicinal plants. Traditional knowledge, like industrial knowledge, has also been accumulated by trial and error; but it has been made public with no patent rights attached. As workers trying to bridge cultures, ethnobiologists and anthropologists are in a position to act as brokers to facilitate a partnership agreement for the benefit of both rural communities and urban-industrial society.

What are the ethics behind recording customary knowledge and making it publicly available without adequate compensation? Surely this perpetuates the historical errors and attitudes that have characterized industrial society's exploitation of other, more tangible resources from developing countries. With the growth of genetic engineering and biotechnology, ethnobiologists need to clarify their code of ethics. Encouragingly, this is already happening. The International Society for Ethnobiology (ISE), the Botanical Society of America (BSA), and the Society for Economic Botany

(SEB) all have established ethics committees to develop professional codes (Boom, 1990)—an important first step. But what strategies need to be adopted to put them into practice, and what pitfalls need to be avoided?

Conservation, Chemical Compounds, and Plant Genetic Resources

The question of rights to tropical-zone chemical or genetic resources is a controversial one, and the debate has grown more heated as biotechnology and genetic engineering become more prevalent (Mooney, 1983). The conservation and social implications of this dilemma make a timely resolution on both issues essential. It has become widely recognized in international funding circles that innovative funding mechanisms will be required to support conservation, and that this support should come from those who benefit from biological resource use. A policy of treating both traditional knowledge and biological material as "free goods" discounts their value; this has important implications for any attempt to justify conservation as a form of land use through economic benefits in addition to aesthetic, religious, and other values.

The more complex a vegetation type in terms of species (or life-form) diversity (and this usually means those with the highest conservation value), the more complex, expensive, and labor-intensive it becomes to manage sustainable use of forest resources such as timber or "minor forest products." In most cases, conservation bodies in developing countries do not have the financial or human resources to carry this out. In instances where demand is high, then, "mining" rather than "managing" occurs, and the fine line between sustainable use and overexploitation is crossed. This negates the rationale behind "sustainable use" being a means for justifying conservation as a form of land use. The primary reason for maintaining core conservation areas is for long-term habitat and species diversity. We see results in Africa, Asia, and South America, particularly for commercially valuable products (whether timber, rattan, medicinal plants, or craftwork resources). The tropical-zone countries, however, are rich in resources that have great value globally and can be harvested with low impact: genes, chemical compounds, and knowledge. The problem is that these resources are largely viewed by urban-industrial society as a "global commons" rather than as a regional resource.

This attitude, often unknowingly fostered by people from temperate-zone countries, thus "devalues" the resource that could best justify maintenance of species-rich vegetation if financial value were placed on those resources. As Scholtz (1989) puts it with regard to the rosy periwinkle plant, the source of a drug used to treat childhood leukemia: "But why should Madagascar preserve the rosy periwinkle? The world community reaps benefits from this plant, but what are the benefits to the local people or to the Madagascan government? The answer is: none at all. No money flows back to Madagascar for the drugs produced, and it is unlikely that the drug itself is available to the poor peasants of Madagascar, should they need it. There is on the face of it no reason whatsoever for Madagascar to preserve the rosy periwinkle."

What Are "Benefits"?

In the past, the sovereignty of renewable (timber, rattan, latex, etc.) and nonrenewable (bauxite and other minerals) tropical-zone resources has been recognized (although prices paid for renewable resources may have borne no resemblance to replacement costs). Why not protect genes, chemical components of plants, and the knowledge that enables them to be collected and identified? The same applies to plants with horticultural potential, such as the US $30 million per year from the sale of African violets (*Saintpaulia*), which come from the Tanzanian forest (Lovett, 1988); none of this money is linked to Tanzanian forest conservation.

If nothing is done, then an already politicized conservation issue will worsen, and we will all lose out. Internationally based researchers will be excluded from collecting either traditional knowledge or plant genetic material. Prolonged war, coupled with economic and ecological devastation in many African countries, will severely limit national capacity to record traditional knowledge or effectively conserve habitat or species diversity in a number of key areas. If neither in situ (in core conservation areas) nor ex situ (in gene banks and botanical gardens) conservation can take place due to a ban on data or seed collection, then the result is a double tragedy where no one wins. We need a mechanism linking the recognition of the origin and value of these resources *and* a mechanism for "capturing" a portion of the profits arising from the use of these resources for local communities and habitat conservation in the tropical zone.

Benefits: Passive Trickle or Active Capture?

At present, what benefits do trickle down to traditional societies or regions when local traditional knowledge is used or when local plant resources are developed? If patent rights are secured, what form should benefits take and how should they be distributed? The answers to these key questions vary by country and therefore need to be resolved at a regional level using a broader ethical framework. Certain generalizations can be made, however.

First, in many of the tropical or subtropical countries concerned, the ratio of MDs to total population is low, even in urban areas (that is, one MD per 16,400 versus one traditional doctor per 110 in Benin City, Nigeria (Oyenye and Orubuloye, 1983). The traditional knowledge that leads to new pharmaceuticals often comes from people with the least formal education and from very remote areas, so there is certainly less access to modern pharmaceuticals, particularly in a barter economy. Certain modern pharmaceuticals can deal with ailments that traditional medicines can not; as Schultes (1988) points out, they are dispensed by mission doctors in certain areas. The constancy of these handouts undoubtedly varies. If a sustained primary health care scheme collaborated with traditional practitioners, the community would have the best of both worlds.

Second, surely it is worthwhile to consider the *active* direction of benefits from new drugs resulting from customary knowledge rather than to rely on the passive trickle-down of modern pharmaceuticals (some of the cake rather than the crumbs)? If 74 percent of the 110 known useful plant-derived drugs have a related use in traditional medicine (Farnsworth, 1988) and the dollar value of prescription drugs sold in the United States containing active ingredients from higher plants totals $8 billion per year (Farnsworth and Soejarto, 1985), then we are looking at a substantial financial resource—even at royalties of a fraction of 1 percent.

Finally, what attraction is there in this for pharmaceutical companies? For those relying on a chemical synthesis of drugs, none. For others, who see the potential for drug development from higher plants with the advances in phytochemistry, genetic engineering, and patent law, they see the opportunity to get ahead of competitors through supporting an equitable partnership between traditional herbalists and urban-industrial society. They would have quicker access to material for new drug development.

Capturing and Distributing Benefits

Labeling Sources

Active "capture" of benefits can take a wide variety of forms depending on local needs and the products involved. Simply recognizing the research input of traditional specialists through a note on a package can be an important—albeit nonmonetary—benefit. Wider recognition of the value of traditional knowledge would be particularly important in countries with racist attitudes and an emphasis on the "superiority" of urban-industrial society. The same would apply to industrial products developed from tropical-zone resources, as this could help highlight the need for conserving biological diversity.

Researchers as Advisers

By more formally recognizing traditional specialists as partners, researchers from a wide variety of fields can facilitate reciprocal arrangements in information flow. This already takes place when scientists provide copies of their reports to the communities with whom they have worked. Researchers can also serve as advisers in land-use conflicts, land-rights issues, or resource-management problems. Chemists and pharmacologists could provide additional detailed information on toxic medicinal plants and their antidotes, and food chemists could give input on the nutritional values of wild food resources. In all cases, referral and information transfer channels need to be set up, and the extent and limits of the assistance need to be defined from the start.

Patents and Legal Contracts

The experience that patent lawyers have built in urban-industrial society certainly provides some useful examples. What needs to be avoided, however, are legal wrangles from which only lawyers will benefit. The past five years have seen a great increase in patent rights applications relating to new drugs, plants, or organisms for industrial use (Crawford, 1988). Discovering plant species that have useful active ingredients (such as those from traditional medicines, dyes, fish toxins, fungicides, and insecticides) is certainly an inventive, intellectual process. Even more so is the selection by trial and error of a few plant species for their synergistic effect from vegetation that may contain hundreds of plant species. The same can apply to specific genes identified from key plant species, which may be used through genetic engineering techniques to produce a particular chemical.

While the ethical arguments behind the patent rights debate may be clear cut, the same does not apply to strategies for capturing benefits; it is essential that false expectations not be raised. On the surface, for example, patenting seems to hold great promise. Again, the vinca alkaloids from the Madagascar rosy periwinkle are a well-publicized recent example. The plant was discovered to have antitumor activity in 1958 (independent of any guidance from traditional medicine) and was patented and marketed by 1963. The sale of pharmaceuticals from this source totaled an approximate $100 million by 1985, 88 percent of which was profit for the company (Farnsworth, 1988). This is a rare case, however. The average value and life of patents is considerably lower. For example, the average value of patent rights between 1951 and 1981 in Great Britain was only $7,000; in France, just over $6,000; and in Germany, $18,000. More than half the patents were canceled after eight years, and only 25 percent survived beyond thirteen years.

Usually patents are applied only to material that has not yet been made publicly available. Published data culled from decades of ethnobiological research, however, have already been made public. The same would apply to genetic material of widespread plants, either as weeds, ornamentals, or crops. (The rosy periwinkle has spread throughout much of the tropical and subtropical worlds as a weed of disturbed areas.) Any claims to rights of published information or already widespread plant resources are a case of shutting the stable door after the horse has bolted, and are all the more reason why guidelines are developed to facilitate capturing benefits from newly recorded, unpublished information and natural resources not found under cultivation or dispersed as weeds.

Legal contract agreements, such as one developed by the National Cancer Institute, provide a very useful alternative mode; but again, any false expectations must be avoided. All groups involved in the research need to know that only a fraction of potentially valuable industrial products will reach the commercial market, since many are unsuitable (due to side effects of new drugs, for example).

Researchers as Brokers

An additional possibility for capturing benefits is by linking the legal approach to a "brokerage role" played by ethnobiologists—who bridge the gap between urban-industrial culture and traditional cultures—and university-based organic chemists and pharmacologists, forming a buffer between ethnobiologists and pharmaceutical companies. Ethnobiologists would provide plant samples for screening, but would maintain confidentiality through identifying the sample by code number only, combined with maceration of botanically identifiable material such as leaves, flowers, and fruits. Once a potentially important new ingredient is identified, these "brokers" can negotiate an agreement with a large company, enabling traditional healers (or other specialists) and ethnobotanists to determine the terms of the contract, not the pharmaceutical company.

"Green Consumerism"

A different approach, taken by Cultural Survival and other groups, is the concept of green consumerism. This could be applied to horticultural products such as the African violet as well as to industrial products, foods, and cosmetics. Companies marketing natural resources would hook up with the people harvesting them to facilitate better prices and therefore benefits to local communities and possibly to conservation.

Distributing the Monetary Benefits

Even if the problems surrounding the capture of benefits are circumvented, the problem of how to distribute and administer them remains. Anders (1989), for example, has documented the social problems among Alaskan peoples as money flowed into communities from oil and land revenues; it would be ironic and tragic if attempts to channel benefits to regions or communities ended up destroying those same communities. Misappropriation of funds has been a feature of many administrations, governmental and nongovernmental alike, and that would have to be guarded against, too.

Incomes from the capture of benefits are unlikely to accrue to a specific community, however (as plant uses are often known through much of the range of a plant species), unless a highly localized, endemic species is involved. Why not base regional funds on biogeographic or phytogeographic boundaries rather than on political ones? A regional fund, perhaps administered by an appropriate NGO through community leaders, would be one way; but the issue requires serious debate. Benefits could take the form of legal resources, primary health care, medicinal plant nurseries for overexploited or popular species, or educational bursaries.

In all cases, however, the position of developing countries in capturing some of these benefits would be greatly improved through access to the training, infrastructure, and technology for screening and developing new products. With few exceptions, Africa does not yet have this expertise; parts of Asia (India, for example) and South America (Brazil) are in a stronger position. The same applies to forming partnerships or legal expertise in developing countries because there is a similar imbalance of power. The majority of patents in developing countries, for example, are owned by foreign corporations—Germany, France, the United States, and Britain. In the short term, partnerships with organizations such as Lawyers for Human Rights need to be explored to improve local access to legal expertise relating to patents and contract agreements.

Clearly there is no single answer to this complex issue that encompasses all research areas or fields. Because patent rights to knowledge involve people, resources, and access to technology, the issue is inevitably politicized. It is essential that ethical guidelines and a strategy for developing equitable partnerships be developed as soon as possible. Encouraging examples such as the Kuna in Panama (the Kuna require researchers working on their land to pay fees, use a Kuna field representative, and provide copies of final reports to the community) already exist. The sooner pragmatic partnerships are developed, the better.

Literature Cited

Anders, J. C. 1989. "Social and Economic Consequences of Federal Indian Policy: A Case Study of the Alaskan Natives." *Economic Development and Cultural Change* 285–303.

Boom, B. M. 1990. "Giving Native People a Share of the Profits." *Garden* 14(6):28–31.

Crawford, M. 1988. "Patent Claim Buildup Haunts Biotechnology." *Science* 239–273.

Farnsworth, N. R. 1988. "Screening Plants for New Medicines." In E. O. Wilson, ed. *Biodiversity*. Washington, DC: National Academy Press.

Farnsworth, N. R. and D. D. Soejarto. 1985. "Potential Consequences of Plant Extinction in the United States on the Current and Future Availability of Prescription Drugs." *Economic Botany* 39(3):231–240.

Lovett, J. C. 1988. "Practical Aspects of Moist Forest Conservation in Tanzania." Monogr. Syst. Bot. Missouri Bot. Gard. 25:491–496.

Mooney, P. R. 1983. "The Law of the Seed." *Development Dialogue* 1–2:1–172.

Oyenye, O. Y. and I. O. Orubuloye. 1983. "Traditional Health Manpower Resources in Nigeria: The Case of Bendel State." *Aman: Journal of Society, Culture, and Environment* (cited in Kemwin and Kemwin. "The Apothecary Shop in Benin City." *African Arts* 22(1):72–83).

Posey, D. A. 1990. "Intellectual Property Rights and Just Compensation for Indigenous Knowledge." *Anthropology Today* 6(4):13–16.

Scholtz, A. 1989. "Conserving Biological Diversity: Who Is Responsible?" *Ambio* 18(8):454–457.

Schultes, R. E. 1988. Letter to the Editor. *Tradition, Conservation and Development: Occasional Newsletter of the Commission on Ecology's Working Group on Traditional Ecological Knowledge* (October):10.

---

22 John O. Browder ◆ Alternative Rainforest Uses

Complex, interlocking economic and social forces, rather than single issues such as population growth, contribute to the destruction of forests. Consideration of the full social dimensions of tropical deforestation must be a part of successful conservation planning. In this 1991 essay, John O. Browder examines three basic strategies for linking economic development and conservation objectives: plantation forestry, agroforestry, and natural forest management. He quickly eliminates plantations as a major player in sustainable development and focuses on agroforestry and natural forest management. In particular, he indicates the value of sustained-yield forest exploitation modeled after the systems developed by indigenous societies or long-term forest dwellers, such as the rubber tappers and Brazil nut collectors of the Amazon. Above all, Browder stresses that no single strategy will work everywhere. Different strategies must be devised

From John O. Browder, "Alternative Rainforest Uses," in *Economic Development and Environmental Protection in Latin America*, ed. Joseph S. Tulchin and Andrew I. Rudman (Boulder: Lynne Rienner Publishers, 1991), 45–54. © 1991 by the Woodrow Wilson International Center for Scholars. Reprinted by permission of Lynne Rienner Publishers.

for the various conditions found in different geographic locations. In other words, public policy must be sensitive to the diversity of ecological and socioeconomic systems in Latin America.

Forests cover more than a quarter of the Earth's surface; 27 percent of these forests are found in Latin America. Although many traditional forms of cutting enable tropical forests to recover cleared areas, the large-scale conversion of tropical forests has become one of the most controversial and widely publicized issues of our time. Estimates of the annual rate of tropical forest conversion range from 113,000 square kilometers—an area roughly the size of the state of Oklahoma—to 205,000 square kilometers.[1] Many legitimate concerns are being raised about the long-term environmental impact of extensive tropical forest conversion on biodiversity and species extinction, indigenous human populations, climate, hydrology, and soil conservation. Although the social costs associated with significant human disturbance of tropical forests are by no means precisely understood, there is a rapidly emerging consensus among scientists, economists, and conservationists that present patterns of tropical forest degradation are portentous. Calls throughout the 1980s for concerted international action to manage an unfolding ecological crisis included the UN Food and Agriculture Organization's Tropical Forestry Action Plan.

Underlying the ecological crisis of tropical forest destruction is a dense amalgam of troubling social, economic, and political issues: rural poverty in developing countries, rapid population growth, food and energy deficiency, territorial sovereignty, foreign debt, and misguided modernization policies. The structure of the "deforestation problem" is multidimensional and organic; no single component of the problem exists in total isolation from the others. Tropical deforestation is not just an event that sets in motion a chain of devastating ecological consequences. It is also a social process, reflecting a continuum of human responses to diverse and changing economic and political conditions—responses that range from desperate hunger to outright greed.

Responsibility for the deforestation problem and its consequences is not confined to the tropical countries of the Third World alone. Effective control of tropical deforestation requires confrontation of numerous seemingly intractable social ills and injustices that are both country-specific and global in nature. Conservationists and enlightened growth economists face the task of finding long-term human uses of tropical forests that are compatible with the economic development objectives of vastly different countries, and land development strategies capable of reconciling the inherent ecological heterogeneity of the forest with the relatively homogeneous, but often conflicting, economic demands placed upon them by differing social groups.

Development Alternatives for Tropical Forests

There are three basic strategies for tropical forest land use that might link economic development and conservation objectives: plantation forestry, tropical agriculture and agroforestry, and natural forest management.

The Limits of Plantation Forestry

Industrial wood plantations are widely considered to be an essential part of any long-term strategy of sustainable forest resource management in the developing world. Annual timber production rates range from ten to twenty cubic meters per hectare. There are currently about thirteen million hectares of plantation forests in the developing world (excluding China), seven million of which are found in Latin America. However, by the year 2000 the developing countries will require approximately fifty million hectares of fuelwood plantations, mainly in the arid tropics.[2] The rate of natural forest conversion currently outstrips the rate of forest plantation establishment by ten to one, making the production and long-term supply of wood to meet energy and raw material needs an issue of strategic concern to both conservationists and development economists. In short, many believe that industrial wood plantations, especially in degraded or secondary forest areas, can be used to reduce pressure on natural forests while providing essential energy for industry and households.

Plantation forestry alone, however, like other tropical forest development alternatives, is not a panacea for Third World energy inadequacy. Nor is it always an appropriate vehicle for achieving economic development objectives. Forest plantations tend to obtain maximum efficiency at high levels of output over relatively long production cycles (seven to thirty-five years), thereby precluding extensive participation by smallholders.[3] They are relatively expensive to establish, although they yield a moderate to high rate of return (10 to 20 percent).[4] Employment on forest plantations is usually cyclical, being more intensive in the early stages of seedling growth. Thus the economics of fuelwood production tends to favor large enterprises over small producers, often requires government subsidization, and offers little promise of significantly serving household energy needs.

Plantation forestry has also been considered or undertaken to produce sawlogs, pulpwood, and fuelwood for electrification of small urban areas in various parts of Latin America. These experiences have not yet been systematically studied, but in most cases the hazards facing monocultural tree production include increased probability of fire damage, reduction in biodiversity, depredations of insects and fungi, short-term decline in soil fertility, soil compaction, and weed competition. These environmental dangers combine with high start-up costs, little permanent job creation, and long-term dependency on excessively hybridized or imported plant stock. Thus monocultural tree farming has, at best, a relatively minor role in sustainable forest use strategy.

Tropical Agriculture and Agroforestry

Because most of Latin America's food supply is produced in small traditional farming systems, conservation development initiatives should seek to stabilize rather than replace small farms. Additionally, the majority of the region's economically active population is engaged in smallholder farming. There are between fifty and one hundred million Latin Americans who make their living from farming, a small fraction of whom live and work on tropical rainforest lands. In many cases, these small farms supply most of the food for domestic consumption.

Although Amazonian smallholder farming systems vary, they share several general characteristics. First, they tend to be low-impact systems; that is, they have low capital/output ratios and low-to-moderate use of labor and industrial inputs. Second, production is commercially oriented toward national markets and tends to be limited to a few commercial food crops. Very few forest products are harvested for sale or consumption. Third, colonist farmers often use agronomic knowledge gained in farming different ecological zones—knowledge that is ecologically inappropriate for the rainforest. Retention and utilization of a natural forest component in farming is, to them, an alien concept. Fourth, these characteristics often reinforce another trait—the sensitivity of smallholders to even minimal exposure to risk. Because risk aversion takes precedence over profit maximization it is difficult to diffuse new agroforestry technology. Finally, unclear land tenure generally discourages smallholder investment in long-term perennial tree-cropping systems. Whereas tree *planting* frequently establishes specific land-use rights in many parts of Africa, tree *removal* usually serves the same function in Amazonia.

There are three main objectives for agricultural development and environmental conservation in most tropical forest areas: increased productivity of agriculture through intensification or increased frequency of cropping; diversification from monoculture to polyculture; and incorporation of productive tree or forest components.

Relatively little attention has been paid to soil management techniques employed by indigenous residents of the Amazon. Recent research suggests that some of these traditional systems are more productive than conventional smallholder agriculture. A comparison of crop yields obtained by the indigenous Kayapó and by smallholder colonists and ranchers in the Brazilian Amazon found that the indigenous farming system produced three times greater yields than the colonist farming system. The difference reflects the fact that the Kayapó recognize many more plant products as crops than do most colonists.

The objective of diversifying crop production is not limited by farm size. In Mexico, for example, small farms ranging from 0.3 to 0.7 hectares are known to produce between thirty-three and fifty-five useful species.[5] Thus farm size alone does not determine farm viability. Smaller farms require intensive management of a more diverse resource base. Short-term yields per unit area in a monoculture will likely exceed the yield of any single crop in a polycultural system, but the total useful yield over the long term may be significantly greater in the polycultural system. Research shows that diversified cropping helps to overcome three important limiting factors to tropical agriculture: soil nutrient depletion, weed competition, and plant disease.

The type of farming system most appropriate to a given area depends on topography, soil and hydrologic factors, access to basic physical infrastructure and consumer markets, and policies that affect market prices for different agricultural products. The key is that a wide range of small-scale agroecosystems exist and tend to share certain characteristics: they produce a wide range of products in a relatively small area, they retain and utilize a significant area of forest, their reliance on natural and locally available sources of fertilizer makes them resource regenerating rather than resource depleting systems, and the sequencing of cropping provides continuity in the supply of food and income. The key issue, therefore, is how to transfer these characteristics successfully to the "modern" smallholders who use resource-depleting monocropping systems on tropical soils.

Natural Forest Management

A wide range of activities, aside from sustained commercial timber harvesting relying on natural regeneration, are now included within natural forest management. Recent research of cultural ecologists suggests that many traditional forms of natural forest management can provide greater financial return on investment of labor than many strictly silvicultural and agricultural activities, provided that they are integrated into larger agrosilvicultural land-use systems or complemented by other small-scale agricultural activities.

One of the best examples of such financial return is seen in northeastern Mexico. A relatively small tropical forest (350,000 hectares) is managed by Huastec Maya and other small farmers. They produce a traditional mix of commercial and subsistence crops (sugar, coffee, maize) through the use of a unique component—the *te 'lom*, or natural forest grove. Ninety percent of the more than three hundred plant species found in the *te 'lom* are used by the Huastec.[6] Although a *te 'lom* alone cannot support a family, its functions within the larger Huastec economy are indispensable. The *te 'lom* produces a wide variety of important subsistence goods that would otherwise be expensive or unavailable to farmers, provides nutritionally important additions to the diet (thus preventing the deterioration of diet quality that generally accompanies a shift to commercial agriculture), provides a variety of marketable goods to supplement farm income, supports the production of livestock (often an important source of cash for women), and serves important ecological functions that farmers value by protecting the region's genetic diversity for future generations. The Huastec agroecosystem is capable of sustaining an averge family on four hectares of tropical forest land. The potential financial benefits of replicating the Huastec production model are especially impressive. If market prices are applied to nonmonetized production factors, the analysis reveals that the average Huastec household earns a net benefit equivalent to $2,459 per year (in 1987 dollars) from farm production, excluding ecological benefits.[7]

Traditional forest management practices are low-input, highly productive uses that can be practiced on either large or small areas of tropical forest lands; they often are more land efficient (that is, they use less land per capita) than many conventional land uses, even though they are associated with low population densities; they have minimal adverse impacts on ecological stability; and they are characterized by a high rate of resource utilization (up to 80 percent of forest tree species) and a diversity of income sources.

Traditional practices are often integrated with various complementary productive activities that ensure continuity of income flows over time. Where such management is a cooperative venture within a large area, the active participation of the local (often indigenous) population is essential. Such areas are generally found in situations where effective private (or tribal) property rights have long been established and recognized, or where public land-use controls have been effectively enforced.

Although these production systems involve the extraction or cultivation of a variety of products, they frequently are dominated by at least one important cash crop, such as sugar for the Huastec. The financial viability of these production systems is constrained primarily by market distance and secondarily by market acceptance, emphasizing the importance of geographic location and marketing infrastructure (not necessarily roads).

The productive potential of low-impact forest management has been demonstrated, but several questions about the possibility of widespread application of these strategies remain unanswered and should be included in any research agenda for natural forest management-based conservation and development: How can such technologies be successfully transferred, in whole or in part, from one cultural group to another? If such systems are replicable, can they be deployed at scales of production that significantly increase employment opportunities without depending upon costly subsidies, swamping local consumer markets with minor forest products, or endangering local habitats from overzealous adoption? What are the likely gender implications (household division of labor) associated with transferred technologies? What is the prospective market demand for the commercial goods produced under managed natural forest systems? What support services (credits, marketing, technical extension) and exogenous inputs (fuel, fertilizers, pesticides) would be necessary to ensure stable production of tranferred or expanded natural forest management systems? And finally, under what circumstances of land use and tenure are such systems socially acceptable, especially when they entail the restricted use of large areas of forest land?

The application of traditional natural forest management strategies relies largely on restrictive land-use zoning (reserves), often in areas where surrounding land uses are incompatible with intended forest management activities. Under these circumstances, reserves must be treated as one component of a larger land-use strategy that accommodates the competing land uses surrounding them. Low-use-intensity reserves favorable to one group of people undergoing rapid land-use transition may unfairly discriminate against others, resulting in social conflict. "Extractive reserves," in which lands are set aside especially for the harvesting of tree products (for example, nuts or rubber) but not for tree cutting, can work, but only if cattle ranchers, landless peasants, and other forest land users pressing at the edges are simultaneously incorporated into complementary solutions to their respective needs for land and forest resources.

Conclusions and Recommendations

Tropical forest destruction in Latin America is largely the result of public policies that promote the expansion of commercial agriculture and ranching, as opposed to in Africa and South Asia where the destruction is caused by timber harvesting and rural poverty. No single land-use strategy will successfully harmonize conservation and economic develop ent objectives for the entire Amazon. Different strategies must be ada ted to diverse local conditions. These strategies should share three common characteristics: they should be decentralized and their benefit widely distributed; they should be diversified to promote heterogeneity, not homogeneity, of production; and they should focus either on activities that can be adapted to small-scale production or on low-impact activities that can be adapted on a socially acceptable large scale.

Brazilian conservation efforts in particular should consider three important realities. First, between five and seven hundred thousand rural households depend on precarious small-scale short-cycle monocropping for their livelihood; thus successful development strategies must provide small farmers with the proper technology and financing to incorporate the lessons about continuous cultivation that can be derived from traditional Amazonian agroecological systems. Second, most of the region's population growth is urban based, so joint poverty and environmental development strategies must consider the implication of growing urban demand for food, energy, and building materials on the region's natural resource base. Third, areas of secondary forest growth are becoming increasingly prominent features of the Amazonian landscape. These degraded pastures and abandoned fallows represent an important untapped resource that appropriate strategies should incorporate.

The following conclusions and recommendations for tropical rainforest regions, especially in the Americas, address small-scale farming, plantation forestry, natural forest management, and diversification of production.

Small-Scale Farming

Appropriate land-use strategies for small-scale farming should promote: (1) expanded low-impact extractive utilization of natural forest remnants on existing productive farm lots; (2) the planting of trees by farmers in conjunction with ground cropping—not only for commercial gain but also planting of those trees that preserve vital ecological functions such as nitrogen fixing; (3) diversification of farm production, especially through the planting of "useful" tree species; and (4) intensification of farm cultivation—continuous cropping with greater reliance on natural fertilizers. Major impediments to all four of these objectives include insecure land tenure, a lack of agroecological knowledge, poorly staffed and underfunded extension institutions with parochial work programs, inadequate technical and ethnological knowledge, and the continued subsidization of monocultural cash cropping and cattle ranching through tax incentives and other governmental policies that promote large-scale forest destruction, often to make way for desultory land uses.

More attention must be given to indigenous agroecological knowledge. Obviously, such knowledge must be blended with modern approaches to tropical agriculture and fit existing sociocultural situations. Much indigenous knowledge is culturally esoteric and alien to contemporary commercial farming. Nevertheless, many indigenous practices do show the way toward techniques that may be able to overcome ecological and financial constraints facing agriculture in moist tropical forest areas. Future funding should emphasize the practical management aspects of applying existing indigenous and traditional knowledge at the farm level.

Plantation Forestry

Four potential applications of plantation forestry will continue to receive attention: electrification of small urban areas, urban household firewood production, industrial fuelwood production, and industrial sawn-wood production. Decentralized small-scale tree farming by rural inhabitants in areas surrounding small towns is an income-spreading and ecologically preferable alternative to centralized or monocultural plantations. An important first step toward the adoption of tree-planting strategies in combination with annual cropping would be a localized response to urban-driven demand for fuelwood and sawlogs.

Natural Forest Management

A number of promising strategies for traditional forest management and agroforestry have been largely neglected by donors in land-use planning for Amazonia. Opportunities to utilize more fully the diverse resources of natural forests in conjunction with agriculture need to be further refined, not only as potential development models for extensive protected forest areas but also for application at the small farm level. Additional research is needed on the following issues: (1) the market potential, both local and national, of promising minor forest products and lesser-known timber species; (2) technical production aspects of local industrial processing of marketable forest products, especially minor forest products; (3) marketing requirements for diverse natural forest products (for example, grouping by general use characteristics); (4) potential uses of different natural forest products as inputs to farm production; (5) financial performance and employment impact of different management procedures that increase yields and minimize damage to natural forest vegetation; and (6) financial analysis of forest management at the farm level and the use of secondary forest growth areas on farm lots for commercial tree planting and agroforestry demonstrations.

Diversification of Production

Diversification of production must become the central and guiding tenet of sustainable tropical forest land use. In one sense, diversity of production runs counter to conventional economic development wisdom advocating specialization around a comparative resource advantage. The reductive conversion of biotically diverse forest communities, supporting tens of thousands of living species for thousands of years, to genetic cesspools capable of supporting one or two commercial species for five or ten years must be rejected as an economic development model. The comparative advantage of tropical forests is their biodiversity.

In those countries where subsidies play a major role in forest land use, the shift from subsidies for commodities to subsidies for biotically diversified land uses should be considered. Instead of rural credit to convert forest land to upland rice fields, policies could entice farmers to productively utilize the biodiversity of the natural forest for financial benefits.

Notes

1. Norman Myers, *The Primary Source* (New York: W. W. Norton and Co., 1984), p. 2; and "FAO's Tropical Forestry Action Plan," extracted from *Unasylva*, Vol. 38, No. 152 (1988): 40.
2. John Campbell, "The World's Third Forest," *Commonwealth Forestry Review*, Vol. 59, No. 4 (1980): 533.
3. Michael Nelson, *The Development of Tropical Lands* (Baltimore: Johns Hopkins University Press, 1973), p. 155.
4. See John Spears, "Replenishing the World's Forests: Tropical Reforestation–An Achievable Goal?" *Commonwealth Forestry Review*, Vol. 64, No. 4 (1985): 318.
5. Stephen R. Gleissman, "Local Resource Use Systems in the Tropics: Taking Pressure off the Forests," unpublished manuscript, n.d.
6. Janis Alcorn, "An Economic Analysis of Huastec Mayan Forest Management," in John Browder, ed., *Fragile Lands of Latin America: Strategies for Sustainable Management* (Boulder, Colo.: Westview Press, 1989).
7. Ibid.

---

23 Rhona Mahony ♦ Debt-for-Nature Swaps: Who Really Benefits?

One of the most promising and highly touted innovations in the conservation world during the 1980s was the idea of the debt-for-nature swap. In these swaps an environmental organization such as World Wildlife Fund purchases deeply discounted loans from creditor banks and then offers to retire the debt if the debtor country implements an agreed-upon conservation project, such as the creation or expansion of a national park. Writing in 1992, Rhona Mahony criticizes the debt-for-nature swap concept as fundamentally flawed, pointing out two major miscalculations. First, the buying and canceling of relatively small amounts of foreign debt will not appreciably help the debtor nations of the Third World. Second, the approach fails to recognize the forces at work against real protection of park land, which leads to the phenomenon of "paper parks"—parks without infrastructure or protection. She argues that because the concept is a

From Rhona Mahony, "Debt-for-Nature Swaps: Who Really Benefits?" *The Ecologist* 22, no. 3 (May–June 1992): 97–103. Reprinted by permission of *The Ecologist*.

top-down approach, it neglects to involve local populations in the land-use decisions that directly affect their livelihoods.

Environmentalists thought they had found a new ally in the 1980s—Wall Street. In 1984, a vice-president of the U.S. World Wildlife Fund, Thomas Lovejoy, suggested that northern environmentalists enter the financial markets, buy up some of the loans which developing countries owed to U.S. or European banks and which the banks were offering for sale at discounted prices, and then cancel those foreign debt obligations in return for good behavior by these countries.[1] Good behavior would include making payments in local currency, equal to the dollar face value of the debt or a little less, to a local environmental nongovernmental organization (NGO).

Scores of environmentalists took up the suggestion. The deals they struck were called debt-for-nature swaps and seemed an excellent idea. By mid-1991, nineteen debt-for-nature swaps had been completed in ten countries. For paying out a small sum in U.S. dollars, environmentalists received a large amount of local currency in return. But, despite superficial appearances, they did not get something for nothing.

The conservation funds generated by the swaps in Costa Rica, the Philippines, Ecuador, and Madagascar account for 95 percent of the total funds generated. They will be used mainly to administer national parks, to buy land to expand the parks, to train park personnel, to research habitats and species, and to carry out environmental education. The environmentalists have worked hard and creatively to arrange these swaps.

From the beginning, however, the effort put into debt-for-nature swaps by environmentalists has been flawed by two miscalculations. The first was their belief that buying and canceling small amounts of debt would help the indebted countries; the second was that simply drawing park boundaries on a map could protect sensitive ecosystems from invaders propelled into them by powerful economic forces, defended by private armies and bribery, and hidden by thousands of hectares of wilderness. Parks supposedly gaining from swaps in all four major beneficiary countries are being invaded by loggers, miners, or the landless.

Third World Debt

Those Third World governments which borrowed heavily during the 1970s from foreign commercial banks, foreign governments, and multilateral institutions, such as the World Bank and the International Monetary Fund, now owe sums of money so staggering that they will never be able to repay them. In 1990, the developing countries' long-term debt totaled $1.05 trillion, of which $293 billion was owed to commercial banks. Developing countries can try to earn dollars to repay these foreign loans by exporting more goods and services than they import. In 1990, however, the developing countries ran a trade deficit of over $28 billion which was projected to rise to $38 billion in 1991.[2]

This disturbing state of affairs is reflected in the low prices the commercial banks have been willing to accept when they sell Third World debt obligations on the secondary, or resale, market. The secondary market began in 1982 after Mexico announced in the same year that it could not make its scheduled loan repayments. Other highly indebted countries, including Argentina, Brazil, Nigeria, the Philippines, Costa Rica, and Peru, soon made the same announcement.

Faced with nonpayment of their loans and therefore keen to reduce their risk by diversifying their portfolios, some U.S. and European banks began selling individual loans at a discount. They calculated the discount by estimating a country's ability to repay in the future, considering aspects such as a country's foreign exchange reserves and its expected net income from foreign trade. Other banks and some private investors, who had made slightly differing assessments of the likelihood that debtor countries would repay, bought up these loans.

By 1989, the total annual volume of debt traded was over $20 billion.[3] The discount on these Third World loans has varied from country to country and over time. Sample secondary market prices, in cents per dollar of face value, in early 1991 were: Colombia 67 cents, Philippines 47 cents, Morocco 46.75 cents, Brazil 26.625 cents, Ecuador 26 cents, Zaire 16.5 cents, Panama 14.25 cents, Ivory Coast 6 cents, Peru 5.5 cents.[4] Most countries participating in debt-for-nature swaps are heavily indebted.

Who Benefits?

Who actually benefits from the purchase of a country's debt? Suppose your best friend has $100,000 in assets, but owes $2 million. You consider going to the lenders and buying back some of the debt so as to cancel it, in effect paying off some of your friend's debt—or so you think. They would sell it to you for five cents on the dollar, a rate calculated on how much your friend, or rather your friend's assets, are worth. If your friend cannot pay the debt, the most the lenders can hope to get back is the assets, their only security. Thus, $100,000 assets divided by $2 million debt equals a discount price of five cents. For only $50,000, you could relieve your best friend of half—$1 million—the burdensome debt ($1 million multiplied by five cents equals $50,000). Should you do it?

The answer is no. If you repurchased half the debt, your friend would still have assets of $100,000, but now owe $1 million. The price of the debt, however, on the resale market, would probably go up to ten cents on the dollar ($100,000 assets divided by $1 million equals ten cents). The lenders would still expect your friend to repay the same amount as before ($1 million debt now multiplied by ten cents is the same as $2 million debt before multiplied by five cents). Your friend would be no better off than before the repurchase. But you would have given $50,000 to some of the lenders, and also increased the value of the debt held by those lenders who did not sell; their IOUs would have doubled in value.

Although this is a simplified example, these price changes do happen in real life. Bolivia repurchased some of its own debt in March 1988. Donors said they would give Bolivia the money to buy back about 46 percent of its debt and cancel it; they did not ask for anything in return, so this deal was not a debt-for-nature swap.

Before the buy-back, Bolivia's commercial bank debt had a face value of $670 million. Its secondary market price was six cents on the dollar, which meant that banks expected Bolivia to repay $40.2 million ($670 million multiplied by six cents).

After the buy-back, Bolivia had only $362 million of commercial bank debt outstanding. The secondary market price, however, had gone up to eleven cents, which meant that after the swap, banks expected Bolivia to repay $39.8 million ($362 million multiplied by 11 cents).

The benefit to Bolivia from the buy-back can be considered as a reduction in the amount the banks *expected* it to repay—$0.4 million. The keenest, most self-interested observers of the situation still expected Bolivia to pay back roughly the same amount as before the debt purchase.

Bolivia, therefore, got very little for its troubles, or for its donors' troubles. In fact, it did not cost the donors some $18.5 million as it would have done when the deal was first mooted (46 percent of the total debt of $670 million multiplied by its discount price of six cents). Instead, it cost them $33.9 million, because news of the impending buy-back had driven the price of the debt on the secondary market up to eleven cents *even before* the purchase.[5]

It was the commercial banks which really received the benefit. Those that sold the debt earned eleven cents on the dollar for something that, until the buy-back, had been worth only six cents, giving them $33.9 million. Those that did not sell suddenly found that the debt they owned had almost doubled in value.[6]

The system works the same way when environmentalists buy back debt. Swap advocates have spent $16.7 million so far to buy debt.[7] That money went directly to such needy institutions as Bank of America, Citibank, National Westminster Bank plc, Dresdner Bank, Banque de l'Union Européene, Crédit Commercial de France, Salomon Brothers, Lazard Frères, and Shearson Lehman. Moreover, for the banks that did not sell, the value of the debt they held went up in value.[8]

Misplaced Enthusiasm

Even if advocates of debt-for-nature swaps realized that the swaps are not a panacea for a country's debt crisis, many of them are still enthusiastic about the conversions because they believe that the discount at which the Third World debt is sold helps multiply the donations. They are confident that they enable the donor to leverage quantities of funds for rainforest conservation at a higher exchange rate than would normally be available, as long as inflation does not whittle away the advantage gained.

Costa Rica carried out a typical swap in February 1988. A Costa Rican NGO, Fundación de Parques Nacionales (FPN), used $215,692, donated by the U.S. World Wildlife Fund (WWF), to buy official Costa Rican debt with a face value of $1.3 million. FPN then cancelled the debt in return for the Costa Rican Central Bank making donations in *colones*—the local currency—equivalent to $978,000 to the Guanacaste and Corcovado National Parks and the Monteverde Conservation League.

WWF paid $215,692 to buy debt for which the Costa Rican government paid the equivalent of $978,000 in local currency to have cancelled. Thus, WWF's contribution resulted in a donation from the government to local environmental groups which was 4.5 times larger, a result that swap advocates enthusiastically call the multiplier effect. But there is nothing magic about it.

The Central Bank's donation to the park authorities and the Monteverde Conservation League was in the form of five-year bonds, denominated in *colones*.[9] These groups will have to wait five years before they can get the funds—assuming the government redeems them. There is no guarantee that Costa Rica will honor these bonds in five years' time any more than it will pay back the rest of its debt. Remember, there is a reason for that secondary market discount in the first place—the Costa Rican government cannot pay its debts. But even if the government did honor this new debt, it could cut its other environmental spending to make up the cost.

What happened in this Costa Rican example, and in most of the other eighteen debt-for-nature swaps worldwide, is that a First World environmental group has given money to First World commercial banks while a Third World country has promised to give money to its environmental groups. No transfer has taken place from north to south.

Unprotected Parks

How do environmentalists spend the money they pry out of Third World governments? They mostly create, enlarge, or administer national parks. Unfortunately, calling an expanse of natural, and possibly threatened, habitat a park by drawing a line around it on a map and issuing uniforms to a few rangers gives it no more protection than it had before. Natural areas will not be safe until governments stop subsidizing the destructive activities of humans, stop theft and violence by the well-off, and fulfill the basic needs of the poor.

Ecuador

The government in Ecuador contributed the equivalent in the local currency, *sucres*, of $10 million, in the form of bonds to an NGO, Fundación Natura. This organization will spend all the money to maintain national parks, mark boundaries, draw up management plans, and carry out environmental education. The parks include the Galápagos Islands; over one million hectares on the western and eastern slopes of the Andes (Cayambe-Coca Ecological Reserve, Cotacachi-Cayapas Ecological Reserve, Sangay National Park, and Podocarpus National Park); and one million hectares in the Amazon (Cuyabeno Wildlife Reserve and Yasuní National Park). They also include Machalilla National Park, a forty-thousand-hectare site on the northwestern coast.[10]

The rangers will face a formidable job in all these places. Poachers and illegal loggers have invaded the Andean Podocarpus Park. Foreign oil companies and landless farmers from western Ecuador, many of whom are part-time oil company employees, are active in both the Amazonian parks. On the Andean slopes, large-scale plantation operators have invaded Cotacachi-Cayapas, while landless farmers threaten Cayambe-Coca and Sangay. Local people's tree-cutting for fuel and overgrazing of goats and cattle may soon desertify parts of northwestern Machalilla.[11]

Many of the people of Ecuador have no other option but to survive in this way. With a per capita GNP of $1,020, Ecuador has a population of 10 million which grows at a rate of 2.8 percent a year; 38 percent of children under five are malnourished.[12] The government depends heavily on its revenues from petroleum, all of which comes from—and is expected to come from—reserves in the Amazon. The roads built by the petroleum industry, which has not been subject to environmental regulation, are the main way the poor colonists enter the rainforest.[13]

Land-tenure laws cause environmental destruction as well. Most of the Amazonian region has been declared "unoccupied," even though indigenous people live there. To receive a title to land, a person must clear the forest, replacing it with crops or pasture. The government gives preferential credit to cattle ranching, even though it is not sustainable on the poor soils of the Amazon.[14] Indigenous people cannot obtain land titles by carrying out shifting agriculture, which is sustainable. When their land rights are granted to them, however, they get no help in enforcing their boundaries against outsiders.[15]

To overcome environmental destruction, the government should help farmers in the coastal areas and mountains produce more for their own consumption and for local sale, or to find city jobs, which at present are too few and pay barely enough for a family to live on, so that they will not be forced to migrate to the Amazon. More spending on education, especially for women, would help as well. . . .[16]

Costa Rica

The Costa Rican wildlife parks cover over 11 percent of the country's land area and have become international tourist attractions.[17] The swap program in Costa Rica has been the largest of any country so far in terms of number of swaps, face value of the debts, the amount paid for them, and the conservation funds generated. As part of swap agreements, the government has contributed the equivalent in *colones* of roughly $42.9 million to environmental projects. But in spite of its reputation as a pioneer in trying to protect national parks, Costa Rica has problems too.

Much of the government's donation will be spent on buying land from private owners and administering parks. Guanacaste National Park, which used to be a tropical dry forest, has been badly degraded by cattle ranching and is still threatened by tree-cutting. Gold miners started working in the Corcovado National Park, part of the Osa Peninsula on the Pacific coast, about ten years ago, many of whom now refuse to leave. Monteverde Cloud Forest in the northwest is beset by illegal loggers. Landless farmers are encroaching on many other parks and reserves.[18]

Reforms

Many environmentalists who have arranged these debt-for-nature swaps know that creating a park is not enough. Some have tried to incorporate social development assistance and reform into their projects. In Madagascar, WWF will help train three hundred villagers to teach contour farming, strip composting, and other techniques to improve farmers' productivity, protecting the local environment in the process. They are considering demonstrating simple, more fuel-efficient cooking stoves, so women would not need to search for, carry, or use so much wood.[19] In Costa Rica, WWF and the Nature Conservancy support environmental lawyers working to issue titles to land on the Osa Peninsula, where only 10 percent of the land is held under secure title.[20]

In another project on the Osa Peninsula, WWF and the Nature Conservancy have come up with an idea called Community and Family Rainforests. Landless farming families living in the forest will be issued land titles and receive a lump-sum payment and annual salary thereafter to become caretakers and guardians of the forest under an agreement to fulfill certain duties. Violators will lose title and possession of the land. The success of such schemes remains to be seen.[21]

To protect sensitive ecosystems in the Third World and the indigenous people who rely on them, the underlying forces causing their destruction, which include extreme poverty, government subsidies for forest clearing, and insecure land tenure, need to be addressed. Development, environment, and economics need to be perceived as indivisible.

Within a wide-reaching framework which attempted to tackle economic, demographic, political, and environmental issues with equal force, debt-for-nature swaps could perhaps play a minor role. But in their current form, despite some good intentions, they are not the mechanism to address or affect any of these problems which have invariably led to the resource degradation in the first place. The only beneficiaries of debt-for-nature swaps at present are the northern banks.

Notes

1. *New York Times*, 4 October 1984, opposite editorial.
2. World Bank, *World Debt Tables, 1991–92*, Vol. 1, *Analysis and Summary Tables*, Washington, DC, 1991.
3. U.S. Agency for International Development (USAID), *Innovative Development Approaches* No. 4, Washington, DC, January 1991, p. 8.
4. Bid prices, that is, the prices buyers were willing to pay, on 29 April 1991. Information taken from Salomon Brothers, *Indicative Prices for Developing Country Credits*, New York. The loans to Colombia, Morocco, and the Philippines are benchmark performing loans, that is, those countries are up-to-date in making their interest payments; other countries are not.
5. The secondary market, like most markets, reacts to supply and demand. The price of the debt is likely to go up if the seller feels there must be an underlying cause for confidence in the country's finances, illustrated by a buyer's eagerness to purchase the debt.
6. Bulow, J. and Rogoff, K. "Buyback Boondoggle," *Brookings Papers on Economic Activity*, No. 2, 1988, pp. 678–682.
7. The donors who contributed the money for the debt-for-nature swaps include foundations, corporations, individuals, the U.S. Agency for International Development (USAID), and the Swedish and Dutch governments. USAID contributed $1.4 million for debt-for-nature debt purchases between 1987 and 1990 and plans to grant another $29.6 million for swaps currently being negotiated, mostly to buy the Philippines' sovereign debt. See USAID, *Innovative Development*, p. 2.
8. Conversation with Kurt Low, U.S. World Wildlife Fund (WWF), Conservation Finance, on 14 May 1991. Information about National Westminster Bank plc, Dresdner Bank, Banque de l'Union Européene, and Crédit Commercial de France from WWF news release, *WWF and Madagascar Announce First Debt-for-Nature Swap for Africa*, 3 August 1989.
9. WWF, *Compliance Review of 1988 Costa Rican DFN Swap*, undated memo concerning review carried out during the week of 5 March 1990.
10. WWF, *Amended and Restated Debt-for-Nature Agreement between WWF (U.S.) and Fundación Natura*, 4 April 1989.

11. Ibid.

12. World Bank, *Social Indicators of Development 1990*, Washington, DC, 1990.

13. World Bank, *Ecuador's Amazon Region: Development Issues and Options*, Discussion Paper No. 75, Washington, DC, 1990, p. 12.

14. As S. Nugent points out, "Exportable beef is simply not the profit inspiration for forest-felling. Amazonian beef production is highly unprofitable, in fact, [with] each hectare of cleared forest producing only twenty-two kilograms of meat. The value of such land from the cattle-ranchers' point of view is that it holds its value well in inflationary times." (Nugent, S. *Big Mouth: The Amazon Speaks*, Fourth Estate Limited, London, 1990, p. 226). For further discussion, see also Hecht, S. B., "The Sacred Cow in the Green Hell: Livestock and Forest Conversion in the Brazilian Amazon," *The Ecologist*, Vol. 19, No. 6, Nov/Dec. 1989, pp. 229–234.

15. World Bank, *Ecuador's Amazon Region*, Annex 2, pp. 35–38.

16. World Bank, *Ecuador's Amazon Region*, p. 23.

17. WWF, *World Wildlife Fund and the Nature Conservancy: A Quarter Century in Costa Rica*, undated, obtained in May 1991.

18. WWF, *Attachment to Debt-for-Nature Agreement*, undated, obtained in May 1991; and conversation on 15 May 1991 with Randy Curtis, the Nature Conservancy.

19. Conversation on 14 May 1991 with Ira Amstadter, WWF.

20. CEDARENA and Fundación Neotrópica, *Towards Community and Family Rainforests*, March 1991.

21. Ibid.; and Curtis, R., conversation.

---

24 David Rains Wallace ◆ Reefs, Rainforests, Caves, Ruins, and Rookeries

Tiny Costa Rica has built a world-renowned national park system in the past few decades and has become a model for other underdeveloped countries striving for sustainable development. David Rains Wallace, an acclaimed naturalist-writer, shows how Costa Rica endeavored to resolve the apparent conflict between conservation and development through nature-based tourism. In this chapter from The Quetzal and the Macaw, *he describes how two dedicated, visionary, and energetic young Costa Ricans struggled to create that nation's park system. They had to negotiate through the minefields of the national political system, institutional competition, local resistance to (or support for) conservation, and the limitations imposed by very scarce economic resources. Wallace reveals that early park service administrators struggled to define the proper role of the parks and decided to stress preservation of ecological resources rather than recreation or tourism. Because they chose conservation of the country's legendary biodiversity, virtually every major type of ecosystem*

From David Rains Wallace, "Reefs, Rainforests, Caves, Ruins, and Rookeries," in *The Quetzal and the Macaw: The Story of Costa Rica's National Parks* (San Francisco: Sierra Club Books, 1992), 36–45. © 1992 by David Rains Wallace. Reprinted by permission of David Rains Wallace.

in Costa Rica has found protection (compared to only 50 percent of eco-systems in the United States). Encouragement of tourism came later—largely from other branches of the government—as a result of the economic crises and structural adjustment policies of the 1980s. Selection 25 provides further information about the ecotourism "boom" in Costa Rica, which overtook traditional exports to become the country's top foreign exchange earner in the early 1990s.

The Costa Rican park system grew so fast in the early 1970s that it seems there must have been some prearranged strategy, some master plan of conquest. A pro-park media blitz in that period strengthens the impression of delibrate promotion. Full-page ads in the dailies boosted Santa Rosa's opening celebration with Madison Avenue brashness. "Begin to enjoy the marvellous experience of visiting the national parks—*un mundo diferente, un mundo fascinante*," they proclaimed, "and remember, bring your camera." Every week, newspapers carried articles about sea turtle slaughter, dwindling quetzal populations, deforestation, endangered species, and other problems, usually with some mention of national parks as a solution.

"Within ten years, there may not be either flora or fauna in the country," said a July 1972 article in *El Diario de Costa Rica*. This article consisted largely of [Mario] Boza's testimony before a Legislative Assembly committee. He said that if parks, then under the Agriculture Ministry's Forestry Directorate, didn't get independent status as a park service, there would be no funds or personnel to develop new parks; and that if new parks weren't created, "within ten years, we'll be like other countries, like El Salvador, virtually without natural resources, with huge economic problems."

The swiftness of this attack seems to have caught potential park enemies off guard. As Boza told me, "There was the usual opposition to parks, but it wasn't strong." The only organized opposition that got media attention at that time was a group called the National Committee for Conservation of Renewable Resources. They got a letter published in *La Nación* in 1972 claiming that a park service would be too expensive and would conflict with existing government bodies. (It would take another five years to get an independent park service.)

The publicity blitz was one of a number of techniques Boza outlined in a little book entitled *A Decade of Development*, published in 1981. The book is a kind of handy, how-to guide on establishing and administering a national park system in a developing country. It explains concisely how to solve the successive problems of a system: how to select parks, staff them, fund them, and get the public to support them. How to "break the vicious cycle between the necessity to develop parks and the lack of means"? Establish parks, publicize them, and thus create a need for means.

How to "avoid wasting the small means available"? Resist the temptation to establish as many parks as possible, and concentrate on areas one can develop and protect. How to get guides, guards, workmen, and cooks to staff parks with the small means available? Recruit Peace Corps volunteers from other government agencies, since parks are "popular with this kind of young person," and thus get a free, insured, Spanish-speaking labor supply. How to get highly qualified planning and research personnel? Borrow them from conservation agencies in developed countries, from international agencies like USAID, or from private organizations like the World Wildlife Fund. How to get operating funds? Charge admission to the parks and get international bank loans. How to get public support? Continually publish short articles in the press (Boza had a Peace Corps volunteer writing articles full-time); escort businessmen, legislators, journalists, and other public figures to the parks; and have friends like Doña Karen Figueres in high places.

It appears that this shrewd strategy came after the fact, however. When I asked Boza in 1990 if he had planned it, he was so taken aback that he mentioned the question in a speech the next day. "*Nothing* was planned," he told me. "We had no experience, although the basic idea of what we wanted to do was clear. But we had to learn by doing it."

Every addition to the system brought with it a new set of problems to learn about. The next two areas on the agenda were Tortuguero, Archie Carr's turtle beach; and Cahuita, a swampy spit of land on Costa Rica's southern Caribbean coast. Costa Rica's biggest coral reef, containing some thirty-five species of reef-building coral, lies offshore from Cahuita. Both areas contained lowland rainforest as well as marine resources, an obvious requirement for a park system within the second largest rainforest region of the Western Hemisphere.

Geographically, Tortuguero and Cahuita are about the same distance from San José as Santa Rosa is. Historically and culturally they were much farther away. Even in 1990 neither park had been integrated into the system to the extent that Poás and Santa Rosa had. Poás and Santa Rosa were about as fully developed as U.S. parks, with paved roads, campsites, visitor centers, and interpretive programs. Cahuita was accessible by dirt road in 1990, so it had a visitor center and camping area, but the government still hadn't gotten around to buying most of the land in it. The much larger Tortuguero was largely in government hands, but remained accessible only by plane, boat, or by hiking for hours through swampy forest, and it contained few public facilities.

Tortuguero and Cahuita were less a part of Costa Rica's colonial-national nucleus than Poás and Santa Rosa, or even than Cabo Blanco. For most of Costa Rica's existence, the Caribbean coast was largely uninhabited because of diseases, pirate raids, and other troubles. In the late nineteenth century, when big foreign companies began developing railroads and banana plantations on the coast, Jamaican blacks came and settled. At first they worked for the big companies; many then went on to develop small cacao and coconut plantations. They developed an English-speaking culture distinct from the rest of the nation. Laws prohibiting Caribbean blacks from immigrating to the Meseta Central helped keep the region distinct into the early twentieth century.

It wasn't surprising, then, that the prospect of the government expropriating land for such an obscure purpose as a national park should have met with even more suspicion on the Caribbean than in Guanacaste or Nicoya. "We are more concerned than anyone else about preserving the area, because it's our farms," said Alphaeus Buchanan, quoted in Paula Palmer's folk history of the Talamanca coast, *What Happen.* "That's what they don't realize, that these lovely coconut groves that they see along the beaches are our farms, something built by our people. They call it 'natural resources,' and it *is* natural resources, but it's our farms!"

It can be difficult for the outsider to distinguish between farms and natural landscape on the Caribbean. Traditional agriculture blends easily with the background of beaches and swampy forest. Farmers grow coconut palms in the sandy strip between beach and swamp, and cacao among the wild trees of inland rainforest. Even the gardens of fruit trees, herbs, and vegetables around towns and houses grade almost imperceptibly into forest. Walking Cahuita's beaches in 1990, I saw little suggestion that a road a few hundred yards inland was lined with farmhouses. The beach apparently belonged to thousands of red and blue land crabs that shuffled over the leaf litter or sat in swamp pools, to hundreds of lizards—geckoes, ameivas, and anoles—and to smaller numbers of howler and capuchin monkeys, three-toed sloths, and small red squirrels. A pair of white-necked puffbirds, a large uncommon rainforest species, seemed to be nesting in a tree above the trail. Similarly, swimming among the squirrel fish, parrot fish, butterfly fish, and wrasse of the reef, I saw little evidence aside from the odd dinghy that subsistence fishing went on.

Traditional farming does have its impacts. At Cahuita's Puerto Vargas visitor center, *guardaparque* Marvin Santamaría told me it has proved impossible to control poaching of iguanas and turtle eggs because of the farms' proximity. The park's nesting turtle population was thus negligible, and I saw no iguanas there. Crocodiles and manatees were no more than a memory. There is a Caribbean tradition that manatees contain every kind of meat—beef, pork, chicken, fish, even bacon—so they don't last long in settled areas. Santamaría also told me that there was some conflict between the park and subsistence fishermen. Spiny lobsters were rare from heavy exploitation. When the park tried to outlaw spearfishing in its waters, fishermen complained that they needed the guns for protection from sharks.

Yet such conflicts have had less impact on the park than such large-scale development as the banana plantations on the Estrella River north of Cahuita. A current carries silt from the plantations southward, and the silt has been smothering the reef since before the park was established. Santamaría told me that living corals remained abundant only at the tip of Cahuita Point. The waters north of the point were a shallow, muddy expanse of dead reef where spiny sea urchins grazed on turtlegrass, and the blue plastic used to bag banana bunches littered the beach.

Vernon Cruz worked on the creation of Cahuita National Park when he was a floating administrator. He told me the streets of the little town of Cahuita north of the park "were grass then, just like a rug. A Chinese lady owned the only hotel, and the theater, dance hall, and grocery store. We had to be refugees with her in bad weather. Alvaro* was in charge in the beginning, but he had some trouble with the local people because of his strong temper. I had to go there and tenderize the situation, because some of them said they'd kill Alvaro."

First created as a six-hundred-hectare marine national monument in 1970, later enlarged to include 1,067 hectares of swamp forest, Cahuita became a political football. In the 1970s it passed from the park system administration to a local agency, the Junta de Administración Portuaria de la Vertiente Atlántica, then back to the parks. Residents and local officials complained that park administrators made arbitrary and unpredictable regulations, such as telling farmers with land in the park to clear brush under coconut plantations, then telling them not to clear it. Locals also complained that the park administration failed to tell them about legislation and plans to start expropriation hearings. Conflict came to a head in the mid-1970s when several hundred people, including the national Legislative Assembly deputy from Limón, gathered in Cahuita town to speak against the park.

The park staff and local people had something in common, however: a desire not to see mass commercial tourist development overwhelm the area. "I don't want to see our people sell it for any tourist complex in the future," Alphaeus Buchanan said, "because we know that if tourism takes over the area, that's the end of our boys and girls. Look at Acapulco. You know what that brings, venereal diseases, crime, prostitution, drugs. . . ." Vernon Cruz told me that Alvaro Ugalde was able to turn around the antipark meeting in Cahuita by pointing out that the likely alternative to a national park would be a mass of hotels, marinas, and golf courses, which nobody wanted except foreign companies waiting on the sidelines.

---

*Alvaro Ugalde, one of the leading figures in the creation and development of Costa Rica's system of national parks.

"I was the only speaker to defend the park," Ugalde recalled. "All the previous speakers had spoken in Spanish, and I saw a possibility open to me in support of the park. The majority of the audience were black men and women who communicated better in English. I started in Spanish, but after a few minutes my desperation forced me to turn to English. . . . I felt I had connected myself to a special communication system with the audience. I told them that in spite of the Park Service's mistakes and serious difficulties in communication between them and the young bureaucrats from San José, our intention was to continue the protection that they and their ancestors had bestowed on those beautiful forests and reefs. I asked them to give us time, and to work with us to solve the many problems.

"Somehow, as if guided by an unseen force, my voice became louder, and I soon was asking them questions, and they were responding en masse. I found myself asking them if they wanted the park to exist, and they said, 'Yes.' The only words I could find after that were 'thank you,' and I shut up. My speech happened to be the meeting's last, to the dismay of my enemies."

In contrast to settled Cahuita, Tortuguero remains one of the wildest regions of Costa Rica. Crocodiles and manatees still inhabit its swampy rivers. On my 1987 visit, I saw caimans, sunbitterns, and sungrebes along the rivers, increasingly uncommon creatures in the rest of Costa Rica. Beaches stretched empty as far as I could see, and an unforgettably large expanse of rainforest was visible from Cerro Tortuguero, an isolated mound just inland. White-lipped peccaries, usually the first mammals to disappear as forest dwindles, still inhabit Tortuguero.

Tortuguero may have been wilder in 1987 than it was when Archie Carr arrived to study green turtles in the 1950s. At that time riverside forests were being logged, and poachers and wild dogs routinely decimated turtle nests. In 1959, Carr and a group of other North American and Costa Rican scientists and conservationists founded the Caribbean Conservation Corporation (CCC) to protect the green turtles' nesting colony, one of only two major colonies in the Caribbean. It was Costa Rica's first nongovernmental conservation organization, or NGO. In addition to starting a hatchery program, the CCC began lobbying the government for official protection for the turtles.

A 1963 executive decree established a turtle nesting reserve under the Agriculture Ministry and also restricted turtle hunting and egg-gathering, but the actual protection it offered was limited. Archie Carr's son David told me that his mother, Marjorie, had to teach the guards assigned to patrol the beach how to camp out, since they were from San José. "I remember her telling them, 'Here's your pots and pans, here's your stove, and this is what you do with this and that,' like sending boys to camp."

When Tortuguero National Park was established by executive decree in 1970, Archie Carr wrote Mario Boza that "the decree has come none too soon. With the penetration of the region by a long-shore canal, the entire ecological organization of the zone will be threatened. . . . The potential of the park in saving threatened species is dramatically shown by the success of your program of sea turtle wardenship during the past two seasons. Three seasons ago illegal exploitation of the nesting colony of the green turtle was esentially out of control, the nesting female turtles were regularly killed for calipee, and there was an extensive open collaboration between turtle boats cruising just offshore and illegal hunters on the beach, who tied buoys to the fins of the nesting turtles so they could be picked up by the boats as they returned to the sea. These inroads, which were quite clearly wiping out the colony, were brought to a halt by the move of your office when it manned two shore warden stations at critical points along the nesting beach and arranged a schedule of coast guard surveillance and of shore patrols by armed guards."

In 1975 more legislation expanded Tortuguero to over eighteen thousand hectares of land, including fifteen miles of turtle nesting beach. Nesting turtles (over twenty thousand greens, three hundred leatherbacks, and lesser numbers of hawksbills and loggerheads) came under threat again in 1979, however, when the Legislative Assembly passed a law reducing offshore turtle hunting limits from twelve miles to three miles. Although the law maintained the twelve-mile limit in park waters, this meant turtles would have to swim through waters full of commercial hunters to reach the park. Archie Carr predicted that this would be the coup de grâce for turtle populations on the brink of collapse. An international letter-writing campaign against the law convinced then-president Rodrigo Carazo to veto it in September 1979.

While Ugalde and Cruz sweated in the lowlands or shivered in the highlands, the Boza publicity mill continued to grind out articles on likely parks. A June 1969 *La Nación* piece boosted the attractions of a place called Barra Honda at the north end of the Nicoya Peninsula, and recommended it as a park. A flat-topped mass of grayish white rock looming over a hilly landscape, Barra Honda had been considered a volcano because sulfurous smells and strange roaring sounds came from holes in its top. A 1967 Mountaineering Club of Costa Rica expedition discovered that the holes were really the entrances to a system of spectacular limestone caves that drop vertically into the mountain to depths of over three hundred feet. Thousands of roosting bats caused the sulfurous smells and roaring sounds.

Apparently nobody had entered the caves before and lived to tell about it because they are sheer drops negotiable only with rappelling ropes. The explorers found blind salamanders and fish as well as rats, birds, crickets, beetles, and snails living in fantastic chambers of stalactites, stalagmites, terrazas, curtains, and other limestone cave formations. In 1970 explorers from the Group of Speleology found a number of pre-Columbian human skeletons in the cave, parts of which were covered with the same calcium carbonate forming the stalagmites.

Early acounts make Barra Honda sound like a bleak place. In *The Geography of Costa Rica*, Miguel Obregón described it as "a white park . . . cones and rocky slopes . . . adorned with shrubs." When I visited in 1990 I found it covered with dense second-growth evergreen forest mixed with occasional gigantic old ceiba, guanacaste, and saman trees. Eroded limestone along the path still resembled "the bones of fantastic animals." When I entered one small cave and looked at the ceiling, I thought a snake was crawling across it, then realized that it was a serpentine calcium carbonate formation. These formations covered the ceiling, twisting in every direction. The cave was close to the surface, and I wondered if the formations were tree roots that had gotten covered with calcium carbonate. At the yawning entrance to one of the deep caves, La Trampa ("the trap"), a tan, fluffy object struggled in an overhanging tree. It was a fledgling mottled owl, evidently just leaving a nest.

La Nación articles in 1971 and 1973 touted the national park potential of Rincón de la Vieja, the most active volcano in Guanacaste Province, located to the southeast of Santa Rosa. The articles dwelt on the value of the mountain's forests for protecting the watershed of the agriculturally vital Tempisque River, and on its scenic wonders, which are impressive. At a place called Las Pailas ("the kitchen stoves"), a belt of fumaroles and hot springs surfaces in mixed dry and evergreen forest at the volcano's western base, creating a landscape out of Arthur Conan Doyle's dinosaur novel, *The Lost World*. Boiling gray mud shoots clots eight feet in the air beside still-living *indio desnudo* trees; steaming pits open under the roots of strangler figs; hidden waterfalls cascade into pools overhung with white frangipani flowers. Farther up the volcano, one stands on windswept, rocky ridges that resemble alpine tundra and looks up thousands of feet at other ridges covered with rainforest. Treeline begins at about 11,000 feet in Costa Rica.

Newspapers in the early 1970s also contained articles about the park potential of two places that both happened to be named Guayabo ("guava tree"). One was an island in the Gulf of Nicoya; the other was a tract of second-growth rainforest near the town of Turrialba southeast of San José. Guayabo Island, along with three nearby islands, provided safe nesting rookeries for the west coast's brown pelicans, magnificent frigate birds, and brown boobies. It also contained the only undisturbed dry forest in the country outside Santa Rosa. The other Guayabo was the main archaeological site in Costa Rica, the remains of a pre-Columbian city of stone mounds, causeways, aqueducts, and tombs. Very little is known about the culture that built it, except that they produced impresive stonework and occupied the site from about A.D. 800 to 1400.

Both Guayabos became part of the park system in 1973. Barra Honda and Rincón de la Vieja became national parks in 1974, although it took many more years to acquire all the land in them. Land acquisition problems would lead to a temporary squatter invasion at Rincón de la Vieja, yet what Alvaro Ugalde wrote about Santa Rosa would apply to the other rapidly acquired parks of the early 1970s as well. Twenty years later, in 1990, they were real parks, with rangers and visitors' facilities, and the trees and wildlife they were created to protect were still there.

Within five years, the Costa Rican system had grown from paper hopes to actual landholdings that included not only some of the nation's most significant scenic and cultural sites, but also what was beginning to be a fair sample of its ecological diversity. It was beginning to catch up with much older systems like the United States' (which grew hardly at all from 1970 to 1975, its budget frozen by the Nixon administration), and it had begun to pass the United States in one respect.

The U.S. park system grew up mainly on the public domain lands of the West, which allowed creation of large parks, but resulted in a lopsided representation of ecosystems. In 1990, only about half of U.S. ecosystems were represented in the park system. From its hasty beginnings, and despite the huge cost of acquiring land not in the public domain, the Costa Rican park system tried to acquire land throughout the country, in every type of landscape and ecosystem possible. It was evolving toward a new kind of park system that would be a repository of a nation's biodiversity and of its ecological capital, as well as a showcase of its scenery.

---

25 Susan E. Place ◆ Ecotourism and the Political Ecology of "Sustainable Development" in Costa Rica

This selection examines in Costa Rica the potential of nature-based tourism to provide a foundation for sustainable development. During the 1980s the country suffered serious economic crises and the imposition of a structural adjustment program. The mandate to diversify the economy and increase foreign exchange earnings led to a new development strategy: attract foreign tourists to Costa Rica's famous system of national parks and nature reserves. Nature-based tourism is widely regarded as a win-win approach that encourages both conservation of natural ecosystems and economic growth in remote, impoverished regions.

This research was made possible in part by a Fulbright-Hays Faculty Research Grant. An earlier version of this paper was presented at the annual meeting of the Association of American Geographers, Honolulu, Hawaii, 1999.

Costa Rica's experience with ecotourism, now the country's top source of foreign exchange receipts, reveals that this development strategy is more problematic than was previously thought. While ecotourism has produced some benefits for Costa Rica, the social impacts on tourist destinations suggest that more attention needs to be paid to the original inhabitants of remote rural regions that undergo tourism development. Ways need to be found to prevent inequality from increasing within communities between those who benefit from tourism and those who bear only its costs. Policies that successfully keep economic multipliers within ecotourism destinations might, in fact, promote both environmental conservation and development. Selection 26, in describing Guatemala's Maya Biosphere Reserve, offers an example of how this might be accomplished.

In the late 1980s the Costa Rican government decided to integrate the country into the global economy through ecotourism, which led to its reinvention as a "natural paradise" for tourists from developed countries. This policy provides us with an opportunity to reflect on some of the major contradictions of capitalist development, especially the commoditization of ever more of the Earth's natural environments and cultures. The example of Costa Rica reveals how places reinvent themselves to meet the expectations of the international market, in this case foreign tourists. It also problematizes the notion of "sustainable development."

Nature-based travel, now generally called ecotourism, began to take off globally in the 1980s and has since become one of the fastest growing segments of the global tourist industry, itself one of the largest industries in the world. Ecotourism represents a response to phenomena occurring at both the center and on the periphery, deriving from the dominant global economic paradigm based on continuous growth. As industrialization contributed to environmental degradation, demand for unspoiled natural areas grew in the developed countries, and affluent people increasingly sought exotic wild places in Latin America, Africa, and Asia, where less space had been fully integrated into the global economy.

On the periphery, stagnant or declining commodity prices and growing foreign debts forced governments to seek alternatives to traditional agriculture-based economies. Pressured to restructure their economies by multilateral institutions such as the World Bank and International Monetary Fund (IMF), many countries sought to diversify production, particularly in terms of exports. Some, such as Costa Rica, decided to promote tourism as a foreign exchange earner (making it, in effect, an export). Banking on its world-renowned national park system, Costa Rica aimed for the niche market of ecotourism, which meant that it needed to promote conservation of its remaining natural areas.

Environmentalists have promoted ecotourism as a nonconsumptive use of nature and a win-win development strategy for underdeveloped rural areas. They see it as offering an economic incentive to protect natural ecosystems and encourage appreciation of nature by local populations. Development theorists and practitioners have touted it as a way to provide local employment and income as well as to promote economic multipliers within the destination country (Boo, 1990: 3). Analysis of concrete examples of ecotourism in countries such as Costa Rica will reveal whether or not, in fact, it generates these benefits.

Tourism as a Development Strategy in Costa Rica

Costa Rica is a good place to examine the role that protected wildlands and ecotourism can play in economic development, and the contradictions that emerge in ecotourist destinations. Since the late 1980s the country has aggressively pursued the promotion of tourism as the centerpiece of its development strategy. A variety of interests were involved in this project: the San José government, multilateral lending and development institutions (including USAID), the travel industry, and some conservation organizations and environmentalists. Because the country was already well known among naturalists and ecologists for its natural beauty, biodiversity, and existing system of protected wildlands, the government astutely decided to promote nature tourism. The success of this campaign is demonstrated by the fact that 75 percent of international tourists visit Costa Rica for its natural areas (Mora, 1996).

The number of foreign tourists rose from 376,000 in 1989 to over 610,000 by 1992 (Leininger, 1993: 5), peaking in 1995 with 792,000 international arrivals (Honey, 1999: 133). The national parks also experienced a rapid increase in foreign tourists, with the number more than doubling between 1988 and 1992, after already having doubled between 1984 and 1988 (Place, 1995: 163). However, the volatility of tourism as an economic base can be seen in the drop in numbers of international arrivals to 555,000 in 1996 (the year after the numbers peaked) and 560,000 in 1997 (Honey, 1999: 133; World Tourism Organization, 1997: 45).

Costa Rica has enjoyed a significant amount of domestic tourism in recent decades, and the national parks have become an important source of civic pride and a focus of this tourism. The number of Costa Ricans visiting the national parks increased from about 130,000 in 1982 to over 300,000 in 1992. By 1998, according to unpublished data from SINAC, this figure had increased to almost 486,000. In the 1980s, Costa Ricans of modest income were able to reach some national parks on public transportation; once there, they could stay in inexpensive lodgings within the means of even working-class families. This fact is important because domestic tourism can help mitigate the effects of volatility in the flow of international tourism. By the early 1990s, however, as the Costa Rican tourist industry shifted its focus toward more lucrative foreign travelers, the cost of accommodations near parks and reserves began to skyrocket, pricing even the middle class out of vacations in their own country. Thus, the current emphasis on attracting foreign ecotourists may erode the ability of domestic tourism to reduce the impact on remote rural destination areas of downturns in international tourism. This potential problem is underscored by the fact that over one-half of the 486,000 domestic entrants to national parks in 1998 visited Poás or Irazu—both easily accessible by day trips from the San José metropolitan area, where the bulk of the Costa Rican population lives.

The tourist boom in Costa Rica serves as a good illustration of the linkages between global, national, and local processes that underlie environmental relations and economic development in general. International tourism in Costa Rica—a small, dependent peripheral state in the U.S. sphere of domination—cannot be understood without looking at the country's role in the global political economy. It has relatively little economic autonomy, especially due to the enormous external debt it incurred as part of its "development" strategy since the 1960s. The economic crisis of the early 1980s (created in part by this development strategy) forced Costa Rica to submit to structural adjustment policies mandated by external multilateral lending institutions, particularly the IMF and the World Bank (Hansen-Kuhn, 1993). USAID also played a key role in Costa Rica's economy, pumping more money into the country during the 1980s than the IMF and World Bank combined. USAID engineered a transnational alliance of local business people and technocrats, the Monge administration (1982–1986), and foreign investors (Clark, 1997). This alliance created the framework for the tourism boom.

Structural adjustment required Costa Rica to increase foreign exchange receipts by promoting an expansion of exports, privatization, and trade liberalization. USAID used the transnational alliance to support the expansion of private investment in and diversification of export production. Initiatives ranged from traditional commodities such as bananas through nontraditional exports such as cut flowers and medicinal herbs to international tourism (which functions as an export because it brings in foreign exchange). The government removed obstacles to foreign investment, paving the way for an influx of foreign-owned hotels and resorts seeking to cash in on rapidly growing tourism. By 1993 tourism had become Costa Rica's leading source of foreign exchange (Honey, 1999: 134). At the same time, the expansion of export-oriented agricultural production caused deforestation that conflicted directly with the growing market for nature tourism, a contradiction that seems to be largely ignored by the architects of structural adjustment.

Draconian cuts in public expenditures were mandated by structural adjustment. Ironically, these included cutting the budget for the national park system. This policy ignored the fact that the tourist industry depended heavily on the existence of the national parks for much of its livelihood. Until recently the parks were so underfunded that most of them were virtually unstaffed and had little or no infrastructure or services for tourists.

Costa Rica also had some well-known private reserves at that time. Probably the most influential were La Selva (owned and operated by OTS, the Organization for Tropical Studies, a consortium of U.S. and Central American universities) and Monteverde Cloud Forest Reserve (owned and administered by the Tropical Science Center, a Costa Rica-based research center, and the World Wildlife Fund). Private reserves began to attract a growing proportion of foreign visitors as the ecotourism boom developed. As a result, private entrepreneurs began to establish new nature preserves for the purpose of tourism. These private reserves provide food, lodging, and interpretive programs geared toward the affluent international market. Due to the higher level of service, increasing numbers of international tourists today visit the growing network of private reserves and refuges, which accounts for as much as 5 percent of Costa Rica's national territory (Honey, 1999: 150). Although ecotourism may have generated modest employment for local populations near private reserves, it has also clearly contributed to growing land hunger in Costa Rica, which will exacerbate the very social and environmental problems that ecotourism is supposed to alleviate. Thus, structural adjustment has encouraged the expansion of agroexport and ecotourist destinations in the past decade and squeezed increasing numbers of small farmers off the land (Vandermeer and Perfecto, 1995). This trend is disturbing because Costa Rica historically has been a country with a relatively high proportion of small and medium-sized farms, which has helped to prevent the political instability and civil unrest that have plagued neighboring nations in Central America.

The tourist industry can wield a powerful influence in the politics and policymaking institutions of destination countries. In Costa Rica the tourism industry has influenced policy in ways that may not be in the nation's long-term best interests. For example, when the national park system suffered an economic crisis due to the deep budget cuts mandated by the structural adjustment agreement, it proposed to institute a dual entrance fee system (charging foreigners more than Costa Rican citizens). Although this is a well-established practice in many countries, the industry pressured the government into greatly reducing the fees for tourists (Honey, 1999). Of even more concern, the San José government now pledges that it will quickly remove squatters from private reserves (Honey, 1999: 164). Historically, the government has followed a policy based in its constitution of allowing landless families to homestead idle land. The practice gave rise to a class of *precaristas* (people living on land without title) who could not be removed without going through considerable legal processes, including payment for "improvements." Since "improvements" usually meant deforestation, this policy led to considerable environmental degradation. However, it also encouraged social and economic equity and slowed down the process of land concentration. The Costa Rican government's commitment to social justice and economic opportunity did much to prevent the political instability that has long characterized neighboring Nicaragua and the rest of Central America. The shift in policy toward protection of big landowners (especially foreigners) represents a significant change in direction for Costa Rica.

The intended beneficiaries of most development policies are ostensibly the poor. Most of the poor in Latin America live in isolated rural areas, which have become target destinations for ecotourists. A growing proportion, however, is to be found in the burgeoning shantytowns that ring virtually every major city in the region. It is generally conceded that structural adjustment policies have increased poverty and migration to urban centers by peasants pushed off the land because of the expansion of commercial activities for the export market. Some observers argue that ecotourism, by creating jobs for local people, promotes rural development while simultaneously preserving the natural environment, and thus should discourage out-migration.

Does ecotourism, in fact, promote development in remote destination areas? The evidence is mixed, as a review of Costa Rica's recent development suggests. Tourist destinations such as Monteverde (with associated communities such as Santa Elena and Cerro Plano) have clearly seen economic growth due to ecotourism, yet they are also experiencing some serious social impacts. Social inequality has increased. Those people with sufficient money to invest in tourist enterprises have benefited, while those without it are struggling. The best that the latter can hope for are low-wage jobs servicing tourist facilities. Meanwhile, the cost of living has increased due to an influx of migrants and entrepreneurs hoping to profit from growing tourism. This growth has caused rapid inflation in land values. As one community leader said, "Now we say we can sell what we have, but we cannot afford to buy. We are losing the properties that we have." (Honey, 1999: 155). All over Costa Rica, small landowners are selling out to foreigners (or to large Costa Rican enterprises), often much too cheaply, and are joining the ranks of rural or urban laborers (Honey, 1999: 164). This shift represents a sea change in a country that prides itself on its heritage of yeoman farmers and democratic traditions.

The tiny Caribbean coastal village of Tortuguero illustrates the complex nature of changes brought by the rapid growth of international tourism in remote underdeveloped areas. In the early 1980s, Tortuguero's population of less than 150 cobbled together subsistence from various natural resources supplemented with sporadic income from sport fishermen and scientists who studied the endangered green sea turtles that nest in the area (Place, 1988). Few tourists visited the remote place, the vast majority of them Costa Ricans, and they frequented the two rustic *cabinas* and *comedores* owned by villagers. In the second half of the 1980s entrepreneurs from San José started package tours to Tortuguero marketed to the Costa Rican middle class, which brought a modest increase in tourism to the village. In the 1990s, in response to government policy promoting international tourism, the number of visitors to Tortuguero started to soar. Most of these people came to experience tropical nature, as can be seen in Tortuguero National Park where the numbers increased from a few hundred in 1983 to 30,000 in 1993 (Place, 1995). Tour operators began to focus on attracting prosperous foreign tourists. By 1998 there were ten fairly large hotels in the area, six of which were foreign-owned (Dennis, 1998). Their high prices effectively prevent most Costa Ricans from vacationing in Tortuguero, and the ratio of foreign to domestic visitors to the area has reversed dramatically.

The social fabric of destination communities is also threatened by tourism. Again, Monteverde illustrates the problems that tourism—even relatively small-scale ecotourism—brings with it. The region has had a long history of cooperative enterprises, particularly in dairying, since Quakers from the United States settled it in the early 1950s. Neighboring communities also embraced a cooperative ethos. Tourism, however, has brought fierce competition. As one community member pointed out, tourism is not a cooperative activity like dairying (Honey, 1999: 156). In Tortuguero, a flood of outsiders, attracted by the prospect of work in the new tourist enterprises, has swamped the little village of 150 people and transformed it. This transformation has not necessarily improved the lives of those living there in the decades before tourism arrived (and presumably the target of rural development policies). It has also diluted the historically Afro-Caribbean cultural identity of the village. By the mid-1990s two souvenir shops, both owned by outsiders, appeared in the middle of Tortuguero. They sold handicrafts made elsewhere in Latin America or Costa Rica, which has recently devised various craft products to sell to foreign tourists.

Tourism can also expose a community to economic volatility over which it has little or no control. In Monteverde, community leaders are concerned about the extent to which tourism has become a "monocrop" because an estimated 65 to 70 percent of the area's income now derives from tourism—up from 10 percent just ten years ago (Honey, 1999: 154). Such extreme concentration is troubling because tourism suffers from ups and downs with the business cycles of wealthy countries. It is also vulnerable to political factors, such as the instability and warfare that embroiled Costa Rica's neighbors during the 1970s and 1980s. Security issues concern the travel industry, as attacks on tourists by armed dissidents seem to occur with increasing frequency around the world, most recently in remote areas of Colombia and Uganda. Even a peaceful and politically stable country such as Costa Rica can be affected. In March 2000 the murder of two young American women near Cahuita sent shock waves through the country's tourism sector. All of these circumstances are beyond the control of tourist destinations, yet their economic fortunes are profoundly affected by them. Even remote rainforest regions are at the mercy of global processes and decisions made in distant places.

Tourist destinations can experience crashes in their economies due to natural hazards such as earthquakes or hurricanes, as seen recently in both Mexico and Honduras. In 1991 an earthquake measuring 7.4 on the Richter scale hit the Caribbean coast of Costa Rica. It caused so much tectonic uplift that it destroyed the transportation infrastructure (bridges, canals, railroad) that brought tourists to the region. The uplift made the coastal canal unnavigable, eliminating public transportation to Tortuguero. The loss impacted locally owned businesses severely because several villagers offered rustic tourist accommodations in *cabinas* and provided typical meals in *comedores* to a predominantly Costa Rican clientele who arrived by train or bus or boat. The owners of these microenterprises purchased fish, game meat, and produce from local people, thus helping to spread the income from tourism.

If tourism is to promote sustainable community development in Tortuguero, it should focus on expanding, improving, and promoting locally owned facilities and services. During the 1980s several local entrepreneurs tried to expand their businesses to accommodate the growing numbers of visitors to the village. These small business owners were hampered, however, by lack of access to capital and the skills needed to offer services suitable for foreign tourists. While they were slowly stockpiling lumber to enlarge their *cabinas*, for example, outsiders quickly moved in and built lodgings to capture the international tourist market. During the early years of tourism promotion, both government and financial institution policies discriminated against small rural enterprises (Hill, 1990; Honey, 1999). However, by the late 1990s several government agencies, including SINAC (which administers all protected areas in Costa Rica), ICT (the tourism office), and INA (the national training institute), were collaborating on policies to provide financing and training for small-scale locally based ecotourism enterprises (León, pers. comm.).

There is some evidence that ecotourism is beginning to produce a few local economic benefits for Tortuguero. For example, several locally owned lodgings had been established in the village by 1997 (Blake and Becher, 1997). Such village-based tourism, oriented toward domestic and foreign tourists on a budget, has the potential to produce more local economic multipliers than the high-priced, tour-package hotels. Moreover, both women and men can participate in the economic spinoffs from this type of tourism. Men, however, are likely to earn more than women by guiding tourists, hunters, and sportfishing enthusiasts.

Conclusion

Ecotourism, at least as practiced in Costa Rica, presents a problematic approach to "sustainable development" because of the social effects that accompany it. Democratic countries with relatively egalitarian social and political traditions, such as Costa Rica, offer hope that a more popularly based form of tourism can develop. However, tourism as a development strategy seems to carry with it the temptation to try to wrest as much money as possible from foreign tourists, thus encouraging overly rapid growth of resorts. Although the San José government has paid lip service to nature-oriented tourism, until recently it has offered little material help to ecotourism microenterprises. In fact, it has promoted mass tourism in order to increase foreign earnings while trying simultaneously to project an image of an ecologically enlightened country with an abundance of unspoiled tropical nature. The result has been a tendency to engage in "greenwashing," with subsequent disappointments on the part of both tourists and environmental organizations—perhaps contributing to a downturn in tourism after international arrivals peaked in 1995.

Furthermore, the capture of most of the profits from foreign tourism by businesses outside the destination area exemplifies the problematic relationship between environment and development. The contradictions revealed by ecotourism-based development suggest that the relationship between the conservation of natural resources and economic development is much more complex than it appears at first glance. With ecotourism, the income generated by the "nonconsumptive" use of local resources flows to the outsiders who bring visitors to ecotourist destinations and provide their accommodations and other services. Travel agencies, transportation companies, tour operators, hotel owners, and souvenir shop owners reap most of the benefits of the protection of nature in ecotourism destinations rather than the locals who used to depend on nearby natural resources, such as tropical forests, for their livelihood. Ecotourism causes nature and rural communities to be commodified for external markets, with the profits flowing outward. Only those local residents able to capture some of the income generated by the tourism boom benefit from it, contributing to widening economic and social disparities within destination communities.

Multiplier leakage is only part of the problem. Ecotourism in Costa Rica has encouraged the establishment of private reserves, which exacerbates land hunger and may increase the potential for social unrest in the future. Tourism exposes host countries to economic volatility over which they have no control. Rural areas that come to depend on a "tourism monoculture" can be devastated if visitors turn their attention elsewhere, whether due to political unrest, natural hazards, or competition from other ecotourist destinations. The impact of declining tourist numbers can be especially devastating to small, family-owned and -operated enterprises in remote rural destinations such as Tortuguero and Monteverde since they have few alternatives to fall back on. Because many Third World countries are jumping on the ecotourism bandwagon, competition is certain to increase.

Ecotourism can provide an economic alternative to natural resource extraction, but this does not happen automatically, or without social and environmental impacts. If it is to be sustainable, local populations must be allowed to capture a significant amount of the economic multipliers generated by tourism. Successful reduction of multiplier leakage requires local participation in development planning and outside assistance with the provision of necessary infrastructure, training, and credit. Community participation is also essential for identifying negative impacts on people who live in areas undergoing ecotourism development. The proliferation of private reserves represents a trend away from community participation in development and land-use planning, which has become standard procedure. It is very rare for landowners to make any attempt to involve the local community in planning the use of their private property. Even where public participation in land-use planning is sought, there are powerful internal and external obstacles to genuine local participation, ranging from factionalism within communities to state policies that promote centralized planning and the accumulation of capital in large tourism enterprises. Finally, negative social impacts such as increasing inequality within local communities and erosion of their cultural practices and values must be acknowledged and solutions sought. When tourism is based on a synthetic cultural and environmental context, it presents neither an authentic experience for visitors nor an authentic form of development for host communities.

Negative effects may not be inevitable, however. Costa Rica appears to have learned from mistakes made during its first decade of tourism-based development. More attention is now being paid to helping local communities restore and protect natural ecosystems and to the promotion of small-scale ecotourism based on these conservation efforts. Grassroots participation in sustainable resource use in several biosphere reserves in Mexico and Central America also serve as models of locally controlled development that promotes environmental conservation (Stafford, 1994 and 1996; Knudson, 1999). Perhaps careful attention to these as well as current problems in ecotourist destinations can lead to more effective policies for tourism-based development that sustain ecosystems, livelihoods, and traditional cultures in Latin America's remaining rainforest regions.

Literature Cited

Blake, Beatrice and Anne Becher. 1997. *The New Key to Costa Rica.* Berkeley, CA: Ulysses Press.

Boo, Elizabeth. 1990. *Ecotourism: The Potentials and Pitfalls.* 2 volumes. Washington, DC: World Wildlife Fund.

Clark, Mary A. 1997. Transnational Alliances and Development Policy in Latin America: Nontraditional Export Promotion in Costa Rica, *Latin American Research Review* 32(2): 71–91.

Dennis, Steve. 1998. Personal communication from a professor in the California State University, Chico, Department of Recreation and Parks Management, who taught in Costa Rica during the fall 1998 semester.

Hansen-Kuhn, Karen. 1993. Sapping the Economy: Structural Adjustment Policies in Costa Rica, *The Ecologist* 23(5): 179–84.

Hill, Carole. 1990. The Paradox of Tourism in Costa Rica, *Cultural Survival Quarterly* 14(1): 14–19.

Honey, Martha. 1994. Paying the Price of Ecotourism, *Américas* 46(6): 40–47.

———. 1999. *Ecotourism and Sustainable Development: Who Owns Paradise?* Washington, DC: Island Press.

Knudson, Tom. 1999. Bighorn Sheep Hunting Helps People, Wildlife of Baja, *The Sacramento Bee*, July 5.

Leininger, Allen. 1993. Algunos aspectos de la geografía turística y su aplicación en Costa Rica. Escuela de Ciencias Geográficas, Universidad Nacional, Heredia, Costa Rica (unpublished).

León, Sergio. 2000. Personal communication from a veteran employee of Costa Rica's National Park Service (now part of SINAC).

Mora Castellano, Eduardo. 1996. El secuestro de una nación, *AmbienTico* (March, no. 38). Revista mensual publicada por la Escuela de Ciencias Ambientales, Universidad Nacional de Costa Rica, Heredia.

Place, Susan E. 1988. The Impact of National Park Development on Tortuguero, Costa Rica, *Journal of Cultural Geography* 9(1): 37–52.

———. 1991. Nature Tourism and Rural Development in Tortuguero, *Annals of Tourism Research* 18: 186–201.

———. 1995. Ecotourism for Sustainable Development: Oxymoron or Plausible Strategy? *GeoJournal* 35(2): 161–74.

SINAC (Sistema Nacional de Areas de Conservación), Government of Costa Rica. Unpublished annual data on national park visitor numbers.

Stafford, Kathryn. 1994. Petén Crafts a Future,* *Américas* 46(5): 29–35.

———. 1996. Breathing Life into the Biosphere, *Américas* 48(3): 24–31.

Vandermeer, John and Ivette Perfecto. 1995. *Breakfast of Biodiversity.*** Oakland, CA: Food First Books.

World Tourism Organization. 1997. *Tourism Market Trends, 1985–96.* Madrid: WTO.

* See Selection 26, this volume.
** For chapter 2 see Selection 2, this volume.

26 Kathryn Stafford ◆ Petén Crafts a Future

Kathryn Stafford describes an experiment in progress at a biosphere re-
serve in the Guatemalan rainforest. Here in the Petén (Guatemala's north-
ern province), local residents earn their living in a variety of ways that
promise to provide for their families while preserving the rainforest.
Family-based woodcarving cooperatives, small-scale ecotourism busi-
nesses, and the harvesting and processing of wild plants all generate a
better income for residents of the Maya Biosphere Reserve than would
cultivating corn or ranching on deforested land. This forest-based mul-
tiple livelihood strategy appears to offer a viable alternative to the tradi-
tional "negative symbiosis" of logging-farming-ranching—the sequence
by which vast areas of tropical forest have been cleared in Latin America.

The future success of this experiment in sustainable forest use de-
pends upon maintaining the Maya Biosphere Reserve's population den-
sity below its carrying capacity. To that end, some local residents are
engaged in an artisan-to-artisan training program whereby they hope to
teach woodcarving to residents of the Guatemalan highlands, a region
characterized by periodic armed struggle and out-migration because of
inequitable land tenure and growing land hunger. The Peteneros hope that
if highlanders can make an adequate living, they will not migrate to the
rainforest frontier in the Petén and add to population pressures there. See
Selections 17 and 25 for additional perspectives on the complexities of
implementing sustainable alternatives to rainforest development.

Islands, by their very nature, are fragile environments—surrounded,
sometimes engulfed, other times stranded. The ancient Maya of northern Guatemala called their island capital in Lake Petén Itzá "El Petén," or
the big island. This was the last refuge for the Itzá, who had fled south
from Yucatán to the tropical forests of Guatemala, and who foretold correctly the year, 1697, when this last Indian stronghold would fall to the
Spanish.

The Spanish, in turn, named their conquered capital Remedios
(present-day Flores), meaning relief or aid, and called the entire northernmost region of Guatemala "El Petén." The name seemed to fit this
isolated area, remote as it was—and it remained so for nearly three centuries—a sparsely populated island of dense forest, cut off essentially from
the rest of the country. But today Petén is an island no more.

From Kathryn Stafford, "Petén Crafts a Future," *Américas* 46, no. 5
(September–October 1994): 29–31, 34–35. Photographs omitted. Reprinted by
permission of *Américas*, a bimonthly magazine published by the General Secretariat of the Organization of American States in English and Spanish.

The population of Guatemala's frontier state has ballooned over the last two decades—from 20,000 to about 375,000. This rapid migration has been aided by logging companies, which have opened up roads in the once impenetrable forest. An area once thought bereft of natural resources and attractions—archaeologist Sylvanus Morley called it "one of the most difficult New World areas in which to live"—is now home to seven logging companies, and has also caught the eye of oil speculators.

The new residents of Petén, or Peteneros, are landless and unfamiliar with Petén's agriculture and forest products. Seeking ways to support themselves and their families, they move north from the highlands to carve a living out of the forest as farmers, or *milperos*. Ranchers, too, over the last two decades, have discovered the last frontier of Petén.

This successive combination of logging, farming, and ranching forms what anthropologist Norman Schwartz, in his book *Forest Society*, terms a "negative symbiosis." He has pointed out that increased deforestation over the last fifteen years has led to longer dry seasons, and that the process appears exponential, that is, the presence of large-sized, contiguous ranches seems to threaten whatever forest patch may be nearby. Perhaps, Schwartz speculates, this is because certain seed-carrying birds and bats, among other animals, will not fly over extensive areas lacking the trees typical of their habitat.

In 1990, in response to Petén's worsening plight, the Guatemalan government legislated fully 40 percent of the department, or 3.7 million acres, as the Maya Biosphere Reserve. The reserve is divided into three areas: multiple use, core (including biotopes and national parks), and buffer, a nine-mile-wide belt, relatively well populated, that surrounds the biosphere and helps protect the reserve. And the government set up an agency to administer the reserve—the National Council for Protected Areas (Consejo de Areas Protegidas, CONAP).

However, as Peteneros, conservationists, and government officials have discovered, designating a reserve is only the first step in the process of forest conservation, reeducation, and retraining. What about life after the biosphere?

~

It is a cloudy afternoon on the shores of Lake Petén Itzá; a light rain has been falling intermittently throughout the day. At Rolando Soto's open-air woodcarving workshop in El Remate, on the road to Tikal National Park, six men are huddled around a table only slightly larger than a chessboard, with knives, saws, and vises, their heads bowed, radio blaring.

Not unlike at a surgical operating table, Rolando is bent over the body of an alligator, while his younger brother Mario scrutinizes the body of a carved, reticulated snake; Mario puts the head in a vise, cuts it in half, and hands the two pieces to the man next to him. At the end of the day the table is swept clean by old and young alike, the radio is silenced, and children gather in the shadows to show Rolando Soto their own carvings.

For the last seven years, Rolando has been working as an artisan in tropical hardwoods, carving objects from fallen trees near his home. He has the eyes and vision of an artist, and speaks quickly and softly about ecologically based woodcarving—showing the beauty of Petén hardwoods as a way of preserving them, teaching artisanry, and [promoting] his ideas for a Petén community supported by income from renewable resources from the forest.

On a wall of his workshop is a list of tropical hardwoods he and his carvers use. *Cericote*, which has a marbled appearance of dark and light swirls, grows quickly and is perfect for carving; *jobillo* is golden-brown, and *mora* is almost blond. This is also where customers—most of them on their way to the Maya ruins of Tikal—come to buy. Two tables are filled with snails of *jobillo*, clam shells of *cericote*, swan-necked spoons of *mora*; an enormous armadillo of *jobillo* seems to preside over everything.

Rolando's parents came to Petén over three decades ago to raise their family of nine children. In that regard, he says, Petén is similar to California: Most Peteneros over the last decades have migrated there from somewhere else.

A boy in soccer gear steps forward shyly, offering Rolando a roughly carved rabbit, which the carver turns over in his hands, then buys, handing the boy a few quetzals. "The idea of artisanry isn't simply a way to make money, but to have people think differently, to have an effect on the way people think. . . . It's not a religion," he states with quiet assurance. "It's a way of life—to live in peace." The idea, the philosophy, behind the cooperative is most important, he says. "The project is more philosophical than material."

Four Soto brothers, as well as seventy residents of El Remate, are employed in the family woodcarving cooperative. According to Rolando, a family of ten can live for one year from the proceeds from the carvings of one tree. The cooperative has also offered workshops to others from outside the area. For example, seven young men from Chimaltenango, in the southern highlands, studied carving techniques with Rolando in a three-week workshop last spring. The idea is to provide skills such that people will be less encouraged to migrate as *milperos*.

"People have become economically and spiritually dependent, but they don't have to live badly because they don't have money. It's because they're not open to new ideas; they're not opening the right doors." The right door, to Rolando, is to understand that work can be communication, not drudgery. "It's a pleasure if you like what you do."

His speech is punctuated with colorful metaphors. Family matters are like cards, he says; there is an ace and a king, with the ace the highest, but it's worth less than the two, and the king is the king. Meaning: Everyone has a role.

All proceeds from the cooperative are shared by the entire family. The family is less concerned with exporting their woodcrafts, but more interested in exporting their ideas for community development. A new woodcarvers' cooperative currently being built nearby on the lake will be supported by a special committee of residents of El Remate. Referring to this new venture, Rolando's younger brother Manuel says: "In the beginning, my father asked me, 'why are you helping those guys to compete?' But I said the better thing is to make everybody competent. Competency isn't competition."

The Soto family also manages a group of bungalows, El Mirador del Duende, which hugs the hillside overlooking the woodcarvers' workshop and Lake Petén-Itzá. More than a half-dozen bungalows are spaced throughout the woods, and their windows open like eyes to view the lake. A main dining hall has not only eyes but a nose too, resembling an ancient Maya god.

Manuel Soto has been gathering citronella, which grows wild throughout Petén; the smell of lemon fills the air. He manages a small ecotourism business, besides the bungalows, taking tourists on camping excursions through the forests of Petén. As he walks purposefully through the woods he knows so well, he identifies the calls of birds as they pass overhead and pierce the morning air—chachalaca, urraca, tordito.

Standing in a grove of *ramón* trees, Manuel rapidly recites what can be extracted or made from the living tree—fruit, flour, soup, cakes, candies. And, like his brother, he speaks in metaphors—to create a continuum, the family cooperative must age like wine that undergoes a fermentation process. He adds: "In other cultures, if you're an architect, maybe your son isn't an architect; but here, if you're an artist, your son is going to be an artist, and a better artist than you."

On the paved road from El Remate, just outside Tikal National Park, are nests of large, colorful birds, oropendolas, a relative of the oriole. About forty nests are clustered together, hanging socks of them, with adult birds coming and going, turning upside down on their branches, their golden tails flashing. Once inside the park, the road north to Uaxactún becomes heavily rutted and muddied. A pair of swallowtail kites, their deeply etched tails like arrows pointing toward their nest atop a tree, are hovering nearby. This is a loggers' road.

Named by Sylvanus Morley, who excavated the Maya ruins nearby— the oldest in Central America—Uaxactún was also one of the most important camps for *chicleros*, those who harvested chicle, a rubber-like substance used in the manufacture of chewing gum, from the *Manilkara zapota* tree. Today, Uaxactún is a village of about seven hundred people located along either length of an airstrip built for the chicle industry, whose heyday existed from about 1890 to 1970. The airstrip is now prime soccer field and horse pasture.

At the thatched hut that is CONAP's district office of the Maya Biosphere Reserve a sign says:

> A tree planted,
> A sign of life.
> A tree destroyed,
> A world diminished.

Here residents talk of developing a tourist route that would extend north from Tikal as far as the less explored ruins of El Mirador and El Perú; they speak knowledgeably about what would be needed: supply stores, horses, trained guides. There is now a guide's course offered their children in the village's only school. Fees could be allocated cooperatively, they say, to support the project's infrastructure, the community, and the forest itself.

They also are exploring ways to derive income from the forest without destroying it, through harvesting plants such as *xate*, a palm used in floral arrangements, which can be collected year-round, and through chicle, which is harvested September through February, allspice (*pimienta gorda*), and medicinal plants.

Says one young resident of Uaxactún with a family: "We know what is in the forest, what we can extract for income besides chicle and *xate*, like medicinal plants and *pimienta*, but someone must help us to extract those things. A *chiclero* feeding his family isn't going to be able to take off a day to harvest medicinal plants and find a market for it by himself. There must be an organization for this."

In fact, Conservation International (CI), a Washington-based nonprofit environmental organization, has been exploring and promoting the economic benefits of Petén's nontimber forest products since the late 1980s. According to Conrad Reining, CI's Guatemala Program director, a family can earn up to three times the average daily wage by harvesting *xate*, chicle, and allspice, versus clearing the forest and planting corn or raising cattle. And, to Guatemala as a nation, these renewable resources could represent from four to six million dollars yearly.

"A tree is concentrated capital, but you must wait many years to obtain that capital," says Reining. "On the other hand, nontimber forest products can be collected from year to year, though their unit value is relatively small. These two can work together: the nontimber forest products provide rent on the land while one waits for the trees to mature. These trees then provide a source of concentrated capital that nontimber forest products cannot easily provide."

At the island capital of Flores, Lake Petén-Itzá is rising, and no one is quite sure why. There are theories: deforestation; the land bridge built two decades ago to connect Flores to Santa Elena disturbed the lake; blocked aquifers; or all of the above. Swallows dive toward the lake's shallows from perches in abandoned buildings on the shore; as a commuter launch from San Andrés passes a tiny outcropping that houses a radio tower, one can't help but wonder how much larger the island was a few decades ago, and how much smaller it will be a few decades hence.

At CI's project offices, called Pro-Petén, Carlos Soza, the organization's in-country director, talks about the importance of determining the carrying capacity of the biosphere—the number of tourists it can serve, the numbers of locals, ranchers, farmers, which are all part of the real picture. As for ecotourism, "it's a process," he says. "It's not the final product. But it's the most direct, quickest way to benefit local people. It's a part of the picture."

Pro-Petén sponsored artisan workshops with the cooperation of the Soto brothers, who pioneered the handicraft effort in El Remate; however, says Soza, wood artisans must be mindful of good management practices. Using *cericote* wood is fine, because it grows quickly, with a mature tree in eight to eleven years, but cedar grows very slowly, and *rosul* is endangered.

Originally, plans for the Maya Biosphere Reserve called for the removal of the residents of the village of El Cruce and further north; however, they resisted, and CI stepped forward with a plan. They offered to place in the village their flagship factory of potpourri products—dried leaves, seeds, barks, and flowers from the forests of Petén, which they would then market.

At the small factory, which opened in April 1993, a group of two men and sixteen women are hand stencilling *jícara* shells that form the holders for the potpourri. Beyond, on the ground, cones are drying, dozens of shells, their rounded skins baking in the noonday sun. The smell of allspice fills the air of the small shop; recycled paper for labels is drying in the back; and natural dyes for leaves are cooking nearby.

Two hundred potpourri baskets are assembled weekly at this small factory. And another ten people are employed collecting species in the forest. Beside the work area, there is a plan for a shop and quarters where visitors may sleep overnight. There are also plans to process allspice oil on-site. CI is currently building a market for the potpourri and other products to be made at the factory, with the plan to eventually transfer ownership to the community of El Cruce. "The whole point," says Soza, "is for the people to take over."

Although Petén is no longer isolated, in many ways it is an island still, an island of refuge. And the question remains: Is the Maya Biosphere Reserve the last refuge, or the first successful incorporation of people living sustainably within its borders?

Suggested Readings

A large and growing literature exists in both the natural and social sciences regarding the tropical forests of Latin America. The following list is nowhere near exhaustive but does represent some of the best sources for further exploration of the causes and consequences of tropical deforestation and alternatives to destruction of the forest in the name of progress.

Anderson, Anthony B., ed. *Alternatives to Deforestation: Steps toward Sustainable Use of the Amazon Rain Forest*. New York, 1990. The essays in this book, written by experts in a wide range of fields, analyze the ecological dynamics of tropical rainforests and the impacts of deforestation. The collection emphasizes appropriate management of tropical forests and contains a number of essays on innovative technologies and approaches that will permit simultaneous use and conservation of the Amazon rainforest. *Alternatives to Deforestation* is written by scholars for readers with some background in ecology.

Browder, John O., ed. *Fragile Lands of Latin America*. Boulder, 1989. This collection of essays grew out of an academic symposium on fragile lands in Latin America, whose goal was to explore strategies for sustainable development. Many of the authors are geographers or anthropologists who analyze nature-society relations from the perspective of cultural ecology. The essays expand on many of the concepts introduced in *Tropical Rainforests: Latin American Nature and Society in Transition*.

Caufield, Catherine. *In the Rainforest*. Chicago, 1991. This book is a good place to start learning about the tropical rainforest. It is a beautifully written, easily accessible account of the social and environmental factors involved in tropical rainforest destruction. Although the scope is global, much of the book is about Latin America—especially the Amazon.

Cowell, Adrian. *The Decade of Destruction*. New York, 1990. This well-researched book documents the destruction of the Amazon rainforest and its traditional inhabitants with a passion born of the author's ten years of work in the region. It is the companion book to the documentary film of the same name that aired in the United States on the *Frontline* television series.

Davis, Shelton H. *Victims of the Miracle*. Cambridge (UK), 1977. The subtitle of this book, "Development and the Indians of Brazil," indicates its focus. The first in-depth analysis of the social and environmental impacts of Brazil's approach to developing the Amazon, it also provides an excellent overview of Brazil's Indian policy since 1940. This book is aimed toward a more academic audience than are the books by Caufield, Cowell, and Head and Heinzman.

Goodman, David, and Hall, Anthony, eds. *The Future of Amazonia*. New York, 1990. This collection of essays, primarily by social scientists, analyzes the ecological and social impacts of Brazil's approach to developing the Amazon. The authors emphasize the social tensions and struggles caused by the destructiveness of current policies in Amazonia. Included are essays that suggest strategies for sustainable development of the Amazon rainforest.

Head, Suzanne, and Heinzman, Robert, eds. *Lessons of the Rainforest*. San Francisco, 1990. Head and Heinzman have put together a comprehensive collection of essays by many of the leaders of rainforest conservation, both academics and activists. The essays are written for the general public by experts in their fields, making *Lessons of the Rainforest* both readable and informative.

Hecht, Susanna, and Cockburn, Alexander. *The Fate of the Forest*. New York, 1990. *The Fate of the Forest* is an exquisitely written, sophisticated analysis of the forces that are destroying the tropical rainforest and indigenous cultures of Amazonia. An excellent example of the perspective of political ecology, which considers how political economy affects the relationship between society and nature, it is written for a general, educated audience.

Meggers, Betty. *Amazonia: Man and Culture in a Counterfeit Paradise*. Chicago, 1971. In this classic of cultural ecology, Meggers analyzes the relationship between the environment and the cultural adaptations of several indigenous groups in the Amazon. Meggers was one of the principal exponents of the theory that the tropical rainforest is fragile and lacking in the subsistence resources that humans need, thereby limiting population growth and cultural development.

Mendes, Chico (with Tony Gross). *Fight for the Forest: Chico Mendes in His Own Words*. London, 1989 and 1992. This fascinating book came out of the last major interview given by Chico Mendes before his assassination. Composed of segments by Mendes interspersed with explanatory material provided by the interviewer, Tony Gross, *Fight for the Forest* provides a good summary of the social history of rubber in the Amazon, with a description and justification of the political resistance by forest-dwellers against environmentally destructive development of the rainforest. The 1992 updated version includes information about the trial of Mendes's alleged assassins and about Brazil's environmental policy under President Fernando Collor de Mello.

Moran, Emilio, ed. *The Dilemma of Amazonian Development*. Boulder, 1983. This collection includes essays by specialists from a wide range of disciplines, including ecology, soil science, geography, anthropology, and economics. The emphasis of the volume is on various strategies for making a living in Amazonia—from traditional indigenous methods to urban middle-class approaches. The authors analyze the social and ecological impacts of various development strategies in a variety of Amazonian environments.

O'Brien, Karen L. *Sacrificing the Forest: Environmental and Social Struggles in Chiapas*. Boulder, 1998. O'Brien uses a political ecology framework to analyze environmental and social struggles in Chiapas, Mexico. In a thoroughly researched but readable form, she shows how deforestation is embedded in a web of social, economic, and political relations with deep historical roots. O'Brien emphasizes the need to recognize both the driving forces of deforestation and the countervailing pressures of conservation in order to understand the contemporary situation in Chiapas.

Painter, Michael, and William H. Durham, eds. *The Social Causes of Environmental Destruction in Latin America*. Ann Arbor, 1995. This anthology provides a wealth of detailed case studies of the factors involved in deforestation in various Latin American countries. It is part of a series that deals with the linkages between local and larger-scale systems. The authors all focus on the social and economic processes that underlie environmental degradation and underdevelopment, especially the gross inequities that allow certain people to control access to resources.

Primack, Richard B., David Bray, Hugo A. Galletti, and Ismael Ponciano, eds. *Timber, Tourists, and Temples: Conservation and Development in the Maya Forest of Belize, Guatemala, and Mexico*. Washington, DC, 1998. The editors have brought together experts from the social and natural sciences as well as conservationists to put together this fascinating anthology. It is a useful synthesis of information on the ecology of the Maya forest, sustainable forestry, extractive reserves, wildlife management, and ecotourism. The book will be of interest to researchers, conservationists, and people working in community development in the region.

Schmink, Marianne, and Wood, Charles, eds. *Frontier Expansion in Amazonia*. Gainesville, Florida, 1984. Based on papers given at a Latin American conference in 1982, this volume focuses on the effects of social change and public policy on development in the Amazon. The authors, primarily social scientists, consider the impact of development on both the environment and on the populations of the region.

Smith, Nigel J. H. *Rainforest Corridors: The Transamazon Colonization Scheme*. Berkeley, 1982. This book exemplifies the approach that cultural geographers use in studying land use and environmental change. Smith analyzes a broad spectrum of impacts on both people and environment created by the construction of the Trans-Amazon Highway during the 1970s. He emphasizes the negative impacts of settlement along its route.

Terborgh, John. *Diversity and the Tropical Rainforest*. New York, 1992. If you could read only one book on the ecology of the rainforest, this should be it. Terborgh, a prominent tropical ecologist, has written a highly readable synthesis of scientific work on tropical forest dynamics intended for the educated layman. He shows how evolutionary processes generate biodiversity and ecological processes sustain it. The volume concludes with an assessment of the current state of, and prognosis for, future conservation of remaining tropical rainforest.

Tomlinson, H. M. *The Sea and the Jungle*. New York, 1964. Tomlinson's witty and eloquent account of his travels up the Amazon to Rondônia on a steamer early in the twentieth century offers modern readers a different perspective than is currently fashionable. Tomlinson was a British journalist who shared his contemporaries' belief in their own cultural superiority and their ambivalence about tropical nature.

Vandermeer, John, and Ivette Perfecto. *Breakfast of Biodiversity: The Truth about Rainforest Destruction*. Oakland, 1995. Although firmly grounded in tropical ecology, this little volume expands its analysis to include the role of the modern world system in rainforest destruction. Based largely on research in Costa Rica, the text compares interesting information about deforestation in Nicaragua, Puerto Rico, and Cuba. The authors also consider strategies for forest conservation.

Wallace, David Rains. *The Quetzal and the Macaw*. San Francisco, 1992. Naturalist-writer Wallace has produced a highly readable account of the history of Costa Rica's acclaimed national park system. In the process he identifies key social and political factors involved in nature conservation. He points out that Costa Rica's efforts to preserve its forests have made it a model for all Latin American countries on how to balance political enlightenment, environmental concerns, and economic development.

In addition, the following journals publish articles on tropical rainforests relatively frequently, and those marked with an asterisk (*) are especially good sources of information on tropical rainforest topics: *BioScience*, *Cultural Survival Quarterly*, *Environment*, *Interciencia*, *International Wildlife*, *Natural History*, *The Ecologist*.

Suggested Films

The tropical rainforest and its rapid decimation have been portrayed in many videos. The following list offers a sample of some that are both interesting and informative. Unless otherwise indicated, most are about one hour long.

"Amazonia: A Celebration of Life." 1984. Director: Andrew Young. Twenty-three minutes long, this is a short but comprehensive introduction to the ecology of the Amazonian rainforest and its value to humans.

"Costa Rica: Paradise Reclaimed." 1987. Director: David Heeley. From the *Nature* series, this video provides a fascinating look at veteran tropical ecologist Daniel Janzen's attempt to recreate an ecosystem that is even more endangered than the tropical rainforest—the tropical dry forest. Filmed in Costa Rica's Guanacaste province, it highlights Janzen's efforts to involve local people in environmental conservation.

"Gertrude Blom: Guardian of the Rain Forest." 1989. Director: Robert S. Cozens. Focusing on photographer Gertrude Blom's long-term relationship with the Lacandón Maya in the Mexican state of Chiapas, this video shows efforts to save the last remaining rainforest in southern Mexico and reveals how the fate of the Lacandón Indians is tied to that of the forest.

"The Hidden Power of Plants." 1987. Director: Kathleen Bernhardt. Part of the *Nova* series, this documentary explores the complex chemical activities of plants and their pharmacological importance. The video focuses on the tropics, although other regions are shown as well. Part of the video emphasizes the importance of the botanical knowledge of rainforest shamans (traditional healers or "medicine men") in helping Western scientists unlock the biochemical wealth of the Amazon rainforest.

"Hope for the Tropics." 1991. Director: Pamela Hogan. Describing various efforts to save the remaining tropical forests in Costa Rica, this *National Audubon* special is somewhat unusual in its focus on the positive aspects of human-forest interactions.

"In the Name of Progress." 1990. Director: Katherine Carpenter. An outstanding example of social ecology, this segment from the television series *The Race to Save the Planet* contrasts the environmental and social impacts of top-down megaprojects, such as Greater Carajás in Brazil, with grass-roots, small-scale development projects, such as extractive reserves in Amazonia. Although the video includes segments on India, these illustrate phenomena that are also part of Amazonian "development" based on the destruction of the rainforest and the culture adapted to it.

"Murder in the Amazon." 1989. Director: Adrian Cowell. From the *Frontline* television series, this documentary explores the forces responsible for the destruction of the Amazon rainforest, concentrating on the conflict between rubber tappers and ranchers. The central figure of the video is Chico Mendes, whose assassination gave the film its title. Cowell also made a five-part series, *Decade of Destruction*, which explores the process of deforestation in the Amazon in more detail. *Frontline* aired the series in 1990.

"Nomads of the Rainforest." 1984. Director: Adrian Warren. This segment from the *Nova* series offers an engaging look at life among unacculturated Huaorani Indians of Ecuador's Amazon region. Their homeland and way of life are now threatened by oil exploration and production and the expansion of African oil-palm plantations. This film may someday represent a historical record of a vanished way of life.

"Rain Forest (Selva Verde: The Green Jungle)." 1985. Director: Phil Agland. Filmed in Belize, Costa Rica, and Panama, this film from the *Nature* series focuses on the various relationships between species that contribute to the biodiversity of the Central American rainforest. It portrays a number of fascinating examples of complex symbioses.

"Rainforest." 1983. Directors/photographers: Carol and David Hughes. Filmed in Costa Rica, this *National Geographic* special provides a good introduction to the ecology of the tropical rainforest. "Rainforest" has the outstanding photography for which *National Geographic* has become famous.